PEOPLE, MAR[...]
ECONOMIES AND SO[...]

Volu[...]

Money and Markets

PEOPLE, MARKETS, GOODS:
ECONOMIES AND SOCIETIES IN HISTORY

ISSN: 2051-7467

Series editors
Barry Doyle – University of Huddersfield
Steve Hindle – The Huntington Library
Jane Humphries – University of Oxford
Willem M. Jongman – University of Groningen
Catherine Schenk – University of Glasgow

The interactions of economy and society, people and goods, transactions and actions are at the root of most human behaviours. Economic and social historians are participants in the same conversation about how markets have developed historically and how they have been constituted by economic actors and agencies in various social, institutional and geographical contexts. New debates now underpin much research in economic and social, cultural, demographic, urban and political history. Their themes have enduring resonance – financial stability and instability, the costs of health and welfare, the implications of poverty and riches, flows of trade and the centrality of communications. This paperback series aims to attract historians interested in economics and economists with an interest in history by publishing high quality, cutting edge academic research in the broad field of economic and social history from the late medieval/ early modern period to the present day. It encourages the interaction of qualitative and quantitative methods through both excellent monographs and collections offering path-breaking overviews of key research concerns. Taking as its benchmark international relevance and excellence it is open to scholars and subjects of any geographical areas from the case study to the multi-nation comparison.

PREVIOUSLY PUBLISHED TITLES IN THE SERIES ARE
LISTED AT THE END OF THE VOLUME

Money and Markets

Essays in Honour of
Martin Daunton

Edited by

Julian Hoppit, Duncan Needham and Adrian Leonard

THE BOYDELL PRESS

First published 2019
The Boydell Press, Woodbridge

ISBN 978-1-78327-445-1

The Boydell Press is an imprint of Boydell & Brewer Ltd
PO Box 9, Woodbridge, Suffolk IP12 3DF, UK
and of Boydell & Brewer Inc.
668 Mt Hope Avenue, Rochester, NY 14620–2731, USA
website: www.boydellandbrewer.com

A catalogue record for this book is available
from the British Library

The publisher has no responsibility for the continued existence or accuracy of URLs for
external or third-party internet websites referred to in this book, and does not guarantee
that any content on such websites is, or will remain, accurate or appropriate

This publication is printed on acid-free paper

Typeset by BBR Design, Sheffield

Printed and bound in Great Britain by
TJ International Ltd, Padstow, Cornwall

Contents

Figures

Tables

Contributors

MARTIN CHICK is Professor of Economic History at the University of Edinburgh. His publications include: *Industrial policy in Britain, 1945–51: economic planning, nationalisation and the Labour governments* (1998); *Electricity and energy policy in Britain, France and the United States since 1945* (2007); and *Changing times: economics, policies and resource allocation in Britain since 1951* (2019). His current research concerns the international conservation of fish and whales after 1945.

SEAN EDDIE wrote his PhD dissertation under Martin Daunton's supervision at the University of Cambridge. He was awarded the Economic History Society's First Monograph Prize and the Royal Historical Society's Gladstone Prize for *Freedom's price: serfdom, subjection, and reform in Prussia, 1648–1848* (2013). His current research focuses on Prussian and German state finance in the nineteenth and early twentieth centuries.

MATTHEW HILTON is Professor of Social History at Queen Mary University of London. He has published widely on the history of charities, social activism, consumption, and NGOs. His most recent book is (with James McKay, Nicholas Crowson and Jean-François Mouhot) *The politics of expertise: how NGOs shaped modern Britain* (2013). He is co-editor (with John Arnold and Jan Ruger) of *History matters: writing history for the 21st century* (2018). He is co-editor of *Past & Present* and is currently engaged on a history of British approaches to humanitarianism.

JULIAN HOPPIT is Astor Professor of British History at University College London. His publications include *Risk and failure in English business, 1700–1800* (1987), *A land of liberty? England 1689–1727* (2000), and *Britain's political economies: parliament and economic life, 1660–1800* (2017). He is currently writing a book about the territoriality of UK public finances from 1707 to 2018.

SEUNG WOO KIM is a Research Fellow in International History at the Graduate Institute, Geneva. He completed his PhD at the University of Cambridge under Martin Daunton's supervision. His dissertation, 'The Euromarket and the making of the transnational network of finance, 1959–1979', examines the history of the Eurodollar market and the role of national sovereignty in the making of global finance. He is currently investigating the political culture of crypto-currencies, the neoliberal contestation on the central banking in the 1960s, and the engagement of the Global South with the Bretton Woods system.

ADRIAN LEONARD is Associate Director of the Centre for Financial History at the University of Cambridge. He completed his PhD at the University of Cambridge under Martin Daunton's supervision. His publications include *Marine insurance: origins and institutions* (editor, 2016), *The Caribbean and the Atlantic World economy* (edited with David Pretel, 2015), and *Questioning credible commitment: perspectives on the Glorious Revolution and the rise of financial capitalism* (edited with Larry Neal and D'Maris Coffman, 2013). He is currently writing a book about 'addictive groceries' and their role in empire.

DUNCAN NEEDHAM is Dean and Senior Tutor of Darwin College and Director of the Centre for Financial History at the University of Cambridge. His PhD dissertation, written under Martin Daunton's supervision, was awarded the Economic History Society's Thirsk-Feinstein Prize. His publications include *UK monetary policy from devaluation to Thatcher, 1967–82* (2014) and (edited with Anthony Hotson) *Expansionary fiscal contraction: the Thatcher government's 1981 Budget in perspective* (2014).

CHARLES READ is Hong Kong Link Fellow and Director of Studies in History at Corpus Christi College, University of Cambridge. His PhD thesis, 'British economic policy and Ireland, c. 1841–53', was supervised by Martin Daunton at the University of Cambridge. He is winner of the Thirsk-Feinstein Prize, the T.S. Ashton Prize, and the New Researcher Prize of the Economic History Society, as well as the International Economic History Association prize for best dissertation in nineteenth-century economic history completed in the world in 2015, 2016 or 2017.

BERNHARD RIEGER is Professor of European History at Leiden University. His publications include *Technology and the culture of modernity in Britain and Germany, 1890–1945* (2005) and *The people's car: a global history of the Volkswagen Beetle* (2013). His current research focuses on the history of unemployment since the 1960s in transatlantic contexts.

RICHARD RODGER is Emeritus Professor at the University of Edinburgh, having been Professor of Urban History and Director of the Centre for Urban History at the University of Leicester. He has published on the urban history of Britain with a particular focus on the socio-economic and legal aspects of housing, property, and land tenure. In addition to books and articles on these and related topics, Rodger has been Editor of *Urban History* (CUP) and General Editor of the Historical Urban Studies series (Ashgate) on European cities. He is currently developing the project 'Mapping Edinburgh' with wide-ranging implications for understanding the spatiality of towns and cities generally.

SABINE SCHNEIDER is the Rank-Manning Junior Research Fellow at New College, University of Oxford, and was previously a Bye-Fellow in History at Fitzwilliam College, University of Cambridge. She has been an ESRC and Ellen McArthur Scholar at the University of Cambridge and a Prize Research Student at the Joint Centre for History and Economics at Cambridge and Harvard. Her research focuses on the history of economic diplomacy and finance since 1800, especially the relations between Europe, Britain and the United States.

HIROKI SHIN is a Research Fellow at the Science Museum, London. His publications include 'At the edge of the network of power in Japan, *c.* 1910s–1960s', in S. Abram, B. Winthereik and T. Yarrow, eds, *Electrifying anthropology: exploring electrical practices and infrastructures* (2019) and (with R. Wright and F. Trentmann), *Power, energy and international cooperation: a history of the World Energy Council, 1923–2018* (2019). His current research focuses on the historical development of energy cultures in Britain and Japan.

DAVID TODD is a senior lecturer in world history at King's College, London. He is the author of *Free trade and its enemies in France, 1814–1851* (2015) which explores French debates about global economic integration in the early nineteenth century. He is currently working on a book on French informal imperialism between 1820 and 1880, *A velvet empire*, to be published by Princeton University Press.

JIM TOMLINSON is Professor of Economic and Social History at the University of Glasgow. His most recent books are *Managing the economy, managing the people: narratives of economic life in Britain from Beveridge to Brexit* (2017) and *Dundee and empire: Juteopolis 1850–1939* (2014). His current research is on the deindustrialisation of Scotland since 1955, and the decline of liberal political economy at the end of the First World War.

FRANK TRENTMANN is Professor of History at Birkbeck College, University of London. His publications include *Free trade nation: consumption, civil society and commerce in modern Britain* (2008) and *Empire of things: how we became a world of consumers, fifteenth century to the twenty-first* (2016). He is currently writing a history of the Germans and their moral transformation since the Second World War.

ADRIAN WILLIAMSON QC wrote his PhD at the University of Cambridge under Martin Daunton's supervision. His publications include *Conservative economic policymaking and the birth of Thatcherism, 1964–1979* (2015) and *Europe and the decline of social democracy in Britain: from Attlee to Brexit* (Boydell and Brewer, 2019). He is a practising barrister at Keating Chambers and sits part-time as a Recorder and Deputy High Court Judge.

Abbreviations

AFDC	Aid to Families with Dependent Children
BAA	British Airports Authority
BEA	Bank of England Archives, London
BEAMA	British Electrical and Allied Manufacturers' Association
BIS	Bank for International Settlements
BISA	Bank for International Settlements Archives, Basel
BL	British Library, London
BOD	Bodleian Library, Oxford
CAA	Christian Aid Archive, SOAS, London
CAA	Civil Aviation Authority
CAC	Churchill Archives Centre, Cambridge
CAFOD	Catholic Agency for Overseas Development
CBA	cost–benefit analysis
DHSS	Department of Health and Social Security
EAW	Electrical Association for Women
EDA	Electrical Development Association
FFHC	Freedom from Hunger Campaigns
FAO	Food and Agriculture Organization of the United Nations
FRBNYA	Federal Reserve Bank of New York Archive, New York
GHL	Guildhall Library, London
GDP	gross domestic product
GNP	gross national product
HC Debs	House of Commons Debates
HMSO	Her Majesty's Stationery Office
IEA	Institute of Economic Affairs
IFS	Institute of Fiscal Studies
IIS	investment income surcharge

IMF	International Monetary Fund
JFS	Joint Funding Scheme
LBGA	Lloyds Banking Group archive, London and Edinburgh
LMA	London Metropolitan Archive
NHS	National Health Service
NRS	National Records of Scotland, Edinburgh
ODA	Official Development Assistance
ODNB	Oxford dictionary of national biography
OECD	Organisation for Economic Co-operation and Development; OECD Library and Archives, Paris
OPEC	Organization of Petroleum Exporting Countries
PFI	Private Finance Initiative
PP	UK Parliamentary Papers
PRONI	Public Record Office of Northern Ireland, Belfast
PSBR	Public Sector Borrowing Requirement
QALY	quality-adjusted life year
SCFA	Save the Children Archive, University of Birmingham
SUL	Southampton University Library
TEDCO	Thames Estuary Development Company
TNA	The National Archive, Kew, England
VAT	value added tax
VPF	value of prevented fatality
VSO	Voluntary Service Overseas

Introduction

DUNCAN NEEDHAM[1]

Frank Trentmann has commented that students could be forgiven for thinking there are four Martin Dauntons:

> There is the Daunton of urban history and housing, then Daunton the author of books on state and taxation, and a third, younger Daunton, who writes about Britain and globalisation. Finally, there is the academic governor Daunton, Master of Trinity Hall, Cambridge, President of the Royal Historical Society, and chair of numerous boards and committees.[2]

There is of course just one Martin Daunton and this volume brings together essays from friends, colleagues, and former students to celebrate his distinguished career.[3] Throughout that career, Martin has focused on the relationship between structure and agency, how institutional structures create capacities and path dependencies, and how institutions are themselves shaped by agency and contingency — what Braudel referred to as 'turning the hour glass twice'.[4] His methodology has variously been described as 'archival narrative', a well-informed, common-sense approach to policy issues and institutions, and as 'a history of linkages'.[5] This is reflected in the contributions to this volume which draw heavily on archival sources to situate their economic, social, political, and

1 I am grateful for comments on earlier drafts from Martin Daunton, Adrian Leonard, and Julian Hoppit.
2 F. Trentmann, 'Review of *State and market in Victorian Britain* by Martin Daunton', *English Historical Review* 125, 517 (2010), p. 1557.
3 This volume was conceived at a 2016 conference held to mark Martin's retirement as Professor of Economic History at Cambridge.
4 M.J. Daunton, 'Time and history', *Balzan Papers* 1 (Florence, 2018).
5 I am grateful to an anonymous referee for the first description. For the second, see Trentmann, 'Review', p. 1558.

cultural enquiry within the policy debates and institutions of periods from the Restoration to the Global Financial Crisis, both in the UK and elsewhere.[6]

In his valedictory lecture, Martin cautioned against constructing narrative arcs that attribute retrospective coherence to a career.[7] In the same lecture, however, he pointed out that his work has often been inspired by the places where he has lived and worked. This is a thread that runs through Martin's career. A second is the link between his publications and the courses he has taught at Durham, University College London, and Cambridge. A third is perhaps best captured in the phrase 'legitimacy and consent'. How did a fiscal-military state that appeared to have reached the limits of its taxable capacity in the eighteenth century earn the legitimacy required to extract ever-higher revenues? And why did the British people consent? This introduction follows these threads, adding biographical and historiographical detail to Trentmann's taxonomy to show how Martin's career as an economic historian sits within the style and tradition of Cambridge economic history.

Urban history and housing

Martin Daunton was born in 1949 on land formerly belonging to the Marquess of Bute, owner of the Cardiff Docks, and grew up in a village owned by the Jenner family, who provided a nineteenth-century predecessor as Master of Trinity Hall.[8] He attended Barry Grammar School, *alma mater* of those other distinguished economic historians Sir John Habakkuk, Professor of Economic History at Oxford, and David Joslin, who occupied the chair at Cambridge while Martin was doing his A-levels.[9] His inspirational history master Teifion Phillips was one of several teachers who had escaped the coal mines.[10] For teachers like Phillips, who walked daily to Swansea University to obtain his degree, history was not an elitist pursuit; it was essential to understanding the local community and broader society.

In 1967 Martin went up to Nottingham to read economic history, then, as was common, housed in its own department. In addition to more traditional history and sociology courses, he took Helen Mellor's final-year option on the Victorian city, thus beginning a long association with urban history.

6   Several chapters follow Martin's lead in deploying quantitative methods without relying upon econometric technique.

7   M.J. Daunton, *Valedictory lecture*, St John's College, Cambridge, 23 Jun. 2015. Mimeo.

8   Sir Herbert Jenner-Fust was Master of Trinity Hall from 1843 until 1852.

9   Sir Bryan Hopkin, Chief Economic Adviser to the Treasury 1974–77, was a classmate of Habakkuk. Archaeologist Gwyn Daniels was a contemporary.

10   Phillips also taught the early modernist Sir Keith Thomas.

His undergraduate dissertation, later published in the *Welsh History Review* as 'The Dowlais Iron Company in the iron industry, 1800–50', explored the extent to which the large South Wales iron firms competed or colluded over labour, orders, and transport links.[11] It showed that sometimes they competed and sometimes they colluded, depending upon 'the flow and direction of the currents of economic life'.[12]

After graduating in 1970 Martin commenced his doctoral research at the University of Kent under the supervision of Mellor's own PhD examiner, Theo Barker. His thesis, 'Aspects of the social and economic structure of Cardiff, 1870–1914', also drew on the place of his upbringing. Examined by urban history 'entrepreneur' Jim Dyos, it formed the basis of his first monograph, *Coal metropolis: Cardiff, 1870–1914*, published in 1977.[13] The first question ('from which everything else follows') is how Cardiff grew from a market town 'of no influence in commerce and with no reputation' in 1850 to become the largest conurbation in south Wales by 1914.[14] The answer lies in the second Marquess of Bute's foresight in developing one of the largest docks in the world in the 1830s. By 1914 the Cardiff docks were in decline, however, with trade diverted to larger facilities such as Barry, which had surpassed Cardiff in export volumes by the start of the twentieth century.

Coal metropolis is much more than an analysis of Cardiff's rise (and decline) as a commercial city and port. The book also focuses on how the city was built, how its physical form was determined, and how its spatial patterns related to its social structure. In particular, Martin shows how the Bute family's leasehold approach, emulated by the neighbouring Tredegar and Windsor estates, created an unusually high standard of housing. Cardiff was over-provided with middle-class housing and underprovided with workmen's dwellings, with more than a third of its (relatively mobile) families sharing subdivided accommodation in 1911. There is also an early exposition of the 'history of linkages'. By examining Cardiff's social and political life, Martin accounts for the unusually low engagement of the commercial elite in local politics compared to cities elsewhere. And alongside the historical statistics, cultural, political, religious, and social practices are all explored to show how the city's inhabitants made sense of, and reacted to, economic change. We may also detect the taproots of the 'second' and 'third' Dauntons here. Calls to municipalise the Cardiff docks and hostility to the Bute family's profits from rising land values fuelled local support for the pre-WWI Liberal land

---

11 M.J. Daunton, 'The Dowlais Iron Company in the iron industry, 1800–50', *Welsh History Review* 6, 1 (1972), pp. 16–48.
12 Ibid., p. 45 (quoting T.S. Ashton).
13 M.J. Daunton, *Coal metropolis: Cardiff, 1870–1914* (Leicester, 1977).
14 Ibid., p. 15.

campaign. And as the largest export port in Britain, Cardiff was a hub of late nineteenth-century globalisation.[15]

In addition to *Coal metropolis*, Martin's doctoral research generated several articles on Cardiff's built environment, economy, and labour relations.[16] These were published after he took up his first lectureship in economic history, at Durham in 1973. There he continued to draw on his surroundings, conducting comparative research on living and working conditions in the South Wales and Great Northern coalfields.[17] Like Nottingham and Kent, Durham then had its own Economic and Social History department. The publication, within five years, of a monograph, five journal articles and a chapter (on eighteenth-century towns and economic growth) in an edited volume appears modest by the standards of Martin's later career. But this level of productivity apparently aroused suspicion in the academic environment of the 1970s.[18] Along with his colleague Ranald Michie, later head of the Department of History at Durham, Martin was accused of 'scribbling'. The then head of history's advice to young academics who wrote was to 'put it in your drawer and let it mature a bit before you put it into print'.[19] All of us who have worked with, read, or been taught by Martin are grateful that he did not heed this advice.

In 1979 Martin moved to University College London, where he completed his second monograph, *House and home in the Victorian city*. This extended the analysis of housing in *Coal metropolis* to Great Britain, to show that, just as Cardiff was atypical (in the British context), so England's preponderance of working-class terraced houses over flats set it apart from the European norm.[20] The focus is on the 'actuality' of developers building working-class housing, largely for a private rental market that still accounted for at least 85 per cent of

---

15   Having been paid off elsewhere, sailors would travel to Cardiff to join outward-bound ships. M.J. Daunton, 'Jack ashore: seamen in Cardiff before 1914', *Welsh History Review* 9 (1978), pp. 176–203.

16   M.J. Daunton, 'Suburban development in Cardiff: Grangetown and the Windsor Estate, 1857–75', *Morgannwg* 16 (1972), pp. 53–66; M.J. Daunton, 'Aristocrat and traders: the Bute Docks, 1839–1914', *Journal of Transport History*, new ser. 3 (1975), pp. 65–85; M.J. Daunton, 'The Cardiff Coal Trimmers' Union, 1888–1914', *Llafur* 2, 3 (1978), pp. 51–67; M.J. Daunton, 'Inter-union relations on the waterfront: Cardiff 1888–1914', *International Review of Social History* 22, 3 (1977), pp. 350–78.

17   M.J. Daunton, 'Miners' houses: South Wales and the Great Northern coalfields, 1880–1914', *International Review of Social History* 25, 2 (1980), pp. 143–75; M.J. Daunton, 'Down the pit: work in the Great Northern and South Wales coalfields, 1870–1914', *Economic History Review*, 2nd ser. 34, 4 (1981), pp. 578–97.

18   M.J. Daunton, 'Towns and economic growth in eighteenth-century England', in P. Abrams and E.A. Wrigley, eds, *Towns in society: essays in economic history and historical sociology* (Cambridge, 1978), pp. 245–77.

19   Institute of Historical Research, 'Interview with Martin Daunton', available at http://www.history.ac.uk/makinghistory/resources/interviews/Daunton_Martin.html, last viewed 12 Aug. 2018.

20   Scottish tenements conform more closely to the European pattern.

dwellings in 1914.[21] Regional differences arose as government policy was interpreted according to local bylaws on space and sanitation, topographies, wages,
and tastes. Again reflecting the 'history of linkages', Martin places the house
at the centre of a web of economic and social ties between, *inter alia*, landlords
(and their agents), tenants, neighbours, financiers, and government officials.
House and home also critiques the teleological assumption that local authority
housing was the inevitable outcome of poor quality privately rented housing
and the limitations of philanthropy.[22] A core theme is the changing relationship
between the public and private domains. As public space was organised into
parks, market places, and sports stadia, so working-class domesticity was
increasingly expressed in enclosed private spaces. A more settled working class
consuming more domestic appliances (such as gas cookers) and luxuries (such
as pianos) moved from the introverted court to the terraced street. There is also
a link to the 'second Daunton' of the state and taxation; rising local government
costs collided with an inflexible tax base to create a municipal funding crisis
that was resolved with more centralised taxation and government subsidies.
This exploration of fiscal policy inspired David Cannadine and John Morrill
to suggest that Martin write a 'short' book on taxation (more on which below).

   House and home was followed in 1984 by an edited volume, *Councillors and
tenants*. This examined the origins of the tripartite pattern of tenure (owner-
occupation, private renting, and social renting) that saw owner-occupation peak
just before the 2008 Global Financial Crisis. In 1939 the majority of English
households still lived in private rented accommodation, but the private landlord
was under siege from a Conservative Party erecting a 'protective rampart' of
owner-occupiers in its broader defence of private property, and a Labour Party
that viewed landlords as exploiters of the working classes. The rise of local
authority housing was not inevitable, however, and Martin's introduction
assesses the social forces that guided Britain down a different tenurial path
from continental Europe, a theme explored in another edited volume, *Housing
the workers, 1850–1914*.[23] As with *House and home*, its emphasis is on the local
as 'all too often in the past, the analysis has ended at the point at which the
[1919 Housing] Act was placed on the statute book, rather than at the point at
which the Council decided to build'.[24] As with Victorian bylaw housing, local
authorities exercised discretion when interpreting national regulations, particularly when deciding how to subsidise their poorest tenants. This is explored

---

21   M.J. Daunton, *House and home in the Victorian city: working class housing 1850–1914*
(London, 1983), p. 1; M.J. Daunton, ed., *Councillors and tenants: local authority housing in
English cities, 1919–1939* (Leicester, 1984).
22   John Patten, then Minister of State for Housing, approved and circulated *House and home*'s
conclusion within his department.
23   In chapters on Paris, Brussels, Vienna, Budapest, Berlin, and North America, M.J. Daunton,
ed., *Housing the workers, 1850–1914: a comparative perspective* (Leicester, 1990).
24   Daunton, *Councillors and tenants*, p. 20.

in case studies, each based on graduate research, of County Durham, Leeds, and Bristol. *Councillors and tenants* advanced the study of urban history in two key respects. First, it shows that housing became a major preoccupation of local authorities as a consequence of the rent controls introduced in 1915 to preserve social stability at a delicate moment during the First World War. Rent controls created a post-war conundrum; it became uneconomic for private landlords to build the working-class housing that was needed to satisfy demand. Without increased supply, rents would rise sharply when controls were removed. A Whitehall committee summarised the problem: 'You will not get the houses until the Act is removed, and, therefore, unless the Act is removed the necessity for the Act remains.'[25] Since the private sector could not resolve the conundrum, local authorities were enlisted to build houses, which they did with varying degrees of enthusiasm.

Councillors and tenants also explores the implications for urban life as tenants 'came to face a public, politically accountable bureaucracy concerned with social policy as well as financial returns, in place of private landlords operating on commercial principles'.[26] As with *Coal metropolis* and *House and home*, urban relations are explored as an arena of complex bargaining between social actors. How did tenants get on with their new landlords? How did local authorities function in their new guise of builders and residential property owners? These concepts were distilled in *A property-owning democracy? Housing in Britain*, published in 1987 as part of Faber's Historical Handbooks series to provide 'short, up-to-date studies in the evolution of current problems'.[27] 'Current problems' in the mid-1980s included rising homelessness and escalating housing prices, especially in London, as the tenurial balance was altered with the sale of council houses to their tenants, and more readily available mortgages. The volume challenged the notion, particularly widespread in North America, that owner-occupancy satisfies some 'innate' human desire. It also takes aim at the suggestion that housing tenures sustain social attitudes and divisions, and that owner-occupation significantly reinforces social stability. The point is also made that investing in existing bricks and mortar (as opposed to new building) may have been an inefficient use of capital for much of recent British history. Once again, Martin drew upon personal experience with this book. He and Claire sold their house in Margaret Thatcher's Finchley constituency while he was writing it.[28]

25   Ministry of Reconstruction, *Report of the Committee on the Increase of Rent and Mortgage Interest (War Restrictions) Acts, 1918*, quoted in Daunton, *Councillors and tenants*, p. 9.
26   Daunton, *Councillors and tenants*, p. 25.
27   M.J. Daunton, *A property-owning democracy? Housing in Britain* (London, 1987), p. v.
28   Ibid., p. x.

The state and taxation

The publication in 1985 of his official history *Royal Mail: the Post Office since 1840* heralds the metamorphosis from the 'first Daunton' of urban history and housing towards the 'second Daunton' of the state and taxation, via the City of London.[29] With characteristic modesty, Martin describes this appointment as owing more to the power of patronage ('something in common with Anthony Trollope') than merit.[30] Since the publication of Howard Robinson's *Britain's Post Office* in 1953, the Post Office had become a public corporation (in 1969), and had hived off British Telecom as a separate entity (in 1981). Typically, the volume is more than a simple administrative history. As the Post Office grew from a conservative government department into a complex bureaucracy with multiple business lines (some operating in competitive markets), management had to reconcile conflicting economic, social, and imperial goals. Britain's largest employer by 1914, the Post Office also came into contact with more individuals from all levels of society than any other government department. So this is also a cultural history, and one that includes a more honest portrait of Rowland Hill – an insufferable egotist whose claims to originality do not bear close scrutiny.

A period of sabbatical leave (and a fortuitous conversation with archivist Penny Pemberton) at the Australian National University in 1985 led to research on Frederick Dalgety, founder of the eponymous commodity trading firm. Dalgety was acutely concerned with the security and status of his family, writing in 1873 that 'I value reputation and social position beyond any amount of profit and will not sacrifice either for gain.'[31] He diversified into property, and incorporated the business, albeit reluctantly, in 1884, thus ensuring the survival of the firm and his family's fortune. On returning from Australia, Martin spent several months in the Guildhall archives, amongst the papers of two prominent Victorian City families: the Hubbards and the Gibbs. While both were concerned to secure the family succession, they followed different strategies. The Hubbards kept the family capital in the business which failed; the Gibbs (like Dalgety) diversified into property and thrived, illustrating there was more to City families buying land than the pursuit of 'aristocratic values'.

These articles on family succession were the preliminaries to a substantial research project on the City that produced several major articles and book chapters while igniting a lively, but friendly, debate with the proponents of

29 Research in the Post Office archive at St Martin's le Grand coincided with Martin's marriage to Claire '[who] cannot have realised that she was marrying St Martin's le Grand', M.J. Daunton, *Royal Mail: the Post Office since 1840* (London, 1985), p. xii.
30 The commission came via Martin's PhD supervisor Theo Barker, ibid., p. xiii.
31 M.J. Daunton, 'Firm and family in the City of London in the nineteenth century: the case of F.G. Dalgety', *Historical Research* 62 (1989), p. 163.

'gentlemanly capitalism' advanced by Peter Cain and Tony Hopkins.[32] Having grown up in a place where aristocratic families were embedded in the industrial landscape, Martin has little sympathy for the notion of separate castes of industrialists and gentlemanly capitalists. Here again we see the history of linkages at work, with ties between aristocrats, financiers, and industrialists laid out. The state did need the City to fund its wars. But it also needed manufacturers to provide war materiel, export earnings, and jobs. Rather than prioritising interests, the state established its legitimacy by *balancing* interests. We see this in the 1853 Budget where Gladstone cemented the income tax as part of a 'social contract' between the classes. We see it again in 1894 when another Liberal Chancellor, William Harcourt, introduced graduated death duties to reduce the burden of income tax at the lower level – 'building from the middle out', to unite rather than divide the classes.[33]

Martin's focus on the City and London's place in the wider economy continued with his appointment as Professor of Modern History in 1989 and then Astor Professor of British History in 1992 (both at UCL). In 1925 J.L. Hammond described the Industrial Revolution as 'a storm that passed over London and broke elsewhere'.[34] This belies the industries that thrived in London (armaments in Enfield, silk weaving in Spitalfields, shipbuilding on the Thames, for example) as well as the businesses linked to the north and midlands through their London head offices. The largest city in Europe from the eighteenth century, London was also Britain's most important manufacturing centre well into the twentieth.[35] This further complicates the notion of a bourgeoisie focused on finance capital in the south and industry in the north.

At a conference about Jeremy Bentham at UCL, Martin was commissioned by Oxford University Press to write a successor to Peter Mathias' classic *First industrial nation*.[36] With *Progress and poverty* he 'rehumanised' this period of British economic history, reconnecting it with social, political, and cultural

32   M.J. Daunton, '"Gentlemanly capitalism" and British industry, 1820–1914', *Past & Present* 122 (1989), pp. 119–58; W.D. Rubinstein, '"Gentlemanly capitalism" and British industry 1820–1914', *Past & Present* 132 (1991), pp. 150–70; M.J. Daunton, '"Gentlemanly capitalism" and British industry 1820–1914: reply', *Past & Present* 132 (1991), pp. 170–87; P.J. Cain and A.G. Hopkins, 'Gentlemanly capitalism and British expansion overseas I: the old colonial system, 1688–1850', *Economic History Review* 39, 4 (1986), pp. 501–25; P.J. Cain and A.G. Hopkins, 'Gentlemanly capitalism and British expansion overseas II: new imperialism, 1850–1945', *Economic History Review* 40, 1 (1987), pp. 1–26.
33   M.J. Daunton, 'The political economy of death duties: Harcourt's Budget of 1894', in N.B. Harte and R.E. Quinault, eds, *Land and society in Britain, 1700–1914: essays in honour of F.M.L. Thompson* (Manchester, 1996), pp. 137–71.
34   J.L. Hammond, 'Eighteenth-century London', *New Statesman*, 21 Mar. 1925.
35   M.J. Daunton, 'Industry in London: revisions and reflections', *London Journal* 21, 1 (1996), p. 1.
36   P. Mathias, *The first industrial nation: the economic history of Britain 1700–1914* (London, 1969).

history. With its roots in his teaching at UCL, the volume portrays the gradualism and complexity of British economic development, emphasising the importance of Smithian growth through mercantile networks, banking, and more efficient transport in reducing transaction costs. As much a work of political economy as economic history, it lays out the linkages between sectors, and describes the role of the state in fostering economic development.

Progress and poverty was originally intended to finish in 1914. But as the manuscript grew, the publishers agreed that a second volume was required to cover the period after 1850. *Wealth and welfare: an economic and social history of Britain 1851–1951* followed in 2007, charting the currents of economic, social, and cultural change in Britain between the Great Exhibition and the Festival of Britain. During this period it became clear that Britain had escaped the Malthusian trap as economic growth outstripped population growth. This generated new debates about how the fruits of growth should be distributed and redistributed. It also reshaped political bargaining between consumers, producers, and shareholders, all of whom were operating in an increasingly globalised system until 1914. This is addressed in the second section, 'Globalization and deglobalization'. The third section addresses the impact of these profound changes on the living standards of the British people, with chapters on 'Births and marriage', 'Death and disease', 'Rich and poor', and 'Cultures of consumption'. After this analysis of history from below, the volume moves on to 'Public policy and the state', examining the changing approaches not only to economic policy, but to cognate areas such as education and the welfare state. The Festival of Britain provides the final vantage point from which to survey the journey from the imperial perspectives of the 1850s to the more insular national perspectives of the early 1950s.

Between *Progress and poverty* and *Wealth and welfare* came Martin's magisterial two-volume history of the British fiscal system from the introduction of the income tax in 1799 to the Great War, *Trusting Leviathan*; and *Just taxes* which extended the analysis up to the election of the first Thatcher government in 1979.[37] As Joseph Schumpeter remarked, 'public finances are one of the best starting points for an investigation of society. The spirit of a people, its cultural level, its social structure, the deeds its policy may prepare – all this and more is written in its fiscal history.'[38] *Trusting Leviathan* is a political history of trust. It shows how the British state established the legitimacy required to extract a higher level of taxation from its people without major unrest. Gladstone's 1853 budget was essential in establishing consent for the income tax on the basis of proportionality; direct taxes on income and land balanced indirect taxes on consumption to pay for limited government expenditure. Martin shows how

37   M.J. Daunton, *Trusting Leviathan: the politics of taxation in Britain, 1799–1914* (Cambridge, 2001); M.J. Daunton, *Just taxes: the politics of taxation in Britain, 1914–1979* (Cambridge, 2002).
38   J.A. Schumpeter, quoted in Daunton, *Trusting Leviathan*, p. 1.

trust was built by involving local elites in tax collection and dividing incomes into different 'schedules' (e.g. income from land, investments, and employment) so that the state could never know an individual's total income.[39] While this settlement was strained by increased military spending and welfare provision before 1914, it was to Britain's great advantage that she could rely on an established and trusted fiscal base during the First World War.

The Gladstonian settlement was intended to reduce corruption by purging politics of disputes over taxation. This approach survived the First World War and reconstruction, albeit a little battered and bruised. In 1913 income tax was an upper- and upper-middle-class tax, falling on around 1.2 million households. After the First World War three times as many households paid income tax, and their discontent forced retrenchment upon the coalition government. As Jon Lawrence points out: 'in 1922 the vision of a "Land fit for heroes" was finally sacrificed in the name of lower taxation for the middle classes'.[40] But the state retained consent for the fiscal constitution at a higher level of extraction, albeit at the price of some fiscal chicanery, especially during Churchill's chancellorship from 1924–29.[41]

The limits of the nineteenth-century fiscal settlement were reached after the Second World War when demographic change and increased welfare expectations rendered the carefully constructed fiscal constitution rigid and inflexible.[42] While the percentage of tax to GDP was broadly in line with the Western European average, the proportion taken by direct taxation was higher, with income tax no longer exhibiting the necessary 'buoyancy'.[43] Increasing the income tax take required higher rates, applied to more people. By 1979 inflation had brought low income households into the net; the tax-free allowance was less than a married man with two children could expect to receive on benefits. Even social democrats such as James Meade could agree that high marginal rates were blunting efficiency and enterprise for high earners, and setting a poverty trap for low earners.[44] In 1979 the newly elected Conservative government

---

39 There were also schedules for commercial occupation of land, and trading and professional income.

40 J.M. Lawrence, 'The First World War and its aftermath', in P.A. Johnson, ed., *Twentieth-century Britain: economic, social, and cultural change* (London, 1994), p. 164.

41 M.J. Daunton, 'Churchill at the Treasury: remaking Conservative taxation policy, 1924–29', *Revue belge de philologie et d'histoire* 75, 4 (1997), pp. 1063–83.

42 M.J. Daunton, '"A kind of tax prison": rethinking Conservative taxation policy, 1960–1970', in M. Francis and I. Zweiniger-Bargielowska, eds, *The Conservatives and British society, 1880–1990* (Cardiff, 1996), p. 290.

43 In a buoyant tax regime, rising national income produces a higher percentage rise in tax revenues as taxpayers move into higher tax brackets and increase consumption.

44 *The structure and reform of direct taxation. Report of a committee chaired by J.E. Meade for the Institute for Fiscal Studies* (London, 1978).

redrew the fiscal constitution with a fundamental shift from direct to indirect tax, reducing the basis rate of income tax from 33 to 30 per cent, and nearly doubling the main rate of value added tax from 8 to 15 per cent.[45]

Britain and globalisation

Martin was elected to the Royal Historical Society in 1979, and served as its Treasurer from 1986 to 1991.[46] In 2004 he was elected President. As is customary, he delivered four Presidential addresses between 2005 and 2008, choosing for his theme 'Britain and globalisation since 1850'. The 'third' Martin Daunton's publications are also firmly grounded in his teaching, by then at Cambridge where he was elected Professor of Economic History in 1997. The first occupant of the chair, J.H. Clapham, was charged by his mentor, Alfred Marshall, with filling the 'empty boxes' of theory with empirical fact.[47] In Martin's case, the theoretical box was the monetary policy trilemma (or 'inconsistent trinity'): a medium-sized nation can have two, but not three, of the following: a fixed exchange rate, capital mobility, and monetary sovereignty. His courses in International Political Economy and his four Presidential addresses analysed the trade-offs made by policymakers in Britain and abroad through the phases of globalisation, de-globalisation, and re-globalisation experienced since the Victorian age of equipoise.

Others have analysed these trade-offs within different theoretical frameworks. Barry Eichengreen, for instance, argues that the classical gold standard was incompatible with mass democracy. After the First World War the newly enfranchised working classes no longer accepted the wage flexibility required to maintain the parity of the currency. But Martin shows this to be a false dichotomy. Alongside free trade and the minimal balanced budget rule, the gold standard was a critical element of a social contract that *included* the working classes. A strong currency ensured cheap food imports, essential for an urban nation that has long been unable to feed itself. There was no firmer believer in the gold standard than Labour's first Chancellor, Philip Snowden.

Identifying the safety valves that insulated national economies from external

---

45   The Thatcher government's tax reforms are explored in M.J. Daunton, 'Creating a dynamic society: the tax reforms of the Thatcher government', in M. Buggeln, M.J. Daunton, and A. Nützenadel, eds, *The political economy of public finance: taxation, state spending and debt since the 1970s* (Cambridge, 2017), pp. 32–56.

46   Martin was elected a Fellow of the British Academy in 1997 (to the Modern History rather than the Economic and Economic History section). He received the degree of LittD from Cambridge in 2005.

47   M.J. Daunton, 'John Harold Clapham (1873–1946)', in R.A. Cord, ed., *The Palgrave companion to Cambridge economics* (London, 2017), p. 439.

shocks is key to understanding the different variants of the gold standard that operated before the First World War. Here Martin enlarges the theoretical box to the 'inconsistent quartet' by adding free trade versus protection. One of the reasons the United States could exercise monetary autonomy while maintaining dollar convertibility and free movement of capital was the high tariff barriers it erected against the rest of the world.[48] The theoretical box can be further enlarged. The 'incompatible quintet' adds labour mobility. Countries on the periphery of Europe such as Sweden experienced mass emigration during economic downturns. Wages could then rise as labour surpluses were exported to the New World.

The attempt to rebuild the Edwardian world of international free trade, contingent upon the gold standard and capital mobility, was understandable given the carnage of the First World War. As Martin explains, the return to gold was 'justified as an employment policy which assumed that recovery rested on the international rather than the domestic economy'.[49] But the facts had changed. The delicate web of trade and capital flows that had evolved during the nineteenth century had been shattered. Even Keynes, the ardent free trader, was arguing by the 1930s that most goods should be 'homespun'.[50] Cosmopolitanism was in retreat; insular capitalism was on the rise. For the state to maintain legitimacy and consent, there had to be a new trade-off. This came with the regime change of 1931–32. Gold was abandoned, and the General Tariff imposed.

The planners of the post-war economy met at Bretton Woods in 1944 to design 'a system of international currency relations compatible with the requirements of domestic stability'.[51] The process and results are analysed in Martin's third Presidential address.[52] According to US Secretary of State Henry Morgenthau, currency disorders had been at the root of the decline in international trade and investment between the wars, causing depression and unemployment, and creating a fertile breeding ground for demagogues and dictators. This required a different trade-off. Free movement of goods and services was deemed a prerequisite of economic growth; unfettered capital movement was not, so capital controls were retained to preserve domestic economic stability. This reflected the perceived change in the nature of capital flows. Before the First World War, capital tended to follow emigrants. But between the wars, capital flows were driven by short-term currency instability and political uncertainty. If legitimacy and consent are essential at the national level, they are just as important at the supranational plane. Keynes lost the argument at Bretton

48   The US also had the 'natural tariff barrier' of distance.
49   M.J. Daunton, *Wealth and welfare: an economic and social history of Britain, 1851–1951* (Oxford, 2007), p. 289.
50   John Maynard Keynes, 'National self-sufficiency', *Yale Review* 22, 4 (June 1933), pp. 755–69.
51   League of Nations, *International currency experience: lessons from the interwar period* (Geneva, 1944), p. 230.
52   M.J. Daunton, 'Britain and globalisation since 1850: III. Creating the world of Bretton Woods, 1939–1958', *Transactions of the Royal Historical Society* 6, 18 (2008), pp. 1–42.

Woods for a more 'symmetric' international monetary system that placed less pressure on the debtor nations to devalue, deflate, or default because the treaty required the consent of the US Congress, which was never going to write blank cheques to deficit nations like Britain. Politics is, after all, the art of the possible.

Martin's fourth Presidential address, delivered in 2008 against the backdrop of the unfolding Global Financial Crisis, chronicled the breakdown of the Bretton Woods system and the creation of the Washington Consensus.[53] By the late 1960s the cracks in Bretton Woods, identified by Robert Triffin in 1959, had become fissures as the United States waged war in Vietnam and constructed the Great Society at home, without raising taxes sufficient to pay for either. In 1971 Nixon calculated that it was not worth deflating the American economy and risking the forthcoming election to save an international monetary system he little understood, and cared for even less. He closed the gold window and negotiated an international currency revaluation that effectively devalued the dollar by around 8 per cent. Decisions like these can always be explained with reference to theory, but as Martin reminds us, they are made by people working within specific economic, political, and social contexts. The theoretical boxes must be filled with empirical facts.

'Academic governor' and Cambridge economic historian

The final element in Trentmann's taxonomy is Daunton the 'academic governor'. In London Martin chaired the Board of Studies in History of the University of London and the Institute of Historical Research. Since moving to Cambridge he has chaired the Faculty of History, the School of Humanities and Social Sciences (twice), the Fitzwilliam Museum (reflecting his keen interest in the Arts) and the academic awards committee of the Leverhulme Trust.[54] He has acted as Trustee of the National Maritime Museum, and is a Commissioner of Historic England. As well as sitting on three Research Assessment Exercise/ Research Excellence Framework panels, he has served on the editorial boards of the *Historical Journal* and the *English Historical Review*, and been a consulting editor of the *Oxford dictionary of national biography*. All this while being Master of Trinity Hall from 2004 to 2014, with the administrative and social commitments that entails.[55]

53   M.J. Daunton, 'Britain and globalisation since 1850: IV. The creation of the Washington consensus', *Transactions of the Royal Historical Society* 6, 19 (2009), pp. 1–35.
54   Martin's interest in ceramics dovetails with regular visits to Japan for the Anglo-Japanese Conference of Historians.
55   A Head of House has a punishing schedule of matriculation dinners, formal halls, graduation ceremonies, alumni events, college committees, etc. With his interest in people, Martin always presided with good humour and humility.

Martin shares the distinction of heading a Cambridge college with his two immediate predecessors as Professor of Economic History, the latter role partially chronicled in his contributions to the *Palgrave companion to Cambridge economics*.[56] These help us to situate his approach within the tradition of Cambridge economic history. The first occupant of the chair in 1928 was J.H. Clapham, a protégé of Lord Acton (Regius Professor of Modern History) and Alfred Marshall (Professor of Political Economy).[57] Clapham's appointment confirmed the armistice between the deductivists, who believed economics should rest on general principles, and the inductivists, who stressed the importance of historical context.[58] Marshall had long argued that both approaches were necessary: 'induction and deduction are both needed for scientific thought as the left foot and the right foot are both needed for walking'.[59] Induction needed theory to establish causation; deduction required historical facts to avoid becoming 'elegant toying'. Clapham agreed, but his sympathies clearly lay with the inductivists; economic history was 'a study of the economic aspects of the social institutions of the past'.[60] The principal methodological difference with mainstream history was the use of statistics: 'it is the obvious business of an economic historian to be a measurer above other historians'.[61]

Martin's approach to economic history aligns most closely with Clapham's successor (in 1938), Michael Postan. Possessed of 'an impish humour' and emanating 'an air of magic', Postan was born in Bessarabia and arrived in Britain in 1920, via Russia and the Balkans. Eric Hobsbawm remembered him 'looking somewhat like a red-haired Neanderthal survivor and speaking through a heavy Russian accent': 'he was nevertheless so brilliant and compelling a lecturer that he filled Mill Lane at nine o'clock in the morning'.[62] Postan's pedagogical approach was to introduce a historical thesis and then dismantle it with empirical evidence. Like his predecessor, he eschewed the universal generalisations of theoretical economists, arguing that theory must be grounded in precise social and institutional settings. As Martin points out, 'Postan's credo is still one that most Cambridge historians could accept.'[63]

---

56   Barry Supple was Master of St Catherine's from 1984 until 1993 and E.A. Wrigley was Master of Corpus Christi from 1994 until 2000; M.J. Daunton, 'Cambridge and economic history', in Cord, *Palgrave companion*, pp. 157–86; Daunton, 'Clapham', pp. 423–54.

57   The chair is based in History with *ex officio* membership of the Faculty Board of Economics; Daunton, 'Clapham', p. 439.

58   The dispute echoed the earlier German *Methodenstreit* between the followers of Carl Menger and those of Gustav von Schmoller.

59   Marshall quoted in Daunton, 'Clapham', p. 431.

60   Ibid., p. 441.

61   Ibid.

62   History lectures were then given in the Mill Lane lecture rooms; Daunton, 'Cambridge and economic history', p. 159.

63   Ibid., p. 165.

Postan retired in 1965 and was succeeded by David Joslin, who died young and was followed in 1971 by D.C. Coleman. Coleman, described as both 'a star and an irritant', arrived from the London School of Economics where, as an undergraduate, he had taken up economic history after informing his economics tutor, Nicky Kaldor, that his experience of running requisitioned hotels in Italy at the end of the war meant he no longer needed to study economics.[64] Coleman shared his predecessors' distrust of universal generalisations, preferring 'middle-order theorizing from an empirical foundation', always aware that 'the past was made by people not processes'.[65] Finding teaching and academic administration increasingly irksome, Coleman retired in 1981 to concentrate on writing. He was succeeded by Barry Supple, who held the chair until 1993. In tune with Martin's analysis of how markets are shaped by economic ideas and how people react to economic change, Supple focused on 'the symbiosis between the way people think about problems and the problems that arise'.[66] An example, taken up in his own *festschrift*, is how people, particularly policymakers, reacted to perceptions of Britain's economic decline.[67] In 1993 Supple was succeeded by E.A. Wrigley, who has done more to fulfil Clapham's injunction that economic historians must be 'measurers' than any of his successors. Wrigley's work, undertaken with colleagues at the Cambridge Group for the History of Population and Social Structure, means we know more about the demographic history of England and Wales than anywhere else. Wrigley has used these findings to produce a major interpretation of the origins and nature of the industrial revolution in England.

The appointment of Martin's successor, Gareth Austin, reflects the global turn in history. Austin's focus is on Sub-Saharan Africa, so for the first time the Professor of Economic History at Cambridge is not a historian of Britain or Europe. While it may no longer enjoy the relative prestige it once did, economic history remains a compulsory element of the History Tripos, attracts graduates from across the globe to its dedicated MPhil programme, and sees its PhD students carrying off more than their fair share of prizes at the annual Economic

---

64   N. Harte, 'Professor Donald Coleman: an appreciation', *Textile History* 27, 2 (1996), pp. 127–31.

65   This was famously expressed in his critique of proto-industrialisation, D.C. Coleman, 'Proto-industrialization: a concept too many', *Economic History Review* 36, 3 (1983), pp. 435–48; P. Matthias, 'Donald Cuthbert Coleman', *Dictionary of national biography*; N. McKendrick and R.B. Outhwaite, *Business life and public policy: essays in honour of D.C. Coleman* (Cambridge, 2009), p. vii.

66   Barry Supple, interview with Alan Macfarlane, available at http://www.alanmacfarlane. com, viewed 31 Aug. 2018.

67   P.F. Clarke and R.C. Trebilcock, eds, *Understanding decline: perceptions and realities of British economic performance* (Cambridge, 1997); see also B.E. Supple, 'Presidential address: fear of failing: economic history and the decline of Britain', *Economic History Review* 47, 3 (1994), pp. 441–58.

History Society conference. There remain the methodological differences with the Faculty of Economics that would have been familiar to nineteenth-century predecessors, but as Martin points out, 'the strength of economic history in Cambridge arises from the fact that there was never a separate department'.[68] This has allowed economic historians to connect with colleagues in related fields, while also surviving the cuts that closed down dedicated departments at other universities in the 1980s.

Despite his heavy publishing, teaching, and administrative workload, Martin has still found time to supervise 34 PhD students, some of whom join friends and colleagues here to fill a number of empty boxes with well-informed 'archival narrative'. These boxes relate to the different phases of Martin's career: urban history and housing, the state and taxation, and Britain and globalisation. Julian Hoppit's essay contributes to the first two research agendas by highlighting the importance of London to the fiscal-military state through an assessment of the tax collected in and around the capital. The fiscal-military state was primarily financed with borrowing, however. Adrian Leonard's study of John Julius Angerstein, doyen of the Lloyd's insurance market and government loan contractor during the Napoleonic Wars, uncovers the links between City merchants and government finance. Richard Rodger picks up the Georgite theme of progress and poverty explored in Martin's work on urban history to show how local property markets were shaped by the nature and extent of landownership, with institutional owners and major utility companies having distortionary effects, particularly in Scotland where urban development (progress) often came at the cost of squalid accommodation (poverty). We return to the topic of the state with Charles Read's essay on 'The political economy of Sir Robert Peel'. Read shows that policies sometimes ascribed to Gladstonian finance owed more to Peel's practical responses to events.

David Todd's essay on 'Champagne capitalism' shifts the focus to the 'third Daunton' of globalisation. Rather than failing to emulate British industrialisation and exports, the French developed a distinctive approach based on luxury and semi-luxury goods that complemented rather than rivalled Britain in the increasingly global economy. The next two essays are on Germany with Sean Eddie highlighting the importance of state finance to the 1848 revolution in Prussia, and Sabine Schneider exploring the debates, political coalitions and diplomatic manoeuvres that characterised the monetary reforms of the new German Empire. We return to Britain for Seung Woo Kim's exploration of the role of the British state, particularly the Bank of England, in nurturing the Eurodollar market in London after 1959.

The next chapters all address 'neoliberalism' in different ways and contexts, with a diversion to the Thames Estuary as Duncan Needham examines the

---

68   Daunton, *Valedictory lecture.*

failed attempt to build an airport at Maplin in the 1970s. Adrian Williamson's essay identifies the continuities in Conservative fiscal policy from the 1960s to the 1980s. Jim Tomlinson also examines fiscal policy during this period to assess the impact of neoliberal ideas in 1970s Britain. Bernhard Rieger explores the impact of neoliberalism on changing labour practices, examining the impact of 'American' workfare on Conservative welfare policy in the 1980s. The welfare theme is further explored in Matthew Hilton's essay, which situates charity in the mixed economy of welfare and neoliberal governance. Martin Chick then shows how the British state has dealt with changing conceptions of time in such practical matters as the allocation of resources to different sectors of public expenditure. In the final essay, Frank Trentmann and Hiroki Shin look at how the state coped with rising demand for electricity, and shortages, in post-war Britain.

Taxing London and the British fiscal state, 1660–1815

JULIAN HOPPIT

This chapter contributes to two of Martin Daunton's main research interests: urban history and the history of taxation.[1] It explores the fiscal importance of London to central government, but not, as is usually the case, with regard to the financial institutions of 'the City', capital markets, and the money supply. Instead it considers the amounts of taxes collected in and around the capital. The spectacular growth in taxation for central government in this period is often ascribed to the ability of the excise service to extract revenue from across the length and breadth of the country. By contrast this chapter shows that very large amounts of taxes were collected in and around the capital. This requires significantly amending usual interpretations both of the nature of Britain's fiscal state and of London's importance to national economic developments.

As is well known, this period saw a dramatic transformation in public finances. In 1670 Charles II was so desperate for funds that he became a pensioner of France; two years later he defaulted on public loans in the 'Stop of the Exchequer'. But from that nadir public finances began to be transformed, if often by adapting earlier innovations, leading Britain to become one of Europe's most heavily taxed societies.[2] Total taxes collected rose eightfold in real per capita terms from 1664 to 1810, and from 4 to 18 per cent of GNP.[3] This was to meet current spending and the charges on a mushrooming national debt: over the same period the debt rose from zero to 160 per cent of national income.[4] Such resources enabled Britain to wage frequent and increasingly costly wars,

1   I am grateful for comments by participants at the conference and my co-editors.
2   K. Kivanç Karaman and Şevket Pamuk, 'Ottoman state finances in European perspective, 1500–1914', *Journal of Economic History* 70, 3 (2010), pp. 610–11.
3   Patrick K. O'Brien and Philip A. Hunt, 'The rise of a fiscal state in England, 1485–1815', *Historical Research* 66 (1993), pp. 161, 174–5. This is of England to 1707, Britain thereafter.
4   B.R. Mitchell, *British historical statistics* (Cambridge, 1988), p. 601; http://www.nuffield.ox.ac.uk/users/Broadberry/Nov2011FinalData1270-1870.xlsx, viewed 27 Jun. 2017.

both European and imperial, becoming in the process sufficiently powerful to survive the tremendous shocks of the American and French revolutions.

Accounts of London's role in that transformation have concentrated on relations between the City and Whitehall, especially regarding the birth and infancy of the national debt between the Glorious Revolution of 1688–89 and the bursting of the South Sea Bubble in 1720.[5] By contrast, the history of taxation in London has hardly been touched on. It is notable, for example, that Miles Ogborn in a chapter about the excise in a book about London pays more attention to the peregrinations of Charles Davenant for the excise in Wales and the west of England than the collection of taxes in the capital itself.[6] Here he follows John Brewer's depiction of the importance of the excise, especially the coherence and effectiveness of the actions of thousands of widely scattered excise officers implementing national tax rates. That it was centred in London is important only in so far as it exerted close administrative control over the provinces.[7] Only in the history of direct taxation has the particular importance of London and south-east England been emphasised.[8]

Stressing the national reach of the excise – much less attention has been paid to other sources of revenues – can ignore the marked regional variations in the amounts of taxes collected in eighteenth-century Britain, while because Scotland enjoyed several lower tax rates, Britain's common market was less complete than is usually said.[9] Building on those studies, here attention focuses first on the amount of taxation raised in London and south-east England compared to the rest of Britain, second on explaining in general terms the striking figures that are revealed, and finally on how these refine our understanding of London's wider role from the late seventeenth to the early nineteenth centuries. Very large amounts of taxes were collected in London during this period, out of all proportion to its population and economy, demonstrating that the British fiscal state was more centralised and metropolitan than is conventionally argued.

Evidence of the geography of taxes collected lies widely scattered, and

5 Foundational was the work of Lucy Sutherland, especially her essays collected in *Politics and finance in the eighteenth century*, ed. Aubrey Newman (London, 1984), but the seminal work remains P.G.M. Dickson, *The financial revolution in England: a study in the development of public credit, 1688–1756* (London, 1967). More recently see, amongst others, Anne L. Murphy, *The origins of English financial markets: investment and speculation before the South Sea Bubble* (Cambridge, 2009).

6 Miles Ogborn, *Spaces of modernity: London's geographies, 1680–1780* (New York, 1998), ch. 5.

7 John Brewer, *The sinews of power: war, money, and the English state, 1688–1783* (London, 1989); recently reiterated by William J. Ashworth, *The Industrial Revolution: the state, knowledge and global trade* (London, 2017), p. 120.

8 E.J. Buckatzstch, 'The geographical distribution of wealth in England, 1086–1843: an experimental study of certain tax assessments', *Economic History Review* 3 (1950), pp. 180–202.

9 Julian Hoppit, *Britain's political economies: parliament and economic life, 1660–1800* (Cambridge, 2017), ch. 9; Julian Hoppit, 'Scotland and the Taxing Union, 1707–1815', *Scottish Historical Review* 98 (2019), pp. 45–70.

Table 1.1. The geography of taxes collected in Britain, 1685–1829, as % of total at given dates

	London	South-East	Rest of Britain
EXCISE			
1685	28	19	53
1741	33	22	46
1783	30	20	50
1796	32	17	51
CUSTOMS			
1710	80	1	19
1750	67	3	30
1780	68	5	27
1829	54	2	44
LAND TAX, 1744	11	32	57
INCOME TAX, 1812	10	25	65

Note: For the excise annual averages are used for 1684–86 and 1782–84, and Scotland is not included in the figures for 1685.

Sources: Excise: BL Harleian 4227; Sandon Hall, Harrowby Trust 525; TNA PRO 30/8/288, ff. 18 and 56; NRS E554/3. Customs: BL Add. 8133A; NRS E231/9/3, E501/43 and 73; J. Marshall, *Digest of all the accounts* (London, 1834), [part 2], pp. 68–9. Land tax: Anon., *Land tax at 4s in ye pound paid by England & Wales in 1702, & 1704* (London, 1745); BL Harleian 4226, ff. 15–16. Income tax, Marshall, *Digest*, [part 2], p. 29.

allows only occasional snapshots to be taken. Moreover, the basis on which the sources, all of them official, were originally compiled means that there is a little less precision in the figures which follow than might be supposed. Even so, the findings are very clear and fairly robust. In what follows I provide figures for three areas: London, defined as the whole metropolitan area; south-east England; and the rest of Britain.[10] The starting point is to set out how much tax was collected in the three areas, expressed first as their absolute share at selected dates (Table 1.1).

Clearly a large amount of Britain's taxes was collected in London and the wider south-east region. The figures in Table 1.1 suggest that during the first half of the eighteenth century London accounted for around one third of total

10   South-east England is defined as in Peter Clark, ed., *The Cambridge urban history of Britain*, vol. 2: *1540–1840* (Cambridge, 2000): Bedfordshire, Buckinghamshire, Essex, Hampshire, Hertfordshire, Kent, Middlesex, Oxfordshire, Surrey, and Sussex.

Table 1.2. Index of taxation per capita (Britain = 100)

	London	South-East	Rest of Britain
EXCISE			
1685	306	108	72
1741	392	147	58
1783	376	130	64
1796	387	111	66
CUSTOMS			
1710	924	6	24
1750	796	18	38
1780	862	33	36
1829	537	18	57
LAND TAX, 1744	133	207	75
INCOME TAX, 1812	109	169	86

Source: Taxes as for Table 1.1. Population, E.A. Wrigley, 'Rickman revisited: the population growth rates of English counties in the early modern period', *Economic History Review* 62 (2009), p. 721; E.A. Wrigley, 'English county populations in the later eighteenth century', *Economic History Review* 60 (2007), pp. 54–5; Phyllis Deane and W.A. Cole, *British economic growth, 1688–1959: trends and structures* (2nd edn, Cambridge, 1969), p. 103; Leonard Schwartz, 'London 1700–1840', in Clark, *Cambridge urban history*, p. 650; Vanessa Harding, 'The population of early modern London: a review of the published evidence', *London Journal* 15 (1990), pp. 111–28; Mitchell, *British historical statistics*, pp. 7–9, 30–1; R.A. Houston, *The population history of Britain and Ireland, 1500–1750* (Basingstoke, 1992), pp. 29–30; John Williams, *Digest of Welsh historical statistics* (Cardiff, 1985), vol. 1, p. 6.

public revenue and south-east England about one fifth, together accounting for a little over half of the total. Those shares fell thereafter, so by 1815 London was providing around one quarter and south-east England one twelfth of public revenue, or about one third in total.[11] Without regional GDP figures, only population distribution provides a useful comparator here. Crucially, the share of Britain's growing population for both London and south-east England changed little in this period: about 8 or 9 per cent for the former, 15–16 per cent for the latter. In 1710 the per capita tax take in London and south-east England was respectively six and two times that of the rest of Britain. By 1800 there was little difference between south-east England and the rest of Britain,

11   Mitchell, *British historical statistics*, pp. 575–7, 581.

Table 1.3. Five most lucrative excise taxes in London, 1741 and 1796, % of total collected

1741		1796	
Beer	25	Tea*	24
Tea*	20	Foreign spirits*	20
Imported liquors*	14	Beer	19
Low wines and spirits	13	Wine*	11
Soap	10	Tobacco and snuff*	9
Sub-total	82	Sub-total	83
Imported goods*	34	Imported goods*	64

Source: Sandon Hall, Harrowby Trust 525; NRS 554/3; TNA PRO 30/8/288, f. 56.

but in London the per capita tax take was over four times higher than both. Table 1.2 puts some detail on those trends.

In the first half of the eighteenth century there was a significant concentration of tax collection in the capital and the south-east. Thereafter, London's absolute and per capita share declined somewhat, but that of the south-east more quickly. London's importance was especially marked with regard to customs duties. Although that dominance declined, even as late as 1829 over half of all British customs duties were collected there. When related to London's population size this importance was overwhelming. This speaks powerfully of London's evolving competitiveness as a port, despite the growth of Glasgow, Hull, Liverpool, and Newcastle, with their rapidly industrialising hinterlands. It is also clear that in terms of customs duties London dominated south-east England, where Portsmouth and Southampton were the only other considerable ports.

London's per capita share of the British tax take declined somewhat in the eighteenth century, but not as quickly as that of south-east England. The capital's achievement here is striking given rapid industrialisation in the Midlands, north-west England, and Scotland's central belt. Usually the excise is considered as a tax on domestic manufactures such as beer, candles, and soap. In that regard it was important that London was a significant locale for such industries, to the extent that it was still, despite rapid industrialisation elsewhere, Britain's largest industrial urban centre in 1815. Yet looking at the commodity composition of the excise adds a further explanatory factor (Table 1.3).

A key factor in the growth of excise receipts in eighteenth-century London was the taxing of imported goods: in London at the end of the eighteenth century, nearly two thirds were levied on imported commodities, whereas elsewhere it was just one twentieth. Plainly the excise was not just a tax on internally produced goods, coming to invade the territory of overseas trade in the eighteenth century, mainly because it was believed to be a much more efficient tax than the customs service. In 1797 nearly 600 excise officers were concerned with import and export duties across Britain, with over half of them in London.[12] Little wonder that Patrick Colquhoun thought that 25 per cent of British tax receipts were collected at the Port of London.[13]

Customs and excise were consumption taxes. For most of the period the land tax, refined in the 1690s, was the main direct tax. Though notionally levied on the value of land, the quotas were little altered after the 1690s, though in 1798 landowners could compound for the tax. That is, the snapshot provided for 1744 holds good for the whole of the eighteenth century in absolute terms, but not relative to population. Given London's economic vitality and high demand for land it is not surprising that the land tax was more productive there, though more striking are the large amounts of land tax collected in the south-east more widely. Together, London and the south-east provided 43 per cent of British land tax receipts. This was not as high a degree of geographical concentration as was the case with the excise, but it was not particularly dissimilar.

Given the unbalanced territoriality of the land tax, from the middle of the eighteenth century the Treasury tried various ways of taxing Britain's growing wealth. A wide range of new taxes on certain types of goods and services – carriages and servants for example – was introduced but rarely produced as much revenue as had been hoped. It was the limitations of these 'assessed' taxes which led to the introduction of the income tax in 1799 as a temporary wartime measure.[14] In fact, this was a tax on different forms of property, meaning wealth was taxed geographically more equally than before. This helps to explain why the new tax was not especially burdensome in the capital – though it was in the wider region. In 1804, by contrast, 27 per cent of British profits from trade and commerce, manufactures, professional earnings, and salaries (Schedule D of the income tax) were assessed as being made in London.[15]

Even in 1815, London remained an extraordinary concentration of revenue collection within Britain. This was associated with a huge concentration of revenue officers. For example, in 1741 there were around 4,200 excise officers in Britain, with 19 per cent based in London, though some in the central offices

---

12   TNA CUST 142/22.
13   P. Colquhoun, *A treatise on the commerce and police of the River Thames* (London, 1800), p. xxxii.
14   Arthur Hope-Jones, *Income tax in the Napoleonic Wars* (Cambridge, 1939).
15   J. Marshall, *Digest of all the accounts* (London, 1834), [part 2], p. 29. Considering the income tax on land (Schedules A–C) qualifies the argument of W.D. Rubinstein, 'The Victorian middle classes: wealth, occupation, and geography', *Economic History Review* 30 (1977), p. 616.

rather than gathering revenue in the capital.[16] In 1780 the geography of customs officers was much the same: 558 were based in London out of a total of around 2,820.[17] Yet these shares fell short of those of revenue collected, meaning that the amounts collected per revenue officer in London were much greater than elsewhere, reaping as they did significant administrative economies of scale in the capital. In 1780 customs officers in London each collected almost nine times as much as those elsewhere; in 1741 London excise officers were twice as productive as those elsewhere.[18]

Having established the large amounts of taxes collected in London and, for much of the period, the south-east, attention now turns to explaining why. In doing so it should be noted that schematically, totals of tax collected are a function of three main factors: tax policy – decisions about what is to be taxed; taxable capacity – the amount of taxable goods and services being produced, traded, and consumed; and the tax gap – the difference between what should have been and what was collected because of maladministration, evasion, and fraud. There is only space here to touch on each of these.

With regard to tax policy it is important to distinguish between the formal and effective incidence of taxes, in the context that customs duties on exports were negligible for most of the period.[19] Importantly a lot of taxes were collected in London, but were paid for elsewhere through higher prices on goods sent up the Thames, overland along improving roads, and, especially, coastwise. This was most obviously the case for the East India Company, which had a complete monopoly of British trade with Asia until 1813 and landed virtually all of its imports in London, paying taxes there before a goodly part were sent elsewhere to be sold. But a lot of Britain's trade with Europe, north and south, also flowed through the capital, if at the behest of market forces rather than political diktat. Indeed, at the end of the eighteenth century, admittedly a period of war, the tonnage of overseas voyages to and from London was distributed thus: 49 per cent with northern Europe, Scandinavia, and the Baltic, 12 per cent with the rest of Europe and the Mediterranean, and 39 per cent with the rest of the world.[20]

Although after about 1700 London was Europe's largest city, with very high real wages (amidst considerable poverty), consuming vast amounts of goods

---

16 Sandon Hall, Staffordshire, Harrowby Trust 525; NRS GD1/54/10. Figures for England and Wales relate to 1741, but for Scotland 1743. I am grateful to Koji Yamamoto for collecting the Scottish figures for me. The excise service in 1800 comprised 300 in the London head office and 966 collecting duties in London, out of a total establishment in England and Wales of 4,844. TNA CUST145/22.

17 Cambridge University Library, Add. 5237; William L. Clements Library, Ann Arbor, Shelburne Papers, box 115, fols 11–30.

18 Numbers of excise and customs officers are from note 16; amounts of excise are Sandon Hall, Harrowby Trust 525 and NRS E554/3; amounts of customs are BL Add. 8133A and NRS E501/73.

19 For this distinction see J.A. Kay and M.A. King, *The British tax system* (Oxford, 1978), p. 7.

20 Colquhoun, *Treatise*, p. 17.

and services of all kinds, the high levels of customs and excise receipts there also reflect on its role as an entrepôt and its developing iterative relationship between overseas and coastal trades. While neither topic has been thoroughly studied, the coastal trade has been more overlooked and is worth exploring a little.[21] Patrick Colquhoun reported from official statistics to the effect that, taking multiple voyages into account, around two thirds of shipping using the Port of London in the eighteenth century was concerned with the coastal trade and around one third with overseas trade – coastal ships were generally of much lower tonnage. In the late 1790s London's coastal trade, excluding colliers, was said to involve 625 vessels, which were twice the size of a century earlier and undertook over 10 voyages per annum. Nearly 90 per cent of those coasting voyages were to or from English out-ports, mainly on the east coast, from Kent to Northumberland, with most of the rest to Scotland and under 2 per cent to Wales. In terms of the number of voyages to individual ports, London's connections to Hull were the most numerous (900 voyages), receiving from there the industrial goods of the West Riding and east Midlands in exchange for overseas goods like tea, sugar, and wine, as well as manufactured goods.[22] But there were also strong connections with rural areas, including nearly 2,000 voyages to or from East Anglian ports, with London consuming and redistributing a large amount of the region's grain, both as flour and as malt.[23]

London's role as Britain's dominant port for both overseas and coastal trade meant that taxes could be collected there which were ultimately paid for across the island. Significant administrative efficiencies were reaped through the relative ease of collecting taxes from a four-mile stretch of the Thames than from those scattered across Britain. Only occasionally, however, is it possible to show that policymakers explicitly acted on such reasoning, though some reasonably supposed that conditions in London and the south-east loomed very large in the minds of ministers and the Treasury.[24] The most important case related to the ways coal was taxed. A tax on coal shipments into London

21   On London and overseas trade C.J. French, '"Crowded with traders and great commerce": London's domination of English overseas trade, 1700–1775', *London Journal* 17 (1992), pp. 27–35; Ralph Davis, *The rise of the English shipping industry in the seventeenth and eighteenth centuries* (Newton Abbot, 1972), pp. 27, 35. On the coastal trade see John Armstrong and Philip S. Bagwell, 'Coastal shipping', in Derek H. Aldcroft and Michael J. Freeman, eds, *Transport in the Industrial Revolution* (Manchester, 1983), pp. 142–76.

22   On Hull's coastal trade see Gordon Jackson, *Hull in the eighteenth century: a study in economic and social history* (Oxford, 1972), pp. 74, 82–6.

23   Colquhoun, *Treatise*, pp. 9, 11–12. East Anglia here is taken to include all ports in Essex, Suffolk, and Norfolk. In 1728, 77 per cent of inward vessels to the Port of London were coasters: Charles Capper, *The port and trade of London, historical, statistical, local, and general* (London, 1862), p. 115.

24   James Anderson, *Observations on the effects of the coal duty upon the remote and thinly peopled coasts of Britain* (Edinburgh, 1792), p. 17; National Library of Scotland, Melville Papers, 640, ff. 33–5.

was introduced in 1667 to help pay for the costs of rebuilding after the great fire, and was subsequently extended. Further local taxes on coal in London were also introduced, but in 1695 a national tax on coastwise shipping of coal began. Unlike London's local taxes on coal, this national tax caused a storm of protest from London, on the grounds that coastwise coal was taxed more heavily than exported coal, that it hampered industrial development in London, and that it hit the colliers' national role as a nursery of seamen. Yet although the tax was soon lifted, it was reintroduced in 1698 and frequently renewed before becoming permanent until its repeal in 1831. Although this was a tax on all coals shipped coastwise, it hit London hardest because much of such coal was consumed in or through the city, with around 60–65 per cent of the tax being collected there.[25]

The coastwise tax on coal stands out as an unusual example of parliament imposing a levy on something that was both a necessity for many and a raw material for key industries. It did so because its needs were great, because this was a relatively easy tax to collect, and because London's vitality seemed inexhaustible. There is certainly no doubt that through the period many were aware of London' immense size and importance as a commercial city, but gradually this scale began to be judged more precisely. Colquhoun's study, first published in 1796, epitomised this, taking to a logical conclusion some of the earlier preoccupations of Sir Charles Whitworth who, as chairman of one of the key finance committees of the House of Commons, accumulated a lot data about overseas trade, and tried (but failed) to establish a quarterly account of London's trade.[26] Such knowledge framed extensions of the excise into overseas trade in the second half of the eighteenth century.

Britain's burgeoning overseas trade in this period, with the majority of it passing through the Port of London, generated not only more customs revenues, but more excise revenues as well. Yet it would be wrong to neglect the fact that London's industrial base also contributed significantly to the capital's taxable capacity. In 1741 beer, distilled spirits, soap, candles, and hides together generated over half of London's excise receipts. The relative importance of these shrank thereafter, but even in 1796 about one third of excise receipts there

---

25   William John Hausman, *Public policy and the supply of coal to London, 1700–1770* (New York, 1976), ch. 3; Michael W. Flinn, *The history of the British coal industry, vol. 2: 1700–1830: the Industrial Revolution* (Oxford, 1984), p. 284. For an earlier attack on the territorial inequality of the tax, Anon., *The mischief of the five shillings tax on coal* (London, 1699), pp. 2–3. Attempts to reduce gin consumption in the middle of the eighteenth century also led to levies that were essentially local to London. Lee Davison, 'Experiments in the social regulation of industry: gin legislation, 1729–1751', in Lee Davison, Tim Hitchcock, Tim Keirn, and R.B. Shoemaker, eds, *Stilling the grumbling hive: the response to social and economic problems in England, 1689–1750* (Stroud, 1992), pp. 25–48.
26   *A register of the trade of the Port of London* (London, 1777); *State of the trade of Great Britain, in its imports and exports* (London, 1776).

were from manufactured goods, with beer, soap, and candles leading the way. In part this reflected direct and indirect consumption in London, with soap, candles, and leather duties a consequence of London's vast consumption of beef, much of it brought on the hoof from as far afield as Scotland. But the continuous significance of London's brewers to the excise needs emphasising. London brewing became highly capital intensive in the eighteenth century, leading to considerable business concentration – by 1800, 80 per cent of London beer was brewed by six giant breweries. This enabled the excise administration to become very efficient in this key London industry.[27] On a lesser scale, much the same was true of distilling, where at the end of the eighteenth century the trade in London was again said to be dominated by just six firms, compared to the many hundreds of small distillers in Scotland.[28]

Discussion of tax policy towards and tax capacity in London has led to two main points: that a significant part of taxes felt across Britain was collected in the Port of London, utilising its strong trading connections to expanding domestic markets; second, that the concentration in London of traders and producers, often much bigger operators than elsewhere, allowed considerable administrative economies of scale to be reaped. Such points imply, of course, that tax avoidance and evasion in the capital were not as serious as elsewhere in Britain. Whether that is true is hard to say; by its very nature, the extent of such activity cannot be pinned down. It would be wrong to say that it did not exist, that the chaotic nature of the Port's wharfs and quays before the building of 'dockland' began in the early nineteenth century did not provide opportunities for smuggling and fraud. In 1796 Colquhoun made much of the scale of pilfering, as have some modern historians.[29] It was certainly argued at the end of the eighteenth century that building the West India Docks would help reduce losses both to the revenue and businesses from the depredations of lightly supervised workers.[30] Yet it appears – clear evidence is necessarily absent – that proportionately revenue avoidance and evasion were less serious in London than elsewhere. Smuggling was more commonly said to be rife, at least for a time, around the Irish Sea, the Channel Islands, and Cornwall, Devon, Kent, and Sussex. Direct smuggling into London appears to have been of limited

27 Peter Mathias, *The brewing industry in England, 1700–1830* (Cambridge, 1959), pp. 339, 346, 350.
28 John Dalrymple, *Address from Sir John Dalrymple, Bart ... to the landholders of England, upon the interest which they have in the state of the Distillery Laws* (Edinburgh, 1786), pp. 6–9; Thomas Smith, *Case of the lowland distillers of Scotland* [Edinburgh?, 1798?], p. 4.
29 Colquhoun, *Treatise*; Peter Linebaugh, *The London hanged: crime and civil society in the eighteenth century* (London, 1991).
30 Walter M. Stern, 'The first London dock boom and the growth of the West India Docks', *Economica* 19 (1952), pp. 59–77.

scale.[31] Some smuggled goods ran the gauntlet of the concentration of revenue officers on and along the Thames via false ships' manifests, with legislation in 1786 seeking to tackle this.[32] Alternatively they came overland, having been landed on the coasts of Kent and Sussex. Because land transportation costs were much higher than by water, this meant that only very heavily taxed goods or those with high value relative to their weight and bulk were profitable to move in large amounts over significant distances. Tea stood out in this regard until duties on it were cut substantially in 1784. It was certainly the case that some businesses in London complained that they were being rendered uncompetitive by smugglers operating in the country.[33]

In the space remaining, some of the general implications of London's great importance as a source of taxation will be considered, under two main related heads: interpretations of London's importance to England and Britain's wider economic development in the period, and London's importance to the nature of the British fiscal state. Some historiographical framing will help set the scene.

In *The perspective of the world*, the third and final volume of Braudel's epic *Civilization and capitalism*, the history of the early modern world economy is depicted as involving clearly discernible shifts in its centre of gravity from southern to north-western Europe.[34] But such changes were not merely those of geography, for Braudel also argued for a fundamental change in economic loci from dominant city-states to national markets. Thus he focused upon the rise in turn of Venice, Genoa, and Amsterdam, if always in their wider settings. But then, changing tack, he moved to consider not London, but the novel importance after c. 1700 of 'national markets', illustrated by the case of France and then of England. While in the latter he gave London some consideration, his unit of analysis had shifted from the city state to the nation state. This is an approach others have taken. Recently the debate over the 'little divergence' has accepted that the centre of economic gravity and vitality shifted to north-west Europe at some point – the debate is about timing – while the older idea of mercantilism developed by Schmoller and others emphasised its nation-building aspects, supplanting more local or regional economies.[35]

31   On the geography of smuggling see Anon., *Observations on smuggling, humbly submitted to the consideration of the right honourable the House of Peers, and the honourable House of Commons* [London, 1779?], p. 6.
32   [George Rose], *A brief examination into the increase of the revenue, commerce and navigation of Great Britain* (1792), p. 5.
33   Clements Library, Shelburne papers, vol. 119, f. 239; Richard Twining, *Observations on the Tea and Window Act, and on the tea trade* (London, 1784), p. 5; NRS CE8/2, fols 93–4, 160–2.
34   Fernand Braudel, *Civilization and capitalism, 15th–18th century, vol. III: The perspective of the world*, trans. Siân Reynolds (London, 1984), chs. 2–4.
35   Gustav Schmoller, *The mercantile system and its historical significance* (London, 1896), pp. 48–50. The belief in an early modern shift in Europe's centre of economic gravity has been especially important to types of Marxist history, such as: E.J. Hobsbawm, 'The general crisis of

In the British case, several arguments have been made about why thinking in national terms is the best way to understand the island's history in this period, notably relating to the Union of 1707, the growth of a national market, and the explosion of commerce, industry, and population away from south-east England. It is telling in this regard that Tony Wrigley's famous 1967 'Simple Model of London's Importance' (uncited by Braudel) considered the period to 1750 only.[36] Although no one would now claim that the industrial revolution was like a 'storm that passed over London and broke elsewhere', no one has successfully extended Wrigley's model to the century after 1750, nor indeed attempted a concerted revision or refinement of it in the light of subsequent research into London's economy and society.[37]

Exploring the tax take in London in this period has confirmed the city's pre-eminence in Britain's overseas trade, industry, and consumption. Rapid economic growth elsewhere, mainly on Britain's coalfields, was diluting this importance through the period, but London maintained its share of the national population before beginning to increase it from the early nineteenth century. Changes in the relative importance of customs and excise receipts in London shed some light on that process. On the one hand, the importance of overseas trade to both underscores the considerable emphasis put upon global connections to Britain's fortunes. On the other, however, the significance of taxes on beer, soap, candles, and leather reminds us of industrial developments that were almost completely untouched by such global connections, at least directly. The great importance of beer and tea to excise receipts in London nicely sums up this duality. Further, this chapter has brought into sharper relief the need to better understand and appreciate the importance of trading connections between the capital and the rest of Britain. Most often that has been done with reference to the development of turnpike roads radiating out from the capital.[38] But this neglects London's role in Britain's vital coastal trade – the best study, published eighty years ago, stopped in 1750.[39] Water remained much more cost

the European economy in the seventeenth century', *Past & Present* 5 (1954), pp. 33–53; Immanuel Wallerstein, *The modern world system* (New York, 1980), vol. 1, pp. 216, 225; vol. 2, p. 37.

36   E.A. Wrigley, 'A simple model of London's importance in changing English society and economy, 1650–1750', *Past & Present* 37 (1967), pp. 711–35.

37   The quote is J.L. Hammond, 'Eighteenth-century London', *New Statesman* 24, no. 621 (21 Mar. 1925), p. 693. David Barnett, *London, hub of the industrial revolution: a revisionary history* (London, 1998). A strong argument for the regional approach is made by Pat Hudson, 'The regional perspective', in Pat Hudson, ed., *Regions and industries: a perspective on the Industrial Revolution in Britain* (Cambridge, 1989), pp. 5–38.

38   William Albert, *The turnpike road system in England, 1663–1840* (Cambridge, 1972); Eric Pawson, *Transport and economy: the turnpike roads of eighteenth-century Britain* (London, 1977).

39   T.S. Willan, *The English coasting trade, 1600–1750* (Manchester, 1938). See also Simon P. Ville, *English shipowning during the Industrial Revolution: Michael Henley and Son, London shipowners, 1770–1830* (Manchester, 1987).

effective for many types of transport through this period, and though London was at the edge of Britain's canal 'network', it was far and away Britain's largest centre of water haulage.

London's economic vitality was, therefore, hugely important to British public income. The contrast here with most other European capitals is marked. As Colley observed, 'Of all the major European powers, only Great Britain – and to a less concentrated degree the Dutch Republic – possessed a metropolis of trade and population that was also its centre of power.'[40] The contrast between London and Paris is especially striking. When travelling in France in the late 1780s Arthur Young was struck by the quietness of the roads around Paris compared to London. Paris was somewhat smaller, within a much larger nation (geographically and demographically), lying a considerable distance from coastal and oceanic trading.[41] It could not play the role that London did. This was contemplated by Jacques Necker, the Swiss-born one-time French finance minister, who somewhat enviously noted 'the reunion in London of almost all the [nation's] specie; that city being at once a sea-port, the capital of the kingdom, the chief trading town, and the place where almost all the exchange operations are made'.[42] London's economic importance, both in its own right and in terms of its connections with the rest of Britain, allowed Britons to be much more easily and heavily taxed. Brewer and Ashworth are right to emphasise the national reach of the excise service in eighteenth-century England, but this should not obscure London's vital role in filling central government's coffers with taxes.

Perceptions of how tax monies flowed and ultimately accumulated within Britain put great store in the fact that the Treasury and Exchequer were in London. It was already common in 1660 for London to be criticised as being too large a head for the national body. Developments thereafter regarding taxes and the national debt encouraged such views to be restated more powerfully.[43] In 1703, one Scottish writer lamented drawing 'the riches and government of the three kingdoms to the south-east corner of this island ... as unnatural', a view given qualified support by David Hume in mid-century and taken up by Cobbett in the early-nineteenth-century English context when he lambasted the tax gatherers of the Great Wen.[44]

40 Linda Colley, *Britons: forging the nation, 1707–1837* (New Haven, 1992), p. 64.

41 Arthur Young, *Travels in France during the years 1787, 1788 and 1789*, ed. Constantia Maxwell (Cambridge, 1929), pp. 16, 49, 72.

42 Jacques Necker, *A treatise on the administration of the finances of France* (London, 1785), vol. 3, p. 275.

43 Briefly summarised in M.J. Daunton, 'Towns and economic growth in eighteenth-century England', in P. Abrams and E.A. Wrigley, eds, *Towns in societies* (Cambridge, 1978), pp. 245–6, 271–2.

44 Andrew Fletcher, *Political works*, ed. John Robertson (Cambridge, 1997), p. 213; David Hume, *Essays, moral, political, and literary*, ed. Eugene F. Miller (Indianapolis, 1987), p. 354; William Cobbett, 'To Mr Canning', *Cobbett's Weekly Political Register*, 22 Feb. 1823, p. 481.

It was natural enough to worry that London might be a monstrous parasite, gorging itself on truly productive provinces, though this was attacked at the time.[45] Yet it is consistent with the view that Britain's fiscal state depended heavily on excises collected nationally. But in terms of the flows of taxes, this chapter has suggested that this interpretation misses the highly centralised nature of much tax collection. It was not just tax collectors sending their receipts from the provinces to the capital, but the business men and women who acted as surrogate collectors by passing on taxes collected in London in the form of higher prices to consumers elsewhere. Handling tax receipts and passing them to London played an important role in the development of 'country banking', but it follows that businesses were doing much the same sort of thing, if less directly.[46] Taxation in the capital affected many consumers nationwide, and aided the greater integration of Britain's financial system. The scale of this is impossible to quantify, but it was very considerable, suggesting that public finances be added to Wrigley's simple model of London's importance in changing the wider economy.

What finally do the findings of this chapter mean for our understanding of Britain's fiscal state at the time? Two major points have been made. Firstly, that while collection from across Britain was increasingly important, London (and for some decades the wider south-east) stands out as an exceptionally fertile tax region. It is certainly right to be struck by the national reach of Britain's revenue services and the fact that most tax rates were applied nationally: the close management of collectors, especially in the excise, was an impressive feature of the central government's wherewithal. But much the most productive revenue officers were those dealing with no more than the ten square miles which London occupied during this period. Secondly, the growing importance of the Port of London to the revenue has been stressed. It has been shown that the excise began to be levied in considerable amounts on imported goods. This then circles back to the previous point, for such goods were taxed in ports, London especially. While rapid industrialisation was mainly taking place outside of London, most of the products of that process were, quite deliberately, not taxed. In the eighteenth century Britain's excise was reoriented significantly towards exploiting domestic consumption of five key imported goods: spirits, wine, tea, coffee, and tobacco. Despite the rise of Liverpool and Glasgow, in 1796, 70 per cent of Britain's total excise duties on those commodities were collected in London.[47]

In discussing the heavy tax burden in Britain in this period Martin Daunton has noted that 'The political acceptability of taxes rested less on their level than

---

45 Roy Porter, *London: a social history* (London, 1994), p. 136.
46 On the flow of taxation to the capital see L.S. Pressnell, 'Public monies and the development of English banking', *Economic History Review* 5 (1953), pp. 378–97.
47 TNA PRO 30/8/288, f. 56.

on their visibility.'[48] It is usual consequently to emphasise the lower profile and importance of indirect taxes as a whole. But this chapter has shown that also important was the fact that many of those taxes were collected disproportionately in London, where the state could exploit its role as an intermediary between consumers spread across Britain and producers, near and far. London's economy and Britain's fiscal state evolved hand in glove.

48   M.J. Daunton, *Progress and poverty: an economic and social history of Britain, 1700–1850* (Oxford, 1995), p. 529.

2

Rents, squalor, and the land question: progress and poverty

RICHARD RODGER[1]

Martin Daunton's contributions to urban history are immense. His earliest works, *Coal metropolis: Cardiff 1870–1914* (1977) and *House and home in the Victorian city: working class housing 1850–1914* (1983), were deeply researched, thoughtful, and influenced me greatly. In this chapter I return to these works, and forty years on still find his insights into the functioning of cities illuminating. This chapter contextualises Henry George's polarity of progress and poverty, also adopted by Martin in another work, and links land values and taxation, two further areas where Martin has made major contributions to urban and economic history. The chapter proceeds from an exploration of the nature and extent of landownership in terms of land prices, and shows that institutional users and major utility companies had important, and previously under-acknowledged, distorting effects on local property markets. Though reference is made to a number of English cities, distinctive Scottish data sources on urban landownership are used to explain the impact on rents and living conditions there. Thus, the pressure of urban development (progress) is at the cost of squalor accommodation (poverty) in Scotland.

> The irresistible disorderly growth of great cities, which may be described in one word as conurbation, is almost as great a social evil as unemployment. It has involved in the past daily waste of life and human energy in needless travel, bad housing and ill health, needless exhausting toil for the housewife in struggling with dirt and discomfort, habituation of the population to hideous surroundings.[2]

---

1 I am grateful to Paul Laxton, Lou Rosenberg, and the editors for their comments on an earlier draft.
2 Advisory Panel on Home Affairs on Reconstruction Problems, 25 Jun. 1942, TNA T161/1165.

It seems that the taxation of land, like the poor, is always with us. From time to time the topic gains political traction, then falters. Rather than focusing on the ownership of land itself, property taxation in Britain has concentrated largely on taxing the combined value of land and buildings. Driven by a sense of social justice, more radical proposals intended to cream off the increment in rising house property prices have come to nought. Such an approach, a 'single tax' to deal with these 'betterment' issues, as promoted by the American political economist and social philosopher Henry George in *Progress and poverty* (1879), were embraced by the Liberal Party as part of land reform in the late nineteenth century. They have since found little resonance in Britain.[3]

The value of property (land, buildings, and improvements to them) has always presented problems as a basis for local taxation. Amongst several reasons for this problem was the revaluation of land which was infrequent, and so lagged significantly behind rising market valuations for house property. Valuations of land for tax purposes in effect were fixed, but were multiplied by a variable, normally increasing annual 'assessment' (the rate in the pound) made by councils to cover their projected municipal expenditure. This was what determined the amount of local tax payable by landlords and tenants. And that remains, broadly, the basis of 'Council Tax' in Britain today, with arrangements made for 'business rates', exemptions for institutional users such as places of worship, and allowances for undeveloped brownfield or derelict land.

The amount raised from property increased appreciably in the second half of the nineteenth century. It was the result, predictably, of twin forces: increasing urbanisation and rising rateable assessments – the amount levied in the pound on properties – to pay for rapidly escalating council obligations. Ability to pay and equality of sacrifice, central principles of Adam Smith's formulation of a tax system in which social justice was considered an important element, were largely absent under this arrangement:

> The subjects of every state ought to contribute towards the support of the government, as nearly as possible, in proportion to their respective abilities; that is, in proportion to the revenue which they respectively enjoy under the protection of the state.[4]

By contrast, capital gains on property accrued to landowners, not just on freehold land, but also on leaseholds. This was because the reversionary period was shortened in the nineteenth century from 999 to 99 years so that capital

---

3   Henry George, *Progress and poverty. An inquiry into the cause of industrial depressions and of increase of want with increase of wealth: the remedy* (1879). Martin Daunton used George's term to encapsulate British economic and social history in his *Progress and poverty: an economic and social history of Britain 1700–1850* (Oxford, 1995).

4   Adam Smith, *An inquiry into the nature and causes of the wealth of nations*, book V, ch. ii.

improvements and real increases in property prices accrued as windfall gains to landowners. Thus urbanisation, the process noted by the Advisory Panel in 1942 by which 'conurbations' were created, itself produced a windfall gain or surplus which was 'unearned', that is, as an economic rent that accrued not generally as a result of landowners' own actions, but as an appreciation driven by population growth, urban development, and workers' needs to live close to their work. Ultimately, lower paid workers and the un- and under-employed and casual workers paid a disproportionate amount of their income in rent compared to other social classes.[5]

The nineteenth-century urban housing market functioned efficiently only in the sense that scarcity and choice were reconciled through pricing. For the regularly employed salaried staff and skilled workforce, the income-rental equation worked tolerably. Where household income was boosted with both husband and wife, or other family members, in work, then late Victorian housing quality was affordable. The unearned increment that resulted due to the pressures of demand and supply accrued to the landowner through rising property prices and land values. For others, interrupted earnings forced households to settle for a standard of squalor that was affordable over a rental period in which bouts of interrupted employment were the norm. For such households 'needless, exhausting toil for the housewife ... dirt and discomfort ... and habituation ... to hideous surroundings' were the consequences for the rest of the family.[6]

Rent control recognised and formalised the essence of these housing conditions. Rents were frozen at the August 1914 level by the Increase of Rent and Mortgage Interest (War Restrictions) Act 1915, which sought to prevent landlords from profiteering during the war years. Nationally, with house-building in the decade 1901–11 as a percentage of gross domestic fixed capital formation running at its lowest for forty years and in further decline by 1914, the result was that English and Scottish urban rents were respectively 20 per cent and 33 per cent above the levels of the mid-1870s.[7] The introduction of the Rent Control Act recognised that the potential to inflate the unearned increment on land values (betterment) was considerable, but considered it to be unacceptable given the exigencies of war. Social justice was invoked to justify regulating rents, and traded for public order. As a Glasgow rent striker's banner proclaimed: 'While my father is a prisoner in Germany the landlord is attacking

5   W. Alonso, 'A theory of the urban land market', *Papers of the Regional Science Association* 6 (1960), pp. 149–57; J.W.R. Whitehand, 'Urban-rent theory, time series and morphogenesis: an example of eclecticism in geographical research', *Area* (1972), pp. 215–22.
6   Advisory Panel on Home Affairs on Reconstruction Problems, 25 Jun. 1942.
7   R. Rodger, 'The "Invisible Hand": market forces, housing and the urban form in Victorian cities', in D. Fraser and A. Sutcliffe, eds, *The pursuit of urban history* (London, 1983), p. 203.

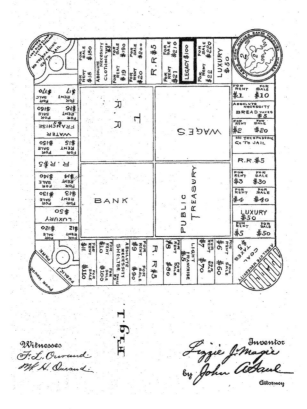

Figure 2.1. The Landlord's Game. Henry George was the inspiration for Elizabeth Magie's board game 'The Landlord's Game' which, she explained, was 'a practical demonstration of the present system of land-grabbing with all its usual outcomes and consequences'. Patented in 1904, it was used as a teaching aid in the University of Pennsylvania Department of Economics (1906). Elizabeth (Lizzie) J. Magie Phillips (1866–1948) contributed (1926) to the Georgist periodical *Land and Freedom*, and was a delegate to the Henry George Congress in Baltimore in 1931. By the 1920s Magie's 'Landlord's Game' was known as 'Monopoly', and a copyright obtained first by Charles Darrow, who paid Lizzie Magie $500 in 1932, and then by Parker Brothers, who reissued Monopoly in 1939.

Source: US Patent 748,626.

our home.'[8] Wartime circumstances forced formal recognition of peacetime inequalities in the housing market. Rather than deal directly with a long-run structural issue – the unearned increment in land values – rent control was designed as a temporary measure. In practice, it remained in operation until the Rent Act 1957, which decoupled rents from the 1914 scale and its subsequent revisions, and permitted controlled rents to be based on gross property values. Rent control fundamentally disturbed the private rented housing market, and obliged city councils to become involved to a greater or lesser degree. Eventually, in 1965, 'fair rents' on regulated properties were set by independent assessors, and all remaining rent controls were removed in 1989.

Rent control was in effect a redistributive policy tool. Rentals were capped, so returns to rentiers (landlords) plummeted in the decade following its introduction in 1915. A ceiling on rents eroded the position of the private landlord for the next half century with consequences both for the returns to capital for landlords, and thus for the quality of the private housing stock for tenants in terms of minimal repairs and maintenance. A seismic shift in political leverage was formalised, therefore, in 1915, and post-war conditions and political expediency rendered it irreversible in the short, medium and long terms. The housing 'crisis' of the early twentieth century has since been seen as indicative of the rise of labour in opposition to the interests of capital, and that binary has been too easily elided with the inevitable introduction of council housing. Martin Daunton explored this forensically in his introduction to *Councillors and tenants*, noting that the landlords' position in the housing market was already untenable.[9]

Land and landownership

Land rather than ideologically driven capital–labour tensions was at the heart of this seismic shift in power relations. The high costs of Scottish housing were the subject of numerous publications and official enquiries before 1915, culminating in the Royal Commission on the Housing of the Industrial Population of Scotland, Rural and Urban (Ballantyne Commission) which, though it reported finally only in 1917, heard compelling evidence from the start of its deliberations in 1911 about the influence of land prices on rents.[10] Indeed, as the terms of reference indicated, covering as they did 'Rural and Urban', it was miners' housing and crofters' housing which were central concerns, tied as they particularly were to issues of landownership in a Scottish postscript to the

---

8   J. Melling, *Rent strikes: peoples' struggle for housing in west Scotland 1890–1916* (Edinburgh, 1983), pp. 84–5.
9   M.J. Daunton, ed., *Councillors and tenants: local authority housing in English cities 1919–1939* (Leicester, 1984), pp. 2–8.
10   For details of sources see Rodger, 'Invisible hand', p. 206.

'Irish Question' in the closing decades of the nineteenth century. The rupture in landlord and tenant relations which finally surfaced in the Red Clydeside rent strike was the climax to years of stress in the peculiarities of the Scottish housing market in which land, landlords, and landowners each played a crucial role.[11]

If rents influenced the quantity and quality of affordable housing it made sense to explore the role of landowners in that process. Were they able to manage the market for land? Did a few landowners monopolise the supply of building land in towns and cities? Was housing quality directly linked to ground rents? David Cannadine concluded when comparing Birmingham and Leeds that 'The fact that one was leasehold [Birmingham] and the other freehold [Leeds] was of little importance.' Nor did it matter in these cities whether the land was owned as a block or highly fragmented – 'it was ultimately irrelevant in determining how the land was used'.[12] Martin Daunton examined 27 different boroughs. Using tithe apportionments for the 1830s and 1840s, he calculated the percentage of land held by the three largest landowners. There was a wide variation between boroughs in the concentration of ownership, and so 'it would be difficult', he concluded, 'to argue that there was more than a tenuous connection between concentration and short leasehold, and between fragmented ownership and freehold'.[13] Taking the analysis forward to 1905, Daunton claimed that 'Variations in rent levels and house form did not obviously arise from the structure of landownership.'[14] At its most extreme were Middlesbrough and Oldham, two boroughs with an almost identical rent index but a landownership concentration in Middlesbrough more than five times that of Oldham. However, if the focus is directed to the *ratio* of land concentration to rent then there is a pattern, and tentatively it *is* possible to conclude that the greater the fragmentation of landownership the lower the rent index. Of the fifteen most fragmented boroughs identified by the Board of Trade data on which Daunton's data is based only one, Stockport, is not also in the lowest fifteen in terms of the rent ratio (Figure 2.2).

There is, then, a degree of correspondence, if not necessarily of causation, between the concentration of landownership and rent. But this is complicated by a number of other local factors: the long-run trajectory and composition of local industry, the extent of the impact of international trade on localities, as in the coalfield towns of South Wales in the decade before World War I, and of a landowner's personal portfolio preferences for a mix of property and financial assets. As Springett commented on the activities of the Ramsden dynasty of

11   R. Rodger, 'Crisis and confrontation in Scottish housing 1880–1914', in R. Rodger, ed., *Scottish housing in the twentieth century* (Leicester, 1989), pp. 25–53.
12   D. Cannadine, 'Urban development in England and America in the nineteenth century: some comparisons and contrasts', *Economic History Review* 33 (1980), pp. 321–2.
13   Daunton, *House and home*, p. 74.
14   Ibid., p. 78.

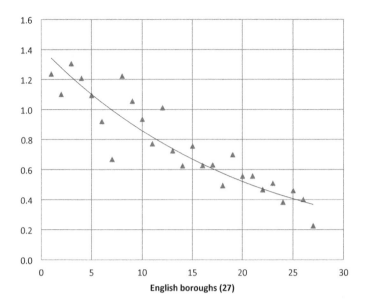

Figure 2.2. Concentration of English urban landowners, 1911. The ratio is derived from the percentage of land in each borough held by the largest three landowners divided by the rent index for that borough.

Source: M.J. Daunton, *House and home*, table 4.4, p. 78.

landowners in Huddersfield, 'it is a fallacy to assume that landowners always make rational decisions when seeking to maximise the potential of their assets, and that they are always sensitive to the needs of the market'.[15] Nor, as Cannadine surmised, were the Calthorpes in Birmingham 'concerned to maximise their profits, and would no doubt have expressed incomprehension or dismay had they been asked if that was their policy'.[16] The development of Eastbourne had much to do with the finances of the Cavendish family's Chatsworth estate, and why would the Fitzwilliams' decision to develop their Sheffield property not take account of the rentals on 100,000 acres held in six English counties and three Irish ones?[17] Undue focus on the major dynastic landed families may not match the scale at which the landowning–rent relationship functions.

15   J. Springett, 'Landowners and urban development: the Ramsden estate and nineteenth-century Huddersfield', *Journal of Historical Geography* 8 (1982), p. 142.

16   D. Cannadine, *Lords and landlords: the aristocracy and the towns 1774–1967* (Leicester, 1980), p. 219.

17   G. Rowley, 'Landownership in the spatial growth of towns: a Sheffield example', *East Midland Geographer* 6 (1975), p. 202; J. Bateman, *The great landowners of Great Britain and Ireland* (London, 1883) provides a wealth of acreages and rental data.

Table 2.1. Landownership in the larger Scottish burghs, 1873

	landowners with 1 acre or more			landowners with less than 1 acre		
burgh	owners (%)	acreage (%)	annual value (%)	owners (%)	acreage (%)	annual value (%)
Edinburgh	2.1	68.4	19.5	97.9	31.6	80.5
Perth	2.5	70.2	31.6	97.5	29.8	68.4
Glasgow	2.8	62.4	26.8	97.2	37.6	73.2
major burghs	3.5	72.1	28.6	96.5	27.9	71.4
Aberdeen	3.7	42.9	27.3	96.3	57.1	72.7
Dundee	4.2	87.7	39.6	95.8	12.3	60.4
Kilmarnock	5.4	87.6	30.3	94.6	12.4	69.7
Leith	5.8	78.0	44.1	94.2	22.0	55.9
Greenock	9.0	87.0	45.2	91.0	13.0	54.8
Paisley	9.8	80.0	43.5	90.2	20.0	56.5

Note: The Crown estates have been excluded since they were never on the market. This is not to say they did not influence rental for adjacent land.

Source: PP 17&18 Vict. C.91, Scotland, Owners of Lands and Heritages.

At first glance data for urban Scotland might offer some corroboration for the concentration of landownership hypothesis. A Survey of Lands and Heritages in Scotland[18] in 1872–73 is summarised in Table 2.1. The survey distinguishes between properties of one acre or more, and those below one acre. Less than 3 per cent of Scottish urban land was held in parcels of one or more acres in Edinburgh and Glasgow; consequently 97 per cent of urban land was held by landowners with less than an acre, and this figure did not fall below 90 per cent in any other of the seven major Scottish burghs. Of 240 Edinburgh landowners, those with holdings greater than an acre (2.1 per cent) accounted for 68.4 per cent of the acreage and 19.5 per cent of the annual value (Table 2.1). However, two thirds of these 240 landowners held between one and four acres only. This, too, seems to leave a small number of influential landowners in a potentially dominant position. More careful inspection shows that many of these larger landowners were trusts, institutions, and utility or railway companies, and so the composition of landownership may be more significant than simply the size of holdings (Table 2.2).

Perhaps the assumption that three landowners might be able to influence

18   PP 1874 C.899, Scotland. Owners of lands and heritages, 17&18 Vict. c.91, Return 1872–73.

Table 2.2. Landowner power: Edinburgh 1873

	name (a)	acreage	name (b)	gross annual value (£)	name (c)	value per acre (£)
1	Trustees of George Heriot's Hospital	180	North British Railway Company	23199	Edinburgh and District Water Trust	8013
2	Edinburgh Town Council	167	Caledonian Railway Company	10363	Edinburgh Railway Station Access Co.	4464
3	North British Railway Company	111	Edinburgh Gas Light Co.	9319	Aitchison & Sons	3109
4	Trustees of Charles Rocheid of Inverleith	96	Edinburgh and District Water Trust	8013	Commercial Bank of Scotland	2804
5	Trustees of Sir William Fettes of Comely Bank	92	Edinburgh Town Council	6983	John Taylor & Sons	2632
6	Lt. Col. Alexander Learmonth of Dean, M.P.	83	Trustees of George Heriot's Hospital	4770	Royal Bank of Scotland	2083
7	Sir George Warrender of Lochend	74	Edinburgh Railway Station Access Co.	4464	Edinburgh and Leith Gas Light Co.	1710
8	Sir Thomas N. Dick Lauder of Fountainhall	68	Royal Bank of Scotland	4166	George Moir	1673
9	Trustees of George Watson's College Schools	53	University of Edinburgh	3566	Andrew Waddell	1589
10	Caledonian Railway Company	44	Edinburgh and Leith Gas Light Co.	3419	William McKenzie	1486

Crown properties have been omitted since such land was unavailable for residential, institutional, or commercial use, though inevitably it affected the value of adjacent properties.

Source: PP 1874 LXXII part III, Owners of Lands and Heritages, 1872–73; pp. 66–9.

rental levels in the housing market is too strict a test. It might be that the top ten, say, were more likely to be in tune with one another, particularly if continuity to hereditary holdings was a strategic priority. Also, different measures of landowner power may be more helpful to an understanding of the complex nature of urban development. A more detailed examination reveals that it was mainly private individuals or their representatives who in 1873 possessed the greatest physical extent of land within Edinburgh (Table 2.2). George Heriot's Hospital (School) trustees managed 180 acres or almost one million square yards, equivalent to about 170 football pitches. The Trust's holdings included much of the desirable residential area of Edinburgh between Princes Street and the northern city boundary with Leith at Ferry Road. Most conspicuous (Table 2.2a) were the trustees, appointed to administer the land and other assets of families owning lands ringing the built-up area in 1873 – the genteel southern suburbs of the Grange (already underway), Marchmont and Warrender (developed in the 1880s) and to the north, the parkland of Rocheid's Inverleith and Fettes' Comely Bank lands. All of these estates were also in the top ten of land valuations a century earlier in 1770, indicating their importance as an asset with a long-term gestation period.[19] What had changed in the interim, of course, was the arrival of the railways, principally the North British and the Caledonian and their various earlier amalgamations, with all the associated infrastructure necessary to operate the passenger and goods networks. The second fundamental change since 1770 was the position of Edinburgh Town Council as reflected in the expansion and diversity of municipal management.

In terms of the gross annual value (Table 2.2b) – the actual rent that property might be expected to command on the open market – this was dominated by companies, headed by railways, and by gas and water utilities.[20] For these companies, as well as the Royal Bank of Scotland which had moved quickly into branch banking after 1850, city-centre sites were crucial to the business model. Such properties also commanded a high rental or gross annual value. The bank branches, like the lots held by the University of Edinburgh and Heriot's School which were once peripheral, commanded a premium as they were increasingly surrounded by the outward march of urban development.

By contrast, the average value per acre (Table 2.2c) contains only business interests, including small specialist firms. Aitchison & Son, confectioner to the Queen, owned a high-value single-acre property; John Taylor & Sons was a firm of cabinetmakers at 109–110 Princes Street with a works at Rosemount and jointly these, too, extended only to an acre. Both Andrew Waddell, builder and contractor, and William Mackenzie, builder and asphalter, operated their business premises from single-acre sites. The nature of the business itself was a significant

19   National Registers of Scotland, Valuation Rolls, Edinburgh 1770, E/106/22/4.
20   Edinburgh and Leith Post Office directories, various volumes. See also National Library of Scotland collection online.

Table 2.3. A typology of urban land use: Scottish burghs 1873, land holdings of one acre or more

Number of owners	Private (%)	Institutions and trusts (%)	Business (%)
Aberdeen (111)	44.1	29.7	26.1
Dundee (188)	56.7	16.6	26.7
Edinburgh (240)	53.8	25.0	21.3
Glasgow (310)	37.0	15.4	47.6
Greenock (102)	49.0	13.7	37.3
Kilmarnock (54)	70.4	9.3	20.4
Leith (127)	57.5	22.9	19.7
Paisley (137)	67.6	16.2	15.4
Perth (47)	58.7	28.2	13.0

Note: Numbers in the left-hand column denote the number of landowners in each burgh with one or more acres.

Source: As for Table 2.2.

influence on the suitability of the site, therefore, and thus of the rental costs. So confectioners and cabinetmakers and those generally with a high value-added skill element to their activities, and for whom the footfall of potential customers was essential, occupied prime city-centre sites with rentals priced accordingly. By contrast, the brewers and distillers, well-known names such as Usher, Younger, and Haig, each located their business on the urban periphery where access to water was essential, as it was for mills and rubber manufacturers.

A conclusion to be drawn from the Survey of Lands and Heritages in Scotland in 1873 is that there were three strands in land use. Firstly, trusts and institutions, as well as some larger private landowners, who sought to optimise the release of property since they had no reversionary rights[21] and who, therefore, retained land until the urban frontier was upon them and they could maximise returns; secondly, business interests with land-extensive requirements, such as utilities and transport, where access to high value central sites was also a core feature of their activities; and thirdly, a category of modestly sized and centrally located businesses located on high value properties of one acre, often with a street frontage, used as sites both of production and of consumption.

The Survey of Lands and Heritages gives a snapshot in 1873 of users' preference schedules for land. The summary in Table 2.3 shows a typology

21 Leaseholding did not exist in Scotland, where the principal tenure was feuing. See below.

of land users in nine Scottish burghs. Though itself simplistic, the tripartite division of the market for urban land and the implications for levels – *plural* – of rent is highly significant. It encourages an alternative perspective to urban rents to that which assumed land to be a relatively homogeneous factor. A moment of reflection regarding personal decisions in a contemporary world is a reminder of the trade-off between amenity/location and price/rent. Some users have more options than others, or are willing to consider site options more flexibly, or have leverage through their local shareholder or political base to influence outcomes over sites. Kellett's masterly account of early railway station development assists an understanding of how the companies interacted with the land market. Kellett states: 'The typical stations of this period [1830s and 1840s] were all ... on the outskirts of the then built-up areas. The main consideration in their siting was to achieve the cheapest and simplest approach and terminus, with the minimum disturbance of property even if ... this involved a final stretch of line served by a tunnel and stationary cable engine.'[22] Liverpool Road (Manchester), Crown Street (Liverpool), Curzon Street (Birmingham), and Haymarket (Edinburgh) were among those that subscribed to this pattern of initial access to the city, and in 1846 the Metropolitan Railway Commission set an exclusion zone for railway access within London which remained a boundary for the central business district for over 150 years.[23]

   It is also worth noting that the process of railway land development fundamentally influenced not just the central business districts: by creating impenetrable deep cuttings and viaducts to obtain access, railways left permanent scars on the landscape, and accordingly affected the prospects for land development. Tracks scythed through existing built-up areas, but they also blighted tracts of undeveloped land. In so doing, the arrival of the railway in the 1830s and 1840s fundamentally influenced the locus of suburbanisation in the second half of the nineteenth century. Proximity to goods yards and junctions appealed to few middle-class residents. Famous intersections, such as at Clapham, created a spaghetti junction of lines with bridges and viaducts that bisected the adjacent land and rendered it the haunt of those marginalised in British society. With between 5 and 9 per cent of land in major British cities directly owned by railways companies, according to Kellett, it is not surprising that they played a critical role in the subsequent development of cities and their neighbourhoods.

---

22   J.R. Kellett, *The impact of railways on Victorian cities* (London, 1969), p. 4.
23   T.E. Bolton, 'Wrong side of the tracks: the development of London's railway terminus neighbourhoods', PhD thesis (University College London, 2017), p. 68. Bolton notes (p. 308) that the viaduct network associated with London Bridge station (19 miles and 878 arches) was probably the largest brick structure in Britain, and that railways were blamed for the rising brick prices in London.

Land tenure and institutional economics

Land hoarding has a negative connotation. It involves restricting the release of land in order artificially to drive up prices and thus rents. In the twenty-first century there is hostility to developers who have option-to-purchase agreements yet display little intention to build. Such is the hostility in Ireland – perennially concerned with the land question – that the Dublin government passed the Urban Regeneration and Housing Act, 2015 which authorised a 3 per cent levy on all properties deemed to qualify under strict criteria for the Vacant Sites Register.

Hoarding land and land banks are not the same thing, however. Land banks may possess a degree of legitimacy. Just as a manufacturer seeks to ensure sufficient stocks from the supply chain in order to guarantee continuity to the production process, so builders seek to acquire, and landowners to supply, sufficient suitable land to maintain a flow of construction work. Since the builder's product is 'lumpy' and takes over a year to become saleable, a smooth supply of land with planning permission is uncertain and unlikely to be achieved easily. A land bank provides a cushion by which to avoid an interruption to construction. A *sufficient* stock of available land is good business practice, therefore, and indeed facilitates the construction process. A *surplus* stock of land, however, constitutes an impediment since it is an idle asset, haemorrhages the supply of land for building, and forces up prices which are transmitted as higher rents which fall disproportionately on the less well off. The culprit may be the landowner, the developer, the builder, or all three. This is why the Irish government seeks only to tax those who hold their land off the market by various devices beyond a reasonable length of time. It is the modern Irish answer to the betterment problem: a single tax on the incremental value that accrues from withholding building land for an unreasonable period.

In nineteenth- and twentieth-century England, urban land was acquired either by freehold or on short lease.[24] That is, an agreed lump sum payment transferred the freehold rights to the land, and to any increased value that resulted. Under leasehold, an annual payment secured the land for a fixed period when it, and any improvements on it, reverted to the owner. The lessor could release the land at a low rent and so encourage development on it, and then had the assurance that they or their heirs would receive any increased value when the lease matured. The prospect of reversionary rights was critical to the decision to lease land, and to the price/rent of the lease.

Neither of these tenures existed in Scotland where, until the late twentieth century, the overwhelming majority of land transactions were completed under

---

24   There were local variations in England, such as the use of copyhold, and ground annuals. There were, similarly, other forms of tenure in Scotland, but these were rare.

the feuing system. Under this distinctive tenure, the feudal 'superior' obtained only an annual sum from his 'vassal' but had no reversionary rights. The Scottish Land Enquiry explained the arrangements: 'Under the feu system … the superior's natural endeavour is to fix his original conditions of feuing so as to get as large a return as possible, once and for all. It is very probable also that the preponderance of tenements of three and four storeys in height in Scotland as compared with England is attributable in part at least to the high ground rents.'[25] The legal system encouraged a front-loading of the cost of land since the feuar (landowner) had no future interest in it.[26]

There were other key features of feuing that affected land prices. One was sub-infeudation (Figure 2.3). Under this system landowners feued to vassals who were also entitled to feu to others, and to charge such a price (feu duty) as would cover the annual payment to their superior. The superior–vassal obligation could and did have many layers. Land parcels, therefore, could be transferred in their entirety or subdivided several times, with the annual feu duty (ground rent) increased on each transfer or subdivision. Payments of feu duties were a first charge on an estate or a bankrupt's assets and so were an attractive 'gold-plated' investment. The most important feature of feuing, however, was the right to create a financial instrument – heritable securities – and few commentators have identified this characteristic and its fundamental significance. As shown in Figure 2.3, a landowner might decide not to develop his land, but to transfer it to a builder or developer who wished to do so. The feu duty was fixed for ever at, say, £20 annually. The builder/developer might simply sit on the asset, declining to develop it for several years, but still had to pay his superior £20 every year. The builder/developer might at some stage decide to feu part of the estate to another builder, and the remainder to an institution, both of whom had to pay a feu duty as determined by the developer, but in this example £15 each. Both the institution and the housebuilder begin work and break the land they have feued into separate plots – three further sub-feued areas by the institution and two plots by the builder – and each of these vassals is obliged to make an annual payment to them as their respective superior.

As the pyramid of sub-feuing develops, so the ground rent/feu duty is increased so that the vassal can meet their own financial commitment to the superior immediately above them, who is in turn also relinquishing an asset for ever. However, a superior might prefer not to have the trouble and expense of collecting feu duties, or might be in need of capital for a business venture. He might, in these circumstances, be prepared to sell his right to receive £25 annually in perpetuity from sub-feuar 4. A solicitor would then find someone – often a widow, a trust, or institution – who was prepared to pay a lump sum for

25   Scottish Land Enquiry Committee, *Report* (London, 1914), p. 1.
26   Exceptionally, if the tenant did not adhere to conditions (burdens) stated in the feu charter then the owner could seek to repossess the lot.

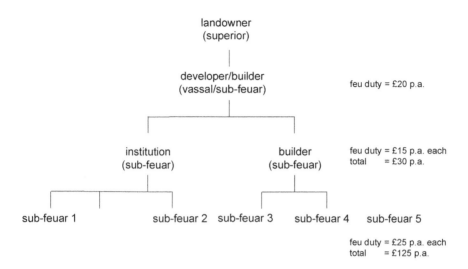

Figure 2.3. Feudal landownership and sub-infeudation: Scotland.

Note: Plots may differ in size and thus by feu duty payable.

the right to receive a sub-feuar 4's feu duty in perpetuity. The amount paid for such heritable securities varied depending on the state of the land market, but normally sold for about twenty to thirty times the annual feu duty, depending on the state of the housebuilding cycle. The builder/superior foregoes the right to receive the feu duty payment if another person, or party, is prepared to pay him a lump sum equivalent to, say, 28 years of feu duty payments – in this case £25×28 or £700.[27] An asset has been created, a small saver's funds have been invested, an annuity guaranteed, and the price of land increased.

Successive upper tiers of the pyramid have the ability to create and then realise financial instruments. No building development need take place. It is possible to generate a lump sum and then invest in a business venture, or in another property, or stocks and shares, or spend on conspicuous consumption. In one sense, therefore, feuing tenure in Scotland is a device to unlock future savings by getting small investors to pay in full and upfront for an asset that then delivers an annuity to them in perpetuity. Not surprisingly, superiors were reluctant to sell their rights to feu duty income cheaply. This added inflationary pressure to the Scottish land market. The premium or economic rent on Scottish land induced by feuing can be estimated, therefore, to be the differential between prevailing rental levels in English boroughs and Scottish ones as revealed by the

---

27 R. Rodger, *The transformation of Edinburgh: land property and trust in the nineteenth century* (Cambridge, 2001), pp. 69–122.

Board of Trade and enshrined in rent control legislation and housing subsidies in the twentieth century. What is also clear is that what was a clever device for annuitants and small investors was a penalty for tenement tenants.

The Royal Commission on Housing, Rural and Urban obtained evidence in 1911 from a highly reputable official, J. Walker Smith, Chief Engineering Inspector of the Local Government Board for Scotland, showing rental payments per square foot for a number of towns and cities. There were not many tenement properties in England to form the basis for an exact comparison, but in an analysis of flatted cottages Smith showed that English tenants paid an average of 8.86 pence per square foot and the Scots paid 10.20 pence, that is, 15.1 per cent more than south of the border.[28] It was arguably a conservative figure, as a more comprehensive study by the Board of Trade the following year showed (Figure 2.5).

Rents and living space

Weak demand squeezed Scottish household budgets and pressurised living space. The retail price index (Figure 2.4) showed that urban Scotland compared adversely with all the major regional centres – Cardiff (99); Newcastle (98); Liverpool (95); Leeds, Manchester Nottingham, Sheffield (94); Birmingham, Bristol (93) – and was even more expensive than central London.[29] Regional rent indices were just as unfavourable. Whereas the overall rent index for England had increased by 20 per cent between 1876 and 1910, the Scottish increase had been 33 per cent over the same period.[30] Again with London as the benchmark of 100, accommodation in ten Scottish burghs was 23 per cent more than ten Yorkshire cities; 28 per cent higher than in seventeen Lancashire and Cheshire boroughs; and 35 per cent above the level of rents in fifteen Midland towns and cities on the eve of World War I (Figure 2.5).

'Rent Control', stated Marian Bowley, 'must be seen in perspective as part of the wartime machinery built up piecemeal to control the prices of the main necessities of "life"' – 'shelter' as it would become in 1942 in Beveridge's five giants of poverty. The disparity between English and Scottish rents meant a differential threshold was necessary when applying rent controls: it applied to all houses with a rateable value not exceeding £35 in London's Metropolitan

28 PP 1917–18 XIV, Royal Commission on the housing of the industrial population of Scotland, rural and urban, report and evidence, Cd.8371, 1917, Appendix CLXVIII, Evidence of J. Walker Smith.
29 Rodger, 'Invisible Hand', pp. 197–200.
30 R. Rodger, 'Rents and ground rents: housing and the land market in nineteenth-century Britain', in J.H. Johnson and C.G. Pooley, eds, The structure of nineteenth-century cities (London, 1982), pp. 61–2.

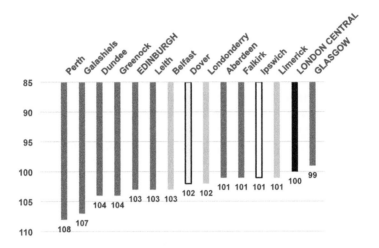

Figure 2.4. Retail price indices, 1912.

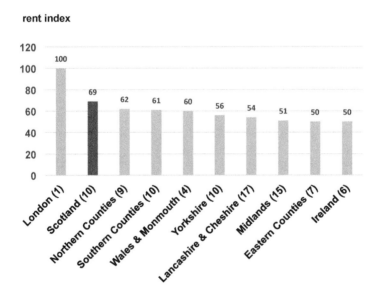

Figure 2.5. Regional rent indices, 1912.

Source: PP 1913, Cd 6955, Report of the Board of Trade Enquiry into Working Class Rents and Retail Prices. See pages xxxvi–xxxvii for the basis of the retail price index.

Police District, £30 in Scotland, and £26 in the remainder of England.[31] This was equivalent to saying that London rents were 35 per cent above those elsewhere in England but only 17 per cent above rents in Scotland. This pattern was extended in 1920, using the same percentage relationships to houses with rateable values respectively of £105, £90, and £78 in London, Scotland, and the rest of England. The regional differential was also recognised in the Housing and Town Planning (Scotland) Act, 1919, whereby the Treasury underwrote losses made by cities on their council housebuilding projects at a level 20 per cent more generous for Scottish councils than for English ones.[32] The preferential treatment for Scotland was justified, according to Bowley, because of the squalid housing conditions there: '73 per cent of the population lived in three rooms or less, including 47.7 per cent in houses with only one or two rooms. The contrast with England is startling … only 7.1 per cent lived in these abnormally small houses; the great majority of the houses, 73.8 per cent had four or more rooms.'[33] Environmentally the living conditions were captured by the Census of 1911: 'The custom of building in tenements reduced to a minimum the light, sunshine and fresh air available, and added extreme density of population per acre to congestion indoors.'[34]

In short, squalor as captured in the Royal Commission of 1917 was explicitly acknowledged and, to an extent, addressed in the rent control and council housing legislation during and after World War I. It was a recognition that for many decades a combination of factors worked against decent living conditions. Squalor was the result. Abject squalor was the result in Scotland, and the longer-term military and economic implications regarding the health of nations was captured during World War I in the statement 'You cannot expect to get an A1 population out of C3 homes.'[35]

There were, however, a number of structural factors that hindered the intentions embedded in the housing legislation of the interwar years. Most obvious was that the prevalence of tenement flats in Scottish burghs and the corresponding shortage of larger houses with amenities limited the extent of 'filtering-up' compared to the situation in England. Conversely, the need for qualitative improvements and slum clearance was more urgent in Scotland, yet these were not a priority until legislation on these qualitative issues was passed in 1930 and 1935. Also, the industrial structure of the west of Scotland was particularly over-committed to heavy industry relative to England and the post-war overcapacity of the steel and shipbuilding industries meant rationalisation

31   M. Bowley, *Housing and the state 1919–44* (London, 1945), p. 5. See also Appendix I 'Scottish housing problems' for further details.
32   L. Rosenburg, *Scotland's homes fit for heroes* (Edinburgh, 2016), pp. 173–5.
33   Bowley, *Housing*, p. 262.
34   PP 1912–13 Census of Scotland; PP 1913 LXXX.
35   R. Reiss, *The home I want* (London, 1918), dustjacket.

and restructuring was problematical. On the demand side, therefore, levels of unemployment and under-consumption were more pronounced than in most places in the United Kingdom. The building industry presented another constraint. Proportionately there were fewer building workers in Scotland compared to England; in 1931 there were just were 16.1 insured building workers per 1000, compared to 19.1/1000 in England. Had there been the same ratio, Bowley explained, housing output would have been 18.6 per cent higher than was achieved in interwar Scotland. The outcome by 1939 of these various limitations meant that, compared to 1911, the number of homes increased by 28 per cent in Scotland and by 52 per cent in England. Bowley concluded: 'after the Great War Scottish housing problems were different to those of England and Wales. This was not recognised and practically the same policy was applied north and south of the border ... uniformity of policy even in England and Wales led to a considerable number of difficulties owing to differences in the economic circumstances of different districts. In Scotland, where there was a peculiarly difficult group of housing problems as well as economic depression, this blind devotion to uniformity of policy led to serious delay.'[36]

Reflections

Land hoarding, rent control, and squalor were interconnected and enduring features of many cities, both nationally and internationally, and the internal structures of cities – networks, relationships, and organisations – formed crucial elements in the development of the study of urban history in Britain. Land- and building-related topics couched often in terms of economic history remain central to that development. Publications by Jim Dyos and David Reeder on Camberwell, Paddington, and west London suburbs, David Cannadine's study of Edgbaston, and Martin Daunton's comprehensive account of the development of Cardiff each contributed significantly to an understanding of the internal dynamics of town and cities. Though there was agreement that there were general processes of urban development, the mix of local factors delivered a distinctive urban identity – an urban 'DNA' specific to place.[37]

Set in the context of the 'Simmering Cities'[38] of the 1970s and 1980s, riven by social divisions and labour disputes, affected by energy crises and significant in-migration, understanding the inner workings of the city had a particular currency, and even urgency. With many historic areas cleared and covered in

36 Bowley, *Housing*, pp. 266–7.
37 R. Rodger, 'The changing nature of urban history', *History in Focus* 13 (2008), 'The City' (with R. Sweet), http://www.history.ac.uk/ihr/Focus/City/articles/sweet.html.
38 J. Beynon and J. Solomos, 'The simmering cities: urban unrest during the Thatcher years', *Parliamentary Affairs* 41, 3 (1988), pp. 402–22.

severe cement structures and pedestrians' interests subordinated to motorists', what made a liveable city came under the policy microscope. High-rise housing stimulated by government grants, and built by the systematised construction companies of Barratt, Laing, Taylor Woodrow, Persimmon, and a dozen others, homogenised the urban realm and crucified smaller building firms. Partly as a reaction, neighbourhood, conservation and civic amenity – qualitative dimensions of the urban sphere – gained momentum in opposition to the quantitative emphasis of post-war housing targets embedded in Labour and Conservative election manifestos. This uneasy contemporary backdrop to urban development in the 1970s and 1980s coincided with the maturing of social sciences in higher education and the quest to understand socio-economic and political processes more generally, and to have an input to them. An urban historical agenda was pursued vigorously through detailed investigations of individual towns and cities, with comparative thematic studies providing an overarching interpretation intended to assist an understanding of place.

To this body of urban historical research Martin Daunton has made many important contributions. Significant amongst them was *House and home in the Victorian City: working class housing 1850–1914* (1983).[39] Significant for several reasons, not least because in building out from his doctoral thesis with its Welsh roots, *House and home* also encompassed an impressive array of regional English towns at various scales in an attempt to explain the differing housing forms and styles that emerged. Reliance on cultural characteristics were discarded as 'a desperate refuge' on the basis that 'differences of taste ... lie behind the quantifiables of price, income, density, costs, rents, returns and land prices.'[40] *House and home* reaffirmed the centrality of economic history to an understanding of the development of towns and cities. For these contributions, for a masterly introduction to the *Cambridge urban history of Britain* (volume 3), and for many works on taxation, postal communications, and a textbook on *The economic and social history of Britain* in the formative years 1700–1850, and for his advocacy of the importance of historical scholarship in a modern world, and many more achievements, Martin Daunton has enriched the scholarly scene we now inhabit. But most significantly, his own patient scholarly techniques and forensic interpretive skills are a reminder of the importance of such qualities in an age of audits.

39   M.J. Daunton, Thesis and *House and home*, p. 60.
40   M.W. Beresford, 'The back-to-back house in Leeds 1787–1937', in S.D. Chapman, ed., *The history of working class housing: a symposium* (Newton Abbot, 1971), pp. 93–132.

3

Marine insurers, the City of London, and financing the Napoleonic Wars

ADRIAN LEONARD

'The market in public loans was at the heart of the financial development of the City of London, and crucial to the success of the fiscal-military state.' So wrote Martin Daunton in *Progress and poverty*.[1] This chapter shows how marine insurers were important to that market, and thus to the fiscal-military state, during what was perhaps its greatest test: the French Revolutionary and Napoleonic Wars. Today a collection of Nelson memorabilia is displayed on the trading floor at Lloyd's of London, the historic insurance market. However, insurance underwriters' subscriptions to state loans – a double use of their capital, which also underwrote the risks of the nation's oceanic trade – were at least as important to Britain's victories as Nelson's successes.

This chapter opens with a very brief introduction to London marine insurance, then describes the underwriter John Julius Angerstein and his little-known government loan contracting activity. It then discusses the subscribers to his loans of 1812 and 1813 to reveal the importance of insurance underwriters' capital in funding the wartime borrowing of the British state. It shows the large contribution made by private, individual insurers – the merchant class – through investment in government loans, in financing the Napoleonic Wars, and that the double use of their capital – simultaneously for state finance and for the business of insuring – eliminate in their example any question of crowding out during this period.

The chapter is based largely on the analysis of two principal and several secondary sources. Primary is Angerstein's loan subscription book, held in the London Metropolitan Archive, where it is identified only as a 'ledger'. The book lists the names of all of the subscribers to Angerstein's portions of the four state loans for which he was contractor between 1812 and 1815. Equally important

---

1   M.J. Daunton, *Progress and poverty: an economic and social history of Britain 1700–1850* (Oxford, 1995), pp. 511–12.

is the 'Roll of Lloyd's', a typewritten volume compiled by Warren Dawson, Lloyd's honorary librarian, in 1931. The two copies made are held at Lloyd's and list all known underwriting members of Lloyd's since its foundation as an independent organisation in 1771, and the date of their election to membership. Additional sources, used to confirm the identity of loan subscribers, include a list of insurance underwriters used by Angerstein, various London commercial directories, and others.

London marine insurance

Marine insurance is unlike other products. Sellers do not know its cost until long after it has been sold, because the total cost of possible claims may not be known until many years after policies are purchased. *Caveat emptor* does not apply, since sellers possess much less relevant information than buyers. Finally, it is unusual because sellers must retain capital to support the product after it has been sold. Insurance underwriters must retain such assets because they provide *contingent* capital, allowing merchants to trade with less capital-in-hand than the peculiar perils of their specific adventures require them prudently to possess.

Captain John Butler confirmed this plainly in a letter to a correspondent in Amsterdam in 1735: 'I could make no insurance here,' he wrote. 'I beg of you that you would get insured for me two thousand pounds, for it is too great a risk for me to run with my little fortune, without insurance.'[2] Collectively, insurance underwriters had to retain sufficient liquid capital to restore insured merchants' fortunes through indemnity when necessary. Like today's insurance companies, private insurance underwriters' accumulated underwriting funds were invariably invested in other ways as well. This practice is known as the double use of capital.

In Britain during the period of the Napoleonic Wars, most marine insurance was underwritten by private individuals, because marine insurance underwriting by companies or partnerships was restricted to two chartered insurers, the Royal Exchange Assurance and the London Assurance, under the so-called 'Bubble Act' of 1720. Many individual underwriters in London (but by no means all) did their business under the banner of Lloyd's, which in 1771 evolved from simply a coffee-house into a self-governing market which controlled its membership, required entrance fees to be paid, and standardised the policy form and language under which its members must contract their risk-taking.

The underwriters of 'New Lloyd's' were not immediately able to secure a permanent location for their institution. In November 1773, 'after many

---

2 Cited in Joseph Inikori, *Africans and the industrial revolution in England: a study in international trade and economic development* (Cambridge, 2002), p. 343.

Fruitless Trials to obtain a Coffee House', they chose to lease from the Mercers' Company 'a very Roomy and Convenient place over the North West Side of the Royal Exchange at the Rent of £180 p Annum'.[3] The choice of venue followed the intervention of the hero of this story, the broker, underwriter, merchant, shipowner, and picture collector John Julius Angerstein.

Angerstein and Baring

Angerstein was born in St Petersburg in 1735. His background is the subject of myth, but it is clear he was naturalised as a British subject in 1770.[4] As a young teenager he was brought to London by the Russia merchant Andrew Thomson (sometimes Thompson), who may have been his father. Angerstein remained close to the Thomson family throughout his life, and by all accounts his demeanour was distinctly English. The Thomsons, who had for generations been in business partnership with the Bonar and Peters families, were with their associates the leading Russia Company merchants at the opening of the wars of 1793–1815. Angerstein began trading on his own account in 1756, and by 1760 he was referred to as 'a gentleman of fortune'.[5]

Angerstein's early role in Thomson's business had been to manage the partnership's insurance affairs. In 1756 Thomson arranged for Angerstein to become a junior partner in the merchant firm of Alexander Dick, which by 1754 is described as an 'insurance office', marking Dick as a broker. By 1758 the firm was styled Dick & Angerstein. The latter dissolved the partnership by 1768, to set out on his own.[6] His subsequent involvement in the establishment of 'New Lloyd's' is well known and need not be recounted here; suffice to say, he is now widely regarded as the Father of Lloyd's. In 1777 he took a new partner, Thomas Lewis, into his business on Throgmorton Street.

He had other interests. As a shipbroker, he has been identified as the third-largest supplier of ships to the Royal Navy during the American war.[7] According to his own testimony before the House of Commons in 1784, from 1775 he 'supplied the Ordinance with Transports, sometimes in consequence of Advertisements, sometimes by Intervention of a Broker, and sometimes by Means of the Intervention of the Superintendent of Shipping'. In 1779 he became a shipowner.[8]

---

3 GHL CLC/B/148/A/001, f. 34.
4 10 Geo. III cap. 19 (private).
5 A.F. Twist, 'Widening circles in finance, philanthropy and the arts: a study of the life of John Julius Angerstein 1735–1823', unpublished PhD thesis (University of Amsterdam, 2002), p. 19.
6 Ibid., pp. 22, 25.
7 David Syrett, *Shipping and the American war 1775–83* (London, 1970), p. 80.
8 Twist, 'Widening circles', p. 30.

The Baring brothers are much better known. The London house of John &
Francis Baring was founded on 1 January 1763 as an extension of the German
Lutheran family's thriving Exeter wool interests. As the West Country business
began to languish, the London operation thrived, with profits reaching a
new high of £13,268 in 1792. Francis, the lead London partner, has a much-
downplayed but long association with insurance. In 1771 he became a director
of the Royal Exchange Assurance. He held the position until 1780, and
possessed £820 in company shares. He was elected MP for the rotten borough
of Grampound in 1784, and was active in politics as an MP until 1802.[9]

The loans

The cash demands of warfare grew to unprecedented levels in the eighteenth
century. Conflicts which cost amounts in the millions in the sixteenth century
were measured in the tens of millions by the seventeenth. During the years
that Angerstein was raising loans for the state, major combatants sometimes
spent £100 million per year on warfare. For Britain, which due to various,
widely understood circumstances was better placed to raise this cash than its
chief rival, France, nearly three pounds in four of the additional cash required
to fund extra wartime-related spending, including vast subsidies to allies,
was raised through loans. Kennedy describes the institutional developments
allowing long-term loans to be raised efficiently, interest to be paid regularly,
and principal repaid where relevant as a 'decisive British advantage' during
conflict years. Daunton observed that 'long-term loans and the capacity to levy
taxes were intimately related ... Since the loans were permanent rather than for
a fixed term, there was a further requirement: an active market so that holders
could sell when they needed cash ... The market in public loans was at the heart
of the financial development of the City of London, and crucial to the success
of the fiscal-military state.'[10] The secondary market was critical to insurers,
since it allowed them to sell government debt instruments very quickly when
their capital was required for its primary purpose, to pay claims.

In 1816, after the final defeat of Napoleon at Waterloo, the accumulated
nominal British national debt was £856 million, more than 210% of national
income.[11] This debt demanded domestic savings roughly on par with the size

9   John Orbell, *Baring Brothers & Co., Limited: a history to 1939* (London, 1985), pp. 1–9; John
Orbell, 'Baring, Sir Francis, first baronet (1740–1810)', *Oxford dictionary of national biography*
(Oxford, 2004), online edn, viewed May 2009.
10 Paul Kennedy, *The rise and fall of the great powers: economic change and military conflict
from 1500 to 2000* (London, 1988), pp. 77–80; Daunton, *Progress and poverty*, pp. 511–12.
11 Bank of England, *A millennium of macroeconomic data for the UK*, p. A29, http://www.
bankofengland.co.uk/statistics/research-datasets, viewed Oct. 2018.

of long-term private investment. Wright calculates that during the years 1811 to 1815, when the extant records of Angerstein's contracted loans begin, government borrowing, excluding considerable redemptions from the sinking fund, averaged £25.3 million per annum.[12]

Borrowing through contracted and subscribed loans was not new for Britain. Contractors had been engaged to circulate English exchequer bills in 1699, and in 1709 the Bank of England advanced money to the state as a loan contractor against an issue of exchequer bills, which it then circulated. An open subscription for 4% annuities raised £4 million in 1747, and subsequent, well-priced subscriptions were popular: in 1756 the crowd of subscribers gathered at the Bank was so enthusiastic that 'the counters were broke by their eagerness to get to the books'.[13]

Angerstein probably learned something of loan contracting from Henry and Peter Muilman, his uncles by marriage, who had been large traders in British state debt instruments for Dutch investors from at least the 1740s. Angerstein received a loan allocation of £3,000 as early as 1781, from a £12 million loan handled by rival shipbrokers Mure & Atkinson (the allocation of which one parliamentarian described as 'a mockery').[14] Barings was already in the business; contracting for government loans yielded the house profits of £19,000 between 1780 and 1784, roughly half its total profit for the period of £37,456.[15]

Pitt came to office in 1782 with a mind to eliminate, through the use of competitive tenders, the notorious corruption of loan contracting and the issue of loans at prices unfavourable to the state. He tested the practice in tenders for lottery issues in 1787.[16] Nine consortia of bankers and one of private gentlemen attended Pitt to bid on an issue on 26 April that year, when the terms offered by 'Messers. Godschall Johnson, and Co. proved by much the most liberal for the public, and far beyond the Minister's expectations'. According to *The Times*, offers were swiftly made for tranches of the issue at a premium of 10 shillings per ticket. Those of the houses of Angerstein, Thompson & Peters (among others) were received immediately.[17] John Julius, merchant-insurer, shipowner, and government contractor, was now in the loan business. With Godschall Johnson, an associate so close that Angerstein was godfather to his children,

12   J.F. Wright, 'British government borrowing in wartime, 1750–1815', *Economic History Review*, new ser. 52, 2 (May, 1999), pp. 355–6.
13   J.J. Grellier and R.W. Wade, *The terms of all the loans which have been raised for the public service*, 3rd edn (London, 1812), pp. 10, 15, 31, 35.
14   *Parliamentary register*, 15th Parliament of Great Britain: first session, 15 Mar. 1781, pp. 256–69.
15   Orbell, *Baring Brothers*, p. 10.
16   Twist, 'Widening circles', p. 60.
17   *The Times*, issue 736, 27 Apr. 1787, p. 2.

he won a competitive tender for the lottery of 50,000 tickets in 1788. Their bid was £15 8s 3d, some 3s and 6d per ticket better than the nearest competitor.[18]

At the outset of the French revolutionary wars in 1793, the public purse was again to be swollen through lottery loans, and Angerstein was back in the business. On 16 May, the governor and deputy governor of the Bank of England 'waited upon Mr. Pitt, to receive the offers of the Lottery, from the persons on that business'. The terms were agreed, and the Bank directors awarded their 'usual £10,000 Tickets'. According to the Bank's Treasury Committee minutes, 'Mr Angerstein, Mr Johnson, Mr Awleby, Mr E.P. Salomon, Mr P. Salomon, & Mr Abraham Goldsmid [the Treasury's bill broker] were the contractors without competition' (although *The Times* reported the involvement only of Angerstein and the Salomons).[19]

Angerstein was unsuccessful in future lottery bids, made solo or with Johnson, but in 1789 he, Johnson, and East India Company chairman William Devaynes (with whom Angerstein worked also on several charity projects) were awarded the contract to operate the first national tontine in several years. The £1,002,500 fundraising, divided into 10,000 shares of £100.5.0 each, was relatively unsuccessful, with shares quickly falling to a discount, but it gave Angerstein useful experience in organising state loans and their subscription, including dealing directly with the prime minister. The loan business was ultimately to be much bigger for Angerstein than lotteries.[20]

Pitt proposed, in 1793, to raise the first long-term loan since 1784. Curiously, interest in the loan was immediately voiced from another quarter of the insurance sector: on 15 March Pitt wrote to the London Assurance, citing their apparent offer to subscribe £300,000 to the new loan. 'As it is my Intention to agree for the whole amount with such Persons as may be willing to take it on such terms as may be most favourable Terms for the Public, I ... cannot therefore enter into any Agreement with respect to any separate Share.' When Pitt met with bidders 'Monday next at Eleven o'clock', the only willing contractors were Angerstein, Johnson & Devaynes. Grellier blamed the lack of bidders on the shortage of money and high interest rates which had plagued the City since about 1790, and on Pitt's decision to switch from the issue of 4% or 5% instruments to the contractors' preferred 3% stock. The £4.5 million loan was issued in 3% consols at a price of £72 for each £100 in consols, and Pitt declared the terms 'much more disadvantageous to the public than might have been expected'. The current market value of the securities was £77, giving 'a bonus to the Money-lenders of 300,000l', the *Morning Chronicle* complained, noting that Angerstein and Johnson had 'lists in which a great number of the

18   *Universal Magazine of Knowledge and Pleasure*, 'Historical chronicle for May 1788', p. 275.
19   Bank of England, G8/5, p. 271, Minutes of the Committee of the Treasury, 16 May 1793; *The Times*, issue 2613, 17 May 1793, p. 2.
20   Grellier and Wade, *Terms of all the loans*, p. 56; Twist, 'Widening circles', pp. 61–3.

Minister's friends are included', although when war was declared the market value of consols dropped immediately by almost 10%; 3% consols fell back to 70½.[21]

Devaynes & Co. split away from their partners for the £11 million loan of 1794. Angerstein and Johnson, with new partners James Morgan and Nesbitt & Stewarts, were awarded the loan in what Pitt described in his budget speech to the House as 'a free and open competition among monied men'. A new structure was for the first time established. The loan was to be issued in a mixture of debt instruments: each £100 bought £100 in 3% consols, £25 in 4 percents, and an 11s. 5d. annuity of 66 years and three months.[22] The combined stock package was described as the 'omnium', and appeared as such in public price lists as a tradeable package until the final instalments on the loan had been paid. Afterwards, subscribers received from the Bank of England 'an engagement to transfer to the person possessing them' the relevant stock 'upon the whole of the instalments being paid at or before the appointed time'. When traded separately, these receipts were known as script.[23] The *Sun* described the loan as 'the most advantageous Bargain ever made for the Public', as Angerstein and Johnson bid 'only a fraction above the Market-price of the Stocks'.[24]

Angerstein and Johnson did not participate in the 1795 loan for £18 million, nor a British-guaranteed loan of £4.5 million for Austria that year, as Pitt chose to grant the contracts without tender to Walter Boyd and Paul Benfield, the former a banker with the ear of Pitt and the latter an East India Company man, who together traded as Boyd Benfield & Co. By summer the loan traded at an 11 point premium. Later in 1795 a new £18 million loan for 1796 was awarded to Boyd. Controversy emerged, following a petition by Angerstein's new contracting partner James Morgan, who complained that the principle of open competition for contracts had been breached. The loans were subsequently the subject of a parliamentary enquiry in which Morgan, the first witness to testify, stated that 'Mr. Godschall Johnson called upon me at Garraway's Coffee House, to acquaint me that he and Mr. Angerstein did not intend to be concerned in forming any List for the Loan' of 1795.[25]

---

21   Pitt to the Governors and Directors of the London Assurance, 15 Mar. 1793, reprinted in G.S. Street, *The London Assurance, 1720–1920* (London, 1920), facing p. 14; Grellier and Wade, *Terms of all the loans*, p. 57; William Newmarch, *On the loans raised by Mr Pitt during the first French war, 1793–1801* (London, 1855), pp. 7–9; S.R. Cope, 'The Goldsmids and the development of the London money market during the Napoleonic Wars', *Economica*, new ser. 9, 34 (May 1942), p. 186; *Morning Chronicle*, issue 7428, 26 Mar. 1793.

22   Newmarch, *On the loans*, p. 10; Grellier and Wade, *Terms of all the loans*, p. 58.

23   Charles J. Hendee, *The mercantile arithmetic* (Boston, 1838), p. 187.

24   *The Sun*, issue 422, 4 Feb. 1794, p. 3.

25   Frederick Wedmore, 'Boyd, Walter', in *Dictionary of national biography*, vol. 6 (London, 1885), pp. 100–1; Alexander John Arbuthnot, 'Benfield, Paul', in *Dictionary of national biography*, vol. 4 (London, 1885), pp. 220–1; *Report from the select committee who were appointed to enquire*

After Pitt went direct to the public with the keenly priced £18 million 'Loyalty loan' of December 1796, a return to conventional contracting for a £14.5 million loan in April 1797 attracted only Boyd, despite paying, according to Newmarch, 'the highest rate paid for any loans … since the American war'. Competition returned for the 1798 loan of £17 million, when four groups of contractors bid against Boyd, who as a result made a very low bid. Boyd Benfield & Co. later collapsed, despite a loan of £80,000 from the Bank of England. Angerstein was among the loan's sixteen guarantors.[26]

Angerstein had remained outside of the direct contracting of loans until 1799, although it is likely that he appeared on successful contractors' lists. However, he was not inactive in raising funds for the state. He was a member of a committee struck in 1798 to organise a 'voluntary subscription for the defence of the country'. Fellow organisers included Lloyd's chairman Brook Watson, Angerstein's close colleagues Thomson Bonar and Henry Peters (now an MP), and subscribers to his 1812–15 loans – Samuel Bosanquet, John Perring, John Brickwood, Jasper Atkinson, Thomas Boddington, George Smith, John Inglis, and Charles Flower. The subscription raised perhaps £2 million.[27]

With his old partner Devaynes, Angerstein bid unsuccessfully for the £3 million loan of 1798 under the banner of Boyd & Co. (which was not yet bankrupt). The winners were a consortium of bankers led by Boldere, who underbid Robarts, Goldsmid, and E.P. Salomons; a consortium for the Stock Exchange under Battye; and Daniel Giles & Co.[28]

Angerstein returned directly to the loan contracting business in 1799 when, with Devaynes & Co. and Sir Francis Baring & Co., he was one of three successful bidders of six (alongside Daniel Giles & Co., bankers Smith Payne & Smith, and Thomas Everett; and Goldsmid & Co., Robarts, Curtis & Co., Thellusson & Brothers, G. Ward, E.P. Salomons, and R. Aislabie). The issue was a £15.5 million loan; Angerstein and his partners bid nil premium in a rising market, ahead of a committee of 24 bankers and the stock exchange consortium. A cryptic passage in *The Times* reports that one bidder – thought to be an agent of Boyd – withdrew his list after 'a long [private] conversation [with Pitt] which it would not be delicate in us to publish'. Documents in the Barings archive confirm this: a blank, printed letter of 15 May 1799 states:

> Although motives of delicacy, arising out of his present situation, have determined Mr. Boyd to take no ostensible part in the Conduct of any List for the approaching Loan, he has however the Pleasure to inform those Friends

---

into the circumstances of the negotiation of the late loan, House of Commons Sessional Papers, vol. 98, p. 4; Newmarch, *On the loans*, p. 12–14.

26   Newmarch, *On the loans*, pp. 17–8; Twist, 'Widening circles', p. 68.

27   'Voluntary contributions', *The Times*, issue 4,111, 5 Feb. 1798, p. 3.

28   Grellier and Wade, *Terms of all the loans*, p. 65.

who have been accustomed to embark with him in familiar Concerns, that his Friends, Messrs. *Walwyn, Strange* & Co. Bankers in Bond-street, Messrs. *Hodsoll* and *Stirling*, Bankers in the Strand, and other Gentlemen of great respectability and fortune, are forming a List, and have assured Mr. Boyd that they will pay particular attention to the Applications of his Friends.

The market price of consols rose immediately, 'so that Mr. PITT actually obtained his Loan under the rising price of the day'. This was the first time Angerstein was in partnership with Baring for a loan contract. Angerstein wrote to Francis Baring on 8 June 1799. 'I have been to the Bank and have written the distribution of the loan', he said. Of the total £15.5 million, £1.7 million was allocated to 'the Directors of different Companies'. Of the remainder, a third, £4.6 million, was allocated to Baring Angerstein and Devaynes. After subtracting relatively small shares for investors including Godschall Johnson, each of the three bidders was left to raise £1.51 million. Barings & Co. recorded a profit on the deal of £21,000.[29] In future Angerstein and his partners would raise much larger sums.

Angerstein was successful again in 1800 for a loan of £20.5 million, this time without Devaynes, but instead with Smith Payne & Smith (who had been successful with Giles the year before), and four members of the Old Committee of the Stock Exchange, including Battye, who bid together under the banner of Sir Francis Baring & Co. They split the loan with Robarts & Co. and Giles & Co., after the bankers and brokers again priced themselves out. The large, £28 million loan of 1801 was again shared by Baring and Angerstein, and another bidding group, which outbid the bankers and brokers Smith Payne & Smith (who appear to have decided to go it alone), and the bankers Newnham Everett & Co.[30]

Amidst stiff competition from seven consortia for the £25 million loan for 1802, Angerstein, Baring & Battye underbid – wisely, since it soon traded at a discount. They did not participate for the £18 million loan for 1803. In 1804 Angerstein made his last bid with Francis Baring as a partner, alongside, for the first time, Baring's son Alexander (a future MP), Battye, Ayton, and Ellis. They group shared the £24.5 million contract with Abraham Goldsmid, Robarts, Sir William Curtis (MP for the City and a former Lord Mayor), the Thellusson brothers, Ward, and Aislabie.[31]

Alexander Baring was involved from 1805, when the Baring/Angerstein consortium took a third of the loan, with the three bidding parties 'agreeing

29 *The Times*, issue 4502, 6 Jun. 1799, p. 2; Barings Archive, WPI A.22.3.2, Angerstein to F. Baring, 8 Jun. 1799; Barings Archive, NP1.A22.3.4, unaddressed letter, 15 May 1799; Philip Zeigler, *The sixth great power: Barings, 1762–1929* (London, 1988), p. 58.
30 *The Times*, issue 4726, 22 Feb. 1800, p. 2; Grellier and Wade, *Terms of all the loans*, p. 67.
31 Twist, 'Widening circles', p. 163; Grellier and Wade, *Terms of all the loans*, p. 68–71; *Morning Chronicle* issue 10,900, 26 Apr. 1804; issue 10,904, 1 May 1804.

to make the same offer'. In 1806 a larger Baring/Angerstein consortium bid successfully with Goldsmid & Co. and Robarts & Co. against John Barnes, James Steers, and David Ricardo, representing brokers of the Stock Exchange, for a £20 million loan. Ricardo and the brokers were successful against the same three competitors in 1807 for a loan of £14.2 million, although Henderson and Davis are incorrect to state that loan contractors had all always been bankers until 1806: clearly the insurers subscribing through Angerstein had a clear and substantial record, and regularly successful bidders such as Battye were fronting Stock Exchange lists.

In 1808 the consortium Baring, Angerstein, Ayton, Ellis & Battye won the entire £10.5 million loan, which traded immediately at a premium, after outbidding Barnes Steers & Ricardo. Goldsmid & Co. took the 1809 loan of £14.5 million, and in May 1810 four groups bid for £12 million, which was divided between Goldsmid & Co. and Baring & Angerstein. By September omnium on this loan was trading at a 6.5% discount, the loss in part prompting Alexander Goldsmid to follow his brother Benjamin's recent example and kill himself with a pistol. The news put the omnium down another four points. Angerstein's consortium was massively outbid in 1811 by a trio comprising: Barnes, Steers & Ricardo; Robarts & Co.; and George Ward. The trio bid too low: by February 1812 the omnium was trading at a discount.[32]

The subscribers

Despite Angerstein's significant loan contracting activity, his role in the business – and the capital of the insurance underwriters he recruited as loan subscribers – has gone almost entirely unacknowledged. Palmer's *Dictionary of national biography* entry on Angerstein makes no mention of the loans, and instead has him retiring in 1811, when his contracting activity was reaching its peak.[33]

Subscription, public or private, was the main means within the City of London to garner broad support for anything from joint-stock company launches to government loans. The term, along with 'underwriting', comes from late medieval Italian insurance practice. It reflects the convention of insurers signing their names below the main text of an insurance contract, making them 'under-writers' or 'sub-scribers'. As an insurance broker, Angerstein had plenty of experience organising insurance subscriptions. He was also an extremely active participant in the arrangement of charity subscriptions. He had, for example, raised funds

32   Grellier and Wade, *Terms of all the loans*, pp. 72, appen. 1–8; John P. Henderson and John B. Davis, *The life and economics of David Ricardo* (New York, 1997), pp. 197–8; *The Times*, 20 Apr. 1805; *Morning Chronicle*, 26 May 1806; *Morning Chronicle*, 28 May 1808.
33   Sarah Palmer, 'Angerstein, John Julius (c.1732–1823)', *Oxford dictionary of national biography* (Oxford, 2004), online edn, viewed 11 Jan. 2008.

Table 3.1. 1812 subscribers to Angerstein's loan, £000

Description	No.	Amount	Share
Insurance underwriters or brokers	104	£3,487	68.0%
Individuals with underwriters in the family	17	360	7.0%
Unrelated to insurance or no connections identified	48	1,143	22.0%
Unknown	4	84	1.6%
Subscriptions for others in Angerstein's name	7	61	1.2%
Total	180	£5,135	

for the London Asylum for the Deaf and Dumb, of which he was a vice president (with William Wilberforce). He, along with loan subscribers Joseph Marryat, R.H. Marten, and Thomson Bonar, comprised the core of a committee arranged to 'carry out the objects' of a subscription, heavily supported by members of Lloyd's, raised 'for the Family off the Late Mr. Palm', a Nuremburg bookdealer tried by the French for dealing in volumes critical of Napoleon. Loan subscriptions were therefore familiar territory for John Julius Angerstein.[34]

The first loan for which Angerstein's subscription list survives is that of 1812. Of £22.5 million, £15,650,000 was to be raised in England, £4,350,000 in Ireland, and £2.5 million from the East India Company. The bidders met with the new Chancellor of the Exchequer, Nicholas Vansittart, to present their bids, to be valued in 3% consols. For every £100 subscribed, bidders would receive a nominal £120 in 3% reduced consols, plus the amount of their bid. Bidders on this occasion were consortia led by Baring & Co.; Reid, Irving & Co. (a leading West & East Indies mercantile firm); Barnes, Steers & Ricardo; and Robarts, Curtis & Co. Wade recorded that three bidders 'coalesced' to bid 56 consols. According to Angerstein's own notes, the winning bidders were 'three partners, viz. Robarts & Co; Baring & Angerstein & Battye & Dawes & Ellis; [and] Ricardo'. The process itself caused a drop in the market price of consols, with 3 percents falling to 59½, and reduceds falling to 58½. The division of the loan changed, according to Angerstein's notes. The East India Company took £1.8 million, and Baring and Angerstein £10,250,000, of which Angerstein took personal responsibility for £5.125 million, a quarter of the total. He immediately planned to take £1.708 million onto his own account, an enormous amount for an individual. The rest he divided between 180 subscribers, including individuals and partnerships.[35]

---

34 *The Times*, issue 5999, 17 Apr. 1804, p. 1; issue 6867, 16 Oct. 1806, p. 1.
35 *The Times*, issue 8626, 13 Jun. 1812, p. 3; Grellier and Wade, *Terms of all the loans*, app. p. 9, Angerstein's subscription book, LMA F/Ang/110, frontispiece.

In total 174 discrete individuals and 46 partnerships subscribed to Angerstein's loans of 1812 and 1813. It is plain that he turned to his familiars, from business, family, and social life, to seek subscribers, and that the underwriting members of Lloyd's comprised the bulk of them. Of the 172 individuals identified with relative confidence, 93 were Lloyd's underwriters, as recorded in the unique 'Roll of Lloyd's'. Another 16 had immediate family members in the market. That makes, in total, 109 subscribers with direct connections to Lloyd's, or slightly less than two thirds of Angerstein's individual subscribers. Further, of 46 partnerships that subscribed in 1812 and 1813, 31 include at least one partner positively identified as a member of Lloyd's. Others, such as 'Thomas Brothers', cannot be conclusively connected to the many Lloyd's members surnamed Thomas. Companies were not permitted to become underwriting members of the market, since partnerships and joint-stock companies were prohibited under the 'Bubble Act' of 1720 from underwriting marine insurance risks, which comprised the vast majority of Lloyd's risks until the twentieth century.

Membership of Lloyd's implies with certainty that an individual acted as a marine insurance underwriter at least occasionally, and probably often, since membership brought associated costs. Some members (like Angerstein) considered insurance their primary occupation. However, underwriting and broking remained a sideline for many individuals and firms, although the business had developed into a primary occupation for some practitioners over the course of the eighteenth century. For example, the merchant Ralph Radcliffe purchased eighteen surviving policies in 1716, underwritten by forty-four discrete individuals. Of these, twenty-eight participated in only one of the eighteen policies, but John Barnard, Richard Cambridge, and William Hayton took a share of the risk under five or more policies. The 'scratch' (or signature) of Cambridge appears on twelve. Barnard is well known in part due to Lucy Sutherland's monograph about him; he was one of what was perhaps London's first generation of full-time underwriters, although he was also a wine merchant, and later an MP.[36]

Fourteen subscribers to Angerstein's loans – all members of Lloyd's – appear on a list of underwriters that were guaranteed by Angerstein eighteen years before the loan of 1812, and they certainly constitute professional insurers. In 1794 Angerstein, Warren & Lock, Angerstein's insurance broking partnership, wrote to John & Francis Baring & Co. regarding an insurance they had arranged to provide £56,500 of cover for goods aboard the vessel *Unity*, on a voyage from Amsterdam to London. For five shillings per £100 of cover, the brokers offered 'in case of Failure … to become your Security for Underwriters'. The list is a who's who of leading underwriters of the day, and includes Miles Peter

---

36   Business records of the Radcliffe family, Hertfordshire Archives and Local Studies Centre, DE/R/B293/1–47; Lucy Sutherland, *A London merchant, 1695–1744* (London, 1933).

Andrews, a partner in gunpowder merchants Pigou, Andrews & Wilkes. (Pigou was also an underwriter, and appears on the guaranteed list, but was not a loan subscriber.) The merchant and insurance broker William Bell appears, as does John Brickwood, a long-standing underwriter.

Loan subscriber Robert Christie, a merchant of 14 New Broad St. according to the *Post Office annual directory* of 1814, was a frequent underwriter, and held a Bank of England joint account with the aforementioned Robert Christie and the underwriters Edward Vaux (also a subscriber), George Henkell (also guaranteed), and Thomas Parry (who appears as both guaranteed and was a subscriber). Guaranteed underwriters Robert Shedden and his son George, merchants of 26 Charlotte Street, Bedford Square, were subscribers, and appear frequently as underwriters in a unique policy register book now held in the vaults at Lloyd's, along with leading underwriters including Vaux, Christie, and others. Other subscribing individuals, such as the East India Company Chairman Sir Henry Lushington Bt, were close to members of the list: guaranteed underwriter William Lushington was Sir Henry's brother.[37]

Absence from Lloyd's membership by no means automatically indicates that Angerstein's subscribers were not underwriters. Considerable volumes of underwriting were carried out by individuals who were not members. Angerstein himself testified in 1810 that 'other underwriters, who do not attend at Lloyd's, carry on the business of marine Insurance at the Jamaica Coffee-house, the Jerusalem Coffee-house, the Coal Exchange, as well as a great number write policies at their own counting houses'. Lloyd's was an exclusive club which imposed restrictions upon the business practised there, from the wording of the insurance policies permitted to the nature of the business which could be transacted in the Underwriting Room; some insurers chose to operate outside these restrictions. Direct evidence that underwriters active outside Lloyd's subscribed to Angerstein's loans is found in a policy of 27 November 1818, in my possession, under which J. Majoribanks grants cover of $50 to Mrs Sarah Wilde's share of the vessel *Frances*, for its voyage from Quebec to Waterford. The policy reached the underwriter through the broking firm Sanderson, Brothers. Jonathan Majoribanks subscribed £3,000 to Angerstein's 1813 subscription. Insurers who did not underwrite marine insurance also appeared as subscribers, such as Thomas Dorrien, a Director of the Sun Fire Office.[38]

Insurance brokers
Among the subscribers, 28 individuals or partnerships have been positively identified as carrying on business as insurance brokers through reference to

---

37 Bank of England Archive, C98/182, Register of accounts 1798–1800, vol. A–C, p. 2; Barings Archive, WPI A1.22, Angerstein Warren & Lock to Barings & Co., 14 Oct. 1794.
38 House of Commons, *Report from the Select Committee on Marine Insurance. (Sess. 1810.)* (London, 1824), testimony of John Julius Angerstein, p. 58.

directories such as *Johnson's London commercial guide* of 1818. All of them are also identified as members of Lloyd's. It was quite usual for individuals to act both as underwriters and as brokers, as indeed Angerstein himself did. Others identified simply as 'brokers' or as 'stockbrokers' may also have dealt in insurance. James Bury, a stockbroker of Throgmorton Street and the Royal Exchange, is one example.

Merchants

Individuals and partnerships identified as merchants in commercial directories very often were prominent underwriters or insurance brokers. For example, Joseph Marryat & Son is listed in the 1814 *Post Office annual directory* simply as 'Merchants', despite Marryat's leading role within Lloyd's; as an MP, he argued vociferously in Lloyd's favour in Parliament. Other merchants, neither Lloyd's members nor listed as brokers in the directories, were known to Angerstein through family connections at Lloyd's. Tullie Joseph Cornthwaite, a wool broker of the Old Pay Office, Old Broad Street, was not a Lloyd's member, and no evidence of underwriting by him has come to light. However, his uncle Robert Cornthwaite was a founding member of Lloyd's.

Angerstein's mercantile business was primarily with Russia, where he had strong family and personal connections. For example, a letter in a private collection of Angerstein documents is from Monsieur de Buschmann, private secretary to the Grand Duchess of Russia (deceased). Angerstein's adopted family, the Thomsons, with the Bonars and Peters, were among the leading Russia merchants of the eighteenth century. Unsurprisingly, Russia merchants featured prominently amongst Angerstein's loan subscribers, including J. Atkinson & Co. of 108 Fenchurch Street, Greenwood & Sons, and Samuel Thornton MP and his cousin William Thornton Astell MP, both of whom were Governors of the Russia Company, as well as Directors of the Bank of England.

Still other subscribers are found among Angerstein's substantial clients, including Glyn Mills Hallifax & Co., bankers at 12 Birchin Lane, and Colonel Charles Herries, a Spain merchant in St Mary's Axe and known slave trade investor. Herries was in a shipowning partnership with Joseph Nailer and James Drummond. Nailer was an underwriting member of Lloyd's, as were many shipowners (including Angerstein), reflecting the continued mutual risk-sharing nature of underwriting.

Others

Angerstein's list was not limited to insurance connections. The aforementioned Herries owed his rank to his position in the Light Horse Volunteers of London and Westminster, first established in 1799 for the defence of the city by Herries and Brook Watson, Chairman of Lloyd's, and also a slaver. The Volunteers included close Angerstein associates Henry Crokatt, John Thomson, and Francis Baring. After a brief interlude the troop was revived in 1794, and perhaps a quarter of the total number of subscribers to Angerstein's loans were members of the Volunteers.

Insurers and the fiscal-military state

Insurance is just one of several ways to address war risk (including mitigation methods such as convoying, fractional ownership of vessels, the division of cargoes over multiple vessels, and the variation of sea routes to avoid dangerous zones). The primary role of marine insurance underwriters in wartime is well recognised: they act as counterparties in risk transfer (rather than risk mitigation), since they provide the contingent capital which allows merchants to continue trading even when the risk of the loss of vessels and cargo is heightened by the activity of enemy vessels. In addition, it is clear their capital – invested and reserved to pay eventual claims – was an important source of the funds supporting state borrowing during the French Revolutionary and Napoleonic Wars. Previously thought to have been the exclusive preserve of bankers and stock exchange principals, the career of John Julius Angerstein, one of Lloyd's leading insurance underwriters and brokers, in loan contracting shows that this critical role in state fundraising was played also by the marine insurance market. Marine insurers in London, who comprised a substantial and savvy group of professional investors, indeed used their capital twice, and twice for the war effort. As the preponderance of insurance men in Angerstein's loan lists shows, they simultaneously supported the state and its merchants, through policies and lending.

4

The political economy of Sir Robert Peel

CHARLES READ

On 24 June 2016 the Electoral Commission announced that the United Kingdom had voted to leave the European Union. Forty minutes later, David Cameron, the Conservative prime minister who had called the referendum to unite his party, resigned. He had campaigned to remain in the bloc. The same week 170 years earlier, on 29 June 1846, the Conservatives' first ever prime minister, Sir Robert Peel, also resigned after splitting his party. While it was the question of Britain's continued membership of the EU which had divided Mr Cameron's Conservative party, Peel's split over his repeal of the Corn Laws, a set of import duties on cereals. Peel had forced the measure through with opposition votes. In revenge, protectionist backbenchers brought their own government down by vetoing its important Irish Coercion Bill. The split became permanent. Peel's parliamentary supporters within the old Conservative party became known as the 'liberal' Conservatives or Peelites, evolving into the modern Liberal party in 1859. The rebels formed a new Conservative party, the direct institutional ancestor of today's organisation of that name.

Historians have long argued over why Peel u-turned over the issue of the Corn Laws and split his party apart over it, in retrospect permanently. In contrast, his role in establishing a new economic-policy paradigm, one that lasted until 1931, has been downplayed. Although Norman Gash praised Peel as 'chief architect' of the mid-Victorian 'age of stability', historians generally see William Gladstone and Benjamin Disraeli as pivotal in establishing a political consensus around 'sound' finance.[1] But as Martin Daunton has pointed out, the historiographical veneration of Gladstone has downplayed Peel's role in establishing the policies Gladstone continued as his protégé.[2] Peel, as chairman

---

1   N. Gash, *Sir Robert Peel: the life of Sir Robert Peel after 1830* (London, 1972), p. 714; H.C.G. Matthew, 'Disraeli, Gladstone, and the politics of mid-Victorian budgets', *Historical Journal* 22 (1979), pp. 615–43.
2   M.J. Daunton, *Trusting Leviathan* (Cambridge, 2001), p. 81.

of the Currency Commission in 1819, a cabinet minister in the 1820s, and prime minister in the 1840s, drove the adoption in Britain of the classic 'gold standard' policies, of which free trade was just one:

1. The value of British currency should be firmly fixed to a gold standard, with the pound freely convertible by the Bank of England.
2. Banknote supply should be limited based on a multiple of gold reserves.
3. Free movement of bullion from 1819, and free trade, or more accurately lower tariffs on food and raw materials, from 1842.
4. Control of interest rates and a balanced budget in order to reduce the national debt.

This chapter re-examines, in the context of his wider economic-policy goals, the intentions behind Peel's repeal of the Corn Laws, and why he was prepared to risk such damage to his party. Daunton, in his survey of the history of tax policy, saw the lowering of tariffs and introduction of an income tax in Peel's 1842 budget as aimed at 'integrating classes and defusing social unrest'.[3] The reassessment of Peel's public statements and private papers presented here confirms this as his primary aim, with the beginnings of free trade merely a tool to achieve it. The repeal of the Corn Laws is therefore an event that should not be seen in isolation, but as part of a consistent economic-policy agenda dating from the 1820s. All of Peel's economic policies were aimed at stability and affordable food prices for the working man. Those policies reigned supreme in Britain, more or less, until the economic crisis of 1931 prompted a dramatic U-turn, but they had important and unintended consequences for some parts of the United Kingdom, particularly Ireland.

I

Historians have long argued over why Peel repealed the Corn Laws. Current academic opinion, though varied, tends to be dominated by a picture of Peel possessing the long-term 'doctrinaire approach to free trade' mentioned in Boyd Hilton's early work.[4] Peel's government was elected in 1841 pledging to preserve the Corn Laws. The editors of Peel's *Memoirs* started off the debate about the intentions behind his decision to abandon this policy by constructing chapters around his most controversial U-turns, including the repeal of the Corn Laws.[5] However, they tended to focus on policies as beliefs rather than as

3   Daunton, *Trusting Leviathan*, p. 81.
4   B. Hilton, 'Peel: a reappraisal', *Historical Journal* 22 (1979), p. 596.
5   R. Peel, *Memoirs*, ed. Earl Stanhope and E. Cardwell, vols 2, 3 (London, 1857), pp. 97–325.

tools to obtain intended outcomes. This has muddied the waters of subsequent historical analysis. The greatest weight in the section of the *Memoirs* about repeal is given to the argument justifying it as a response to the Irish famine. Peel openly stated that he presented it in that way because he thought to emphasise this reason would be most persuasive.[6]

Contrary to his expectations, many historians have since found it unconvincing. Richard Gaunt has recently summarised the resulting debate amongst historians as a contrast between an acceptance that policy was 'the outcome of immediate stimuli such as the failure of the Irish potato crop' and a belief in 'Peel's long-term and premeditated commitment to the repeal of the Corn Laws'.[7] Gash has maintained that there was a 'fundamental connection between the Irish potato disease and the abandonment of the corn laws'.[8] Gash defended Peel's sudden U-turn over the Corn Laws in 1845 by pointing out his 'instinct was always to the practical measure rather than the political gesture', what Robert Stewart referred to as his 'pragmatic temperament'.[9] This position has come in for substantial criticism in recent years. Robert Blake has argued that 'the repeal of Corn Laws did not make – and could not have made – much difference to the famine', and that 'Peel was already converted to free trade'. Blake asked: 'why did he do it with such alacrity and glee' when, at the end of 1845, he could have left it to Russell who had at that time supported full free trade?[10] David Eastwood has gone further: Peel 'deliberately engineered' the destruction of the Conservative party to make him the natural leader of a Whig-Liberal government.[11]

In forming these viewpoints, historians have tended to consider only the Corn Laws, with little analysis of his wider economic-policy agenda. At first these appear contradictory. Supporters of free trade, such as James Wilson of *The Economist*, opposed the state regulation of banknote issues. In contrast, protectionists in trade, such as Robert Torrens, supported such limits. Peel adopted an ideologically incoherent mix of the two positions: he came to support freer trade and stricter controls on banknote issue as his career progressed. But the policies pursued by Peel throughout his lifetime are consistent if his overall economic aim of benefiting the labouring classes by ensuring low and stable prices, without lowering wages or hurting the agricultural sector, is taken into consideration. Such an aim is referred to in Peel's *Memoirs*, and it was his declared preoccupation from c. 1830 to 1850. The variation in his support for

6   Ibid., p. 107.
7   R. Gaunt, *Sir Robert Peel: the life and legacy* (London, 2010), pp. 104–5.
8   Gash, *Sir Robert Peel* (London, 1972), p. 565.
9   Ibid., p. 297; R. Stewart, *The politics of protection* (Cambridge, 1971), p. 34.
10 R. Blake, *The Conservative Party from Peel to Churchill* (London, 1970), p. 53.
11 D. Eastwood, 'Peel and the Tory Party reconsidered', *History Today* 42 (1992), p. 33.

free trade was due to uncertainty about whether it would produce his desired aim of stable prices at the time. Peel was consistent in aim – if not in policy – and he acted as much *pro bono publico* as politically.[12]

II

Historians other than Daunton have touched upon Peel's aim of benefiting the labouring classes. Derek Beales noted Peel's prioritisation of 'the comforts of the labouring classes' and Gash thought 'concern for the masses was never far away from his economic philosophy'.[13] Even Hilton identified his early concerns about 'food supply', and Daniel Verdier put Peel's actions down to 'scarcity of foodstuffs'.[14]

In contrast to the political historians who saw Peel as dogmatically driven, Douglas Irwin noted particularly his 'long' concern with 'the welfare of labour'.[15] This concern for the poor can be seen clearly in Peel's writings and speeches, and traced throughout his career. Peel was Home Secretary when J.C. Herries replaced a fixed duty on corn with a sliding scale.[16] But Peel's first real policy initiative on free trade, with Herries and Henry Goulburn (later his Chancellor of the Exchequer), came in 1830 when he tried to cut taxes on beer, hops, and sugar, and replace the lost government receipts with a property tax. Its presented aim was to reduce the weight of indirect taxes, and therefore prices, placed 'on the shoulders of the middling and labouring classes'.[17] In 1834 when he spoke against free-trade proposals, he said the Corn Laws protected the 'moral and social interests of the whole community' because landowners helped to pay for the Poor Law.[18] Again in 1839, when he still supposedly spoke in support of the Corn Laws, he required that they 'be consistent not only with ... the maintenance of the landlord's interest but ... especially with the improvement of the condition of the labouring classes'.[19]

In 1839 Peel argued for a better Corn Bill to assist the working classes. Later, in 1842, describing his plans for reduced tariffs that year, Peel was even

---

12   Ibid., p. 27.

13   D. Beales, *From Castlereagh to Gladstone 1815–1885* (London, 1971), p. 135; Gash, *Sir Robert Peel*, p. 565.

14   B. Hilton, *A mad, bad, and dangerous people?* (Oxford, 2006), p. 268; D. Verdier, 'Between party and faction', in C. Schonhardt-Bailey, ed., *The rise of free trade*, vol. 4 (London, 1997), p. 309.

15   D. Irwin, 'Political economy and Peel's repeal of the Corn Laws', *Economics and Politics* 1 (1989), pp. 53–5.

16   Importation of Corn Act 1828, 9 Geo. IV c.60.

17   Memorandum by Herries on free trade, n.d. [c. 1830], Wellington papers, SUL, WP1/1164/11.

18   *Hansard*, XXII, 19 Mar. 1834, c.443.

19   *Hansard*, XLVI, 15 Mar. 1839, c.757.

more focused: 'the great object ... is the welfare and benefit of the great body of people'.[20] Describing 1846 in his *Memoirs*, Peel cited the interests of 'the whole community' and his 'serious doubts whether ... cheapness and plenty are not [better] ensured for the future' by free trade than protection.[21] His main emphasis in his *Memoirs* on the role of the famine in his decision-making may well have been because the wider aim of lower prices seemed weak and unsubstantiated by comparison. Yet even in 1850 he argued that the 'condition of the working classes' was still 'the test by which the merits of the question must be decided'.[22]

Peel's views were strengthened by a fear of revolution, which was common among politicians of his generation. Eastwood highlighted Peel's 1842 belief 'that if prices and unemployment continued at the current levels the security of property would be imperilled'.[23] Cobden claimed that Peel, on hearing of the overthrow of the French government in the 1848 revolution, had said:

> this comes of trying to govern the country through a narrow representation in Parliament, without regarding the wishes of those outside. It is what this party behind me [the protectionist Conservatives] wanted me to do in the matter of the Corn Laws [in 1846], and I would not do it.[24]

As Stewart puts it, Peel pre-empted the demands of the mob, taking care not to 'excite the feelings and inflame the passions of the people'.[25] Peter Ghosh also emphasised that Peel's 'oddity' in attending to the needs of the impoverished addressed 'a serious danger to the aristocracy' and Peel's apprehension at the expansion of the electorate.[26]

Peel's attitude to free trade as a policy varied according to whether he believed it would produce the outcome he understood that the masses wanted. He had defined their demand in his Tamworth Manifesto of 1841. In that election speech he sympathised with 'the poor manufacturers of Nuneaton' and their hope for 'increased employment, and a reduction in the price of bread'.[27] However, he emphasised that altering the Corn Laws required great care in

---

20 *Hansard*, LX, 16 Feb. 1842, c.592.

21 Peel, *Memoirs*, vols 2/3, p. 102.

22 R. Peel, 'Taxation of the country debate, 12 March 1850', *Speeches, IV: 1842–50* (London, 1853), pp. 835, 833.

23 D. Eastwood '"Recasting our lot": Peel the nation and the politics of interest', in L. Brockliss, D. Eastwood, eds, *A union of multiple identities: the British Isles c.1750–c.1850* (Manchester, 1977), p. 35.

24 J. Bright and J.E.T. Rogers, eds, *Speeches on questions of public policy by Richard Cobden, M.P.*, vol. 2 (London, 1908), pp. 580–1.

25 Stewart, *The politics of protection*, p. 35; *Hansard*, XIII, 5 Jun. 1832, col. 426.

26 P. Ghosh, 'Gladstone and Peel', in P. Ghosh, L. Goldman, eds, *Politics and culture in Victorian Britain: essays in memory of Colin Matthew* (Oxford, 2006), pp. 47–51.

27 R. Peel, *Tamworth election: speech of Sir Robert Peel, June 28, 1841* (London, 1841), p. 12.

order to achieve the desired results, because even the experts did not agree.[28] Peel was wary of taking action that would cause increased fluctuations in prices which would outweigh any price reduction. Fluctuations in food prices, he argued, were greater than the fluctuations in the supply which were supposed to cause them. In 1840 he believed 'a greater steadiness [existed] under the sliding scale, as it was called, than could be hoped for under any other system'.[29]

At this time he did not believe that full-blown free trade would stabilise prices. 'I have great doubts whether your expectations, that free trade in corn will produce a great fixity in price will be realised ... The main object to be attained is a comparatively fixed price.'[30] In 1842 he still believed that 'prices are more peculiarly affected by influences which fluctuate, and must of necessity be uncertain ... it appears to me that the strict principles of free trade cannot be applied without danger to the interests of the community'.[31]

Initially, between 1841 and 1844, he was influenced by his President of the Board of Trade, the Earl of Ripon. Ripon advised Peel against unilateral reductions in tariffs, counselling that the Corn Laws provided food security and that 'reciprocity' was the only way to get other countries to reduce their tariffs.[32] But Ripon's deputy, Gladstone, was a more driven supporter of unilateralism, and challenged Peel on 'corn law revision', threatening resignation when he did not get his way.[33] Ripon avoided conflict within the Board of Trade by deferring arguments with Gladstone to the prime minister, which gave Gladstone an opportunity to persuade Peel of the correctness of his views.[34] As a result of this access, Peel came to be convinced that his principal aim, to lower prices, would not be put at risk by slight trade imbalances, which Ripon's slow path to free trade through bilateral agreements was intended to avoid.

The 1842 budget, in which Peel's new government cut 750 out of 1,200 import duties and reintroduced the income tax, was mainly intended to eliminate the government budget deficit.[35] The Whig experiment of raising tariffs to reduce the deficit in 1840–41 had failed to produce sufficient revenue.[36] Peel quoted

28   See Irwin, *Political economy*, p. 45 for more examples of Peel's opinion of political economists as disagreeing on this subject.
29   *Hansard*, LIII, 3 Apr. 1840, c.523.
30   *Hansard*, LIX, 27 Aug. 1841, c.419.
31   *Hansard*, LX, 16 Feb. 1842, c.604.
32   W.D. Jones, *Prosperity Robinson* (London, 1967), pp. 249–51; Ripon to Peel, 7 Oct. 1841, Peel papers, BL Add. MS 40464, f. 28; Ripon to Peel, 29 Nov. 1841, Ripon papers, BL Add. MS 40863, f. 254.
33   H.C.G. Matthew, *Gladstone 1809–1874* (Oxford, 1991), p. 66.
34   Ripon to Gladstone, Oct. 1842, Gladstone papers, BL Add. MS 44731, f. 5.
35   Gash, *Sir Robert Peel*, p. 319; A. Howe, *Free trade and Liberal England 1846–1946* (Oxford 1998), p. 4.
36   D. Steele, 'Baring, Francis Thornhill, first Baron Northbrook (1796–1866)', *Oxford dictionary of national biography* (ODNB), 2004; online edn, Jan. 2008; L. Brown, *The Board of Trade and the free-trade movement 1830–42* (Oxford, 1958), p. 219.

this experience as evidence in Parliament to support the tariff-reducing and income-tax-raising strategies of the 1842 budget.[37] The 5 per cent increase in excise duties had only increased revenues by £206,715 – 'but a little more than half per cent' – and not the £1,895,575, or 5 per cent, that Baring, the Chancellor, had originally hoped for.[38] Conversely, the 10 per cent increase in assessed taxes increased revenues by 11.75 per cent.[39] Raising other taxes was a more effective way to cut the deficit than increasing excise duties.

The driving motive behind this desire to balance the budget was to stop adding to the national debt. In 1842 Peel berated the Whigs for their spending, and for adding £2 million to the enormous £800 million of national debt, the interest on which consumed over half of annual government expenditure.[40] After seeing a list of the 'comparative advantages and disadvantages of an Income Tax' prepared by Goulburn, Peel had confirmed his decision in favour of an income tax, to compensate for reduced import duties, 'in point of reason and sound policy'. Peel hoped lower food prices, 'a great public advantage', would follow without an increased national debt.[41]

In early 1844 Peel believed that his economic policies to date were working, and that the benefits were shared by Ireland. That situation confirmed to him that he was correct in the way he thought the economy functioned. This included Ricardo's belief that high food prices only benefited the landlords. Peel had studied Ricardo's work in 1819–20 when he was chairing the Currency Commission, and in particular Ricardo's arguments that landowners benefited unfairly from the Corn Laws in the form of rent, or profit, and that the poorer tenants did not benefit from the higher prices.[42] The assumption followed that if tariffs were reduced the landowner rather than the tenant or farmer would suffer because 'a low price of produce may be compensated to him [the farmer] by a great additional quantity'.[43]

These views struck a chord with Peel, who privately disliked the Irish landowners in particular as they believed themselves to be 'a superior and privileged class'.[44] However, Peel adopted these economic ideas with care, aiming for moderate price reductions which he hoped would benefit the

37 *Hansard*, LXI, 11 Mar. 1842, c.432.
38 Ibid., c.588.
39 Ibid.
40 *Hansard*, LXII, 8 Apr. 1842, c.156.
41 Peel to Goulburn, 28 Jul. 1841, Goulburn papers, Surrey History Centre, 304/A1/1/2/548/1; Peel to Ripon, 1 Apr. 1842, Ripon papers, BL Add. MS 40863, f. 323; Howe, *Free trade*, p. 7; N. Gash, *Sir Robert Peel*, p. 321.
42 D. Ricardo, *An essay on the influence of a low price of corn* [1815], published in *The works of David Ricardo*, ed. J.R. Murray (London, 1888), p. 378.
43 Ibid.
44 Draft, Peel to De Grey, 22 Aug. 1843, Peel papers, BL Add. MS 40478, f. 160. These words were deleted in the draft.

labouring classes without antagonising the agricultural interest. This was still true in 1846, when the 'repeal of the Corn Laws' actually still retained part of the sliding scale.[45] He planned that increased demand for produce and labour would benefit the great body of the people, without prejudice to the interests of agriculture.[46] He anticipated that the measure would so increase consumption that the reduction in the prices of agricultural produce would be slight.

Peel carefully considered whether a fall in prices would cause a fall in wages in both agricultural and commercial sectors, and came to the conclusion that 'the wages of the agricultural labourer did not vary in a direct ratio with the price of corn ... but ... in many cases the wages of the manufacturing labourer had varied in an inverse ratio to the price of corn'.[47] Therefore he assumed a fall in prices would benefit workers in both sectors.

Peel adopted allegiance to full free trade from only June 1846, when, facing resignation, he pondered in cabinet a strategy with which to fight a general election, and decided it would be 'Free Trade and the destruction of Protection'.[48] This sudden decision is what has prompted accusations that he acted politically. Yet his intention was to beat the Whigs – who were offering full free trade immediately – so he could implement the policy in a more gradual way to benefit all parties.[49] He blamed Richard Cobden, a free-trade campaigner, for the change because his activism had made it inevitable.[50]

III

Generally supporters of free trade also supported free banking, but Peel was seemingly inconsistent in this respect. However, a general aim of reducing food prices can be seen as consistent with Peel's Banking Acts of 1844–45 because he adopted the Currency School's belief that the gold standard with a limited circulation of notes would cause a fall in the general level of prices.[51] Peel, between the 1820s and the 1840s, had seen plenty of evidence to suggest that a gold standard reduced price levels. After his term as chairman of the Currency Commission, he had the gold standard restored to the high pre-war parity in three stages between February 1820 and May 1823, ending a period of

45   Rarely noticed by political historians, although some economic historians have drawn attention to it. See K.H. O'Rourke in 'British trade policy', *European Journal of Political Economy* 16 (2000), pp. 832–3.
46   *Hansard*, LXXXIII, 27 Jan. 1846, c.305.
47   *Hansard*, LXXXVI, 15 May 1846, cols 631–2.
48   Cabinet memorandum, 21 Jun. 1846, Peel papers, BL Add. MS 40594, ff. 23–37, trans., ff. 38–55.
49   Ibid.
50   Eastwood, 'Peel and the Tory party', p. 33.
51   Noted but not agreed with by *The Economist*, 7 Sep. 1844, p. 1178.

suspension enacted by Pitt's government in 1797. As a result of this return to gold, prices fell sharply, causing distress as small note circulation was reduced by seven-eighths between 1819 and 1822.

Peel avoided the blame for these events by stating only obliquely his belief that restricting note circulation would keep down prices. In 1826 Peel was attacked by all sides for causing a slump in prices with his legislation. This viewpoint came from Huskisson's theory that 'we have Bank notes as a substitute for gold, and that it is by an abundant supply of them that prices at home are raised and improved'.[52] It followed that by removing banknotes from circulation, prices would fall. Peel fought back against the attacks by claiming that changes in prices caused the issued number of banknotes to change, the reverse of Huskisson's theory.[53]

In 1844 Peel followed the same line, but was unclear about the direction of causation.[54] However, his belief that a gold standard lowers prices is clear from other explanations. In answering the question, still often asked today, why he only controlled banknotes and not other forms of money with the Bank Charter Act, he answered that it was mainly notes (promissory notes) that had an effect on the prices of commodities, his main target.[55] Moreover, the position was made clearer in the House of Lords by Ripon. He argued against the suggestion that Peel's Act of 1819, returning convertibility, was responsible for recent price increases (rather than the immediate decreases it was originally believed to have caused) and distress amongst the working classes, but he was very clear that he believed it was note issue that increases prices. By inference, limiting note issue was beneficial to labourers.[56]

Peel's views on this matter were influenced by the theories of S.J. Loyd, the leader of the Currency School.[57] He believed that if the 1819 Act on a gold standard had been properly constituted 'considerable fluctuations in prices ... would have been avoided'.[58] Peel reflected the Lloyd line in Parliament, both being unwilling to predict price movements but showing an underlying belief that a gold standard exerted a downward pressure and brought stability to prices.

Peel did not wish for deflation to depress the economy, but he hoped for moderate increases in sales by farmers to counterbalance any loss from low prices and for expanding employment, driven by a greater volume of trade. In

52   W. Huskisson, *The question concerning the depreciation of our currency stated and examined* (London, 1810), p. 42.
53   *Hansard*, XIV, 13 Feb. 1826, c.289.
54   *Hansard*, LXXIV, 20 May 1844, c.1342.
55   *Hansard*, LXXIV, 6 May 1844, c.733.
56   *Hansard*, LXXVI, 12 Jul. 1844, cols 714–15.
57   M. Reed, 'Loyd, Samuel Jones, Baron Overstone (1796–1883)', *ODNB*, 2004; online edn, Jan. 2008.
58   *Report from Select Committee on Banks of Issue*, PP 1840 (602) IV.1 para. 2935, 258.

a letter to Peel in 1841 Gladstone identified one of Peel's 'main propositions' that he used to justify lower tariffs as 'stimulating consumption'.[59] In 1846 when arguing for repeal, Peel had said to agriculturalists that 'we must take some measures, therefore, to increase the produce of your farm'.[60]

The attitude amongst policymakers thus differed from the 'static self-regulating economy' which Hilton has defined as 'liberal-tory economic policy' before 1830.[61] This echoed J.S. Mill's vision of the endgame of long-term growth: 'the increase of wealth is not boundless ... at the end of ... the progressive state lies the stationary state'.[62] By contrast Peel looked to an immediate expansion of trade, living standards and government income, and his choice of economic policy was driven by a search for the tools to encourage it whilst maintaining stability. Peel realised by the end of the 1840s that low tariffs and competition meant that the farmer needed to make up income lost because of low prices by increasing volumes of turnover brought about by increased efficiency. He published an open letter to his tenants in *The Times* suggesting the solution to foreign competition was agricultural improvement and efficiency.[63] In other words growth was necessary to maintain, let alone increase, incomes. This is why Peel is often referred to as the 'father of globalisation' and modern economic growth.[64]

The Bank Charter Act was also intended to solve the problem of bullion 'drains', the movement of excessive amounts of bullion out of the country to pay for foreign goods such as corn. Hilton has described in detail Peel and Ripon's investigation of data to try to find a link between wheat imports and bullion reserve depletion.[65] The worry, at first, was that the corn-law sliding scale caused sudden bursts of wheat imports, and consequent exports of bullion to pay for it, as the tariff changed. But it was soon realised, even by the supporters of free trade, that the same problem might apply to the lowering of tariffs under free trade.[66] Peel relied on the theory that restricting the note issue according to bullion reserves would create a self-balancing system in which low bullion reserves caused a low number of notes, increased the value of money, and decreased prices, which would attract foreign purchasers and return bullion. Higher reserves would then increase prices, encouraging foreign

---

59 Gladstone to Peel, 4 Nov. 1841, Peel papers, BL Add. MS 40545, ff. 76–8.
60 *Hansard*, LXXXIII, 16 Feb. 1846, cols 1031–2.
61 B. Hilton, *Corn, cash and commerce: the economic policies of the Tory governments 1815–1830* (New York, 1977), vii–ix, pp. 3–30, 303–15.
62 J.S. Mill, *The principles of political economy*, II (New York, 1868), p. 334.
63 R. Peel, letter to his tenants 24 Dec. 1849, *The Times*, 28 Dec. 1849; although it was sympathetic to farmers, *The Economist* approved of it: *The Economist*, 5 Jan. 1850, p. 8.
64 *The Economist*, 30 Jun. 2007.
65 Hilton, 'Peel: a reappraisal', pp. 602–3.
66 C. Villiers, *Hansard*, LXXV, 25 Jun. 1844, c.1391.

A CANDIDATE FOR PARLIAMENT.

ROBERT DUSTY, Esq.—Gemmen—(loud cheers)—should I have the honnor to be elected, yer representator in the kommon House o' Parleyment, (deafening cheers) for the Dust-hills, (repeated cheering) depend on it I will do my utmost endeavours to throw dust in the eyes of yer enemies—(vehement cheering). I'll wote for cheap Bread—(enthusiastic cheering). In fact, I'll propose that yer shall have Bread for nothin'!—(tremendous cheering)—I'll wote for Sugar to be given away—(reiterated cheering). In short, that it shall be brought home to yer, that yer shall have only the trouble of popping it into yer Tea—(thundering cheers). And, as to cheap vood, vy I'll undertake to say that, if yer send me to Parleyment, yer shall have, in no time, broom-sticks and shovel-handles laying about in all directions, hollowing out to yer—"Come and take me!"—(vociferous cheering).

Figure 4.1. A candidate for parliament. Peel is depicted as a clown dustman, 'Dusty', because of his claim to represent the wishes of the working man, by promising cheap food and goods. The cartoon is a satire of Peel's Tamworth election speech of 28 June 1841. (10 July 1841). From Cleave's Penny Gazette of Variety and Amusement. *Cleave's Penny Gazette of Variety and Amusement.* © a part of Cengage, Inc. Reproduced by permission. www.cengage.com/permissions

PEEL'S CHEAP BREAD SHOP,
OPENED JANUARY 22, 1846.

Figure 4.2. Peel's cheap bread shop. *Punch*, 24 January 1846, p. 46.
The cartoon links Robert Peel, 'R.Peel' of the Corn Laws and cheap bread.
From PEEL'S CHEAP BREAD SHOP. *Peel's Cheap Bread shop.* © a part of
Cengage, Inc. Reproduced by permission. www.cengage.com/permissions

imports and, eventually, an outflow of bullion. All this was built on Peel's conviction that 'Bullionist' theory was correct in proposing that gold was a reasonable standard for value.

However, Peel had no conception of the long timeframes required for equilibriums in economic systems to be reached; Charles Wood, Chancellor of the Exchequer in Russell's government, pointed out to him what Smith had said on the subject only in the year before his death.[67] In spite of prices being part of this balancing system, the provisions of the Banking Acts were designed to exert a downward pressure on prices by restricting notes and by preventing a free-for-all expansion, but prices would not always decrease overall, which explains Peel's reticence about future price movements.

IV

The interpretation of Peel's general economic policy as one of a carefully controlled manipulation of price levels downward was very much how it was perceived at the time. Cartoons in the comic papers made fun of Peel's election promise of cheap food and goods. 'A candidate for parliament' in *Cleave's Penny Gazette* of 10 July 1841 depicted Peel as 'Dusty', a clown dustman, because he claimed to represent the wishes of the working man. The cartoon is a satire of Peel's Tamworth election speech in 1841 and 'Dusty' promises if elected: 'I'll wote for cheap Bread. In fact I'll propose that yer shall have bread for nothin!' Later, *Punch* satirised 'R.Peel' as the owner of a cheap-bread shop, declaring that the establishment has 'no connection with a person of the name of Russell'. More seriously, a popular book from 1850 assembled quotations from Peel's published speeches to show a consistent theme of concern about lowering food prices.[68]

Contrary to common perception, both Peel's trade and banking policies did not take extreme positions. The 'repeal' of the Corn Laws, and also the Banking Acts, was only partial in nature, demonstrating Peel's gradualist approach. Privately, in 1845 Graham explained to Croker the overall aim of a gradualist approach to benefit all, and how it seemed to have succeeded so far.[69] The idea was to moderate and stabilise food prices without harming agriculture. Most notably, Peel's 'repeal of the Corn Laws' was in fact only a half measure. In the 1846 legislation, it can be seen from Figure 4.3 that duty still rose as prices dropped below a certain level. That arrangement was intended to ensure that food prices would drop far enough to help agricultural areas, including Ireland,

---

67 Wood to Peel, 26 Sep. 1849, Graham papers, BL Add. MS 79713, f. 36.
68 A. Hall, *The opinions of Sir Robert Peel* (London, 1850), pp. 164, 166, 183, 185, 187, 188, 488–9.
69 Graham to Croker, 22 Mar. 1845, Graham papers, BL Add. MS 79618, f. 59.

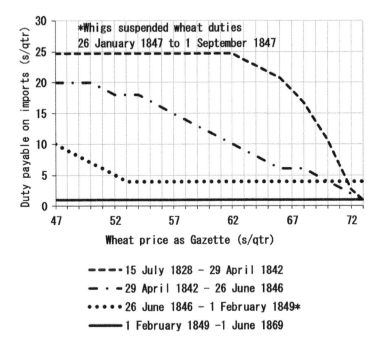

Figure 4.3. Duty payable per quarter for foreign imports of wheat according to price in shillings/quarter, 1828–69.

Note: Concept from: P. Sharp, '1846 and all that', *University of Copenhagen Department of Economics Discussion Paper 06–16* (2010), p. 7.

Sources: 9 Geo. IV. c.60; 5 & 6 Vict. c.14; 9 & 10 Vict. c.22.

while not destroying the livelihoods of farmers. Repeal of more of the sliding scale was provided for in the legislation, but had to wait until 1849. And even then a duty of one shilling per quarter was retained.

His phased approach to introducing low tariffs in 1846 resulted in attacks from both sides of the debate – from the Whigs for not bringing in free trade in one step and from the protectionists for doing it at all. Peel believed the one-step approach would harm agricultural districts, and that it was better that free trade was introduced slowly by a Conservative government than all at once by a Whig government, who, he worried, were more guided by liberal *laissez faire, et laissez passer* dogma than well-thought-out economic aims.[70] Peel had explicitly stated in 1845 that such ideas did not drive him when he said that he 'was not prepared to apply to the rural population of this country those principles

---

70   Russell explains '*laissez-faire*': *Hansard*, CIV, 2 Apr. 1849, c.215.

of political economy which many hon. Gentlemen were disposed to do'.[71] In contrast, Russell, the leader of the opposition Whigs, had written an open letter on 22 November 1845 to his constituents in the City of London declaring 'observation and experience have convinced me that we ought to abstain from all interference with the supply of food', and urging the government to unite to put an end to 'a system which has been proved to be the blight of commerce, the bane of agriculture'.[72] On failing to form a government in January 1846, Russell accused Peel of acting out of fear that the Whig leader 'would have formed his Ministry on the basis of a complete free trade in corn, to be established at once, without gradation or delay'.[73]

In response Peel said he would ignore all other points except 'the question whether it be desirable that the repeal of the corn duties should be immediate, or whether they should continue, as Her Majesty's Government propose, for a period of three years', showing how important the issue was for him.[74] He explained that the legislation was dual purpose, helping Ireland and changing permanently the import duties. Although tariffs were only to be slowly reduced on grain, immediate and complete reductions on Indian corn and rice were designed to help Ireland.[75] The three-year delay before a further reduction was, he said, to avoid 'a panic greatly depressing the price of wheat' and to 'meet the wishes ... of the agricultural interest'.[76] Peel proposed several measures, including government loans and relief to rural districts from the cost of pauperism, to help boost agricultural efficiency so as to 'enable the landed interest to meet the competition' from foreign corn producers over this time.[77] Peel had explained his plans in much the same way to Prince Albert, who had noted:

> Sir Robert has an immense scheme in view ... He will deal with the whole commercial system of the country. He will adopt the principle of the League, that of removing all protection and abolishing all monopoly, but not in favour of one class and as a triumph over another, but to the benefit of the nation, farmers as well as manufacturers.[78]

Peel's actions after 1846 show his continued commitment to gradualism. The Russell government passed the Corn Importation Act,[79] which suspended

---

71   *Hansard*, LXXXI, 2 Jul. 1845, cols 1426–7.
72   *Morning Chronicle*, 26 Nov. 1845; *The Times*, 27 Nov. 1845.
73   *Hansard*, LXXXIII, 22 Jan. 1846, c.107.
74   Ibid., c.450.
75   Ibid., c.451.
76   Ibid., c.455.
77   *Hansard*, LXXXIII, 27 Jan. 1846, cols 264–71.
78   Prince Albert memorandum, 25 Dec. 1845, Royal archives microfilm 95709/5; A.C. Benson and Viscount Esher, *Letters of Queen Victoria*, vol. II (London, 1908), pp. 65–6.
79   10 & 11 Vict. c.1, 26 Jan. 1847.

the duties on corn completely from then until 1 September 1847. Peel, in 1849, blamed any 'evil effects from the repeal of the Corn Law before 1st February 1849' on this suspension, which interfered with his policy of gradualism.[80] In an attempt to defend Peel's gradual approach, in March 1848 he and his followers voted against the Whigs' increased income tax, which would have enabled funding for an immediate and complete abandonment of corn tariffs.[81] This move, although it again confirms Peel's opposition to introducing free trade immediately, seemingly contradicts his realisation at the time that Ireland needed more relief funding, which would have been supplied by increased income-tax rates. However, private correspondence with Charles Wood shows that Peel had been trying to get Wood to set a deficit budget, which would have enabled a higher income tax to have been set with little risk of immediate total free trade. Any extra receipts from increased income tax would have been needed to make up the deficit rather than compensate for decreased tariffs. Wood refused, so the Peelites had to vote against a proposal to increase the income tax.[82]

Similarly, the Bank Charter Act of 1844 was also only a half measure. The legislation required that notes issued only over a fixed limit had to be backed by bullion, the rest by government securities. The Bankers (Ireland) Act 1845 of 21 July 1845 decreed that Ireland's fixed-issue limit was the average issued in the year up to 1 May 1845. It did not require any security. Only notes issued above this limit had to be backed by bullion. Both sets of legislation differed from the Currency-School thinking of the time that a full gold standard required banknotes to be backed 1:1 with gold. There was, and still is, great confusion as to why the Banking Acts did not follow a full gold standard and why exceptions were built into them.[83] However, it does make sense if the aim of Peel's policy was to use the price-depressing effect of a gold standard in only a moderate way.

In his speech at the opening of Parliament in January 1846 Peel justified his conduct in office by claiming that he had 'used it for the benefit of the public interest and national good'. He had had to 'consult the public interest'.[84] He repeated the same theme in his *Memoirs*, placing 'public interests' above 'party attachments'.[85] Such an attitude fits with the evangelical milieu of his confidantes, such as Lady de Grey, who placed a striking emphasis on public service, truthfulness, and practical results as the methods through which decisions should be made.[86] It is difficult to reconcile this attitude, for which there is

---

80   *Hansard*, CVI, 6 Jul. 1849, c.1433.
81   *Hansard*, XCVII, 13 Mar. 1848, c.534.
82   Wood to Peel, 26 February(?) 1848, partial letter, Graham papers, BL Add. MS 79713, f. 34.
83   Thomas Tooke, *On the Bank Charter Act of 1844: its principles and operation; with suggestions for an improved administration of the Bank of England* (London, 1856), pp. 21–2.
84   *Hansard*, LXXXIII, 22 Jan. 1846, c.93.
85   Peel, *Memoirs*, vols 2/3, p. 182.
86   Henrietta (Lady de Grey) to Lady Hardwicke, 28 Sep. 1833, Caledon Papers, PRONI, D2433/D/5/200.

overwhelming evidence in his correspondence of concern for Ireland and the search for data to understand the effect of policy on prices and wages, with an historical assessment of Peel which suggests that he used the Irish famine as an 'excuse' for passing legislation to repeal the Corn Laws for reasons of ideological dogmatism or personal political gain.[87] That would have involved an extended untruth for which there is little evidence in his correspondents' private papers.

An analysis of the Peel papers reveals no striking revelations about his reasoning other than the continuity of the theme of food prices and supply. The sources support Cormac Ó Gráda's approach in taking Peel's explanations at face value.[88] The original letters in the Peel papers, Peel's original manuscript of his *Memoirs*, and the edited published version all agree and have not been altered significantly. There is therefore no reason to view the aim of Peel's repeal of the Corn Laws as anything other than what he describes.

Peel's actions were intended to safeguard food supplies for Ireland by keeping prices down and preserving economic and political stability. Peel considered the alternative would hinder relief spending for Ireland politically and practically. He asked, 'Can we go into the Liverpool market and raise the price of oats by Government purchases, leaving the Corn Law in full operation at the time?' He also foresaw the prospect of 'additional difficulty if the prices of food should range very high, and if we resolve to maintain during the period of pressure the existing Corn Law.'[89]

Peel's consistent aim in favour of the working population was not necessarily based on liberal views, but was intended to ensure the survival of the aristocracy while forcing them to contribute to improving the lot of the general populace. Manufacturers and landowners were expected to gain from a release of tension between classes and from increased commercial activity. The policy of gradualism was to placate landowners, whose counterparts in Europe were almost as quarrelsome as the workers.[90] It was the failure to communicate this message which gave Peel his political difficulties. Lady de Grey, who had previously discussed with Peel his temper and impatience in explaining policy aimed at moderation, wrote to him in December 1845 that though she did not fear a repeal of the Corn Laws, she did not understand why it was more necessary in December than in July.[91] Yet, he was so concerned

87 For the 'excuse' opinion, see Gaunt, *Sir Robert Peel*, p. 122; example of data collection, 'Workers wages in Barnstable Union', Peel papers, BL Add. MS 40566, ff. 64–377b.
88 C. Ó Gráda, *The great Irish famine* (Cambridge, 1997), pp. 43–4.
89 Peel, *Memoirs*, vols 2/3, pp. 193–4.
90 R. Bidelux and I. Jeffries, *A history of Eastern Europe: crisis and change* (London, 1998), p. 295.
91 Lady de Grey to Peel, 19 Jun. 1844, Peel papers, BL Add. MS 40547, ff. 130–5; Peel to Lady de Grey, 21 Jun. 1844, Peel papers, BL Add. MS 40547, ff. 136–9; Lady de Grey to Peel, 18 Dec. 1845, Peel papers, BL Add. MS 40581, f. 15.

about gradual implementation that he sacrificed the unity of his own political party to control the way the legislation was enacted. Informed by the ideas of Ricardian economics and the Currency School, Peel believed that his policies of free trade and a firmly controlled currency would lower and bring stability to food prices. In addition the transfer from indirect to direct taxes and downward pressure on interest rates would get the country out of economic difficulties and enable a balanced budget to stabilise or reduce the national debt. In these ways, Peel's policies were aimed at satisfying all the various conflicting demands and interests that besieged him.

V

This conclusion accounts for many puzzling features of the development of Peel's economic policies. The aim of low prices explains why he sometimes spoke for free trade and sometimes against. His concern for the agricultural sector and Ireland is shown by his method of staged or partial introductions of legislation. This approach was intended to help the agriculturalists in his party, but as Stewart noted, they were not persuaded this was the case.[92] The consistent way in which he pursued his approach nevertheless shows the integrity that he claimed, and explains why he was so anxious to implement the policy himself in 1846 when the Whigs were equally willing to do so, but immediately and in one step. Abolish the Corn Laws too fast and the result would be economic instability and agrarian revolt, he thought, but without any change the result would be political and civil unrest in urban areas. The answer to this problem – gradualism designed to lower food prices and maintain economic stability – makes his seemingly ideologically-inconsistent support for lowering tariffs and regulating banking look far more coherent. Other intended effects of his policies, including the control of bullion drains and the amendment to tax legislation in order to run a balanced budget and reduce the national debt, were aimed at producing stability and prosperity in the country which would benefit all classes.

Nevertheless Peel's economic plans had not been thoroughly tested and were to have unexpected outcomes. It is true that, unlike continental Europe and America, Britain avoided revolution and civil war, but Peel did not fully understand the wider macroeconomic or longer-term consequences of his reforms. He was unaware of the extent of his lack of knowledge. He took an economic rebound from 1843 as a sign that his budget of 1842 had worked promptly, and never considered Smith's warning that events which change prices

---

92   Stewart, *The politics of protection*, pp. 37–8.

could take twenty years for their effect to work through.[93] His policies were a great leap into the dark. The Bank Charter Act contributed to financial crises in 1847, 1857, and 1866, some of the most severe of the nineteenth century. And the combination of economic policies he had established as the paradigm of the period meant that fiscal and monetary policy could not be fully used to relieve the Irish famine, the worst humanitarian disaster in the modern history of the British Isles.[94] The split in the Conservative party resulted in three decades of weak and wobbly governments, and their descendants – the Liberal Democrats and Conservatives of today – have never healed their divide. The question remains, therefore, whether Peel really does deserve to be remembered as the 'chief architect' of the mid-Victorian 'age of stability'.

93   The UK economy grew after 1842, see B.R. Mitchell, *British historical statistics* (Cambridge, 1988), p. 837; Wood to Peel, 26 Sep. 1849, Graham papers, BL Add. MS 79713, f. 36.
94   C. Read, 'Laissez-faire, the Irish famine, and British financial crisis', *Economic History Review* 69 (2016), pp. 411–34.

5

Champagne capitalism: France's adaptation to Britain's global hegemony, 1830–80

DAVID TODD

In 1882 Henry Vizetelly asserted that if the taste for the wine of Champagne had spread on a planetary scale, with aficionados from Africa to Japan, nowhere and not even in France had it acquired as prominent a status as in Britain. Indeed, its success 'in oiling the wheels of social life' among Britons was such that 'its eclipse would almost threaten a collapse of our social system'. Not only had it become the 'obligatory adjunct' of countless formal public and private occasions, from the inauguration of new railway junctions to the breakfast of every respectable wedding, but 'the part that Champagne plays in the City' was fundamental:

> The amount of business ... transacted by the aid of the wine is incalculable. Bargains in stocks and shares, tea and sugar, cotton and corn, hemp and iron, hides and tallow, broadcloth and shoddy, are clinched by its agency. On the other hand, many a bit of sharp practice has been forgiven, many a hard bargain has been forgotten, many a smouldering resentment has been forgiven for ever, and many an enmity healed and a friendship cemented, over a bottle of Champagne.[1]

Vizetelly, an editor of the *Illustrated London News*, was only half-guilty of journalistic exaggeration. Nearly nine out of ten (88 per cent) of the 20 million bottles of French champagne purchased in 1880 were sold outside France, and Britain was by far the largest market. Between 1860 and 1880, British sales represented between 50 and 60 per cent of the exports of Moët & Chandon, the leading producer of champagne, and it was in response to the demand of British consumers that the firm, along with its competitors, began to produce

---

1   Henry Vizetelly, *A history of champagne, with notes on the other sparkling wines of France* (London, 1882), pp. 109–10.

the drier types of champagne (*sec*, *brut*) that are today the commodity's most common iterations. Champagne was produced in France, and intensive advertising endowed the wine with supposedly French qualities such as a sophisticated *joie de vivre* and 'sparkling' wit, but Britons and other Anglo-Saxons were its chief consumers.[2]

Champagne, this chapter shows, was typical of France's adaptation to nineteenth-century globalisation. It has now been forty years since a revisionist current in economic history contested the traditional view of French economic 'backwardness' or 'retardation' in the nineteenth century, by comparison with the allegedly more rapid and successful industrialisation of the British economy. As shown by Patrick O'Brien and Caglar Keyder, the growth of per capita incomes in France matched, and perhaps even slightly surpassed, their growth in Britain between 1815 and 1914. The earlier conception, they claimed, was based on an excessive focus on highly visible industries in which Britain excelled (cotton textiles, coalmining, etc.) and did not allow for France's much slower demographic growth. A broader approach considering all sectors of the economy showed that France had performed well given its specific resource endowment, such as limited coal supplies and abundant skilled manual labour. France, they concluded, had not failed to emulate Britain, but followed an alternative path to high per capita incomes.[3]

Despite some criticisms that have focused on France's economic slowdown after 1880, this revisionist account, in its broad lines, has not been refuted.[4] Drawing on more recent approaches in global economic history, such as the redefinition of the nineteenth century as 'the great specialisation' of the world's economies and the novel emphasis placed on the study of commodity chains, this chapter examines the international dimension of France's relative economic success in the nineteenth century.[5] Instead of competing with British industries that increasingly dominated the global market for cheap mass-produced goods, French producers came to dominate the fast-growing market for luxury and

2   Claire Desbois-Thibault, *L'extraordinaire aventure du Champagne: Moët et Chandon, une affaire de famille, 1792–1914* (Paris, 2003), pp. 128–31; Kolleen M. Guy, *When champagne became French: wine and the making of a national identity* (Baltimore, 2003), pp. 15–17, 51.
3   Patrick O'Brien and Caglar Keyder, *Economic growth in Britain and France, 1780–1914* (London, 1978); for a summary of the debate, see François Crouzet, 'The historiography of French economic growth in the nineteenth century', *Economic History Review* 56 (2003), pp. 215–42, and on the elaboration of France's path as the product of political preferences, see Jeff Horn, *The path not taken: French industrialization in the age of revolution, 1750–1830* (Cambridge, MA, 2006).
4   Jean-Pierre Dormois, *L'économie française face à la concurrence britannique à la veille de 1914* (Paris, 1997).
5   Ronald Findlay and Kevin H. O'Rourke, *Power and plenty: trade, war, and the world economy in the second millennium* (Princeton, 2007), pp. 365–428; Steven C. Topik and Allen Wells, 'Commodity chains in a global economy', in Emily Rosenberg, ed., *A world connecting, 1870–1945* (Cambridge, MA, 2012), pp. 593–812.

above all *demi-luxe* (semi-luxury) commodities.[6] In other words, France – paradoxically given the ritual invocation by contemporary writers and politicians of French egalitarianism – turned into the global procurer for a bourgeoisie that still aped the manners of the old aristocracy. This champagne capitalism – again *contra* the traditional emphasis on Anglo-French rivalry, in both contemporary discourse and the historical scholarship – was also highly dependent on the development of British capitalism in Britain and its expansion overseas. At least until the 1870s, France followed a path of economic development that was complementary, as much as alternative, to Britain's.

This brief survey of France's adaptation to the new 'highly global economic order' that emerged in the mid-nineteenth century is intended to echo and pay homage to Martin Daunton's own work on global political economy, including his analysis of Britain's successive adjustments to globalisation since 1850.[7] Drawing inspiration from Martin's elegant syncretism, it also seeks to pay due attention to the role of political and cultural factors in processes of economic change: champagne capitalism no doubt reflected France's specific factor endowment in an increasingly globalised world economy, but its development and eventual decline after 1880 were also the product of ideas, institutions, and events.

The other country of free trade

Historians of ideas have often drawn a sharp contrast between the ideological triumph of free trade in Britain and the prevalence of protectionist ideas in French politics in the nineteenth century.[8] These politico-economic discourses imperfectly reflected the reality of British and French commercial policies. By some measures at least, Britain's trade policy remained more restrictive than France's until the 1850s, while France more discreetly but steadily and effectively dismantled its own mercantilist legislative arsenal between 1830 and 1860.[9] Contrary to a still-widespread impression, the 1860 Cobden treaty that

6   Patrick Verley, 'Essor et déclin des industries du luxe et du demi-luxe au XIXe siècle', in Jacques Marseille, ed., *Le luxe en France: du siècle des 'Lumières' à nos jours* (Paris, 1999), pp. 107–23; see also Patrick Verley, *L'échelle du monde: essai sur l'industrialisation de l'Occident* (Paris, 1997), pp. 543–615.

7   M.J. Daunton, 'Britain and globalisation since 1850', *Transactions of the Royal Historical Society*, 6th ser., 16 (2006), pp. 1–38; 17 (2007), pp. 1–33; 18 (2008), pp. 1–42; and 19 (2009), pp. 1–35.

8   Anthony Howe, *Free trade and liberal England, 1846–1946* (Oxford, 1997); Frank Trentmann, *Free trade nation: commerce, consumption and civil society in modern Britain* (Oxford, 2009); David Todd, *Free trade and its enemies in France, 1814–1851* (Cambridge, 2015).

9   John V. Nye, *War, wine, and taxes: the political economy of Anglo-French Trade, 1689–1900* (Princeton, 2007), pp. 1–19.

reformed British indirect taxes (especially on alcoholic beverages) and repealed French protectionist legislation was a French initiative, designed to bypass domestic parliamentary opposition to reform. The idea of a treaty originated with Michel Chevalier, a former adept of Saint-Simonianism (a religious movement dedicated to the spread of industrial capitalism) and a professor of political economy at the Collège de France, while Richard Cobden and other British free traders only reluctantly overcame their dislike of commercial bilateralism, which smacked in their eyes of the old mercantile pursuit of national power. Furthermore, in the subsequent six years it was France that played the leading part in establishing what some historians have described as Europe's 'First Common Market', since it concluded similar free trade treaties with eleven other European powers (in contrast to Britain's four).[10]

The free trade policy of the Second Napoleonic Empire (1852–70) facilitated an extraordinary commercial boom. Between 1850 and 1870, French exports (excluding re-exports) more than trebled in value. This boom was arguably more significant than the strong commercial growth of the 1770s and 1780s, which had relied almost exclusively on re-exports of West Indian commodities (sugar, coffee, etc.).[11] Remarkably, in terms of participation in world trade, its roaring exports allowed France to close much of the gap with Britain. As shown by Figure 5.1, despite the rapid increase of Britain's own foreign trade after 1850 (and much slower demographic growth in France), the ratio of French to British exports rose from 50 per cent in the late 1840s to 90 per cent in the mid-1860s. This ratio then stabilised around a respectable level of 70 per cent until the late 1870s (the dip of 1870–71 corresponded with the Franco-Prussian war), before abruptly falling under 50 per cent in the 1880s. France's export boom was extraordinary, but it was relatively brief. A comparison with the fast-growing exports of the United States or Germany would show an even more precipitous decline after the mid-1870s.

The mid-century boom of French exports was grounded in a process of divergent specialisation rather than emulation. In the case of Britain, commercial expansion, as well as industrialisation, was closely associated with the trade in cotton yarns and textiles, with manufactured cottons goods representing 50 per cent of the estimated real value of British exports in 1830, and 36 per cent in 1860.[12] Starting from a lower level of output, the French cotton industry had also experienced rapid growth between 1780 and 1830.[13] Yet from the 1840s

10   Peter T. Marsh, *Bargaining on Europe: Britain and the first Common Market* (New Haven, 1999), pp. 28–61.

11   Guillaume Daudin, *Commerce et prospérité: la France au XVIIIe siècle* (Paris, 2005).

12   James A.H. Imlah, *Economic elements in the 'Pax Britannica': studies in British foreign trade in the nineteenth century* (Cambridge, MA, 1958), p. 104; Ralph Davis, *The industrial revolution and British overseas trade* (Leicester, 1979), p. 15.

13   Serge Chassagne, *Le coton et ses patrons, 1760–1840* (Paris, 1991).

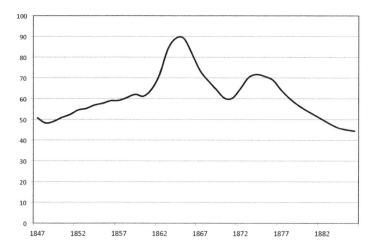

Figure 5.1. Ratio of French to British exports, 1847–86 (three-year moving average, excluding re-exports, per cent).

Sources: Direction générale des Douanes, *Tableau décennal du commerce de la France avec ses colonies et les puissances étrangères*, 13 vols (Paris, 1838–98); Brian R. Mitchell, *British historical statistics* (Cambridge, 2011), pp. 520–1. Calculations based on estimated value and an exchange rate of £1 = 25 francs.

onwards, its expansion slowed down and the share of cotton manufactures in total French exports declined from 10 per cent in the 1820s to 2 per cent at the end of the 1860s. The emphasis placed by many recent works on the role played by the commercial circuits of raw and manufactured cotton in the advent of modern capitalism is of limited applicability to the French case.[14] If one textile industry played a significant part in integrating France in the global market, it was the manufacture of silks, France's leading export industry with nearly 20 per cent of all French exports in the 1850s and 1860s. As shown by Figure 5.2, while exports of cotton textiles stagnated, exports of silk textiles trebled between 1847 and 1861. In the south-east of France after 1850, proto-industrial cotton weaving was replaced by the cultivation of mulberry trees (the host of silkworms and therefore the source of raw silk) and the throwing of silks, while merchant houses which had specialised in the cotton trade since the 1780s abandoned their former activities to dedicate themselves to the silk trade.[15]

The silk industry was in many respects typical of the champagne capitalism that flourished in mid-nineteenth-century France. Relying on a highly qualified

14 See especially Sven Beckert, *Empire of cotton: a global history* (New York, 2014).
15 Jean-François Klein, *Les maîtres du comptoir: Desgrand père & fils (1720–1878): Réseaux du négoce et révolutions commerciales* (Paris, 2013), pp. 227–8.

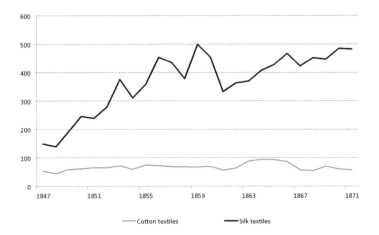

Figure 5.2. French exports of cotton and silk textiles, 1847–71, real value, in millions of francs.

Source: Douanes, *Tableau décennal.*

workforce and concentrated in the Lyon and Saint-Etienne region, it provided luxury products to a mostly well-to-do clientele, aristocratic in the eighteenth century and increasingly bourgeois in the nineteenth, although from the 1830s it was not uncommon for rural peddlers to sell small silk products such as ribbons.[16] Economic historians have traditionally scorned the silk industry in the nineteenth century, on the grounds that its narrow custom and reliance on skilled labour made it untypical of the processes of 'economic modernisation' or 'industrialisation'. For instance, Claude Fohlen, in his classic study of the French textile industry, excluded silk from the scope of his inquiry because it constituted 'an aberrant branch' of the French economy.[17]

The shift of focus in the historiography of the past thirty years, from industrialisation to the advanced international division of labour that characterised the world economy in the second half of the nineteenth century, should instead encourage historians to give silk manufacturing pride of place when they examine the French path of economic development. The Lyon silk industry undeniably displayed some 'archaic' features, in the sense that they were

16   Pierre Cayez, *Metiers Jacquard et hauts fourneaux: aux origines de l'industrie lyonnaise* (Lyon, 1978) and *Crise et croissance de l'industrie lyonnaise* (Paris, 1980); see also Giovanni Frederico, *An economic history of the silk industry, 1830–1930* (Cambridge, 1997), and on the usages of silk textiles, see Natalie Rothstein, 'Silk: the industrial revolution and after' and Penelope Byrde, 'Dress: the industrial revolution and after', in David Jenkins, ed., *The Cambridge history of western textiles* (Cambridge, 2003), vol. 2, pp. 790–808, 882–909.
17   Claude Fohlen, *L'industrie textile au temps du Second Empire* (Paris, 1956), pp. 51–2.

inherited from the eighteenth century, such as the continued reliance on commissioning merchant-manufacturers and an organisation of semi-independent small workshops. Yet as shown by Charles Zabel and Jonathan Zeitlin, who used the French silk industry as the main example of their reappraisal of flexible modes of production in the industrial era, French silk producers were anything but averse to technological innovation. Their dominance of the global market relied on the early adoption of the sophisticated Jacquard loom, with its punched card system, as much as workers' traditional *savoir-faire*. From today's post-industrial perspective, the prevalence of small units of production pursuing the capture of small but lucrative market segments appears extremely rational and even forward-looking.[18]

The other industries that pulled French exports forward in the period also combined skilled labour aided by mechanisation, with a focus on the luxury and semi-luxury markets. For example, between 1850–52 and 1864–66, while exports overall grew 164 per cent, wine exports (aided by new technologies such as bottling machines, a delicate operation for effervescent wines such as champagne) grew 213 per cent, exports of ornamental knick-knacks ('articles de Paris') grew 251 per cent, and exports of garments ('confection', aided by sewing machines) grew 313 per cent. Together these three industries contributed 18.5 per cent to French exports in the mid-1860s, about the same as silk manufacturing. Tellingly, the fastest growing single export item was 'lingerie' products (a subheading in the broader *confection* category that referred to all underwear clothes), with a growth of 580 per cent between 1850–52 and 1864–66. In 1866, *lingerie* exports reached 50 million francs, or £2 million.[19] The commercial success of *lingerie* and silk fabrics suggests that the French export industries targeted a female as well as a wealthy clientele. Even champagne was viewed, at least in Britain, as '[the ladies'] wine *par excellence*'.[20] Paris dictated women's fashion in the nineteenth century, but the standards of male fashion, increasingly sober and uniform, continued to be set in England.[21] The disparagement or relative neglect of French champagne capitalism in the existing literature may therefore be construed as reflecting, in part, a gender bias, under the form of an excess of attention given to more masculine industries or commodities,

18   Charles Sabel and Jonathan Zeitlin, 'Historical alternatives to mass production: politics, markets and technology in nineteenth-century industrialization', *Past & Present* 108 (1985), pp. 133–76; see also Alain Cottereau, 'The fate of collective manufactures in the industrial world: the silk industries of Lyons and London, 1800–1850', in Charles Sabel and Jonathan Zeitlin, eds, *World of possibilities: flexibility and mass production in western industrialization* (Cambridge, 1997), pp. 75–152.
19   My calculations, based on Douanes, *Tableau décennal*.
20   Vizetelly, *History*, p. 112; see also André Simon, *History of the champagne trade in England* (London, 1905), pp. 106, 150–5.
21   Philippe Perrot, *Fashioning the bourgeoisie: a history of clothing in the nineteenth century* (Princeton, 1994), pp. 25–33.

although given the eventual stagnation and decline of the French export model, other factors were certainly at play.

As is well known, France's export boom between 1850 and 1870 extended to capital as well as commodities. Thanks to a high savings rate, the emergence of new deposit banks, and fast-rising export earnings, France after 1850 turned into a major capital exporter. In the 1860s its exports of capital probably surpassed Britain's.[22] It is noteworthy that in Peter Cain and Anthony Hopkins' magnum opus *British imperialism*, the quotation of the financier George Goschen that opens the chapter on foreign investment – a foremost instance of their argument on the role of financial and other services in the development of British capitalism and overseas expansion – spoke, in 1865, of 'English *and French* banking principles' as being 'on a crusading tour throughout the world'.[23] The shift of emphasis from manufacturing to services as a major fount of British economic dynamism and expansionism, which formed the crux of Cain and Hopkins' argument, could also be applied to France. Although France had no merchant navy or insurance industry comparable to Britain's, not only was it a major exporter of capital, but it pioneered in the 1850s and 1860s new forms of services, such as department stores and mass tourism, which brought a crucial invisible complement to the sale of commodities in the French balance of payments.[24] Even the sale of French luxury and semi-luxury commodities should be seen as incorporating a substantial services element, since their popularity depended on the cultivation of an image encouraged by new marketing and advertising techniques. Champagne capitalism was a close cousin of gentlemanly capitalism.

Economic and imperial collaboration with Britain

Even when historians have acknowledged the external dynamism of the French economy in the mid-nineteenth century, they have tended to stress its increasing focus on European markets, drawing a contrast with the more global orientation of British foreign trade.[25] The available statistical evidence offers strong support for this view, since French trade with Europe (from Britain to Russia)

---

22   Maurice Lévy-Leboyer, 'La balance des paiements et l'exportation des capitaux français', in Maurice Lévy-Leboyer, ed., *La position internationale de la France: aspects économiques et financiers, XIXe–XXe siècles* (Paris, 1977), pp. 75–142.

23   P.J. Cain and A.G. Hopkins, *British imperialism, 1688–2000*, 2nd edn (Harrow, 2002), p. 160 (my emphasis). Cain and Hopkins mistakenly date Goschen's assertion to the 1880s, although it was part of an article originally published as 'Seven Per Cent', *Edinburgh Review* (1865), repr. in George Goschen, *Essays and addresses on economic questions* (London, 1905), p. 22.

24   Lévy-Leboyer, 'La balance des paiements', pp. 92–111.

25   Rondo Cameron, *France and the economic development of Europe, 1800–1914* (Princeton, 1961).

Figure 5.3. Share of Britain and the German Zollverein in French exports (re-exports excluded), 1830–70, per cent.

Source: Douanes, *Tableau décennal*; official values until 1846 and estimated values from 1847.

appears to have grown more rapidly than that with the rest of the world. It is natural that most consumers of French luxury and semi-luxury commodities lived in European countries or 'New Europes', with fast-growing middle classes and a cultural predisposition for equating Frenchness with luxury. Yet closer analysis of the data suggests that champagne capitalism had more significant connections with the world beyond Europe than at first appears. The fall in the share of the extra-European world in French trade was almost entirely due to the relative decline of France's commercial exchanges with the United States, its leading trading partner until the 1840s, but this reflected the declining French specialisation in cotton manufacturing rather than a profound change of geographical orientation. Conversely, the rise in the share of 'Europe' in French trade can be entirely attributed to the phenomenal growth of French exports to Britain. The Europeanisation of French foreign trade was a statistical phenomenon relying on the inclusion of Britain in Europe, while the share of continental European countries stagnated or even declined. As shown in Figure 5.3, even the share of the Zollverein (the German customs union founded by Prussia in 1834), continental Europe's fastest growing economy at the time, increased only moderately after 1850, and stagnated overall between 1830 and 1870. By contrast, the share of Britain in French exports nearly trebled, from 10–15 per cent in the 1830s to 30–35 per cent in the 1860s.

The real specificity of France's foreign trade in the mid-nineteenth century was its Anglicisation rather than its Europeanisation. Between 1847 and 1866, the rise of French exports to Britain contributed an extraordinary 42 per cent of the overall increase in French exports. A detailed analysis would certainly show that the British contribution to the export boom of champagne-capitalist industries was even larger. Given the lack of information in contemporary statistics about the actual origin or final destination of exchanged commodities, and the persistence of a large entrepôt trade in Britain, this statistical Anglicisation is likely to conceal an increase in indirect exchanges between France and the extra-European world. Unfortunately, the actual extent of such indirect exchanges is very difficult to assess. The small and declining proportion of silk textiles imported into Britain (originating, in large part, from France) that was re-exported – 17 per cent of £2.4 million in 1854 and 1 per cent of £15.2 million in 1870 – suggests that most were consumed in Britain.[26] However, the transit (or 'transhipment') trade, excluded from the main export statistics because goods in transit were not cleared by customs, was heavily dominated by shipments from France: 80 per cent of goods in transit via Britain in 1852–54 and still 50 per cent in 1862–64 originated from France. The vast majority (c. 90 per cent) of goods in transit via British ports were 'manufactured products', and were destined for southern or northern America.[27] The trace is therefore faint in official documents, but Britain's role as an intermediary for the exportation of French commodities beyond Europe was probably not insignificant.

Britain played an even more important and more easily traceable role as an intermediary for the supply of extra-European commodities, including essential raw materials, to France. While re-exports represented only 18.5 per cent of overall British exports to the world between 1854 and 1870, they made up 52 per cent of overall British exports to France, as illustrated by Figure 5.4. (Despite this extraordinary level of re-exports, Britain's trade deficit with France grew from an annual average of £1 million in 1854–56 to £10.5 million in 1867–69.)

An outstanding and well-documented example of such re-exports is the case of the fast-growing importation of 'British' raw silk in France after 1850, which of course comprised the British re-export of Asian raw silk to France. Until the 1850s, France had produced on her own soil (in the Rhône valley) about 50 per cent of the raw silk her industry needed and imported the rest from Italy (40 per cent) and the Levant (10 per cent). Yet just as French manufacturing was booming, and partly as a result of the intensive cultivation of mulberry trees, *pébrine* ('pepper disease'), a disease of silkworms, more than halved the French and Italian output of raw silk.[28] In response to the crisis, British re-exports of mostly Asian raw silk to France leapt nearly eightfold in value, from £679,000 in 1852 to £4.4 million in 1862.[29] French direct imports from Asia, mostly China, also grew, but these 'French' purchases were mediated by British firms such as

26   My calculations, based on *Annual statement of the trade and navigation of the United Kingdom with foreign countries and British possessions*, 17 vols (London, 1855–71).
27   My calculations, based on *Annual statement*.
28   Debin Ma, 'The modern silk road: the global raw-silk market, 1850–1930', *Journal of Economic History* 56 (1996), pp. 330–55.
29   *Annual statement*.

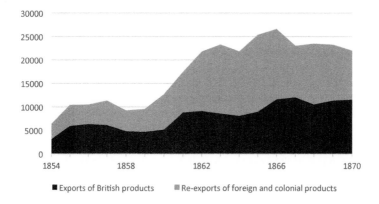

Figure 5.4. British exports to France, 1854–70 (in millions of pounds).
Source: Annual statement; estimated values.

the Hong Kong-based Jardine Matheson & Co. In Lyon, Desgrand père et fils, a firm which pioneered this direct trade, acted only as a consigner, selling raw silk transported from Shanghai to Marseille by British steamers via the overland route of Egypt (the transportation also often included transhipments in British Indian ports) on the account of Jardine Matheson, and the merchandise was insured by underwriters at Lloyd's.[30] The new maritime silk road from Shanghai to Lyon, which prevented a crisis of France's leading export industry, either passed by Britain or remained firmly ensconced in the global web of British capitalism. Only in the 1870s, after the French silk industry began to lose its global dominance, did Lyon merchants begin to establish direct relations with Chinese producers.[31]

The high dependence on Britain of France's commercial boom after 1850, both as an export market and as a provider of crucial raw materials, helps understanding of the extraordinary level of Anglo-French collaboration in foreign and imperial policy between 1850 and 1870. Mid-nineteenth-century British global policy has often been described as 'free trade imperialism' consisting of a preference for gunboat diplomacy and informal dominance over

30 See European correspondence of Jardine & Matheson (Hong Kong) with Desgrand père & fils (Lyon, Marseille) and Wilson & Poy (Lyon) between 1854 and 1863 in Cambridge University Library, MS JM/C11/18–31, especially first order for sixty-five bales of Jaysaam raw silk and twelve bales of thrown silk, in Jardine & Matheson to Desgrand père & fils, 25 Mar. 1854, JM/C11/18, fol. 448.
31 Robert Eng, *Economic imperialism in China: silk production and exports, 1861–1932* (Berkeley, 1986); Jean-François Klein, 'Soyeux en Mer de Chine: stratégies des réseaux lyonnais en Extrême-Orient (1843–1906)', unpublished PhD dissertation (University of Lyon II, 2002).

territorial conquest as the most economical means of securing new markets.[32] This free trade imperialism was also arguably an imperial partnership with France. Britain and France fought Russia together during the Crimean War (1853–56) to maintain their dominance over the Ottoman Empire, and fought China together during the Arrow or Second Opium War (1856–60) to confirm the opening of East Asia to Western trade. Britain and France were also the main joint protagonists of the international interventions in Syria in 1860–61 (to protect indigenous Christians) and initially in Mexico (1862–66), and they consulted each other before adopting a policy of non-intervention in the American Civil War (1861–65).[33] Much has been made in the literature of Lord Palmerston's hostility to the cutting of the Suez Canal (1857–69) by a nominally international but in reality French-dominated company, but the British business world was supportive of a venture that considerably curtailed transport costs between Europe and Asia. *The Economist*, for instance, applauded the opening of a canal 'cut by French energy and Egyptian money for British advantage'.[34]

It may therefore be possible to speak of a French free trade imperialism that acted often in collusion with Britain and sometimes independently, as in Mexico after Britain withdrew from the intervention in 1863. It is significant that one of the main supporters of the strange French attempt to turn Mexico into a client monarchical state was the ardent promoter of free trade Michel Chevalier, who wished France to sponsor another interoceanic canal in central America, and to increase the global supply of silver (Mexico had the largest known deposits); the rapid increase in the global stock of gold resulting from the Californian and Australian rushes from the end of the 1840s was endangering the French bimetallic gold-silver standard. France's attempt to establish its hegemony in Central America failed due to the military resistance of Mexican Republicans and pressure from the United States after the end of the Civil War in 1865, but the scheme had earned the plaudits of free trade imperialism connoisseurs such as Palmerston or *The Economist*'s editor-in-chief Walter Bagehot.[35] Defenders of the French path of economic development have suggested that domestically, the lower level of anarchic urbanisation and a smaller large-scale manufacturing sector had resulted in less social disruption and lower human costs than Britain's, but externally, champagne capitalism proved as, if not more, prone to gunboat diplomacy and other forms of aggression against extra-European societies as British capitalism.

32   John Gallagher and Ronald Robinson, 'The imperialism of free trade', *Economic History Review*, new ser. 6 (1953), pp. 1–15.
33   David Todd, 'A French imperial meridian, 1814–1870', *Past & Present* 210 (2011), pp. 155–86.
34   'The Suez Canal', *The Economist*, 20 Nov. 1869.
35   Edward Shawcross, 'French imperial projects in Mexico, 1820–1867', unpublished PhD dissertation (University College London, 2016), pp. 190, 213.

Causes and fragilities

Although revisionist historians have offered persuasive statistical evidence for the relatively strong performance of the French economy in the nineteenth century, they have been more vague about the ultimate factors that shaped the course of French economic development. True, they have pointed at major structural factors, which, in contrast to the British experience, delayed urbanisation (prevalence of peasant landownership) or rendered large-scale manufacturing cost-ineffective (absence of large coal deposits).[36] Yet such factors are still inspired by an implicit British norm, and do not provide a satisfactory explanation for the abrupt flagging of the French development model after the 1870s. There is no room in this chapter for an adequate exploration of this issue, but I would like to put forward two not mutually exclusive hypotheses: firstly, the persistence of a 'courtly' model of economic growth, through the Revolution and until the definitive abolition of monarchical institutions with the fall of the Second Napoleonic Empire in 1870; and secondly, the influence of France's regime of quasi-demographic stagnation after 1830, which enabled France to reap a temporary Malthusian dividend until the 1870s.[37]

In French economic as well as political history, the Revolution has often been treated as a fundamental rupture, one which laid the foundations of modern capitalism according to Ernest Labrousse and his disciples, or durably retarded its flourishing according to his conservative opponents.[38] Yet it is striking that many of the myriad French industries which prospered in the mid-nineteenth century owed their competitiveness to advantages gained under the Old Regime, as privileged providers to the court at Versailles and the still often-aristocratic Parisian elite. The champagne and silk industries are outstanding examples. The Lyon silk industry took off in the early eighteenth century in close coordination with the growth of Paris as a consumer market, and sparkling champagne wine became fashionable at court during the Orléans Regency of 1715–23: until late in the eighteenth century, most of the wine produced in the Champagne region was a low quality red, often destined for Parisian working-class consumers, but this connection with Paris facilitated its reinvention as an upmarket wine. Until the Revolution, both industries relied heavily on this courtly Parisian market, complemented by exports towards the smaller courtly economies of the Germanic and Italian worlds.[39]

---

36   See esp. O'Brien and Keyder, *Economic growth*, pp. 185–98.
37   On the demographic factor, see Crouzet, 'The historiography', pp. 237–8.
38   Ernest Labrousse, *La crise de l'économie française à la fin de l'Ancien Régime* (Paris, 1943).
39   William H. Sewell Jr, 'The empire of fashion and the rise of capitalism in eighteenth-century France', *Past & Present* 206 (2010), pp. 81–120; Thomas Brennan, *Burgundy to Champagne: the wine trade in early modern France* (Baltimore, 1997). On the dynamism of the Old Regime's economy, see also Philippe Minard, *La fortune du Colbertisme: État et industrie dans la France*

The Revolution unsurprisingly dealt a severe blow to these luxury industries, due to the reduction of aristocratic consumption and, in the case of silk, the bloody repression of a Girondist insurrection in Lyon in 1793. Both silk and champagne, however, experienced a resurgence under Napoleon, thanks to the restoration of a lavish court life and the revival of exports towards continental markets. This pattern of development suggests that the persistence of monarchical institutions in France after the fall of Napoleon (Bourbon Restorations of 1814–30; July Monarchy of 1830–48; Second Napoleonic Empire of 1852–70) played a non-negligible role in fostering these industries' growth. Indeed, as late as under Napoleon III, champagne producers and silk manufacturers enjoyed a great deal of official patronage, and were showered with official honours. As these luxuries became semi-luxuries and monarchical institutions took on a more and more bourgeois exterior, the centralised promotion of high quality French products took new middle-class forms, such as a slew of national exhibitions of industrial products, usually held in Paris, or the emergence of the Parisian *magasins de nouveautés* (selling a wide range of dry goods) in the 1830s. After 1850, this system of promotion culminated with the universal exhibitions (held in London in 1851 and 1862, with a strong French participation, and in Paris in 1855 and 1867), the frequent sponsoring of lavish festivities throughout the reign of Napoleon III ('la fête impériale'), and the creation of the first department stores in the 1860s.[40]

If the maintenance of monarchical institutions and values underlay the growth of champagne capitalism, it is possible that their definitive downfall, with the advent of the Third Republic in the 1870s, contributed to its decline. As late as the mid-1890s, Paul Leroy-Beaulieu, Michel Chevalier's son-in-law and his successor as professor of political economy at the Collège de France, still championed the economic benefits of luxury in a language reminiscent of its defence in the eighteenth century.[41] But even if most of Leroy-Beaulieu's career took place under the Third Republic, he was an *Orléaniste* royalist who had become reconciled with the liberal Bonapartist Empire, and his effusiveness in favour of luxury and his staunch support for free trade are again suggestive of a link between monarchism and the French model of economic development before 1880.[42]

des Lumières (Paris, 1998) and Jeff Horn, *Economic development in early modern France: the privilege of liberty, 1650–1820* (Cambridge, 2015).

40   Anne-Laure Carré, ed., *Les expositions universelles en France au XIXe siècle: techniques, publics, patrimoines* (Paris, 2012); Michael B. Miller, *The Bon Marché: bourgeois culture and the department store* (London, 1981).

41   Paul Leroy-Beaulieu, 'Le luxe. La fonction de la richesse: caractère et variété du Luxe. Son rôle économique', *Revue des Deux Mondes* 126 (1894), pp. 72–100; on the persistence of French debates about luxury in the nineteenth century, see Jeremy Jennings, 'The debate about luxury in eighteenth- and nineteenth-century French thought', *Journal of the History of Ideas* 68 (2007), pp. 79–105.

42   Dan Warshaw, *Paul Leroy-Beaulieu and established liberalism in France* (DeKalb, IL, 1991).

As part of his defence of luxury, Leroy-Beaulieu also drew an interesting connection with birth limitation, arguing that the taste for luxury was an effective remedy for the Malthusian danger of 'overpopulation', because the pursuit of 'convenient and pleasurable objects' stood in natural opposition to 'the excess of procreative force'. Leroy-Beaulieu even felt that France, whose relative share in Europe's population was shrinking fast, had made excessive use of the preventative check. This, the reader was left to infer, was probably because it had shown such a predilection for luxury industries.[43] Nor was Leroy-Beaulieu the only contemporary writer on political economy to suggest an intimate connection between luxury and low birth rates. In 1868, for instance, Walter Bagehot, while commending the British mastery of the processes of economical production, admitted France's supremacy in what he described as 'demand-producing articles … which can hardly be said to satisfy a previously felt want, but create a desire for themselves by a choiceness in workmanship and a perfection in indescribable detail'. He cited as examples French cooking, female clothing, modern urban *appartements*, and 'the endless incidentals and *et ceteras* of ornamentation and civilisation'. To account for this French superiority over Britain, he mentioned the possible negative influence of Puritan Protestantism on the latter, but claimed that 'the principal cause of the difference' lay in the contrast between Britain's rapid demographic growth and France's near stagnation. While in Britain there was 'a struggle and hurry and strain' just to maintain the standard of living of a fast-growing population, the French, unburdened by large families, had 'time and leisure and, so to say, mind to enjoy'.[44]

The psychological dimension of Bagehot's demographic interpretation would be given short shrift by demographers and economists today, although it was less unscientific than the then common belief in the innate superiority of French taste. However, Leroy-Beaulieu and Bagehot's intuition that France's demography was a major underlying factor of its path of development overlaps with some important findings in French economic history. Whatever the actual impact of a greater amount of leisure in stimulating the production of finer commodities, it is almost certain that France's low birth rate facilitated an increase in the savings rate. Together with the limited capital needs of small French firms, this enabled France to export much more capital than was justified by its level of development. The very foundation of the revisionist thesis on French economic development is predicated on a shift of emphasis to per capita

---

43 Leroy-Beaulieu, 'Le luxe', pp. 98–9; on the role of demographics in Leroy-Beaulieu's economic thought, see Georges P. Tapinos, 'Paul Leroy-Beaulieu et la question de la population: l'impératif démographique, limite du libéralisme économique', *Population* 54 (1999), pp. 103–24.
44 [Walter Bagehot], 'One difference between France and England', *The Economist*, 12 Sep. 1868; on the emergence of demand enhancement and the origins of consumerism in France, see Sewell Jr, 'Empire of fashion'.

growth, to take into account its demographic regime. In other words, if Britain avoided the Malthusian trap of falling per capita incomes thanks to contingent factors such as its large coal deposits and extensive colonial empire, as suggested by Kenneth Pomeranz, France more simply avoided it by Malthusian means, with a voluntary reduction in the number of births.[45]

Yet the economic boon of a reduction in the birth rate is arguably temporary, lasting one or two generations; even in Malthus' model, it delays rather than prevents the onset of stagnation. After a long decline began at the end of the eighteenth century, the French birth rate began to stabilise between 1860 and 1880, and this stabilisation may have been a contributing factor in the abrupt stagnation of France's champagne-capitalist economy. By almost any measure, the Great Depression of 1873–96 struck France harder than other European countries (including Britain, despite the focus of historiographical debates on Britain's relative decline at the time), and hit its export-oriented luxury and semi-luxury industries harder than others.[46] Between 1871–73 and 1891–93, French total exports stagnated in value at c. 3.4 billion francs, while exports of silk textiles fell from 467 million to 240 million francs.[47] Other factors besides politics or demographics account for this crisis of French champagne capitalism. Firstly, just as luxury industries tend to outperform others in good times due to a high income elasticity, they fare worse in bad times: France's specialisation in superfluities exposed it to a sharper downturn. Secondly, the period saw the emergence of new competitors for the exportation of semi-luxury commodities, especially in southern and central Europe (Italy, Switzerland, Austria-Hungary). The traditional story of Britain's relative decline due to the spread of industrial capitalism to the United States and Germany needs to be adapted in the French case, since champagne capitalism spread in other directions. In any case, this crisis proved terminal for the French model of development, since even when the French economy recovered in the 1890s, growth relied much less on the luxury sector.

Revisiting the revisionist interpretation of French economic development through the lens of the global division of labour strengthens it in some respects, but suggests the need for qualification in others. A focus on foreign trade, especially in the mid-nineteenth century, shows that by most accepted measures,

---

45   Kenneth Pomeranz, *The great divergence: China, Europe, and the making of the modern world economy* (Princeton, 2000); on the Malthusian rather than modern traits of the French demographic regime until the 1880s, see E.A. Wrigley, 'The fall of marital fertility in nineteenth-century France: exemplar or exception?', *European Journal of Population/Revue Européenne de Démographie* 1 (1985), pp. 31–60, 141–77.

46   Yves Breton, Albert Broder and Michel Lutfalla, eds, *La longue stagnation en France: l'autre grande dépression, 1873–1897* (Paris, 1997).

47   My calculations, based on Douanes, *Tableau décennal*.

the French economy was exceptionally dynamic and outward-looking. The French export boom of 1840–70 is hardly compatible with the traditional view of the nineteenth-century French economy as sluggish and lacking in entrepreneurship. However, the high level of Anglo-French interconnection, with Britain absorbing up to a third of French exports and British trade becoming a major French provider of extra-European raw materials and other commodities, undermines the revisionist notion that France followed an alternative path of development, in conscious or unconscious opposition to the British path. Rather, French champagne capitalism became an adjunct of British industrial or gentlemanly capitalism, just as France tended to perform the role of a useful auxiliary of British imperial domination overseas.

The problem is partly one of chronological scope, with the extant literature on the nineteenth century often focusing on the years 1870–1914, for which statistical evidence is more abundant. Yet in the case of France's economic relations with the world, the 1870s were arguably a watershed, more significant in the long term than the revolutionary and Napoleonic era or even the First World War. It was then that a model of economic growth still heavily indebted to the Old Regime's predilection for luxury ran aground. Nor was this profound shift confined to foreign trade, since it was also at the end of the 1870s that the new Third Republic turned away from collaboration with Britain – especially after British occupation put an end to the informal Anglo-French condominium over Egypt in 1882 – and began to build a vast colonial empire. Yet these new colonial possessions, sparsely populated and with low income levels, proved much less lucrative markets than the global middle classes of the mid-nineteenth century.[48] If there was a specific path of French economic development after 1815, it owed more to the onset of nineteenth-century globalisation than is allowed by the historiography, but it did not successfully adjust to its intensification after 1870.

---

48 Jacques Marseille, *Empire colonial et capitalisme français: histoire d'un divorce*, 2nd edn (Paris, 2005).

6

The 1848 revolution in Prussia: a financial interpretation

SEAN EDDIE

When it comes to revolutions, the gold standard is 1789 in France. By that measure the events in 1848 have been found wanting, the farce to 1789's tragedy. But should all the revolutions that year be tarred with the same brush? True, the issues at stake were the same in Berlin as in Paris: how to help the unemployed while ensuring that taxpayers were not abused. What differed was the Prussian solution, which was as bloodless it was enduring. The roots of British state power in the nineteenth century have been traced by Martin Daunton to its gradual cultivation of taxpayer and creditor trust.[1] The roots of Prussian state power resulted from a much shorter but similarly effective process, one called the 1848 revolution.

Before the revolution: social issues

By the 1840s social pressures were mounting in Prussia. Its population had grown by 58 per cent between 1816 and 1849. With landownership relatively immobile, the landless labouring class swelled and the number of artisanal *Handwerker* grew by 133 per cent.[2] This left a large group of Prussians vulnerable to crop and economic failure. In 1845 and 1846 potato blight and a disastrous harvest led to food prices doubling and more. The result was food riots: in Prussia 158 such riots occurred in April–May 1847 alone.[3] Famine was averted by the

---

1 M.J. Daunton, *Trusting Leviathan: the politics of taxation in Britain* (Cambridge, 2001).
2 W. Fischer *et al.*, eds, *Sozialgeschichtliches Arbeitsbuch* (Munich, 1982), vol. 1, pp. 22, 56–7, 89, 121.
3 C. Clark, *Iron kingdom* (London, 2006), pp. 455–6.

bountiful harvest of 1847, but the resultant squeeze on discretionary income caused a deep recession and credit crisis.[4]

With unemployment rising sharply, welfare was pressing.[5] But who bore responsibility for poor relief? Prussia's *Allgemeines Landrecht* of 1794 had acknowledged the state's duties. But this was a contingent responsibility, for in the first instance the local community and in the second, wealthy locals were liable.[6] Even before the crisis, the costs of providing for the growing class of poor had been mounting. After 1846 the local communes struggled to meet their obligations.[7] In Berlin, for instance, the population doubled between 1830 and 1851, but poor relief increased threefold, swallowing nearly 40 per cent of Berlin's budget in 1847.[8] That March commentators such as Koenig worried about relying on the wealthier, for 'nest-eggs have been consumed'.[9] Increasing recourse to the central state was the result.

Historians (and some contemporaries) have lamented Prussia's dilatory response to the welfare problem as reflecting dogmatic *laissez faire* principles.[10] But principles were not sacrosanct: the government had been compelled in the 1820s to relieve distress through emergency employment or food provision.[11] So why was the Prussian state so reluctant to spend more money?

Political issues

While some Prussian officials promoted *laissez faire* reform, they were opposed by many conservatives.[12] That the king, not the government, remained the lynchpin was clear from the speed of the revolving door as four foreign, four finance, and three interior ministers followed each other between 1840 and 1848. Frederick William IV's views were anyway hardly those of a *laissez faire* zealot: he saw Prussia as a paternalistic order, its freedoms guaranteed by historic estates not newfangled written constitutions, and was convinced that his authority was divinely ordained.[13]

---

4   J. Sperber, *The European revolutions, 1848–51* (Cambridge, 1994), pp. 105–7, 246–9; Fischer, *Arbeitsbuch*, vol. 1, p. 180; H. Obenaus, *Anfänge des Parlamentarismus in Preußen bis 1848* (Düsseldorf, 1984), pp. 522–3.

5   J. Hansen, ed., *Rheinische Briefe 1830–1850* (Cologne-Bonn, 1942), vol. 2/1, p. 129.

6   R. Koselleck, *Preußen zwischen Reform und Revolution* (Stuttgart, 1975), pp. 621, 630 n. 256; Hansen, *Briefe*, vol. 2/1, pp. 128–40.

7   Koselleck, *Reform*, pp. 635–6.

8   M. Gailus, *Straße und Brot* (Göttingen, 1990), pp. 319–20, 378–9.

9   Hansen, *Briefe*, vol. 2/1, p. 141.

10   Gailus, *Straße*, pp. 319–20; Koselleck, *Reform*, p. 625.

11   Koselleck, *Reform*, p. 630.

12   E. Dorn Brose, *The politics of technological change in Prussia* (Princeton, 1993), pp. 251–9.

13   D.E. Barclay, *Frederick William IV and the Prussian monarchy 1840–1861* (Oxford, 1995), pp. 20–2, 35ff.

The actual issue behind Prussia's frugality was the promises of a national constitution which Frederick William III had made in 1810, 1815, and 1820. In 1810 he had exhorted his subjects to greater sacrifices to meet Napoleon's exactions, but his vague promise of 'national representation' remained unfulfilled. Amid the need for more sacrifice to defeat Napoleon in May 1815, the king made a rather more explicit promise: an assembly of representatives drawn from the provincial estates would advise on all legislation concerning personal and property rights, including taxation. A constitution would also be drawn up. Frustrated by the lack of progress, Chancellor Hardenberg's State Debt Law of January 1820 approached the matter differently. Prussia promised that its debts should be capped: new state debt required the approval of an Estates General. Hardenberg's 'tactic' amounted to a third promise, a 'time bomb' ensuring a gradual shift towards a constitution.[14]

That these promises continued *after* 1815 shows that the real agenda was to assuage creditors' concerns as Prussia approached bankruptcy (debt service consumed nearly a quarter of the budget). In addition, the royal domains were 'nationalised' as security for Prussia's debts. Creditors were duly impressed, and two large loans were raised in London. Once securely refinanced, the king had less need for new taxes, and promptly reneged on his promise to his citizens: a law of June 1823 established only consultative provincial diets. The 1820 law was thus a self-denying ordinance sustaining monarchical control. Yet the promises were not forgotten, and the provincial diets reminded Frederick William IV of them on his accession in September 1840. His response was to dismiss the whole idea of a 'parchment constitution'.[15] Frederick William's unshakeable convictions thus coincided with his interest.

The first tremors: financial problems amass

Prussia's priorities gradually provoked unhealthy side effects. Naturally, one priority was a reserve to avoid new debts, and the Treasury amassed 19.5 million talers by 1847. Another was debt reduction, and as a third of the debt was repaid, debt servicing fell to 11 per cent of the budget by 1848. But with the political cost of new taxes now high, state income lagged population growth, rising only 22 per cent between 1821 and 1847. Direct taxes such as the land tax, which comprised a third of revenues, were especially inflexible, compensated by faster growth in consumption taxes.[16] These priorities meant that spending

14   Clark, *Iron kingdom*, pp. 458–9.
15   R.M. Berdahl, *The politics of the Prussian nobility 1770–1848* (Princeton, 1988), pp. 317–23.
16   D.E. Schremmer, 'Taxation and public finance: Britain, France and Germany', in P. Matthias and S. Pollard, eds, *The Cambridge economic history of Europe*, vol. III (Cambridge, 1989), pp. 434–8.

growth had to be even slower: despite domain sales, this equates to an average annual budget surplus of 5 to 6 per cent.[17]

Creditors were satisfied with these priorities, but citizens had less to cheer. Precisely those consumption taxes disproportionately borne by those unrepresented in the estates grew disproportionately. And what did taxpayers get for their money? The most visible element was the standing army, which consumed 40 per cent of the budget. Unsurprisingly, the cost of the army was a major grievance during 1848.

Lack of funds also meant that Prussia relied on private investment to build railways. Infracting the 1820 Debt Law, a small fund offered co-investors dividend guarantees, which sparked an investment mania.[18] But the government's perverse incentives created perverse outcomes. Concerned that state bonds should not suffer, a series of laws attempting to control the issue of securities culminated in the Stock Market Edict of May 1844, which forbade purchases of shares on margin. The *sauve-qui-peut* panic caused a crash and a credit crisis.[19]

The result of these self-inflicted wounds was that private railway investment dried up, a grave problem given its welfare role: railways had employed tens of thousands at limited cost to the state itself. These governmental *démarches* also began to redound on the state's own finances. The budget turned to deficit during 1845, and in 1846 tax shortfalls meant that the Finance Ministry needed a loan from the Rothschilds (to bypass the 1820 law, issued through the state's private investment vehicle, the *Seehandlung*).[20] With state debt the only way to secure public welfare from railway construction, on 16 March 1847 the king summoned a United Diet to approve funding for the largest railway project, the *Ostbahn* between Berlin and Königsberg.[21]

The warning tremor: 1847

The Patent convoking the United Diet revealed the king's selective memory when it came to his father's promises. The Diet was the fulfilment of the 'Estates General' promised in 1823, and the 'Imperial Estates' promised in 1820. However, it avoided reference to the promise of a 'constitution' and a

---

17   Derived from E. Richter, *Das preussische Staatschuldenwesen und die preussischen Staatspapiere* (Breslau, 1869), pp. 38, 49, 51, 55, 67; Obenaus, *Anfänge*, p. 257; G. von Schmoller, 'Die Epochen der preußischen Finanzpolitik', in idem, *Umrisse und Untersuchungen* (New York, 1974), pp. 225–6.
18   Berdahl, *Nobility*, pp. 378–9; J.M. Brophy, *Capitalism, politics and railroads in Prussia, 1830–1870* (Columbus, OH, 1998), pp. 37–44, 109; Koselleck, *Reform*, p. 618.
19   H. von Poschinger, *Bankwesen und Bankpolitik in Preußen*, vol. I (Berlin, 1878/9), p. 260.
20   Schmoller, 'Epochen', p. 216; Obenaus, *Anfänge*, p. 524.
21   Brophy, *Capitalism*, p. 47.

body to 'represent the people' in 1815. Ominously, the king refused the Diet annual sittings ('periodicity'). Malign intent was also detected in his ability to dismiss the Diet and to rule with an advisory standing committee instead.[22]

The gap between promises and reality did not go unnoticed and found voice in a riposte drafted by Rhineland financier Ludolf Camphausen.[23] Having reluctantly rejected a boycott, liberals were met by the king's confrontational opening harangue: 'There is no power on earth that can succeed in making me transform the natural relationship between prince and people ... into a conventional constitutional relationship, and I will never allow a written piece of paper to come between the Lord God in Heaven and this land.'[24]

Stances now hardened on all sides. Repeal of the urban milling and slaughter tax as an unjust burden on the poor and the introduction of a fairer income tax failed within the Diet. So did a motion establishing the claim to annual Diet sittings. Incensed by Interior Minister Bodelschwingh's assertion that its approval was needed for loans, not guarantees,[25] the Diet majority developed its own selective memory. Since the 1815 promise remained unfulfilled, the Diet claimed that it lacked the competence to approve a railway loan. On 26 June the *Ostbahn* loan guarantee was decisively defeated.[26]

So, far from enabling new welfare relief, therefore, the Diet led to work on the *Ostbahn* being halted, putting thousands out of work.[27] Governmental frustration was evident in Bodelschwingh's threat to charge recalcitrant deputies with criminal proceedings for *lèse majesté*.[28] The wells of political trust, already dangerously shallow, began to be poisoned.[29]

March 1848: the earthquake

When news of the Paris Revolution of 22–26 February rippled through Prussia, therefore, it seemed that the time for action was finally at hand. As President Birck of Trier in the Rhineland reported, 'people have completely lost confidence in the government, and so do not believe its promises, demanding action not words'. The cause was clear in the Trier's citizens' demand for 'the rights withheld from us for thirty years'.[30] Basic mistrust was only exacerbated

---

22 Obenaus, *Anfänge*, pp. 651, 658; Berdahl, *Nobility*, pp. 334–8; Brophy, *Capitalism*, pp. 47–8.
23 Brophy, *Capitalism*, pp. 47–48; Hansen, *Briefe*, vol. 2/1, pp. 167, 174–5.
24 Clark, *Iron kingdom*, pp. 459–61.
25 Obenaus, *Anfänge*, pp. 709–10; Hansen, *Briefe*, vol. 2/1, pp. 252–3, 273–9.
26 Obenaus, *Anfänge*, p. 692; Berdahl, *Nobility*, pp. 336–40.
27 Obenaus, *Anfänge*, p. 707.
28 Hansen, *Briefe*, vol. 2/1, p. 290.
29 R. Stadelmann, *Social and political history of the German 1848 revolution* (Ohio, 1975), pp. 43–4.
30 Hansen, *Briefe*, vol. 2/1, pp. 560, 685–7.

by the want of timely concessions. The king's first reaction to the events in Paris was truculent.[31] He conceded United Diet periodicity only on 6 March, and a spiral of disappointed expectations developed. On 14 March Koblenz President von Auerswald thought that 'The government's measures which at other times, and only a few weeks ago, would be called rampant progress, are now … denounced as deliberate procrastination.'[32] Such concessions as were made seemed wilfully ambiguous. The artfully conditional press freedom conceded on 8 March was regarded as 'an insult'.[33] On 17 March the king had another go, promising an immediate free press and a constitution.

These fresh concessions prompted 'frenetic ovations' for the king in Berlin's Palace Square the following morning. However, the wary crowd demanded the removal of the troops. Amid conflicting advice, the king instead decided to clear the square entirely. In the confusion, two shots rang out. However accidental, these were construed as a betrayal of the royal promises at the very moment of their concession.[34] Barricades were thrown up, and the troops' inability to clear them compelled the king to withdraw the army. During his conciliatory ride through Berlin on 21 March, Frederick William gave a speech at the Armoury, where renewed vows were interrupted by a heckler shouting 'Don't believe him, he is lying! He has always lied and is lying again now!'[35]

Financial distress and the logic of concessions

Despite the seeming panic, there was a pattern to the timing of Frederick William's concessions. Only one of the 'March demands' made by students at the Brandenburg gate on 7 March was met immediately and unconditionally – the recall of the United Diet.[36] Unconditional press freedom and a constitution were delayed until 17 March, the creation of a civic guard until 21 March. The reason was the increasing difficulty of raising money.

By 1 March, the stock market was 'in shock and distress'.[37] On 8 March the financier Otto Camphausen worried about signs of a bank run and foresaw a full-blown recession.[38] He was right. As loans were now called in, bankruptcies and unemployment mounted. Railways were a particular problem.[39] Many communes began to lack the funds to support the poor, just at the moment

31 K.A. Varnhagen von Ense, *Journal einer Revolution* (Nördlingen, 1986), p. 47.
32 Hansen, *Briefe*, vol. 2/1, p. 570.
33 Varnhagen, *Journal*, p. 53.
34 Stadelmann, *Revolution*, pp. 58–60.
35 Varnhagen, *Journal*, pp. 121, 129.
36 For the March demands, see Varnhagen, *Journal*, p. 50.
37 Varnhagen, *Journal*, pp. 47, 63.
38 Hansen, *Briefe*, vol. 2/1, p. 541.
39 Brophy, *Capitalism*, pp. 50–2.

when they were becoming a public order menace. Municipal revenues were also threatened by popular tax revolts. In Trier, amid a tax boycott, the town had 'fully exhausted our means'. Aachen officials drew the implication 'as long as workers can continue to be employed, absolutely no further disorder is to be feared. How it will look in a few weeks, however, if no more resources are created, God knows.'[40]

The result was that central government was inundated by requests for loans, but central funds were themselves running out. In January 1847 the Treasury had 19.5 million talers at its disposal, but had used 11 million on emergency grain purchases and to support Lombard and discount markets. Of the 8.5 million left at the beginning of 1848, 2 million had been needed to increase troops, and 1 million used for public works. Together with projected tax shortfalls, this left a mere 3.5 million talers.[41] Normally part of the solution, at the same moment the *Seehandlung* investment vehicle became part of the problem, and received an emergency advance of 1 million talers from the state Treasury.[42] By 28 March the Royal Bank had only 258,000 talers left.[43]

Where might funds be found? In 1818 and 1846, emergency loans were raised by the Rothschilds. But now even they were over-extended, selling off their loan books at alarming discounts.[44] And if the French revolution started the crash, the March days in Berlin created 'a full paralysis on the money market'. Losses ranged from 30 to 45 per cent, and banks stopped discounting bills.[45] Government bond prices were not exempt, as Figure 6.1 shows.[46]

The bond market was closed, and with it the escape hatch of 1818. From early March there was only one way out: the United Diet had to sit, and Frederick William had been quick to concede it. Next, a liberal Camphausen-Hansemann ministry was formed on 29 March to re-establish confidence in the credit-worthiness of the Prussian state and its major banks.[47] The following day the king reversed his initial refusal to support the Prussian Bank, agreeing a 2 million advance.[48] To secure the funds, the same day the king urged his new premier, Camphausen, to allow troops back into Berlin 'to bring out the state treasury' under cover of night.[49] He did so: given the events of 18 March, this was highly risky, but securing those funds was worth it.

40   Hansen, *Briefe*, vol. 2/1, pp. 668, 685–7.
41   E. Bleich, ed., *Verhandlungen des zum 2, Apr. 1848 zusammenberufenen Vereinigten Landtages* (Berlin, 1848), pp. 127–9.
42   Hansen, *Briefe*, vol. 2/1, p. 355.
43   H. Rachel and P. Wallich, *Berliner Grosskaufleute und Kapitalisten* (Berlin, 1967), pp. 261–2.
44   Count Corti, *The reign of the house of Rothschild* (London, 1928), pp. 251–3, 261–3.
45   Rachel and Wallich, *Kapitalisten* (Berlin, 1967), pp. 261–2.
46   Source: Richter, *Staatsschuldenwesen*, p. 272.
47   Wolfram Siemann, *Die deutsche Revolution von 1848/49* (Frankfurt, 1985), p. 67.
48   Rachel and Wallich, *Kapitalisten*, pp. 261–2.
49   E. Brandenburg, ed., *König Friedrich Wilhelms IV. Briefwechsel mit Ludolf Camphausen* (Berlin, 1906), pp. 24–32.

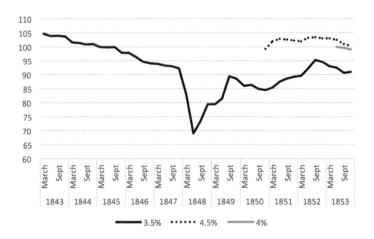

Figure 6.1. Price of Prussian bonds, 1843–53.

All power to the ministry?

The second United Diet was tasked with creating an electoral law for the new National Assembly: matters of policy should await this new body. But given the financial crisis, the government could not wait. On 4 April the king asked the assembly to invest full powers in his ministry to raise emergency funds. The 'desperate situation' also made relief of the social situation urgent. Pending wider reform, the milling tax was abolished in favour of a new direct tax (from which manual workers and day-labourers were made exempt), at two-thirds of the prior amount.[50]

The government's proposals to raise 15 million talers for the military and 25 million for loan guarantees to provide credit-market liquidity were debated in the United Diet on 10 April.[51] From the ultra-conservative wing, a young Bismarck questioned allowing the ministry to raise a sum worth half the annual budget 'on the basis of a sheet of paper containing only general hints and rounded millions'. Berlin merchant Schauß found the 25 million taler guarantee 'freakish'. Outside the Diet, critical voices were also heard. The Cologne Workers' Club, for example, asked: 'Who is more deserving of state support, the rich merchants and factory-owners or the starving and bare workers?'[52] Still, most delegates agreed that emergency funding was a necessary

50 Bleich, *Verhandlungen*, pp. 70–3, 83–4, 146, 168–72.
51 H. Mähl, ed., *Die Überleitung Preußens in das konstitutionelle System durch den zweiten Vereinigten Landtag* (Munich and Berlin, 1909), pp. 205–10.
52 Hansen, *Briefe*, vol. 2/2, pp. 44–5.

evil. The difficulty of forming an alternative ministry also helped focus minds.[53] Accordingly, both the 15 million talers for defence and the 25 million of guarantees were approved with near unanimity.[54]

A financially literate ministry had been granted almost unprecedented financial powers. This stabilised markets thrown into further turmoil by the failure of the Schaaffhausen bank on 29 March. Standing at 61 before the opening of the United Diet on 1 April, by 10 April state bond prices had recovered to 80. The 15 April law establishing loan societies extended these gains.[55] But was this recovery sufficient for the ministry to actually raise the funds the Diet had approved? The market rally prompted the cabinet order of 25 April to raise the 15 million talers for defence through a voluntary ten-year loan at 5 per cent, but on 16 June the banker Oppenheim lamented the ongoing lack of interest.[56] Finance Minister Hansemann had wanted to cover the deficit of 30 million talers with a foreign loan, but on 3 July the London banker Nilsen informed him that English investors regarded Germany as insufficiently stable.[57]

All power to the revolution?

The National Assembly opened on 22 May, the anniversary of the constitutional promise of 1815. The remarkably wide indirect franchise had excluded only welfare recipients and those inhabiting their abode for fewer than six months. This was defended by Gottschalk, self-styled plenipotentiary of the Cologne workers: 'Why should the people not help create the laws, which they defend with their property and blood?'[58] Yet the exclusion of welfare recipients was also justified by the need for those exercising political rights to fulfil corresponding obligations.[59] The resulting assembly was predominantly liberal and left-liberal. It was entrusted with the task of agreeing a new constitution with the king, which proved difficult. Successive ministries produced successive constitutional drafts, which failed as democratic critics bayed for more.[60] The revolution was approaching its high-water mark.

In Berlin a serious challenge from the mob came with the storming of the Berlin Armoury on 14 June. Those excluded from the civil guard because

53 Mähl, *Überleitung*, pp. 201–2, 218, 221.
54 Bleich, *Verhandlungen*, p. 153.
55 Mähl, *Überleitung*, pp. 229–30, 238.
56 Hansen, *Briefe*, vol. 2/2, p. 235 n. 2.
57 Hansen, *Briefe*, vol. 2/2, p. 307.
58 Ibid., vol. 2/1, pp. 500–1.
59 G. Schilfert, *Sieg und Niederlage des demokratischen Wahlrechts in der deutschen Revolution 1848/49* (Berlin, 1952), p. 64.
60 Clark, *Iron kingdom*, pp. 477–80.

they lacked the means to arm themselves (students and journeymen) decided to help themselves. And yet the raid proved a setback for the revolution, affording a reason to double the garrison to 10,000, to place 25,000 troops within a day's march, and to establish a uniformed police force, all without provoking disorder.[61] It also prompted the king to write to Camphausen that 'the gradual retrieval of the remaining treasury by night to Spandau must be begun'.[62] Conservative resistance was sparked by Hansemann's July plan to end noble exemptions from land taxes; he was reviled as, among other things, 'a bastard'.[63] The *Junkerparlament*, which first met on 18 August, appealed to the king, claiming that the proposed legislation amounted to a wanton attack on property rights. The proposals were shelved.[64]

Having ceded control over finances, the king clung to his last powers, and in June threatened abdication if ministerial co-responsibility for the army was introduced. The cabinet backed down.[65] On 31 July a clash between garrison troops and the civil guard at Schweidnitz prompted the Assembly to compel officers to swear allegiance to it. For conservatives, since parliament did not in principle control the army, this implied parliamentary tyranny; for the left, it was the cabinet's duty to follow parliamentary will.[66] With the king threatening to clear the city by force, the ministry resigned. Two weeks later a new ministry was assembled under the former military governor of Berlin, General von Pfuel. By September, therefore, counter-revolutionary straws were in the wind.

The importance of public works in 1848

One problem for radicals after March was that the king was finally making good on some of the most important promises. Progress was slow on the constitution, but workers had been exempted from indirect taxes in April. Meanwhile the wide suffrage for elections to the National Assembly had split the opposition.[67] Peasant concerns were largely met in July with the proposal to eliminate residual feudal ties without compensation and allow rents to be bought out.[68] Whereas in France in 1789 delayed concessions promoted ever-increasing radicalisation, such concessions divided the already fissiparous revolution.

61 Hansen, *Briefe*, vol. 2/2, pp. 250, 323.
62 Brandenburg, *Briefwechsel*, pp. 138–40.
63 Varnhagen, *Journal*, p. 177.
64 Berdahl, *Nobility*, pp. 378–9.
65 Barclay, *Frederick William*, p. 162.
66 M. Boitzenhart, 'Das preußische Parlament und die deutsche Nationalversammlung im Jahre 1848', in G.A. Ritter, ed., *Regierung, Bürokratie und Parlament in Preußen und Deutschland von 1848 bis zur Gegenwart* (Düsseldorf, 1983), pp. 30–4.
67 Schilfert, *Sieg und Niederlage*, pp. 79–83.
68 Berdahl, *Nobility*, pp. 378–9.

But the real force which gradually defused the revolutionary mood was the deployment of the vestiges of the state's Treasury to meet welfare relief. Already on 9 March a new 'Work Detection Agency' was instituted in Berlin: between March and May, 2,500–3,000 were employed daily.[69] Attempting to exploit the market rally, the king gave the necessary permission for municipalities to issue new bonds (Cologne and Berlin for 200,000 each on 31 May).[70] In April, 1 million talers were used to establish provincial support funds (*Unterstützungskassen*), and a further 1 million was approved to supply merchants and manufacturers with bridge financing via loan societies (*Darlehenskassen*). Prioritising businesses employing manual labour, the first opened on 16 May in Berlin, followed by twenty more.

Still, funds remained tight, and public relief had to be flexed accordingly. Initially the plight of the needy workers evoked sympathy among the wealthier, but gradually the beggars and menacing crowds of young men made honest *Bürger* distinguish the virtuous from the idle poor, while the antics of the rowdier element wore patience thin. Partly by intimidation, the Berlin navvies managed to increase their daily pay to 15 groschen, up from 12.5 (and 9 in October 1847). This outraged taxpayers, and the city started to winnow out the worst offenders and reintroduce piece-rates, sparking conflict.[71]

Indeed, the pattern of protest correlates closely with public works activity. Matters deteriorated during May and June when the loan societies' well began to run dry (955,000 of the 1 million was quickly paid out), and amid the disappointing subscription to Hansemann's voluntary loan. Just at the moment when programmes including the *Ostbahn* had to be scaled back the navvies became prominent on the streets, and the Armoury was stormed.[72] The very same day, the king dipped further into his reserves and ordered the resumption of work on the *Ostbahn* by emergency decree, simultaneously employing 2,000 and removing the radicalised from Berlin.[73] This was thus an important part of the turning point in the summer of 1848.

The Suicide Parliament

While the king was drawing the sting of the mob, Prussian democracy was losing credibility. Ministries came and went in an increasing whirl: the Camphausen ministry lasted twelve weeks, the Auerswald-Hansemann ministry eleven, and General von Pfuel's only six. Each change occasioned prolonged uncertainty, as

69 Gailus, *Straße*, pp. 378–9.
70 Hansen, *Briefe*, vol. 2/2, p. 235.
71 Gailus, *Straße*, pp. 380–5.
72 Ibid., pp. 378–9.
73 Brophy, *Capitalism*, pp. 49–50; Gailus, *Straße*, pp. 385–90.

fewer candidates would serve, and with ever weaker Assembly support. By early November 1848 a minority government under Count Brandenburg was formed.

Coinciding with another reduction in *Ostbahn* work, fresh riots in late October offered the count grounds to more troops into Berlin, and to inform the outraged National Assembly that it had to move to Brandenburg on 27 November.[74] While soldiers remained loyal, only a half of the militia was sufficiently armed to defend the city, and only a half of those committed to do so. Hence there was no resistance when, on 11 November, the king dissolved the Assembly and put Berlin under a state of siege. To the surprise of most local officials, Berlin remained in 'imperturbable calm'; the Rhineland, too, remained peaceful even as the militia were disarmed.[75]

Determined to resist the ministry, but baulking at insurrection, the Assembly majority voted for a tax boycott.[76] This fatally misjudged the mood. Sympathy with the Assembly, anyway fraying, finally gave way. In radical Cologne and Trier little actual tax refusal resulted. Left-wing papers, having approved the tax strike early on, quickly turned against it: these funds were needed for welfare, after all.[77] Even in Trier the feeling was that 'an end must be brought to the useless farce into which the National Assembly had descended'.[78] A tax boycott may well have worked in March, but by November support had dissipated. Bismarck observed drily that 'Passive resistance turns out more and more to be cover for weakness.'[79]

Imposed constitution

If this was a *coup d'état*, all that remained was the *coup de grâce*. As Finance Ministry official Delbrück pointed out, the Assembly 'killed itself off though its own mistakes'.[80] The dilemma about whether to attend in Brandenburg became intolerable to the moderates when the democrats reversed their opposition to attending. Before they could, on 1 December an inquorate minority of only 73 members adjourned the Assembly until 7 December. The king once again seized his chance. On 5 December he dissolved the Assembly and imposed a new constitution.[81]

74   Gailus, *Straße*, pp. 385–90.
75   Hansen, *Briefe*, vol. 2/2, pp. 503, 504–25, 528, 531, 539; V. Valentin, *Geschichte der Deutschen Revolution 1848–1849* (Berlin, 1931), vol. II, pp. 269–71.
76   H. Wegge, *Die Stellung der Öffentlichkeit zur oktroyierten Verfassung und die preußische Parteibildung 1848/49* (Berlin, 1932), pp. 22–6.
77   Wegge, *Öffentlichkeit*, pp. 26–30.
78   Hansen, *Briefe*, vol. 2/2, pp. 585–8, 593, 598.
79   J. Steinberg, *Bismarck* (Oxford, 2011), p. 98.
80   Delbrück, *Lebenserinnerungen*, p. 213.
81   Boitzenhart, *Parlament*, p. 40.

Almost anything might have been better than the Assembly, but the imposed constitution had liberal elements. Prussians were equal before the law, personal freedom and property rights were inviolable, and suffrage was universal for independent adult males not in receipt of poor relief. And yet, beyond the power to dissolve either chamber, the king retained control of the army, foreign policy, and civil service personnel. Further, existing taxes would continue to be levied and altered only through legislation, over which the king had a veto. Even a minority government thus had the funds to continue, at least until new taxes or loans became unavoidable. It says much about expectations that this constitution was welcomed as liberal, but welcomed it was. The democrats Waldeck and Varnhagen were astonished by its liberal aspect.[82] Albert von Thimus was perhaps more realistic in welcoming it as 'the lesser evil', the only way out of the labyrinth.[83]

The king vacillated about imposing a constitution. On 21 November the imperial commissar was informed of the intention to proceed. Two days later Frederick William dismissed the plan as 'dangerous, bad and impractical'. But on the evening of 4 December, just three days after the Assembly's inquorate sitting, the final decision was taken.[84] What decided it? Army loyalty had been a constant, so not that. The sense that the revolution had run out of steam, the parliament a shambles, played its part. But by November Prussian finance was also decisively on the mend.

Finance tips the balance?

The recovery was slow. During the summer Hansemann had to extend the deadline for the voluntary loan several times.[85] By 23 August his view was simple: 'Since state bonds are once again at 74, we can once again venture something.'[86] By early November even Cologne finances had improved, and the city increased the number of public workers by 400 to 1,150. In December, Trier President Sebaldt also celebrated 'the boom in Saarbrücken public works, which is likely to eradicate all … worker hardships during the coming winter'.[87]

As political tension subsided markets rallied, most steeply during November 1848.[88] The government now became bolder. On 4 December the king gave his permission for Cologne's long-delayed 1 million taler loan 'for various public

82 Wegge, Öffentlichkeit, pp. 56–7, 66–8.
83 Hansen, Briefe, vol. 2/2, pp. 580, 581, 582.
84 Ibid., pp. 570, 578.
85 Mähl, Überleitung, pp. 262–3.
86 Varnhagen, Journal, pp. 187–8.
87 Hansen, Briefe, vol. 2/2, pp. 498, 601.
88 Rachel and Wallich, Kapitalisten, p. 264; Varnhagen, Journal, p. 232.

works and other extraordinary expenditure'. The same day he permitted Berlin to raise its million taler at 5 per cent, repayable over thirty years. To cover shorter-term requirements, 600,000 talers of three-month bills were issued. That same evening, having dithered for weeks, the king gave the order to impose a new constitution. The *Kölnische Zeitung* reported on 8 December 1848 that market participants were jumping for joy.[89]

1849 and beyond: new electoral suffrage

Even with the revolutionary dust settling, public finance refused to vacate the stage. By May 1849 the democratic suffrage of April 1848 and January 1849 was rescinded. Instead of votes counting equally, they would be weighted in three classes according to the amount of direct tax paid each year. Each class voted for one-third of the electors, who in turn elected the deputies to the parliament.[90]

How was Prussia's wide suffrage reversed so quickly? The argument was once again about taxation and representation. In December 1848 the *New Prussian* weekly argued that those who paid little or no tax should not enjoy the same political weight as those who paid more.[91] Prince Wilhelm zu Löwenstein objected that the appalling outcome of universal suffrage could only be taxation of the propertied until they were bled dry.[92] Such arguments were pressing, given the taxpayers' burdens in public welfare schemes. For the July 1849 elections a new election law was debated. The problem was the inviolability of the March 1848 promise of the 'widest basis' of popular participation. Gradually the view emerged that the way out of the conundrum would be the general but unequal votes introduced for communal elections in the Rhineland in 1845.[93]

In the ensuing elections steep tax-paying differentials meant that the first class (4.7 per cent of voters) and the second (12.6 per cent) had the same voting weight as the third (82.7 per cent).[94] In Berlin there were an estimated 2,000 voters in the first class, 7,000 in the second, and 70,000 in the third. The result was a swing from democratic towards conservative and liberal views. Judgements about the popular reaction are hampered by the continuing emergency rule. One thing is clear: voter turnout was low, and only three towns saw a majority turnout. In Brieg, 57 per cent of voters from the first class, 42 per cent from the second, and 23 per cent from the third turned up; in Cologne the turnout was

---

89 Brophy, *Capitalism*, p. 52.
90 Barclay, *Frederick William*, pp. 194–5.
91 Wegge, *Öffentlichkeit*, p. 87.
92 Schilfert, *Sieg und Niederlage*, p. 155.
93 Ibid., pp. 158–9, 257–60, 265, 268.
94 Clark, *Iron kingdom*, p. 501.

similar.[95] Opponents once again floundered on the question of a boycott, but the feeling that votes did not count for much or a general despondency about parliament after 1848 are equally likely explanations.

Disenchantment was not universal. The jurist Rudolf Gneist recalled that 'the property-owning classes welcomed the three-class suffrage calmly ... the Borse, with an unequivocal rally'.[96] There was good reason, for the new suffrage aligned the Prussian taxpayer with the needs of its creditors. The liberal *Aachener Zeitung* pointed up the paradox: the numerical dominance of the propertyless meant that equal suffrage actually 'destroyed equality'.[97] With taxpayers now controlling parliament, the circle had been squared into the closest imaginable relationship between taxation and representation. This notorious system lasted until 1918.[98]

Prussia's new constitution(s)

Whatever else it was, the revolution in Prussia emerged from a battle for control of finance. Of the many factors at work, state finance provided the preconditions (an executive choosing power over flexibility) and the precipitants (inability to meet the growing social welfare challenge). The mounting distrust of the authorities which resulted from this tension also provided the fuel at the crucial moment. Public finance also shaped the revolution, even down to the ebbs and flows of violence, and provided a resolution which endured in the constitution of January 1850 and fiscal reform of 1851.

That resolution was a complicated balance. The king retained control over the army, foreign policy and ministerial appointments. Legislation required the agreement of the king and both chambers. Yet new loans and guarantees required approval, budgets were to be presented annually, and any deficits also required subsequent approval. Compromises were found on tax privileges (to be abolished, but later) and on periodicity (the king could dissolve either chamber, but elections were to be held within three months).

This constitution thus represented a new settlement, in which all parties had to accept a compromise. Democratic ultras had been undermined gradually by the provision of emergency welfare, and fatally by the tax boycott debacle. Nobles had to accept peasants' gains, formalised in March 1850, though they did manage (in 1852) some restoration of manorial police and advowson powers.[99] The new suffrage offered moderate conservatives and liberals control

---

95   Schilfert, *Sieg und Niederlage*, pp. 255–7, 309–16.
96   Ibid., p. 283.
97   Wegge, *Öffentlichkeit*, pp. 89–91.
98   Barclay, *Frederick William*, pp. 194–5.
99   Ibid., pp. 216–19.

over a permanent second chamber and a veto over legislation. For these gains they had to accept contingent, not absolute, parliamentary control over the executive on financial matters.

Nevertheless, the settlement suited taxpayers, whose civic obligations were recast in May 1851. Matching the suffrage, those in receipt of welfare remained excluded from tax, but the emergency exemption of manual and day labourers from indirect tax was ended. Ordinary Prussians were once again subject to milling tax, but its perceived injustice was now ameliorated by the introduction of an income tax averaging 3 per cent on the wealthy few. Taxpayers' satisfaction might be judged by taxes rising 36 per cent per capita between 1847 and 1867. Fears that the suffrage would shift tax onto the poorest were allayed by the 61 per cent increase in direct taxes, led by the new graduated tax (+81 per cent), against a 25 per cent increase in indirect taxes: under the new suffrage, the wealthiest were indeed prepared to pay more.[100] By 1861, even the nobles accepted the ending of their tax exemptions, albeit with compensation.[101]

This settlement suited creditors even better. The recovery in state bonds received a further fillip from the new three-class suffrage: that existing (rather than new) taxes were no longer subject to the sort of parliamentary wrangling seen in 1848 was a relief, implying secure coupons. By June 1852 all the ground lost since 1846 had been recovered. With lenders happy to lend, Prussia's overall debt rose from 182 million talers in 1850 to 248 million by 1855.[102] And who were these creditors? In short, those with savings to invest, the same sort of Prussians who enjoyed disproportionate parliamentary control. Political and financial power structures were thus interlocking.

This did not mean that workers were left out. Taxpayer generosity was not limitless, and the emergency public works were wound down after November 1848.[103] But cuts to municipal aid were compensated by the central government's proposed 5.7 million taler spending on public works in 1849. The month before Berlin's employment agencies were closed, in December 1849, an *Ostbahn* law permitted the government to build three railway lines. With financial markets open, the 107 million talers invested in Prussian railways by 1849 jumped to 273 million in 1856. The new settlement therefore formalised temporary public welfare into a more permanent policy of public investment. Beyond these immediate jobs, the knock-on effects on coal and iron were substantial: coalmine employees in the Ruhr valley, for example, doubled.[104] Together with the expansion of the banking system after 1848, this represented the Prussian

---

100   Schremmer, 'Taxation', pp. 439, 456.
101   Berdahl, *Nobility*, pp. 378–9.
102   Richter, *Staatsschuldenwesen*, pp. 61–2.
103   Mähl, *Überleitung*, p. 246.
104   Barclay, *Frederick William*, pp. 217–18.

economic 'take-off'.[105] Within twenty years, Prussia's financial power would allow Bismarck to sweep aside both Austria and France, and to unify Germany around Berlin.

Famously for Marx, the 1848 revolution in France was the farce to 1789's tragedy. But compared to its Prussian equivalent, the 1848 revolution in France was itself a tragedy. There was no Prussian analogue of the bloodshed of the June days in Paris, and for good reason. That violence was prompted by the dissolution of the National Workshops workers had established to provide welfare relief: taxpayers baulked at 'socialist' experiments. In Berlin workers made similar demands, and the Prussian state's inability to afford relief spelled trouble in March 1848. However, the king compromised, and workers' demands were soon heeded: the provision of public works gradually drew the sting from the revolution, and continued long afterwards. Taxpayer demands to control state expenditure were also heeded, finding expression in the constitution of 1850. The longevity of this overall settlement and the financial power it unleashed far exceeded those of the French version, and without having to plumb tragic depths. Although historians have mostly been sceptical, therefore, there are grounds to regard the 1848 revolution in Prussia a success, though they are certainly not ones that Marx himself would have celebrated.

---

105   J.M. Brophy, 'Eisenbahnbau als Modernisierungsstrategie?', in T. Stamm-Kuhlmann, ed., *Pommern im 19. Jahrhundert* (Cologne, 2007), pp. 253–4; Barclay, *Frederick William*, pp. 217–18.

7

Imperial Germany, Great Britain and the political economy of the gold standard, 1867–1914

SABINE SCHNEIDER

For Ludwig Bamberger, the chief political architect of German monetary union, the Reichstag's decision to suspend the minting of silver in December 1871 appeared like the 'de-thronement of a world monarch'.[1] Foreshadowing an age of gold-backed currencies, Germany's coinage laws of 1871 and 1873 marked a caesura in the first phase of globalization. The preceding decade had seen a succession of international conferences and diplomatic efforts to establish a pan-European currency under French leadership. Germany's victory in the Franco-Prussian War of 1870/71 sealed the fate of European monetary integration by inaugurating a multi-polar system of gold standards that persisted until the outbreak of the First World War. Imperial Germany's adoption of a national gold currency has principally been attributed to a 'modernizing' desire to emulate Britain's commercial ascendancy.[2] The British Empire's global trading network had long projected national strength, while the pound sterling was revered as an epitome of fiscal prudence.[3] For German liberals and free traders, Britain's currency and banking arrangements constituted a model of 'enlightened institutional' practice and a blueprint for industrializing nations.[4] When the German states unified in 1871, the Reich ushered in unparalleled liberal reforms to integrate its federal economies and public

---

1 Ludwig Bamberger, *Gesammelte Schriften*, 5 vols (Berlin, 1894–98), vol. IV, p. 311.
2 Patrick Karl O'Brien, 'The Pax Britannica and American hegemony: precedent, antecedent or just another history?', in Patrick Karl O'Brien and Armand Clesse, eds, *Two hegemonies: Britain, 1846–1914, and the United States, 1941–2001* (Aldershot, 2002), pp. 22–4; Alan S. Milward, 'The origins of the gold standard', in Jorge Braga de Macedo, Barry Eichengreen and Jaime Reis, eds, *Currency convertibility: the gold standard and beyond* (London, 1996), pp. 89–95, 100.
3 Martin J. Daunton, 'Britain and globalisation since 1850: I. Creating a global order, 1850–1914', *Transactions of the Royal Historical Society* 16 (2006), pp. 21–3.
4 Harold James, 'Monetary and fiscal unification in nineteenth-century Germany: What can Kohl learn from Bismarck?', *Princeton Essays in International Finance* 202 (1997), p. 16; Giulio

finances. In December 1871, the German Empire founded the gold Mark as its common currency, and in 1876 the Reichsbank opened its doors as Germany's central monetary authority. Thirty years after Bismarck's reforms, Georg Friedrich Knapp first ascribed Germany's espousal of a gold standard less to economic calculation than to a fateful tendency to imitate 'England's successful institution'.[5] Since Knapp's *State theory of money*, the Reich's currency laws have been portrayed as an artifact of Bismarck's 'Western orientation' in his 'foreign trade policy', which enabled a raft of liberal measures to pass into law during the founding years of the German Empire.[6]

Emulating Britain's mercantile success was an integral aspect of Bismarckian trade policy, yet there were also crucial domestic and geopolitical motives that have so far eluded analysis. This chapter revisits the Reich's currency reforms by considering how national politics and foreign precedent shaped Germany's monetary constitution. It reinterprets the Reich's currency politics as a strategic move towards financial independence through emulation and rivalry. In examining how the Reich's monetary and foreign policies intersected, the chapter recovers a critical dimension of Anglo-German competition that predates the countries' naval and industrial rivalry in the twentieth century. Germany's choice of gold was bolstered by the prospect of establishing the Mark as a key international trade currency: one that could challenge sterling's predominance in the world economy. By tracing Germany's incentives for currency reform, the chapter posits that the origins of the pre-war gold standard were deeply rooted in the Reich's institutional legacy and its financial reliance on Britain.

Germany's territorial fragmentation prior to 1871 had entrenched a decentralized monetary system, which was widely recognized as an impediment to domestic economic development and overseas trade (Table 7.1). The twenty-five German kingdoms, duchies and city-states that formed the Reich in 1871 consisted of no fewer than six currency zones. With the foundation of the Zollverein (Customs Union) in 1834, the pursuit of political unification had gone hand in hand with efforts to foster deeper economic integration. Successive coinage treaties, in 1837, 1838 and 1857, pursued this aim by harmonizing the mint conventions and metallic weight of Germany's standard coins. Guided by divergent political interests, the North and South German states opted for incremental steps towards integration in place of more ambitious schemes for

Gallarotti, *The anatomy of an international monetary regime: the classical gold standard, 1880–1914* (Oxford, 1995), p. 9; Milward, 'Origins of the gold standard', pp. 93, 95, 100.

5   G.F. Knapp, *Staatliche Theorie des Geldes* (Leipzig, 1905), pp. 265, 349–52.

6   Knut Borchardt, 'The industrial revolution in Germany, 1700–1914', in C.M. Cipolla, ed., *The Fontana economic history of Europe: the emergence of industrial societies*, 6 vols (London, 1973), vol. IV, p. 152; Gustav Stolper, Karl Häuser, Knut Borchardt and Toni Stolper, trans., *The German economy: 1870 to the present* (London, 1967), p. 18; Wilhelm Rieger, *Die Gründe für den Übergang zur Goldwährung in Deutschland* (Strasbourg, 1918), pp. 68, 74–5.

Table 7.1. Germany's money stock in 1870 and 1885, in millions of Mark

Circulating medium	Net value		Percentage	
	1870	1885	1870	1885
German gold coins	91	1,500	4.0	49.2
Gold bars and foreign coin	–	72	–	2.4
Old silver coins	1,500	450	65.7	14.7
Imperial silver coins	–	442	–	14.5
Subsidiary coins	85	40	3.7	1.3
Foreign coins	40	–	1.8	–
Hamburg banking currency	36	–	1.6	–
State paper money	171	–	7.5	–
Imperial Treasury notes	–	145	–	4.8
Uncovered bank notes	359	401	15.7	13.1
Total	2,282	3,050		

Sources: Estimates from Adolph Soetbeer, *Gegenwärtiger Stand der Währungsfrage und die Zukunft des Silbers (April 1885): eine Abhandlung* (Berlin, 1885), pp. 36–7, reprinted in J. Laurence Laughlin, *The history of bimetallism in the United States* (New York, 1886), pp. 136–7, 144.

centralizing monetary sovereignty. From the mid-1860s, German financial and industrial circles petitioned the Zollverein parliament to introduce a common decimal currency based on a gold standard. Their demands were championed by a number of supra-regional pressure groups, foremost among them the German Trade Assembly (*Deutsche Handelstag*) and the Congress of German Economists (*Kongreß deutscher Volkswirte*). Germany's national unification in the wake of the Franco-Prussian War put an end to the states' currency diversity and the disparities in the country's note circulation. Bismarck's peace treaty with France provided a short-lived opportunity to reorder Germany's currency affairs, with minimal fiscal repercussions.[7] The 5 billion francs indemnity levied on France in May 1871 was the 'game changer' that supplied the Reich with the necessary financial resources to complete its costly transition.[8] With the funds

7   Rudolph von Delbrück to Heinrich von Itzenplitz, 11 Feb. 1871, Geheimes Staatsarchiv Preußischer Kulturbesitz (GStA PK), I. HA Rep. 120 Ministerium für Handel und Gewerbe, AX, Nr. 27 Bd. 2, fols 240–50.
8   Milton Friedman, 'Bimetallism revisited', *Journal of Economic Perspectives* 4 (1990), p. 90; Marc Flandreau, 'The French crime of 1873: an essay on the emergence of the international gold standard, 1870–1880', *Journal of Economic History* 56 (1996), pp. 873, 890.

remitted by France, the German Chancellery replenished its war chest, and acquired the requisite gold for minting Germany's new coinage.

The German Coinage Acts of 1871 and 1873 jointly created a national money market and consolidated the Reich's commitment to a gold-convertible currency. Preliminary legislation passed by the Reichstag on 4 December 1871 authorized the minting of the Mark as a decimal gold coinage for the German Reich.[9] It sanctioned the issue of 10- and 20-gold Mark, and suspended the minting of silver coins across the federal states. The second Coinage Act, of 9 July 1873, formally rejected the old silver *régime* and declared the Reich's intention to convert to gold monometallism.[10] It approved the Reich's withdrawal of the states' silver coins and decreed that, from 1 January 1876, the gold Mark would become the common unit of account in all German territories. In the framing of the 1871 law, Prussia's political and economic dominance in the Reich prevailed over the interests of the smaller Southern states.[11] The common German currency was crafted in the image of Prussia's currency, the Thaler, and the timing of its transition to gold was shaped decisively by the great power rivalry between Prussia and France.[12] Bismarck's government not only secured a preferential conversion rate between the Thaler and the Mark, Prussia's former leading coin also continued to assume legal tender status until 1907.[13] Beyond the states' domestic power struggle, the Reich's unilateral shift to gold thwarted France's plans for a supra-national currency. Under the auspices of Napoleon III, the Latin Monetary Union had established, in 1865, a bimetallic franc zone in Central and Southern Europe. Napoleon III and his economic advisors envisaged the creation of a 'universal coinage' to simplify foreign exchange and cut transaction costs in cross-border trade.[14]

9 'Gesetz, betreffend die Ausprägung von Reichsgoldmünzen, 4. Dezember 1871', *Deutsches Reichsgesetzblatt* (Berlin, 1871), pp. 404–6.

10 Karl Helfferich, *Die Reform des deutschen Geldwesens nach der Gründung des Reiches*, 2 vols (Leipzig, 1898), vol. 1, pp. 206–36.

11 Frank Otto, *Die Entstehung eines nationalen Geldes: Integrationsprozesse der deutschen Währung im 19. Jahrhundert* (Berlin, 2002), pp. 516–18; Harold James, 'Zwischen Welt- und Nationalwährung: Die Mark und das Kaiserreich, 1873–1914', in Carl-Ludwig Holtfrerich, Harold James and Manfred Pohl, eds, *Requiem auf eine Währung: Die Mark 1873–2001* (Stuttgart, 2001), pp. 71–2.

12 Marc Flandreau, *The glitter of gold: France, bimetallism, and the emergence of the international gold standard 1848–1873* (Oxford, 2004), pp. 183–4, 209–10; Luca Einaudi, *Money and politics: European monetary unification and the international gold standard (1865–1873)* (Oxford, 2001), pp. 184–5.

13 The Prussian Thaler's privileged status in the coinage laws established a 'limping' gold standard in the German Empire, see Richard Tilly, 'On the history of German monetary union', in P.L. Cottrell, G. Notaras and G. Tortella, eds, *From the Athenian tetradrachm to the euro: studies in European monetary integration* (Aldershot, 2007), p. 47.

14 Einaudi, *Money and politics*, pp. 3–4, 7.

As Vice-President of the Conseil d'État, Félix Esquirou de Parieu championed a European monetary alliance based on the franc and backed by a pure gold standard. His scheme formed the cornerstone of the International Monetary Conference of 1867 in Paris, which conference delegates from twenty countries attended on the invitation of the French monarch. Parieu's aspiration was to establish a fixed exchange rate regime from Greece to Finland, in which the 10-franc coin would become a truly 'international' unit of account.[15] In the German states, Parieu's proposal gained many sympathizers in the kingdoms of Bavaria, Hesse, Baden and Württemberg, as well as in the financial centre of Frankfurt am Main.[16] Southern Germany had close commercial and financial ties to France, and France's 'universal coinage' promised to be highly beneficial to its continental trade. Prussia's government, however, as well as the Hanseatic cities, remained unreceptive to France's internationalist scheme, favouring instead the creation of a small-German (*kleindeutsche*) monetary union.[17]

In the aftermath of the Franco-Prussian War, Prussian opposition to France's scheme, coupled with a popular tide of anti-French sentiment in the Reichstag, put a swift end to the notion of harmonising the Mark with the currency of its recently defeated neighbour. Rudolph von Delbrück, the President of the Imperial Chancellery, and the National-Liberal delegate Ludwig Bamberger emerged as the leading advocates for a national gold coinage.[18] Both had strong reservations against sacrificing monetary sovereignty to a council of nations, arguing that it would render Germany highly vulnerable to other nations' financial follies – especially to the debasement of their currencies through over-issue of specie.[19] When Delbrück and Bamberger advanced their case in the Reichstag, France's *assignats* crisis of the 1790s still resonated bleakly in

15   Ibid., p. 51.

16   Ibid., pp. 179, 186; Carl-Ludwig Holtfrerich, *Frankfurt as a financial centre: from medieval trade fair to European banking centre* (Munich, 1999), pp. 185–7. See the writings of the Württemberg Master of the Mint, Friedrich Xeller, and the financial journalist S. Eichelberg: F. Xeller, *Die Frage der internationalen Münzeinigung und der Reform des deutschen Münzwesens* (Stuttgart, 1869); S. Eichelberg, *Vorschlag für eine Einheit in Münze und Währung für alle grossen, handelstreibenden Staaten* (Frankfurt am Main, 1870).

17   Prussian Ministry of Trade to Otto von Bismarck, 21 Sep. 1867, GStA PK, III. HA Ministerium der auswärtigen Angelegenheiten, Abt. 2, Nr. 1877, fol. 198. For the case in favour of a small-German monetary union, see the pamphlet of the Deutsche Handelstag's Vice-President: A.G. Mosle, *Das teutonische Münzsystem: ein Beitrag zur Lösung der deutschen Münzfrage* (Bremen, 1870). On the antagonism between Prussia and France, see Einaudi, *Money and politics*, pp. 179–88.

18   See Dieter Lindenlaub, 'Confidence in a new currency: the introduction of the Mark in Germany', in P.L. Cottrell, Even Lange and Ulf Olsson, eds, *Centres and peripheries in banking: the historical development of financial markets* (Aldershot, 2007), pp. 137–8.

19   Ludwig Bamberger, *Reichsgold: Studien über Währung und Wechsel* (Leipzig, 1876), pp. 69–73; Lindenlaub, 'Confidence', p. 138; Rieger, *Goldwährung*, pp. 45–7.

Europe's collective memory. The emission of *assignats* – paper money secured against plots of land confiscated from the Church – acted as a financial lifeline to the First French Republic.[20] In 1795 the market for *assignats* collapsed and wiped out the savings of France's lower and middle classes.[21] Seventy years later, German policymakers still referred to *assignats* as a byword for fiscal imprudence, political corruption and moral hubris. But contemporaries needed to look no further than the neighbouring Habsburg monarchy to appreciate the dangers of an over-reliance on paper money to re-finance government debt. Austria lost its own battles with runaway inflation during the Napoleonic Wars and the revolutionary uprisings of 1848–49.[22] German officials hence judged the uncertainties attached to a pan-European monetary union with France and Austria as too high a price to pay. National gold coinage, according to their rationale, guarded against the evils of 'imported' inflation and potential conflicts with treaty partners. While it was desirable that currencies should circulate internationally, German and British statesmen shared the view that the power to mint and issue money was lodged within nations' economic borders. Consequently the 'classical gold standard' satisfied both national and internationalist aims: it facilitated economic exchange in an age of rapid globalization, while remaining heavily rooted within the nation state.[23]

By joining Britain's 'gold club', Germany laid the foundations for a multipolar monetary order, as well as stabilizing its exchange rate with the British Empire – its principal creditor and the leading importer of German goods. Coordination with Britain's currency zone promised to lower transaction costs with the world's largest trading bloc, a policy that enjoyed the firm backing of free traders in the Reichstag.[24] Karl Braun, the President of the Congress of German Economists, echoed the prevailing sentiment that a gold currency was best placed to advance Germany's stake in global commerce, since London

---

20   Charles Kindleberger, *A financial history of western Europe* (London, 1984), p. 99.

21   Gerlof D. Homan, *Jean-François Reubell: French revolutionary, patriot, and director (1747–1807)* (The Hague, 1971), p. 87.

22   Convertibility of the Austrian Gulden into silver was suspended in 1848 and attempts to restore convertibility were twice cut short by the onset of war in 1858 and 1866. See Barry Eichengreen and Marc Flandreau, 'The geography of the gold standard', in Braga de Macedo *et al.*, *Currency convertibility*, p. 117.

23   Eric Helleiner, 'Denationalising money? Economic liberalism and the "national question" in currency affairs', in Emily Gilbert and Eric Helleiner, eds, *Nation-states and money: the past, the present and future of national currencies* (London, 1999), pp. 139–45.

24   German exports and imports from the British Empire purportedly accounted for as much as 20% of the trade of the Zollverein and the Hanse towns prior to unification, see Paul Kennedy, *The rise of Anglo-German antagonism 1860–1914* (London, 1980), p. 46; Guido Thiemeyer, 'Die deutschen Liberalen, die Reichsgründung und die Entstehung des internationalen Goldstandards 1870–1873', in Eckart Conze, Ulrich Lappenküper and Guido Müller, eds, *Geschichte der internationalen Beziehungen: Erneuerung und Erweiterung einer historischen Disziplin* (Köln, 2004), pp. 163–4.

constituted 'the centre of trade for all five continents'.[25] Securing exchange rate stability with Germany's largest trading partner was a crucial factor in favour of a gold currency; however, a gold anchor was also perceived as a *panacea* for the Reich's inherited institutional weaknesses. Bamberger repeatedly made the case in the Reichstag that gold was both a guarantor and a precondition for a prudent fiscal policy and a resilient banking system. Only a gold anchor would be capable of reining in the expansion of Germany's sprawling paper note circulation. When devising the Reich's monetary constitution, German legislators drew extensively on Britain's monometallic orthodoxy. Of the classical economists, it was John Stuart Mill and, in particular, his *Principles of political economy* (1848) that elaborated on the gold standard's technical workings in Britain.[26] In 1844, Mill declared in *The Westminster Review* that 'Gold is not an ideally perfect standard – a commodity absolutely unchangeable in cost of production; but it approaches nearer to that abstract perfection of a measure of value, than any other production of nature or industry'.[27] Sterling's relative price stability in the nineteenth century had recommended Britain's gold standard as a paragon of order and fiscal restraint. When Bamberger thus quipped that Germany had 'chosen gold not because *gold* is *gold*, but because *England* is *England*', he exalted Britain's commitment to gold convertibility as the foundation of a stable and efficient monetary system.[28] By steadfastly upholding gold convertibility, the British state guaranteed that the operation of its currency was liberated from party politics and insulated against short-term fiscal pressures.[29] Both of these aspects appealed to German liberals and many Prussian conservatives, who sought to eliminate the fiscal excesses of the smaller German states. Gold monometallism was presented as an effective instrument to eradicate the Reich's *Papierwirtschaft*, a term contemporaries coined for the large circulation of uncovered notes emitted by the states and private issuing banks (*Zettelbanken*). The gold standard as a 'good housekeeping seal of approval', to use Bordo and Rockoff's terminology, imposed a welcome dose of fiscal rectitude on the federal states, as well as on the central government in Berlin.[30]

Throughout the nineteenth century, the emission of unsecured state and bank notes had flourished unchecked in Germany, leading to periodic bank runs

25   *Stenographische Berichte über die Verhandlungen des Deutschen Reichstages*, 17 Nov. 1871, p. 327.
26   Michael D. Bordo, 'The gold standard: the traditional approach', in Michael D. Bordo and Anna Schwartz, eds, *A retrospective on the classical gold standard, 1821–1931* (Chicago, IL, 1984), pp. 40–3.
27   J.S. Mill, 'The currency question', *Westminster Review* 41 (Jun. 1844), p. 581.
28   Gert von Eynern, *Die Reichsbank* (Jena, 1928), p. 3 [emphasis added].
29   Daunton, 'Britain and globalisation', p. 24.
30   Michael D. Bordo and Hugh Rockoff, 'The gold standard as a "good housekeeping seal of approval"', *Journal of Economic History* 56 (1996), pp. 389–428.

and financial contagion. While in 1851, 9 *Zettelbanken* held licences to print bank notes, by 1870 their number had risen to 32, and their issue of uncovered bank notes totalled 359 million Mark.[31] Especially in the smaller German states, rulers had often turned to seigniorage and inconvertible paper money in order to rehabilitate their battered finances. Johann Ludwig Tellkampf concluded in 1873 that the German credit system would have been tested to breaking point had the German army suffered defeat in the wars against Austria in 1866 and France in 1870/71.[32] Cautionary tales of the hazardous effects of unsecured notes turned to outright vilification in the mid-1870s, bordering on 'Papierophobie'.[33] Reichstag speeches regularly compared the large circulation of small bank notes to 'pestilence' or infectious diseases that slowly threatened to destroy commerce and distort social relations.[34] Even the financially adroit Bamberger professed that 'Paper money, like war, is the suspension of culture', while the author of a popular pamphlet series evoked Goethe's *Faust* to portray paper money as a Mephistophelian invention.[35]

Political expediency aside, German parliamentarians also ascribed potent cultural and moral attributes to gold currencies. Gold's prestige as a monetary metal had emanated, since the early nineteenth century, from the prosperity of Britain's open economy and its financial centre, the City of London.[36] Britain's economic experience had invested the gold standard with a host of normative assumptions about *laissez-faire* governance and the growth effects of capital mobility. The metal's cosmopolitan analogy with 'peace, prosperity and civilisation as part of the wider political culture of free trade' resonated positively in Germany with a nascent commitment to Smithian economic liberalism.[37] Since its *de facto* adoption in Britain in 1717, the gold standard came to epitomize the commercial traits of the country in which it first took root. On the heels of the Industrial Revolution and the extension of the British Empire, the pound sterling established itself as the world's leading trade currency and the preferred medium of international credit. Britain's prosperity had given rise to the notion that gold was 'the wholesale money of mercantile nations', a narrative that

31   See Table 7.1, 'Germany's money stock in 1870 and 1885'; Karl Erich Born, 'Der Ausbau der Reichsinstitutionen und das Notenbankproblem: Die Herstellung einer Währungseinheit und die Entstehung der Reichsbank', in Johannes Kunisch, ed., *Bismarck und seine Zeit* (Berlin, 1992), p. 262.
32   Johann Ludwig Tellkampf, *Erforderniss voller Metalldeckung der Banknoten* (Berlin, 1873), p. 35.
33   Rieger, *Goldwährung*, p. 37.
34   See, for instance, Moritz Mohl, *Stenographische Berichte*, 18 Nov. 1871, p. 348.
35   Bamberger, *Reichsgold*, p. 142; August Eggers, *Die Fehler der deutschen Münzreform und Vorschläge zu deren Abhülfe* (Berlin, 1876), p. 20; Rieger, *Goldwährung*, pp. 38, 43.
36   Daunton, 'Britain and globalisation', pp. 21–3.
37   Ibid., p. 23; M.J. Daunton, *State and market in Victorian Britain: war, welfare and capitalism* (Woodbridge, 2008), pp. 7, 237.

served to cement its association with progress and modernity.[38] From the middle of the century, it increasingly became a staple in political economy that industrializing states required high-value gold coins to conduct large volumes of world trade.

Gold had undergone a remarkable change in social perception since the eighteenth century, as classical economics overturned its early modern associations with idolatry, avarice and greed.[39] In his *Wealth of nations*, Adam Smith envisioned 'a progression' of gold from 'originally being valued as "frivolous ornaments of dress and furniture," then successively as a signifier of status and a facilitator of trade, before finally reaching its apotheosis as the basis for Britain's credit economy'.[40] Biblical and Darwinist references to gold's qualities also proliferated in nineteenth-century literature, art and political economy.[41] Silver, by contrast, was ever more relegated to the small-change currencies of agrarian societies. Alexander Meyer, the editor of the *Deutsches Handelsblatt*, noted in 1867 that the present 'impulse towards a gold currency should be considered from a cultural-historical [perspective] as the final stage of an ancient, evolutionary process'.[42] In a similar vein, Bamberger's Reichstag speech on the Coinage Act of 1871 predicted that 'gold is more and more destined to endow the circulation of civilized nations'.[43] Both statements are characteristic of a teleological belief that as nations progressed from agrarian societies to industrializing economies, they gradually abandoned copper and silver coinage for gold.[44] Such crude civilizational rhetoric was by no means unique to the economic discourse of Britain and the German Empire.[45] The tendency to portray credit and monetary innovations in the West as 'universal' signifiers of 'modernity' abounded across the nineteenth and early twentieth centuries.[46]

Critics of Germany's new monetary regime challenged the myth of gold's moral superiority, by rejecting the popular notion that Britain's strong economic trajectory stemmed from its pure gold standard. Bismarck's private banker and

---

38   *The Economist*, 27 Oct. 1866, p. 1252; James, 'Zwischen Welt- und Nationalwährung', p. 69.
39   Recent studies on the cultural history of gold have traced the metal's moral associations in Britain, see, in particular, Deborah Valenze, *The social life of money in the English past* (Cambridge, 2006); Timothy Alborn, 'Money's worth: morality, class, politics', in Martin Hewitt, ed., *The Victorian world* (London, 2012), pp. 210–12; Timothy Alborn, 'Coin and country: visions of civilisation in the British recoinage debate, 1867–1891', *Journal of Victorian Culture* 3 (1998), pp. 252–81.
40   Timothy Alborn, 'The greatest metaphor ever mixed: gold in the British bible, 1750–1850', *Journal of the History of Ideas* 78 (2017), p. 428; Adam Smith, *An inquiry into the nature and causes of the wealth of nations*, 2 vols (London, 1776), vol. I, pp. 218, 388.
41   Alborn, 'Gold in the British bible', pp. 427, 446–7.
42   Quoted in Rieger, *Goldwährung*, pp. 29–30.
43   *Stenographische Berichte*, 11 Nov. 1871, p. 229; Rieger, *Goldwährung*, p. 61.
44   Rieger, *Goldwährung*, p. 29; Gallarotti, *International monetary regime*, p. 9.
45   Daunton, 'Britain and globalisation', pp. 23–4.
46   Milward, 'Origins of the gold standard', pp. 89–91.

long-time advisor Gerson von Bleichröder was among a few leading German financiers and officials who remained sceptical of the merits of a gold currency. Bimetallists like Bleichröder maintained that Britain's commercial success owed a large part to France's costly maintenance of a joint standard of silver and gold.[47] The French government had awarded its gold and silver coins equal standing as legal tender in 1803 at the ratio of 1:15.5. Its bimetallic constitution acted as a 'currency buffer' between Britain and the European silver economies, as well as facilitating easy access to the metal for the settlement of Britain's balance of trade with silver-using countries in East Asia. Bleichröder heavily criticised what he saw as the unpatriotic and misguided application of Smithian economic principles to the German currency question. His chief concern, however, was that a gold standard would come at the price of an inflexible money supply, increased volatility in interest rates and periodic credit contractions.[48] Rather than making Germany more independent from its largest creditor, he anticipated that Germany would become still more reliant on London as the hub of the world gold and money market.[49] Bleichröder's judgement revealed extraordinary foresight at a time when the opposing view held sway – that the gold Mark would enable German commerce to gain financial independence from London.

National unification and its aftermath spawned a short-lived euphoria that a gold currency would allow German exporters and importers to sever their ties with British finance.[50] In the prosperous years preceding the stock exchange crash of 1873, the German press frequently lamented how London dictated the terms of global trade to the disadvantage of German merchants, and thus deprived Germany of a considerable share of its profits from overseas trade.[51] Karl Braun reminded the Reichstag in November 1871 that Britain's financial centre controlled the cost of trade credit for German commerce and industry:

> Who governs our exchange rate? Who has so far exploited us by the rate of foreign exchange? London. Where is the price ratio of gold to silver fixed? In London. By introducing the gold standard alongside England and America and adopting the shilling under the title 'Mark', we shall set limits to this exploitation and so save all the money which we have lost so far.[52]

47 'Hervorragende Punkte betreffend einfache Goldwährung und Doppelwährung', Bleichroeder Bank Collection, Box XXXI.II. Baker Library, Harvard Business School.
48 Fritz Stern, *Gold and iron: Bismarck, Bleichröder and the building of the German Empire* (New York, 1977), pp. 180–1.
49 Gerson von Bleichröder to Otto von Bismarck, 11 Dec. 1874, OBS B 15, Otto-von-Bismarck-Stiftung; Stern, *Gold and iron*, p. 180.
50 Youssef Cassis, *Capitals of capital* (Cambridge, 2006), pp. 110, 133; Manfred Pohl and Kathleen Burk, *Deutsche Bank in London 1873–1998* (Munich, 1998), p. 7.
51 Richard H. Tilly, 'International aspects of the development of German banking', in Rondo Cameron and V.I. Bovykin, eds, *International Banking 1870–1914* (New York, 1991), p. 106.
52 *Stenographische Berichte*, 17 Nov. 1871, p. 327.

Deutsche Bank's managing director Hermann Wallich shared Braun's patriotic zeal for liberating German trade from foreign financial intermediation. He was eager to remedy the situation by which:

> Until 1870 not a single bale of cotton had been able to enter Germany without having been financed by British mediators on the way. The same was true of all the other raw materials on which German industry depended for its basic supplies. Britain was also the main channel for German exports. All this cost Germany many millions annually in unnecessary commission charges, and it was a good idea to try [to] put an end to this tribute and enable the country's trade to stand on its own feet.[53]

Contemporary estimates suggest that commission charges on British acceptances and trade credits to Germany totalled around £5 million annually in the mid-1880s.[54] Anglo-German merchant banks in London – like Frederick Huth & Co. and Kleinwort, Sons & Co. – had cultivated profitable relationships with German companies by offering lower rates than could usually be procured in Berlin, Hamburg and Frankfurt.[55] Wallich's intention, and that of Deutsche Bank's founders, was to repatriate a share of this highly lucrative business.[56] Their commercial endeavour sprang as much from a healthy business instinct as from a patriotic ambition to secure the 'introduction of the German currency in overseas markets'.[57] National aspirations to ascend to be a world trading power certainly played a significant part in Deutsche Bank's strategy, which fell on fertile ground in the Chancellery and secured Bismarck's approval for its incorporation in 1870.[58] But Germany's financial relationship with London was not only seen as costly; many also sought to limit their country's vulnerability to financial contagion. Since the railway manias of the mid-1840s, German investors and merchants had periodically experienced the disruptive effects of financial crises, originating from London and New York. Hamburg, 'the continent's most English city', relied on acceptance credits and overdrafts from

53 Quoted in Manfred Pohl, 'Glimpses of Deutsche Bank's early days – through the papers of Hermann Wallich', in M. Pohl, ed., *Studies on economic and monetary problems and on banking history* (Mainz, 1988), pp. 382–3; see also *Geschäftsbericht der Direction der Deutschen Bank* (1871), p. 3.
54 Maximilian Müller-Jabusch, *Franz Urbig* (Berlin, 1954), p. 73.
55 Stanley D. Chapman, *The rise of merchant banking* (London, 1984), p. 123; Harry Arthur Simon, *Die Banken und der Hamburger Überseehandel* (Stuttgart, 1909), p. 60.
56 Christoph Buchheim, 'Deutsche Finanzmetropole von internationalem Rang (1870–1914)', in Hans Pohl, ed., *Geschichte des Finanzplatzes Berlin* (Frankfurt am Main, 2002), pp. 117–18.
57 *Geschäftsbericht der Direction der Deutschen Bank* (1873), p. 3; Richard H. Tilly, 'Berlin als preußisches und deutsches Finanzzentrum und seine Beziehungen zu den anderen Zentren in Ost und West', in W. Ribbe and J. Schmädeke, eds, *Berlin im Europa der Neuzeit* (Berlin, 1990), pp. 203–4.
58 Cassis, *Capitals of capital*, p. 110; Buchheim, 'Finanzmetropole', pp. 117–18.

British banks, which City houses liquidated when credit seized up in the London market.[59] If a tightening of money rates occurred in London, it could be felt as far as the Prussian hinterlands of Saxony and Silesia. Industrialists in these areas relied principally on Hamburg bankers for their working capital, but also drew directly on London to settle their overseas trade.[60]

When, in 1857, a credit crisis of worldwide proportions transmitted shockwaves from the United States over Britain to Scandinavia, several Hamburg merchant houses found themselves 'on the verge of collapse'.[61] The Hanse town's position at the crossroads of mercantile trade with Central, Northern and Eastern Europe rendered it particularly susceptible to sharp changes in the global financial climate.[62] Overtrading in blank acceptances[63] further augmented the severity of the credit crunch and resulted in 'the accept-ances of the most respectable houses' being treated 'little better than scrap paper'.[64] The 1857 crisis dealt a lasting blow to the perceived trust in Hamburg's marketplace and the solidity of its currency, the Mark Banco.[65] The last episode of financial panic to hit Germany before unification – the Overend & Gurney Panic of 1866 – again caused trepidation and alarm on German shores. Open market rates in Hamburg climbed to 7–9% in the wake of Overend's collapse, while discount rates in Berlin stood at 7% and 6% in Frankfurt am Main.[66] The fallout from the 1866 panic, as Flandreau has argued, 'played an essential part in convincing Germans of the problems arising from dependence upon a foreign credit system, and of the need to provide one's own source of liquidity'.[67] Both crises affirmed the desirability of 'free[ing] German traders from British go-betweens', and of shielding the Reich from periodic credit shocks from overseas.[68]

The ambition of bankers like Hermann Wallich, Georg von Siemens and Ludwig Bamberger was to elevate the German currency to a position where 'the

59   Marc Flandreau, 'Does integration globalize? Elements of nineteenth-century financial geography', in Richard Tilly and Paul J.J. Welfens, eds, *Economic globalization, international organizations and crisis management* (Berlin, 2000), pp. 112–13.

60   Richard Tilly, '"Los von England": Probleme des Nationalismus in der deutschen Wirtschaftsgeschichte', *Zeitschrift für die gesamte Staatswissenschaft* 124 (1968), pp. 192–3.

61   Charles P. Kindleberger, *Manias, panics and crashes: a history of financial crises*, 6th edn (Basingstoke, 2011), pp. 164, 237; Charles P. Kindleberger, 'Germany's overtaking of England, 1806–1914, Part I', *Weltwirtschaftliches Archiv* 111 (1975), p. 279.

62   Helmut Böhme, *Frankfurt und Hamburg: Des Deutschen Reiches Silber- und Goldloch und die allerenglischste Stadt des Kontinents* (Frankfurt am Main, 1968), p. 237.

63   Blank acceptances are bills endorsed with incomplete information, such as leaving blank spaces for the date by which payment is due or the sum endorsed.

64   Böhme, *Frankfurt und Hamburg*, pp. 273–4.

65   Ibid., pp. 273–4.

66   *The Economist*, 12 May 1866, p. 564.

67   Flandreau, 'Financial geography', p. 113.

68   Ibid.; quoting Hermann Wallich, in Pohl, 'Deutsche Bank's early days', p. 382.

mark could take its place beside the pound as a mainstay of financial stability in the West'.[69] Establishing the Mark as a major international currency promised to challenge sterling's hegemony, reduce exchange rate risks and assist the expansion of German exports. While Berlin merely occupied a subsidiary role in international finance prior to 1871, German financiers glimpsed an opportunity to transform the new capital into a hub for overseas lending. Berlin's domestic financial business was to develop in tandem with an expansion in the presence of German banks abroad, whose foreign branches were 'to serve as bases for Germany's trade and Germany's currency'.[70] Its overseas banks and their sponsors – the large universal banks, led by Deutsche Bank, the Disconto-Gesellschaft and Dresdner Bank – would become crucial for the promotion of the Mark.

The development of German trade finance and the international spread of the Mark proceeded through four distinct channels. *Kommanditgesellschaften* (limited partnerships)[71] and overseas branches[72] were gradually supplemented by specialist foreign and colonial banks, like the Deutsche Übersee-Bank and the Deutsch-Asiatische Bank. German overseas and colonial banks sprang up in South America, Africa and Asia from the mid-1880s, primarily to finance exports and imports, before extending their business to state loans, as well as railway and mining finance. The Hongkong & Shanghai Banking Corporation and the Comptoir d'Escompte served their founders as blueprints. Whereas several of these early ventures were liquidated after a few years, the second generation of German overseas banks – established between 1886 and 1906 – successfully claimed market share from their British and French counterparts.[73] Outside Europe, the number of German foreign and colonial banks rose from 4 in 1896 to 12 in 1914, with 106 branches.[74] Competition for international trade finance was dominated by the long-established British foreign and colonial banks, of which there were 50 in 1904.[75] Their core business consisted of acceptance credit, arbitrage and advances at rates that were consistently

---

69   Theodore S. Hamerow, *Restoration, revolution, reaction: economics and politics in Germany, 1815–1871* (Princeton, NJ, 1958), p. 254.

70   Quoting Wallich, in Pohl, 'Deutsche Bank's early days', p. 383; Pohl and Burk, *Deutsche Bank*, p. 7.

71   The earliest *Kommanditen* in London were set up by Deutsche Bank in 1871 (German Bank of London Ltd), and the Commerz- und Disconto-Bank in 1873 (London & Hanseatic Bank Ltd).

72   Deutsche Bank established its London agency in 1873, while Dresdner Bank and the Disconto-Gesellschaft opened branches in the City in 1895 and 1899.

73   Herbert Feis, *Europe: the world's banker 1870–1914* (New York, 1964), p. 66.

74   Jacob Riesser, *The German great banks and their concentration in connection with the economic development of Germany*, 3rd edn (Washington, DC, 1911), pp. 459–60; Karl Strasser, *Die Deutschen Banken im Ausland* (Munich, 1925), p. 181.

75   France and the Netherlands likewise developed extensive overseas banking networks; Riesser records 16 Dutch and 18 French overseas and colonial banks for 1904/5. See Riesser, *German great banks*, p. 460.

Figure 7.1. Open market discount rates in London and Berlin, 1876–1913 (annual averages in per cent, not seasonally adjusted).

Sources: Open market rates of discount in London (NBER Macro History Database, Series m13016) and Private discount rate on prime banker's acceptances in the open market, Berlin (NBER Series m13018), retrieved from FRED, Federal Reserve Bank of St. Louis Economic Data.

cheaper than those offered by German banks. Between 1876 and 1913, Berlin's private discount rate was on average 0.5% higher per annum than open market rates in London (Figure 7.1). So long as sterling bills remained cheaper and more liquid financial instruments, local merchants were hard pressed to accept bills denominated in Mark. With a view to loosening the hold of British intermediaries, German banks offered longer terms of credit by replacing the usual 3-month acceptances with 4- and 8-month bills.[76] Syndicates of German banks also acquired shareholdings and controlling stakes in European and international banks, such as the Banca Commerciale Italiana (formed in 1894) and the Banque Internationale de Bruxelles (1898). Their establishment was chiefly motivated by the desire to open up new markets for German goods and gain financial footholds in the Mediterranean, the Ottoman Empire and the Balkans.

Not uncommonly in this period, the German government and the Ministry of Foreign Affairs gave express support and encouragement for overseas banking projects and foreign state loans.[77] For the German Chancellery, the Mark's standing on foreign exchanges was as much a geopolitical as a purely economic issue. Bismarck's bid for colonial possessions in the mid-1880s and the outspoken imperialist tendencies of Wilhelm II increasingly aligned the

76   Strasser, *Banken im Ausland*, p. 22; Philip Barrett Whale, *Joint-stock banking in Germany: a study of the German credit banks before and after the war* (London, 1930), p. 87.
77   Feis, *World's banker*, pp. 73, 160–88; Strasser, *Banken im Ausland*, pp. 28–9.

spread of the Mark with the Reich's expansion of its spheres of influence.[78] In 1884, the German Chancellery sounded out sponsors for a *Reichsüberseebank*, a government-backed institution to finance German exports and imports, and in 1904/5 it considered the desirability of a *Reichsbank* for its colonies.[79] While both proposals failed to get off the ground, financial intermediation remained a key to German *Weltpolitik*, as conveyed by Georg von Siemens, managing director of Deutsche Bank (1870–1900):

> Every bank or railway ... that is established in foreign lands is at the same time a pioneer for the activities of [German] industry and for the formation of permanent relationships between the two economic areas. Such connections account for a great deal of English influence outside Europe, [and] of French influence in Spain, Portugal, Italy and the Orient.[80]

If the German Reich intended to capture overseas markets, it was paramount that the Mark commanded not only domestic legitimacy but also external confidence among foreign investors. Within the Chancellery, Delbrück repeatedly voiced concerns about the link between the Mark's credibility and the Reich's commitment to a fully convertible gold standard. Germany's adherence to gold, he thought, remained in doubt as long as Prussian silver Thaler pieces circulated alongside the gold Mark. Shortly before his resignation in 1876, he testified to the Bundesrat's Committee on Trade, Transport and National Accounts:

> So long as the holders of acceptances on German places cannot be sure that they receive, under all circumstances, payment in gold coins as the internationally [recognized] payment medium in Germany, then the German currency cannot enjoy the full trust at home and abroad, which constitute[d] one of the primary purposes of the currency laws.[81]

When Bismarck ordered a stop to Germany's silver sales in May 1879, the Mark's reputation on foreign exchanges suffered a severe blow. The sudden cessation of the Reichsbank's silver sales raised doubts over the government's adherence to its gold standard and to currency convertibility.[82] Bimetallism and protectionist tariffs had gained vocal proponents among Bismarck's conservative supporters since the economic recession of the mid-1870s. In the Reichstag,

---

78 Buchheim, 'Finanzmetropole', p. 117.
79 Strasser, *Banken im Ausland*, p. 2.
80 Quoted in Richard Rosendorff, 'Die deutschen Überseebanken und ihre Geschäfte', *Blätter für vergleichende Staatswissenschaft und Volkswirtschaftslehre* 3 (1908), pp. 242–3.
81 Rudolph von Delbrück to the Bundesrat's Committee on Trade, Transport and National Accounts, 27 Nov. 1875, GStA PK, I. HA Rep. 120 Ministerium für Handel und Gewerbe, AX, Nr. 27 Bd. 6, fols 57–8.
82 *Stenographische Berichte*, 19 Jun. 1879, pp. 1710–11.

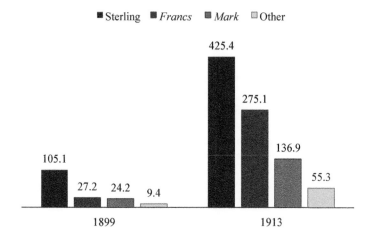

Figure 7.2. Foreign currency reserve holdings in official institutions, 1899 and 1913 (end of year, in millions of dollars).

Source: Peter H. Lindert, *Key currencies and gold 1900–1913* (Princeton, NJ, 1969), p. 22.

Bismarck justified the decision to suspend the sale of silver on account of the price fall of the metal on world markets and the resulting loss of profit to the Imperial Chancellery.[83] Even so, the timing of the announcement – during the parliamentary debate on the imposition of rye and iron tariffs – fuelled distrust in the financial markets. Speculative rumours that the Reichsbank prepared to exchange its bank notes against silver triggered a short-term flight from the Mark among European banks. The whole episode cast a shadow over Germany's promotion of its gold currency as a credible alternative to sterling.[84] It would take another two decades to rebuild and consolidate external trust in the Mark.

By the eve of the First World War, the German Mark had established itself as the world's third major reserve currency after sterling and the franc (Figure 7.2). Its pre-war use in international trade finance, however, was geographically limited to parts of South America, the US, Scandinavia, Italy, Romania and Austria-Hungary.[85] The British Empire continued to be impenetrable for Mark acceptances, and in the Mediterranean and across North Africa francs

83 Ibid., p. 1712; see also Steven P. Reti, *Silver and gold: the political economy of international monetary conferences, 1867–1892* (Westport, CT, 1998), p. 103.

84 See *Geschäftsbericht der Direction der Deutschen Bank* (1884), p. 3.

85 Cassis, *Capitals of capital*, p. 113; Tilly, 'German banking', p. 109; Richard Rosendorff, 'Die deutschen Banken im überseeischen Verkehr', *Jahrbuch für Gesetzgebung, Verwaltung und Volkswirtschaft im Deutschen Reich* 28 (1904), p. 102.

credits still predominated.[86] As a US Department of Commerce report from 1913 confirms:

> [O]wing to London's eminent position in the world market and the preference of over-sea customers, the sterling currency [continues to be] almost universally used by German exporters in their dealings with Australia, South Africa, China, Japan, and the British and Portuguese colonies in Africa. The mark is used to a larger extent than … sterling in German dealings with South American countries. It is almost exclusively used in transactions with the exporters' own branches oversea[s]. In dealings with Egypt, Morocco, and Asia Minor the German exporters employ the French currency.[87]

While Germany was the third-largest capital exporter in 1914, its financial reliance on the City of London had not diminished – in fact, the opposite was true.[88] When demand for trade credit expanded during Germany's industrial 'take-off', the proportion of German business handled by London banks only increased further in absolute terms.[89] German joint-stock banks nevertheless prospered by taking a sizable stake in the British market for sterling bills. Deutsche Bank's and the Disconto-Gesellschaft's combined issue of sterling acceptances was estimated at over £4 million in 1900 and £10.5 million in 1912.[90] Whereas German banks secured profitable footholds in the City, the high hopes for Berlin as an international financial centre failed to materialize. Neither Berlin nor Frankfurt matched the pre-war depth, liquidity and international orientation of the London money and discount market. Berlin's pre-war reputation as a financial centre continued to be built largely on domestic securities and industrial finance.[91]

From the German Empire's inception, the gold Mark proved a potent symbol of national unity and of the country's ambition to position itself as a global trading power. The liberal agenda of Germany's currency reformers had converged with a nationalist drive for modernization that sought to establish the Mark as a strong medium of international credit. Not only did a gold-convertible currency complement the agenda of cosmopolitan free traders; it also appealed to those harbouring patriotic ambitions to challenge Britain's leadership in

---

86 Simon, *Hamburger Überseehandel*, pp. 60–1, 73–4.

87 Archibald J. Wolfe, *Foreign credits*, US Department of Commerce, Special Agent Series, No. 62 (Washington DC, 1913), p. 24.

88 Tilly, 'German banking', p. 108. In 1913, British capital exports totalled £3.5 to £4 billion, compared to £1.8 billion for France and £1.1 billion for Germany. See Youssef Cassis, 'Financial elites in three European centres: London, Paris, Berlin, 1880s–1930s', *Business History* 33 (1991), p. 54.

89 Cassis, *Capitals of capital*, p. 113; Tilly, 'German banking', pp. 108–9.

90 Müller-Jabusch, *Urbig*, p. 83; see also 'Entwicklung des Akzepts der Deutschen Bank', HADB, SG3/19b/1, Historical Institute of Deutsche Bank.

91 Ranald Michie, *The global securities market* (Oxford, 2008), pp. 147–8.

global commerce and finance. This dual nature of the gold standard – as both a national and an internationalist construct – held a particular appeal for German policymakers and business leaders. Between 1871 and 1914, Germany's overseas banking network and its steep export growth succeeded in consolidating the Mark's status as a key trade and reserve currency.[92] Beyond Europe, however, sterling's predominance in trade finance remained unchallenged, as the Mark's trajectory fell short of Germany's industrial 'catch-up' with Britain before the First World War.

---

92   Tilly, 'German banking', p. 109.

8

Knowledge, contestation and authority in the Eurodollar market, 1959–64

SEUNG WOO KIM

In *Worlds of political economy*, Martin Daunton (with Frank Trentmann) proposes a new political economy to explore 'the large and often neglected universe of economic knowledge and practices, and the way the two have shaped each other'.[1] This approach 'supports the political repositioning of economic subjects' and moves beyond 'the political and institutional settings of economic life' to analyse the economic knowledge deeply embedded in milieus, its contested nature, form of authority, and transnational dynamics.[2] In this way Daunton reappraises political economy 'as a system of ideas, value, meanings'.[3]

This chapter explores the Eurodollar market, an offshore market in US dollars, from the perspective of this new political economy. Historians and international political economists regard the nascent international money market as emblematic of the re-emergence of global finance that evaded controls on capital mobility after the return to convertibility of Western currencies in December 1958, the 'real post-war turning point for the foreign exchange market'.[4] Schenk highlights the role of innovative bankers in the City of London in the mid-1950s in inventing Eurodollars. These bankers offered higher interest rates on foreign dollars in London than American banks handicapped by the Federal Reserve's Regulation Q – the limit on the interest payable on domestic deposits.[5] Others, notably Burn, stress 'the historic specificity of

1 Frank Trentmann and M.J. Daunton, 'Worlds of political economy: knowledge, practices and contestation', in M.J. Daunton and Frank Trentmann, eds, *Worlds of political economy: knowledge and power in the nineteenth and twentieth centuries* (Basingstoke, 2004), pp. 1–23.
2 Ibid., p. 2.
3 Ibid., p. 9.
4 William M. Clarke, *The City in the world economy* (Harmondsworth, 1965), p. 75.
5 Catherine R. Schenk, 'The origins of the Eurodollar market in London: 1955–1963', *Explorations in Economic History* 35, 2 (1998), pp. 221–38. Regulation Q was introduced as a

the British state' in which the Bank of England ('the Bank') and financial elites embraced the Eurodollar market to promote the interests of financial capital by promoting the City of London's standing as an international financial centre.[6]

Beyond the institutional and political approach, this chapter examines the production of knowledge in and about the Eurodollar market in its formative years by concerned practitioners as well as various observers, monetary authorities, and international organisations. In the absence of a centralised institution for collecting information on Eurodollar business they proposed various explanations for its operations and prospects. Their opinions evolved into contestations over the present and future of the nascent market. Each discourse had its own unspoken practices, norms, and visions for the Eurodollar. Thus, the challenges not only highlight divergent understandings of the market, they were part of the market-making process itself.

This chapter shows how the Bank exerted authority over the contestations on the Eurodollar market on two levels. First, it set the regulatory framework of the City of London. Observers were sceptical about the market from the moment it was 'discovered' by financial journalists in 1959. Relaxation of Regulation Q in 1962 generated pessimism about the future of the market. Also some market participants called for the imposition of regulations, fearing the 'speculative' nature and inherent dangers – as they saw it – of the Eurodollar. The Bank, as City regulator, repeatedly affirmed its support of the new business because it believed it would revive the City of London as the international financial centre.

Second, the Bank extended its authority to the Bank for International Settlements (BIS), a forum for the central bankers from major industrial countries. The growth of the Eurodollar market challenged the Bretton Woods consensus on capital mobility, or 'hot money', as Eurodollar flows increasingly constrained autonomous domestic monetary policy, especially after the widespread return to convertibility in December 1958. When central bankers understood the dangers posed by these capital flows, the Bank thwarted the production of uniform statistics on the Eurodollar market that might have provided a foundation for regulations. The success was highlighted in 1964, when central bankers recognised the market's usefulness, despite two defaults of Eurodollar borrowers in the late 1963, which seemed to have substantiated the suggested risk by pessimistic critics. In this way, the legitimisation of the Eurodollar market embodied the shift in cultural assumptions on short-term capital movements, and paved the way for the globalisation of finance in the late twentieth century.

---

result of the Banking Act of 1933. The Federal Reserve Board, on 29 Aug. 1933, imposed interest rate ceilings on various types of bank deposits to restrict excessive competition among banks for deposit funds.

6   Gary Burn, *The re-emergence of global finance* (Basingstoke, 2006), p. 227.

I

Financial journalist Paul Einzig brought the Eurodollar market to wider attention with his July 1959 *Economist* article 'Dollar Deposits in London'.[7] Einzig reported that London banking houses were converting dollars into sterling (to lend to local authorities) and borrowing and re-lending dollars. An 'unexampled network of correspondent banks and agencies' had developed and in the absence of a lender of last resort they were running the risk of a sudden withdrawal of funds.[8] Subsequently, journalists writing about the City of London struggled against 'a remarkable conspiracy of silence' on the part of practitioners in a market 'likely to appear clouded in an aura of mystery'.[9] As Poovey suggests in her analysis of disclosure and secrecy in the culture of investment, it was characteristic of bankers to protect their secrets for fear that publicity would attract rivals, press criticism, and 'unhelpful' responses from the authorities.[10]

Financial journalists relied on personal contacts in the City for knowledge of the Eurodollar market. The relationship was reciprocal, with bankers also using information from the media. For example, in 1962, an American banker sent a letter to Einzig with his remarks on the journalist's book on foreign exchange.[11] Many bank review articles in this period also cited writings by Einzig to introduce the Eurodollar market. In the absence of a clearing house or centralised exchange for Eurodollar business, the monetary authorities also relied on contacts with practitioners and the media for market information. In the absence of reliable information, contemporary periodicals presented diverse accounts of the new market to their different audiences. In this way financial journalists were able to exert a measure of authority.

From 1960 articles on the Eurodollar consistently (re)produced contemporary discourses. Most linked the new market to the future of the City. William M. Clarke introduced the new market with the term 'Eurodollar' to *Times* readers, explaining that London bankers' 'traditional skill, experience, and agility' had enabled them to exploit Regulation Q to build up a profitable business with short-term dollars.[12] He saw the increasing presence of foreign, particularly

7   'Dollar deposits in London', *The Economist*, 11 Jul. 1959.

8   Ibid.

9   Paul Einzig, *Foreign dollar loans in Europe* (London, 1965), p. vi; Letter from G.W. Parkinson to Paul Einzig (17 Feb. 1964), CAC ENZG 1/23. Papers of Paul Einzig.

10   Mary Poovey, 'Writing about finance in Victorian England: disclosure and secrecy in the culture of investment', in Hancy Henry and Cannon Schmitt, eds, *Victorian investments* (Bloomington, 2009), pp. 39–57.

11   Letter from Herbert J. Rosenstern [Assistant Vice President of the Philadelphia National Bank], 30 Mar. 1962, CAC ENZG 1/21, Papers of Paul Einzig.

12   'London – centre of the Euro-dollar market', *The Times*, 24 Oct. 1960; David Kynaston, *The City of London*, vol. 4: *A club no more, 1945–2000* (London, 2003), p. 269.

American, banks' branches and subsidiaries in the Eurodollar market contributing to London as a 'leader in the foreign exchange market of the world'.[13] This vision of the internationalisation of London banking was one response to left-wing critics who blamed the Square Mile's failure to channel capital into domestic industries, and criticised the burden of the Sterling Area on the British economy. It was contended that the use of sterling in member countries of scheduled territories, which in return demanded the UK's mandate to maintain the pound sterling as an international reserve currency, 'starved British industry of capital by allowing free movement of funds to the Commonwealth'.[14] The new business would create additional 'invisible earnings', a statistical indicator of the economic contribution made by the financial industry. By shaping the early discourse, financial journalists strategically appropriated the emergence of the Eurodollar market in the future of the financial district.

Interest in the Eurodollar market went beyond the City of London. In 1960, the New York Clearing House Association argued that Eurodollars were a 'straitjacket of Regulation Q'.[15] They claimed the cap on deposit rates undermined the American free market system and the status of New York as an international financial centre by diverting business to Canadian and European banks.[16] Continental Europeans were also involved in these discussions. In April 1961 *Banque* introduced the Eurodollar market to French readers, explaining that it put pressure on US dollar acceptance business in Paris.[17] This article anticipated that the Eurodollar market might facilitate a 'financial European community' alternative to the Treaty of Rome.[18]

In June 1960 the Federal Reserve Bank of New York (FRBNY) despatched a team to Europe investigate the Eurodollar market.[19] Recognised as the 'first authoritative investigation', this study provided a comprehensive account of dollar deposits in Europe, already in excess of $1 billion, as well as their geographical reach into the Communist Bloc, the Middle East, and South Asia (although it did not enumerate the size of London's market).[20] It explained the burgeoning business in Europe as the corollary of the relative decline of New

---

13   Kynaston, *City of London*, p. 269; 'Japan bids high for dollars', *The Times*, 8 Aug. 1960; 'Transatlantic ties with the City', *The Times*, 24 Oct. 1960.
14   Jim Tomlinson, 'Labour party and the City 1945–1970', in Ranald Michie and Philip Williamson, eds, *The British government and the City of London in the twentieth century* (Cambridge, 2004), pp. 174–92, p. 184. See also Andrew Shonfield, *British economic policy since the war* (Harmondsworth, 1958).
15   *A study of Regulation Q as it applies to foreign time deposits* (New York, 1960), p. 12.
16   Ibid.
17   Paul Turot, 'Le marché des capitaux à court terme en Europe et l'Euro-dollar', *Banque* 178 (1961), pp. 215–18.
18   Ibid., p. 218.
19   'Euro-dollar team move on', *The Times*, 16 Jun. 1960.
20   Alan R. Holmes and Fred H. Klopstock, 'The market for dollar deposits in Europe', *Federal Reserve Bank of New York Monthly Review* 42, 11 (1960), pp. 197–202.

York as an international lending centre, but argued that the market enhanced the status of the dollar as an international currency.

International organisations were also focusing on the new markets. In 1961 the BIS discussed Eurodollars in its 1961 annual report, and the International Monetary Fund (IMF) published a series of articles in its *Staff Papers*.[21] The IMF reported that large dollar holdings by US residents and foreigners made the market increasingly independent of the US balance of payments. It also observed that the Eurodollar market was becoming an important determinant of interest rates, creating arbitrage opportunities between different countries' domestic financial markets.

Commercial bank reviews were another important platform for practitioners for whom disclosure to targeted audiences could be as important as secrecy. These periodicals functioned as 'mouthpieces' for banks to publicise their views on financial issues in the 1960s.[22] The December 1961 issue of the *Morgan Guaranty Survey* addressed the anxiety of the US clearing houses, predicting the active participation of American banks 'in what may some day be called Americo-currencies'.[23]

These publications show how various actors in the international financial community interpreted the Eurodollar market. Depending on the publication, its target audience, and the interests of the authors and organisations including monetary authorities and international organisations, they provide discursive representations of the market. These discourses provided a platform for debates regarding the future of the Eurodollar market, including the regulatory framework.

II

The Bank relied on the leading London banks, as well as the financial press, for information on Eurodollar markets. The relationship was reciprocal, with the banks able to influence the regulation of Eurodollars as they shared their opinions with the central bank. The Bank's concerns about the market, especially after convertibility in 1958, were conditioned by its experience of the 1930s when short-term flows of internationally mobile funds added to turmoil in the international monetary system. In April 1961 the Bank undertook a

21   Bank for International Settlements, *Thirty-first annual report: 1st April – 31st March 1961* (Basle, 1961), pp. 137–8; for example, Oscar L. Altman, 'Foreign markets for dollars, sterling and other currencies', *IMF Staff Papers*, Dec. 1961, pp. 313–52.

22   Richard Roberts, 'A special place in contemporary economic literature: the rise and fall of the British bank reviews, 1914–1993', *Financial History Review* 2, 1 (1995), pp. 41–60.

23   Morgan Guaranty Trust Company, 'The Euro-Dollar market: dollars that go abroad – but not really', *Morgan Guaranty Survey*, Dec. 1961, pp. 4–6.

major investigation of the Eurodollar market. While precise measurement was difficult because of cross-trading and double counting, the size of the market was estimated in excess of £5 billion at the end of 1960.[24] For the Bank the substantive questions were the Eurodollar market's usefulness and the dangers posed to the domestic economy. While the former appeared self-evident, the latter was difficult to assess, because it could only be verified under 'the extraordinary circumstances such as revolution, moratorium or war, such as the loss of currency deposits in Russian banks in 1917 and German banks in 1931'.[25] Nonetheless, the Bank considered that 'such dangers would be naturally restricted by banking prudence'.[26] Policy towards short-term dollars was consistent with the Bank's position on the City's standing as the international financial centre.[27] Meanwhile the UK Treasury assessed the Eurodollar market for its implication for the balance of payments from the conversion of Eurodollars in and out of sterling. In an internal memo to the Bank, the Treasury expressed the view that the Eurodollar market was weakly linked to US and UK international payments, but that New York and London benefited from the extensive use of dollars and sterling.[28] The Bank agreed.[29]

The Bank's position reflected a softening of its long-standing hostility – shared by monetary officials elsewhere – towards short-term capital movements. In April 1961 the Economic Policy Committee of the Organisation for Economic Co-operation and Development (OECD) agreed that short-term capital movements had become a permanent feature of the international payments system. Indeed, the committee encouraged cross-border flows by introducing convertibility on current accounts. As the Belgian Cecil de Strycker explained, 'short-term capital movements must not be condemned *a priori*'.[30] His confidence rested on recent examples of central banking co-operation such as reciprocal swap arrangements, which had proved effective in neutralising hot money flows.[31] Memories of the 1930s appeared to be fading.

London banks were in the vanguard of Eurodollar business.[32] One of the principal names was the Bank of London and South America (BOLSA), a British overseas bank which was outside the banking cartel of British clearing

---

24 'The Euro-Dollar market', 20 Apr. 1961, BEA EID10/19.
25 Ibid.
26 Ibid.
27 'Hot money', 19 Oct. 1961, BEA EID10/19.
28 'Euro-dollars and Euro-sterling', 16 Jun. 1961, BEA EID10/21.
29 'Euro currencies', 21 Jul. 1961, ibid.
30 'Economic Policy Committee, record of the 6th meeting held on Tue. 18 and Wed. 19 Apr. 1961', OECD ECO/EPC:WP3(1990)01.
31 Ibid.
32 See Stefano Battilossi, 'Banking with multinationals: British clearing banks and the Euromarkets' challenge, 1958–1976', in Stefano Battilossi and Youssef Cassis, eds, *European banks and the American challenge* (Oxford, 2002), pp. 103–34.

banks and free of reserve requirement obligations.[33] Under the chairmanship of George Bolton, a former Bank of England deputy director with experience in the foreign exchange market, BOLSA had been one of the pioneers. Bolton believed that Eurodollars would replace sterling whose role as a reserve currency was 'doomed'.[34] Under his direction, BOLSA grew its Eurodollar business, particularly with Japan and the Communist bloc.[35] The chairman's close links to the Bank established BOLSA as a reliable institution in the eyes of the monetary authorities.[36]

By the end of 1961 the Eurodollar market appeared to be an accepted part of the City of London. Einzig wrote, 'there is every reason to believe that the new facilities have come to stay'.[37] Paul Bareau, editor of the *Statist*, saw the market as 'a most promising indication of the growing internationalisation of the money markets of the free world', and attributed the rigidity of banking practices in the US to the emergence of Eurodollars.[38] It was not long, however, before market participants began to question the Eurodollar market – even its very existence.

The emergence of a sizeable US balance of payments deficit, and its impact on the international payments position, had been a growing concern since 1958, prompting a bout of speculation against the dollar in the second half of 1960.[39] US officials blamed the interest rate differential between New York and Europe for capital outflows.[40] In January 1962 the Board of Governors of the Federal Reserve announced that American commercial banks would be permitted to offer higher interest rates on deposits of more than one-month duration, effectively loosening the constraints of Regulation Q.[41] London bankers began to speculate on the impact of the liberalisation of interest rates on the Eurodollar market, as Regulation Q was understood to be the key factor underpinning the Eurodollar market. In practice, the impact was small, with only a modest reduction in the outflow of American capital.[42] But

---

33 Ibid., p. 115; 'Currency deposits', 20 Mar. 1962, BEA EID10/21.
34 Geoffrey Jones, *British multinational banking, 1830–1990* (Oxford, 1993), p. 264.
35 'A meeting of the board', 23 Jan. 1962, LBGA F/2/D/Boa/1.11.
36 'Currency deposits', 9 Jul. 1962, BEA EID10/21.
37 Paul Einzig, 'Towards an international money market', *Statist*, 17 Nov. 1961.
38 Paul Bareau, 'Fifty years of international banking … Will London hold its place?', *Statist – International Banking Supplement*, 8 Dec. 1961.
39 'International payments position of the United States', 24 Jul. 1959, *Foreign relations of the United States, 1958–1960, Foreign economic policy, volume 4*, ed. Suzanne E. Coffman, Edward C. Keefer, and Harriet Dashiell Schwar (Washington DC, 1992); 'The economic situation and the balance of payments: a special report to President-Elect Kenney by Allan Sproul, Chairman, Roy Blough, and Paul W. McCracken, Jan. 18, 1961', in Robert V. Roosa, *The dollar and world liquidity* (New York, 1967), pp. 271–99.
40 Ibid., p. 282.
41 'Amendment to Regulation Q', *Federal Reserve Bulletin*, Jan. 1962, p. 7.
42 'Euro-dollar deposits an active market', *The Times*, 5 Feb. 1962.

the perceived effect of US interest rate policy galvanised debate regarding the Euromarket's future, even its *raison d'être*. In May 1962 Charles Hambro of Hambros Bank argued that the abandoning Regulation Q would weaken the new market, suggesting Eurodollars were 'likely to be a temporary phenomenon in the European economy'.[43] Against such claims, foreign exchange dealers in London argued that 'Regulation Q is now only a subsidiary reason for the market's continued existence and that the market is likely to flourish as long as the American payments deficit pumps dollars into foreign hands'.[44] Also, they could rely on the absence of any currency to challenge the position of the US dollar in the world economy.

European bankers were aware of the risks even as they added to their Eurodollar exposures. At a May 1962 meeting of the International Institute of Banking, one Swiss banker described Eurodollars as 'black' (i.e. hot) money that had escaped the control of US authorities, and said they were now under no one's control.[45] Hermann Abs of the Deutsche Bank blamed central bankers for assisting the growth of the market. He suggested that the high reserves on foreign deposits and the exchange rate guarantee from the central bank encouraged German banks to borrow abroad.[46] However, British, Belgian, and Italian bankers emphasised the utility of Eurodollars as a relatively cheap resource, and accused the US monetary authorities and banks of being 'the real causes of trouble'.[47]

In July 1962 the *Financial Times* suggested that opinions on the Eurodollar market turned on two issues.[48] On the supply side, there was uncertainty about the dollar and future US monetary policy that flowed from disequilibrium in the US balance of payments. On the demand side, there was 'the growing tendency for the monetary authorities' in countries of major borrowers of Eurodollars 'to impose restrictions on the freedom of their banking systems to drink at this financial well'.[49] In short, at this stage the Eurodollar market was inextricably linked to international monetary politics.

Monetary authorities shared the growing disquiet in the international banking community about Eurodollars, namely the impact of short-term capital movements on domestic monetary policy. In March 1962, during a conversation

---

43   Hambros Bank Limited, 'Britain cannot afford to stay out of the Common Market and they need us says Sir Charles Hambro', 22 May 1962, LMA 2007/015 ITEM 17/516 (temporary reference number).
44   'Euro-Dollar's future', *The Economist*, 26 May 1962.
45   'Note of discussions of Madrid – EURO-DOLLARS', 5 May 1962, BEA EID10/21.
46   Ibid. Under his directorship, Deutsche Bank had no debts or claims in Eurodollars until Nov. 1963. Lothar Gall, Gerald D. Feldman, Harold James, Carl-Ludwig Holtfrerich, and Hans E. Büschgen, *The Deutsche Bank, 1870–1995* (London, 1995), p. 625.
47   'Note of discussions of Madrid'.
48   'Lombard – the shadow over the Euro-dollar market', *Financial Times*, 6 Jul. 1962.
49   Ibid.

with the Bank of England, US Treasury Under-Secretary for Monetary Affairs Robert Roosa compared the 'dubious pyramiding of inter-related credits to the conditions that preceded the 1929 collapse'.[50] He considered a bill 'to check the growth of the Euro-dollar market by increasing the attractiveness of times deposits'.[51] In June 1962 Banca d'Italia Governor Guido Carli complained that the increased mobility of short-term money defeated measures to control internal liquidity and exacerbated balance of payments problems. Carli stressed the responsibility of central banks and commercial banks to maintain the monetary stability of the Western world and urged commercial banks to set limits on their Eurodollar business.[52] The Bank of Japan, which had initially welcomed domestic borrowing of Eurodollars, now admitted that such short-term capital movements tended to 'obstruct efforts to damp down economic activity as well as to leave the country vulnerable on external payments'.[53] The Japanese introduced new reserve requirements to discourage 'the use of foreign hot money for internal financing'.[54]

The Bank was more enthusiastic, spelling out the principal issues in a July 1962 memo.[55] On the changes in interest rates, one official commented, 'a rise in U.S. short-term money rates would make the Euro-dollar market even more attractive for the ultimate foreign user ... the Euro-dollar rate in London would rise, thereby nullifying the attraction of the higher rates in New York'.[56] In August 1962 the Bank reviewed the regulatory framework of the Eurodollar market, focusing on the risks to the domestic banking system and the UK reserves.[57] The Bank decided to collect information on the initial lenders and the ultimate borrowers of US dollars, and the maturity both of deposits and advances, while continuing to rely on 'moral suasion' to shape commercial bank decisions.

Nevertheless, some City bankers remained sceptical. In late 1962 Hambro repeated his fear of a sudden withdrawal in the event of a loss of confidence abroad. Within the Bank, J.B. Selwyn dismissed this criticism, asserting that there was 'nothing wrong' with the market.[58] In his reply to Hambro, Deputy Chief Cashier Roy Bridge explained the Bank's standpoint:

50 'Meeting in Room 4425, Treasury, Mar. 8, 1962', 23 Mar. 1962, FRBNYA 615845.
51 Ibid.
52 'A central banker's hot money worries', *Statist*, 15 Jun. 1962.
53 'Japan and the hot money', *Statist*, 22 Jun. 1962.
54 Ibid.
55 'Euro-Dollars', 24 May 1962, BEA EID10/15.
56 'Your note on Euro-dollars of 24th May', 25 May 1962, BEA EID10/15.
57 Catherine Schenk, *The decline of sterling* (Cambridge, 2010), p. 229; 'Currency deposits'; J.S. Fforde, 'Currency deposits', 12 Jul. 1962, BEA EID10/21.
58 'Eurodollars: Sir Charles Hambro's discussion with the Deputy Governor', 10 Dec. 1962, BEA C48/28.

we have not however thought that the existence of such risks provided any reason for our seeking to restrict the development of this market. We have rather felt that we ought to be able to rely on the judgment of London banks to conduct their operations in accordance with sound banking principles.[59]

Bridge defended the Bank's belief in sound operations in the Eurodollar market – prudent lending, suitable geographical distribution of deposits, the maintenance of adequate liquidity, and a reasonable spread of maturity dates.[60]

The Bank's reply – the first official policy statement to one of the principal banks – explicitly endorsed the Eurodollar market. The Bank explained that it did not wish to lose the market since 'to drive the business from London would be wrong as it would continue in other places and the reputation of London as a monetary centre would suffer in the process'.[61] As the *Economist* noted in May 1963, the London financial community believed that the Eurodollar market was 'here to stay'.[62] The decision enhanced the standing of London in international finance for other centres suffered restrictions by monetary authorities.

The transnational nature of the Eurodollar business constrained the ability of national monetary officials to frame regulation. This required an institution where central bankers could discuss policy responses. The Bank for International Settlements had since 1930 provided a locus for central bankers to share their experiences and normative ideas on international finance. In May 1961 it shed light on the Eurodollar market in a paper, delivered to member central banks' governors, about short-term capital movements. At a meeting a month earlier Charles Coombs of the Federal Reserve drew attention to the threat to monetary stability posed by Eurodollars to which the BIS was sympathetic.[63] The following year an economic adviser to the BIS, Milton Gilbert, approached member central banks and the US Federal Reserve with the 'design of a possible BIS survey on the Euro-dollar market'.[64] However, as Klopstock of the FRBNY noted, a balanced and careful approach was necessary to reconcile the two goals of obtaining meaningful data for analytical purposes and avoiding placing an undue burden on participating banks. At the same time it was imperative to eliminate 'the large amounts of duplications arising from the pyramiding of deposits'.[65] He suggested 'a uniform and logical coding system'.[66]

---

59   'Euro-Dollars', 22 Jan. 1963, BEA C48/28.
60   Ibid.
61   Ibid.
62   'All about Euro-dollars', *The Economist*, 25 May 1963.
63   Kynaston, *The City*, p. 269; Gianni Toniolo, *Central bank cooperation at the Bank for International Settlements, 1930–1973* (Cambridge, 2005), p. 458. The US central bank was not a formal member of the BIS, but was invited to attend meetings.
64   Letter from Fred H. Klopstock to Milton Gilbert, 28 May 1962, BISA 1.3a(3).
65   Ibid.
66   Ibid.

In June 1962 BIS officials requested a meeting and the collection of statistical information to arrive at 'a clear view of [the] size and workings of the Eurodollar market.[67] Meanwhile Working Party No. 3 of the OECD's Economic Committee was proposing a similar inquiry.[68] In London, the Bank wished to avoid simultaneous discussions on what was 'essentially a banking matter'.[69] Nor did the British want 'the staff of the O.E.C.D. and the B.I.S. asking regularly for either the same or slightly different statistical information'.[70] At this stage the BIS prioritised statistics over policy discussions, expressing its dissatisfaction with existing data on the size of the market.[71] Officials hoped that newly compiled statistics would function as a reference for further discussions on policy measures. Ahead of the October 1962 meeting Gilbert circulated an agenda for discussion of the nature, supply and use of Eurodollars, actual and potential problems, and possible future work.[72] Internally, the Bank concluded that, while collecting information was desirable, it would 'be very reluctant to call for details of maturities for fear of giving the impression that it was thought that some banks were not acting according to prudent banking practice'.[73] Its priority was the City of London. By deliberately avoiding the completion of statistics which would provide a basis for further discussions on international regulations at the BIS, the Bank of England sponsored the Eurodollar market.

The BIS convened five meetings on 6–8 October 1962.[74] The discussions focused on two areas: statistics on the Eurodollar market and a general exchange of views.[75] Each country provided statistics on Eurodollar flows in its domestic money market, but each applied a different category to represent the object. For example, Germany identified exchange positions according to currency and country, while Switzerland collected figures for each foreign currency. The Bank categorised data by types of bank in current and deposit accounts and loans to local authorities. The US complained that these figures 'had made nonsense of U.S. statistics', and that they could not yield reliable information on dollar foreign holdings by country or by ownership.[76] It rendered any assessment of the current status of the Eurodollar market impossible. To pool information in

67   'Proposal for a meeting of Central-Bank officials at the B.I.S. to discuss the Eurodollar market' (14 Jun. 1962), BISA 1.3(a)3.

68   'Dr. Holtrop's proposal for a meeting at the B.I.S. in October on Euro-Dollars', 3 Jul. 1962, BEA EID10/21.

69   Ibid.

70   Ibid.

71   Letter from Dealtry to M. Gilbert, 19 Sep. 1962, BISA 1.2(a)3.

72   'Suggested question for discussion' undated, BISA 1.3(a)3.

73   'Meeting on the Euro-Dollar market in Basle Milton Gilbert's questionnaire', 1 Oct. 1962, BEA EID10/21.

74   Delegates from nine central banks attended the meeting: Belgium, UK, France, Germany, Italy, Netherlands, Sweden, Switzerland, and the US.

75   'Euro-Dollar: Basle – 6th/9th October', 11 Oct. 1962, BEA EID10/21.

76   'Euro-Dollars Basle – 6th/9th October', 22 Oct. 1962, ibid.

unified form, the French proposed strict reciprocal exchanges between central banks. However, as noted above, the British central bank already limited the level of its international co-operation.

The BIS recommended that members should make 'a concerted effort to improve statistical data on the Euro-dollar market by a mutual and reciprocal exchange of information through the B.I.S.'.[77] Officials agreed that the BIS would provide a snapshot of the Eurodollar market with a dummy table, which would record the holding of Eurodollars in individual countries but without information on geography or maturity. Nonetheless, the meetings confirmed that the central bankers held different positions. They failed to reach a consensus on a definition of Eurodollars. Even the compilation of data suffered practical difficulties and resistance from individual central banks, particularly the institution best placed to collect information – the Bank. In December 1962 BIS officials visited London.[78] Gilbert wanted the Bank to divide its data between non-resident banks and other non-residents, something that proved impossible since, as the Bank's Thompson-McCausland warned, the figures varied according to the purpose of gathering it.[79] While Selwyn questioned the accuracy of data received from several banks, the Bank was itself unwilling even to grant the BIS permission to use the statistics published in the June 1964 issue of the *Bank of England Quarterly Bulletin*.

In contrast with the Bank's uncooperative approach, the BIS regularly obtained information from other central banks. In June 1964, in its 34th annual report, it published tables and charts on the Eurocurrency market.[80] However, despite a warm reception in the London press, these statistics provided no more than estimates.[81] The problem of eliminating duplication from the pyramiding of deposits and identification of the end users that would leverage discussions for a regulatory framework was left unresolved. Instead, a series of events in 1963 triggered a comprehensive re-examination of the Eurodollar market at the central bankers' club.

The trouble came first from Germany, not the City of London, with the failure of the industrial firm Hugo Stinnes in the autumn of 1963. The firm had financed short-term credits from the Hugo Stinnes Bank, which was active in the Eurodollar market. When it got into difficulties, a withdrawal of funds

77   'Euro-Dollars meeting of central bank officials on the Euro-Dollar market summary of discussion', 7 Nov. 1962, ibid.
78   'Euro Dollars', 6 Dec. 1962, ibid.
79   Letter from L.P. Thompson-McCausland to Milton Gilbert, 21 Feb. 1963, BISA 1.3(a)3.
80   It conducted the survey for its own purpose because 'to know what London is doing would be a great advance on the present position'. L.P. Thompson-McCausland, 'Euro-Dollars', 2 Dec. 1963, BEA EID10/22; Bank for International Settlements, *Thirty-fourth annual report: 1st April–31st March 1961* (Basle, 1961), pp. 127–41.
81   'Lombard – lights on the vital statistics on the Euro-Dollar traffic', *Financial Times*, 17 Jun. 1964; Paul Bareau, 'The Euro-currency market', *Statist*, 19 Jun. 1964.

embarrassed German bankers and other firms which had been heavily reliant on Eurodollars.[82] In a private talk with the German Secretary of State, Herman Abs again expressed his misgivings about the Eurodollar market.[83] He was angry that about $400 million Eurodollars had been used for long-term investment, and demanded that the central banks carefully monitor the incident and adopt a firm position on it. Bank Director Maurice Parsons believed the issue was one of 'under-capitalisation of Germany industry, not the Euro-currency market'.[84] The problem, according to Parsons, was the interest rate differentials, not the Eurodollar market itself, because 'euro-dollars are not inherently evil'.[85]

The Stinnes bankruptcy was swiftly followed by another fraud, one that originated in New York and spread to the London market. In November 1963 the commodity dealer Allied Crude Vegetable Oil and Refining Company suspended payments. When its collateral turned out to be nil, the New York Stock Exchange suspended two New York banks one of which, Ira Haupt and Co., had significant Eurodollar exposure. This transmitted the crisis to London, when Brandt, a British merchant banking firm, was 'getting into difficulties'.[86]

These incidents, which seemed to confirm Abs's fears, did little to alter the Bank's attitude. At first, of course, the memory of 1931 loomed large, a point raised by L.T.G. Preston, Principal of the Dealing and Accounts Office in the Bank. His interpretation of recent events was 'too much speculation, a tendency to inflation everywhere and what seems to be an increasing lack of integrity'.[87] Bridge found Preston's note disquieting, for he had regarded the Ira Haupt bankruptcy as no more than 'an amber light [that] caused a number of banks here and elsewhere to review the way they were doing their business'.[88] Regarding Allied Crude, the Bank viewed that 'this trouble had arisen quite apart from the use or misuse of Euro/dollar facilities'.[89] The problem of the soundness of the end-borrowers, the general explanation for the cases in Germany and the US, was 'essentially a matter for the banker's own judgment'.[90] The Bank maintained its 'green light' for the Eurodollar market. Other central banks were more alarmed. At the December 1963 BIS governors' meeting attendees offered various thoughts on the implication for

---

82   Herman Nickel and Robert Sheehan, 'Germany's financial coronaries', *Fortune* (Jun. 1964), pp. 130–1, 48, 52, 54–5.
83   Letter from J.F.J. Jardine to S. Littler, 20 Nov. 1963, BEA EID10/22.
84   Letter from D.F. Stone to S. Litter, 6 Dec. 1963, ibid.
85   'Germany: Euro-Dollars', 25 Nov. 1963, ibid.
86   'Euro-Dollar Market', 2 Dec. 1963, TNA T 295/239. The following London banks had extended loans to the Ira Haupt: Kleinworts $1,500,000, Ansbachers $500,000, Brandts $3,000,000, Japhets $500,000. 'Note for Record', 25 Nov. 1963, BEA C20/5.
87   Memo to Bridge from Preston, 4 Dec. 1963, BEA EID10/22.
88   Memo by Bridge, 5 Dec. 1963, ibid.
89   'Ira Haupt and the Euro/Dollar market', 5 Dec. 1963, TNA T 295/239.
90   Untitled document, 6 Dec. 1963, ibid.

the Eurodollar market, but refrained from making a final judgement.[91] The Bundesbank's Karl Blessing blamed the absence of re-discount facilities, while the French referred to their own plans to restrict Eurodollar loans.[92] The Banca d'Italia's Paolo Baffi warned against curtailing the integrated money market because the two incidents represented only a small part of the whole. His more positive assessment came from the expediency of the Eurodollar market in financing Italy's balance of payments deficit and alleviating the liquidity squeeze of 1962–63.[93] The Bank's J.M. Stevens also rejected the 'condemnation of the Eurodollar market'.[94] At the Basle Group of Experts meeting the following day, Bridge told the US delegate that the recent 'tight' market was simply 'a natural feature in face of end-year window dressing'.[95] He added 'if underlying danger there were, it might lie in the direction of development of a lack of business confidence rather than doubts as to the monetary system'.[96] The Bank resisted any suggestion that credit information obtained through the BIS be centralised.[97]

At the January 1964 BIS meeting Governor Cromer reported that while losses had been incurred in New York, no serious difficulty had arisen so far, and that the banks were performing soundly.[98] President of the FRBNY Alfred Hayes hinted at possible cautionary action 'if contradiction of Euro-dollar credit became desirable'.[99] At this point, however, Blessing sided with Cromer. He disagreed with some observers' comparisons between the present situation in the Eurodollar market and what had happened in the early 1930s.[100] Furthermore, the governor noted that the Bank was not worried about German commercial banks participating in the Eurodollar market. Gabriel Ferras, General Manager of the BIS, concluded 'the general view seemed to be that there might be problems in connection with the Eurodollar market but they were not essentially different from the problems that existed in relation to international short-term capital movements in general'.[101] The market was neither speculative nor a by-product of US regulations, but a normal part of the international financial market, with increased capital mobility since the return to convertibility. By the end of the meeting, the central bankers had agreed that the market followed a logic of its own, just like the other financial markets.

91   Ibid.
92   Letter from Julien Koszul to Milton Gilbert, 19 Dec. 1963, BISA 1.3(a)3.
93   Toniolo, *Central bank cooperation*, p. 460.
94   Ibid.
95   'Extract from a note for record by R.A.O. Bridge of 11.12.63', 11 Dec. 1963, BEA EID10/22.
96   Ibid.
97   Letter to Cromer from Preston, 7 Jan. 1964, ibid.
98   Letter from G. Ferras to Masamichi Yamagiwa, 23 Jan. 1964, BISA 1.3.(a)3.
99   Ibid.
100 Ibid.
101 Ibid.

The governors adopted a resolution, 'Group of Ten: The Euro-Currency Market and the International Payments System', which addressed the major issues in the Eurodollar market.[102] The Group of Ten dismissed the possible risks and endorsed the market's usefulness: 'because of its efficiency, the Euro-currency market has an exceptional potential for expansion which may create a special problem for monetary authorities in the future; but so far this does not seem to have been the case and on the whole it appears clear that the market has served a useful purpose'.[103]

Although central and private bankers continued their discussions thereafter, the resolution indicated central bank approval of the Eurodollar market as a part of the international money market.[104] Later, in a speech to the Association Cambiste Internationale (the club for currency dealers), the Banque de France's Koszul acknowledged that 'the market exists and clearly it answers a need'; 'the end of the Euro-dollar market is not yet in sight'.[105]

III

The post-war international monetary order established at Bretton Woods in 1944 was designed to counter the speculative and destabilising capital movements experienced in the 1930s.[106] 'Many monetary experts have accused capital flight movements of being the main cause of monetary troubles', one international banker succinctly summarised it in 1956.[107] At the same time, however, Western countries moved toward a multilateral global economic order with the introduction of convertibility in 1958 to revive the capital mobility for the multilateralism in the world economy. Short-term capital movements in Eurodollars illustrated the conflict between two Bretton Woods assumptions. In fact, the practice of Eurodollars was to exploit the Regulation Q which limited the competition for deposit funds.

The Eurodollar market, in the eyes of contemporary practitioners and observers, presented a challenge. It was 'purely a telephone market',[108] without

---

102   'Group of ten: the Euro-currency market and the international payments system', 20 Jan. 1964, BEA 6A123/1.

103   Ibid.

104   Abs and Koszul proposed establishing an international centre of risks in the Eurodollar market. 'Mr. Koszul's paper on Euro-currencies', 26 Jun. 1964, FRBNYA 615851.

105   J.P. Koszul, 'Viewpoint: thoughts on Euro-dollars', *Opera Mundi Europe*, 21 May 1964.

106   See M.J. Daunton, 'The future direction of British history: thinking about economic cultures', *History Workshop Journal* 72 (2011), pp. 222–39.

107   'The use of a currency of account in international loans, by Fernand Collin', Lecture delivered at Yale University, 4 Oct. 1956, Box 20, Papers of Robert Triffin, Manuscripts and Archives, Yale University Library.

108   Kynaston, *The City*, p. 268.

an authoritative institution or exchange to delineate the realm of the nascent market. Practitioners added to the mystery as they sought to keep their Eurodollar business from others. The market's growth, owing to its implications for the City's revival, the resumption of 'hot money' movements, and relevant regulatory concerns, attracted attention from various observers including financial journalists, monetary authorities, and international organisations. The Eurodollar market started with various ideas concerning the definition, measurement, and assessment of the market, which resulted in the contestation.

The Bank of England was at the centre of the contestation. As a regulator of the City, the international centre of Eurodollar business, it had comparative advantage not only in accessing the information, but also in setting the regulatory framework. It exerted authority over the contestation, and granted legitimacy to short-term capital movements in Eurodollars, despite anxieties even within the Bank, to facilitate the revival of the City as the international financial centre. Furthermore, by deliberately avoiding the production of coherent and complete statistics by the BIS, the Bank was able to protect the Eurodollar market from attempts to introduce international regulations. The production of statistics, a particular representation of the market, implied the control of the scope of knowledge by the Bank.[109] By 1964, once the contestation had been settled, the market was given the green light for further development by monetary authorities, something taken up by even its most vociferous dissenter when Abs allowed the Deutsche Bank to participate. The Eurodollar market, the embodiment of the shift in cultural assumptions about capital mobility, set a foundation for the resurrection of global finance in the late twentieth century.

109   On the relationship between statistics and financial practices, see Marieke de Goede, *Virtue, fortune, and faith: a genealogy of finance* (Minnesota, 2005), pp. 87–95.

9

Continuity and change in British Conservative taxation policy, c. 1964–88

ADRIAN WILLIAMSON

In March 1988 the UK Chancellor of the Exchequer, Nigel Lawson, introduced the first budget of the 1987–92 Parliament. The centrepiece was the abolition of all rates of income tax over 40 per cent. There were at that time five such rates, with a maximum of 60 per cent. Lawson, Chancellor from 1983 to 1989, was a key figure in a Conservative government which had just won its third successive election victory. He was in a triumphant mood, boasting that he had 'radically reformed the structure of personal taxation, so that there is no rate anywhere in the system in excess of 40 per cent'.[1]

Others were less impressed. Alex Salmond, a Scottish National Party MP, interrupted Lawson to declare that 'this Budget is an obscenity', and was suspended.[2] Shadow Chancellor John Smith described the budget as 'an outrage ... immoral, wrong, foolish, divisive and corrupting'.[3] When Lawson announced the abolition of the higher rates, grave disorder arose in the House, and the Speaker suspended the sitting for ten minutes, an almost unprecedented event during a budget speech.

Press comment upon the changes was likewise not all favourable. Hugo Young in *The Guardian* wrote that the budget represented 'the final disappearance of the last vestiges of the post-war consensus ... [such that] fairness and social justice, as registered through the tax system, have ceased even to be the pretended aspiration of the Conservative Party'.[4] *The Financial Times* (with more than a few wealthy readers itself) noted 'dramatic gains for the

---

1   HC Debs, 15 Mar. 1988, vol. 129, c. 1,013.
2   HC Debs, 15 Mar. 1988, vol. 129, c. 1,008.
3   Ibid., c. 1,116.
4   *Guardian*, 16 Mar. 1988.

rich'.[5] Scholarly analysis has been similar. Sven Steinmo thought that 'Margaret Thatcher was perhaps Britain's toughest bully ... [she and her ministers] plotted a head-on attack on the distribution of the tax burden' to help the rich.[6] Martin Daunton echoes this in his comprehensive history of the politics of taxation in Britain from 1914 to 1979, detecting a distinct shift in the Conservative approach between the 1960s on the one hand and the post-1979 period on the other, 'from an opportunity state to an enterprise society'. During the 1960s policy was not based on 'crude anti-statism', but sought to combine competition and compassion. By 1979, 'the pursuit of incentives at the cost of social integration became possible'.[7] Monica Prasad has similarly argued that 'monetarism became sales tax increases': a neoliberal government sought to control the budget deficit while reducing income tax.[8]

In contrast, I suggest that 1979 (and 1988) represent much less of a watershed in Conservative taxation policy than has been widely assumed. In the three central respects examined in this chapter, one may discern notable continuities with enduring Tory instincts. The first is a preference to shift the burden from direct to indirect taxation. The second marks a strong aversion to the idea that earned and investment income should be treated differently for tax purposes. Finally, and to the horror of the Opposition in 1988, Conservatives were unashamed in seeking to secure a massive lightening of the burden on high earners, in keeping with their long-standing distrust of progressivity. Each of these developments is considered in turn, but first it is helpful to put these themes into the wider context of taxation policy.

Rhetoric and reality in Thatcherite taxation policy

The Conservative Manifesto in 1979 was blunt as to its priorities, arguing that 'The State takes too much of the nation's income; its share must be steadily reduced ... the British people must be given more incentive ... We shall cut income tax at all levels to reward hard work, responsibility and success.'[9] Mrs Thatcher's first Principal Private Secretary understood that her 'aim must be to reduce substantially the cost of government'.[10] Four years later, Lawson's

5   Quoted in Sven Steinmo, *Taxation and democracy: Swedish, British, and American approaches to financing the modern state* (New Haven and London, 1993), p. 170.
6   Steinmo, *Taxation and democracy*, pp. 172–4.
7   M.J. Daunton, *Just taxes: the politics of taxation in Britain, 1914–1979* (Cambridge, 2002), pp. 302, 322, 328.
8   Monica Prasad, *The politics of free markets: the rise of neoliberal economic policies in Britain, France, Germany, and the United States* (Chicago, 2006), p. 118.
9   Conservative Party, *Conservative general election manifesto* (London, 1979).
10   Note by Kenneth Stowe, 'Cabinet: Tuesday 8 May points to make', undated, Cambridge, the Thatcher Papers, CAC THCR 2/6/2/7.

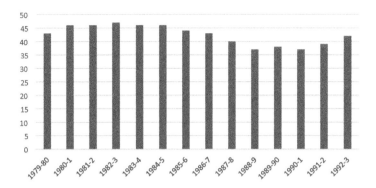

Figure 9.1. UK government (central and local) spending as per cent of GDP, 1978–93.

Source: http://www.ifs.org.uk/tools_and_resources/fiscal_facts/public_spending_survey/total_public_spending, fig. 1b, viewed 17 Nov. 2016. For a more detailed analysis of the performance of the UK economy over this period see https://visual.ons.gov.uk/uk-perspectives-trends-in-the-uk-economy/, viewed 24 Mar. 2018.

Special Adviser Adam Ridley (who had performed the same role for Geoffrey Howe, Chancellor from 1979 to 1983) reminded him that 'The Government's long-term tax objective ... is <u>above all</u> to bring down the <u>total</u> burden of taxation ... as a percent of GDP.'[11]

These objectives were not achieved. Indeed, public spending, and therefore taxation, continued to grow in real terms throughout the Thatcher years and subsequently. Thus, total outturn public spending for fiscal year 1978/79 was £371 billion (at 2015 prices), but this rose to £421 billion by 1989/90 (and to £742 billion by 2014/15).[12] The state rolled on rather than being rolled back. The principal determinant of the 'per cent of GDP' taken was the state of the economy, which was broadly in recession from 1979 to 1983 and 1989 to 1993, and enjoying the 'Lawson boom' from 1983 to 1989 (although there was some reduction of the national debt in the 1983–89 period, see Figure 9.1 above).

As Lawson (never one to hide his light under a bushel) was obliged to accept, 'the Conservative Governments of 1979–92 cannot claim to have reduced the burden of tax as a proportion of GDP ... the tax take was in fact a couple of percentage points higher in 1991–92 than it had been in 1978–79, the previous Labour Government's last year'. Lawson found this 'understandably disappointing'; he might have added that this was particularly so given the windfall

11   Memorandum, Ridley to Lawson, 6 Oct. 1983, CAC THCR 2/6/3/70, emphasis in original.
12   http://www.ifs.org.uk/tools_and_resources/fiscal_facts/public_spending_survey/total_public_spending, fig. 1a, viewed 17 Nov. 2016.

benefits that the Thatcher/Major governments enjoyed from North Sea Oil, privatisation receipts, and council house sales.[13]

Lawson went on to argue that 'despite the inability to reduce the overall burden of taxation, a substantial measure of tax reform was carried out'. The tax reform took a number of guises. For example, a flagship policy was developed to reform local government taxation, culminating in the ill-starred and swiftly abandoned poll tax. This reform was highly controversial, but at the other end of the spectrum, changes to the taxation of married women were widely regarded as long overdue.[14] No subsequent government has sought to reverse these reforms. In between these two extremes were, for example, significant changes to national insurance, corporation tax, and capital taxes.[15]

This chapter therefore concentrates on certain reforms which were highly contentious, distinctively Conservative, and which have so far proved enduring. Increasing reliance upon value added tax (VAT) as a source of revenue certainly meets these criteria. Between 1978 and 2008, the proportion of government spending funded from VAT doubled, from 8 per cent to 16 per cent.[16] Tory governments have been at the forefront of this development, and have always been ready to increase the rate of VAT to resolve fiscal difficulties. One can see from Table 9.1 that it was a Tory government which introduced VAT in 1973, then nearly doubled the rate in 1979. The Major government raised VAT in 1991–92 in order to ease the introduction of the council tax (successor to the poll tax). Likewise, the Cameron administration twice increased the rate of VAT as part of its austerity programme.

A similar pattern is apparent in relation to marginal rates of taxation and the treatment of investment income. Table 9.2 identifies key changes: the reduction of the highest marginal rate of tax in 1979 to 60 per cent and its further reduction in 1988/89 to 40 per cent, and the abolition of investment income surcharge (IIS) in 1984/85.

If their anti-state language was largely presentational, what did the Conservatives believe in, and how did they make these beliefs capable of acceptance beyond their own ranks? Although Thatcher and her Conservative successors often appeared in thrall to a 'neoliberal' or Hayekian ideology, the ideas that drove these policies were somewhat more prosaic. The starting point for most Conservatives was the need to improve incentives for hard work and enterprise. Nothing was new about this sentiment. In 1947, Quintin Hogg made the case for the beneficial effects of inequality. An 'Opportunity State' would create 'the incentives to make oneself unequal [which] are a necessary part

13   Nigel Lawson, *The view from No. 11: memoirs of a Tory radical* (London, 1992), p. 339.
14   Lawson, *View from No. 11*, pp. 881–7.
15   For a summary: Steinmo, *Taxation and democracy*, p. 170.
16   http://www.ifs.org.uk/uploads/mirrleesreview/dimensions/ch1.pdf, fig. 1.3, viewed 17 Nov. 2016.

Table 9.1. Rates of VAT since introduction, selected years (Conservative governments in bold)

Year	Standard	Higher
1973–74	10	–
1974–75	8	25
1976–77	8	12.5
1979–80	15	–
1991–92	17.5	–
2009–10	15	–
2010–11	17.5	–
2011–12	20	–

Source: http://www.ifs.org.uk/ff/vat.xls, viewed 17 Nov. 2016.

Table 9.2. Highest marginal rates of income tax, 1973–2015, selected years (Conservative governments in bold)

Year	Rate	IIS	Total
1973/74	75%	15%	90%
1974/75	83%	15%	98%
1979/80	60%	15%	75%
1984/85	60%	–	60%
1988/89	40%	–	40%
2010/11	50%	–	50%
2013/14	45%	–	45%

Source: http://www.ifs.org.uk/uploads/publications/ff/income.xls, viewed 1 Dec. 2016.

of the mechanism of creating new wealth'.[17] A generation later, Keith Joseph advanced very similar arguments: 'confiscatory rates of tax discourage the creation of wealth [so that] the poor are actually worse off than they would be in a society of sharp contrasts'.[18] Lawson's credo as Chancellor was 'to improve incentives … to reduce marginal tax rates, so that an extra pound of earnings or profits was really worth having'.[19]

17 Quintin Hogg, *The case for Conservatism* (Middlesex, 1959 [1947]), p. 112.
18 Keith Joseph and Jonathan Sumption, *Equality* (London, 1979), p. 23.
19 Lawson, *View from No. 11*, pp. 334, 339.

This belief in the positive effects of incentives was not based upon any rigorous research. It was simply common sense to most Conservatives that reducing the burden of income tax would promote enterprising behaviour: Conservative rhetoric abounded with talk of 'pacemakers', 'the people with particular skills, greater imagination, foresight, inventiveness, administrative ability who can give a lead'.[20] The levels of taxation on the rich in the 1960s and 1970s did promote interest in incentives, and, for example, the Institute for Fiscal Studies (IFS) set up a committee under Michael Edwardes, a high-profile industrialist, to examine the allegedly debilitating effects of very high marginal rates on business people. However, as John Kay, then Research Director of the IFS, recalled:

> The reason the thing was a disaster, was there wasn't actually any evidence … there were endless stories about British executives, who were leaving the UK, because of the crippling rates of taxation in the UK. What became clear was, that there wasn't any evidence for that at all. Indeed, all of the stories about it turned out to relate to one man.[21]

Most Conservatives were also conservative in fiscal matters, believing that cuts in any given tax would need to be matched by increases elsewhere or reductions in spending. They were sceptical about the so-called Laffer curve and unwilling to gamble that tax cuts would produce sufficient compensatory surges in revenue.[22] It followed that as one tax fell, another would have to rise in compensation. These conversations took place against a more general backdrop of condemnation of the size of the state by, at least, some Conservatives, coupled with threats to reduce its scale. However, this rhetoric and these threats fell some way short of a coherent programme to roll back the state. As Samuel Brittan, a sceptical observer of, and occasional adviser to, policymakers, points out:

> If you asked [Conservatives] did they want to shrink the State they would say 'Yes.' If you said 'Does that mean curbing your health service?' They would say 'No, no, that is sacred.' Everybody wants to shrink the size of the State. Nobody wants to shrink anything in particular.[23]

Conservative policymakers approached taxation, therefore, with instincts rather than ideology. Incentives were good and inequality the motor of economic progress. Taxes on the incomes of those who drove those motors

20   Heath at 1965 Party Conference, quoted in Andrew Roth, *Heath and the Heathmen* (London, 1972) p. 191.
21   John Kay interview.
22   Geoffrey Howe, *Conflict of loyalty* (London, 1995), p. 128.
23   Samuel Brittan interview.

should therefore be reduced, and these reductions would have to be paid for by increases elsewhere. The state should be made smaller in theory but not in practice.

How, then, were these long-standing concepts to be sold in the political marketplace? There were not, by definition, many pacemakers, let alone wealthy investors. How was the party of the rich to persuade the electorate that their prosperous fellow citizens should pay much less tax, and that this burden should be distributed more widely? It was one thing to suggest airily that the state had become too big, quite another that the very rich should pay less tax and the middling more.

In one respect this was less of an uphill task than it might have appeared, since it was not only Conservative policymakers who thought that the British tax system as it had developed to the 1970s was a 'mess', full of 'abuses, anomalies and loopholes'.[24] Of course free market ideologues like the Institute of Economic Affairs (IEA) said this, but it was not only those on the Right who so argued. The IFS (whose first Director, Dick Taverne, had been a Labour Treasury minister) pointed out that tax started at lower levels and at a higher rate than in any other Western country, and that the top rates were the highest in the industrialised world.[25]

Even in some Labour circles doubts had begun to creep in as to the balance between direct and indirect taxation, and as to the burden of marginal taxation. In 1977 Bernard Donoughue, Head of the Prime Minister's Policy Unit, advised the Prime Minister that the poor image of the British tax system derived largely from high marginal rates at the top. He suggested that 'A reduction in the top rate to 75% – as a first step – would cost only £80m.'[26] The next year a reduced rate band of 25 per cent was introduced on the first £750 of taxable income. This formed part of a conscious policy of 'reduce[ing] tax payments right across the income scale'.[27]

The Conservative case also enjoyed some good fortune in the high inflation of the 1970s. This meant there would be problems indexing income-based taxes to account for inflation.[28] The solution was to adopt 'tax measures, that are based on cash flows rather than calculations of income. Because inflation makes a whole variety of measures of income harder and less meaningful.'[29] All in all, the wind seemed to be blowing in the Conservative direction on the need to cut marginal rates and to pay for these cuts through increased indirect

24 John Kay and Mervyn King, *The British tax system* (Oxford, 1978), pp. 246–7.
25 Taverne interview, *Daily Telegraph*, 24 Feb. 1975.
26 Note Donoughue to Prime Minister, 26 Sep. 1977, CAC PU/306, the Papers of Lord Donoughue, CAC DNGH 1/1/19 (emphasis in original).
27 Note Donoughue to Prime Minister, 26 Sep. 1977, CAC PU/306, CAC DNGH 1/1/19.
28 Thelma Liesner and Mervyn King, *Indexing for inflation* (London, 1975).
29 Kay interview.

taxation. As Chris Patten (Director of the Conservative Research Department 1974–79) recalled, 'there was quite a large body of opinion that tax rates had become intolerably heavy. So I don't think there was as much caution as you might suppose about cutting top rates of tax.'[30]

Switching from direct to indirect taxation

As will be seen, throughout this period the Conservatives were determined to reduce reliance upon direct taxation, particularly income tax, and place greater reliance upon indirect taxation, especially VAT. In respect of this approach, two things should be noted at once. The first is that this was not inherently part of an attempt to bring down the total burden of taxation as a proportion of GDP. Rather the aim was to find a more satisfactory way, from the point of view of a Conservative government, of funding essentially the same expenditure. The second is that such a shift obviously raised distributional questions, since a proportional, even progressive, levy would be replaced with an essentially flat-rate charge. This aspect of the change was the subject of critical comment and scholarly analysis.[31]

This preference for indirect taxation did not begin in 1979. A 1957 Bow Group paper suggested the adoption of an expenditure tax 'on a wide range of goods and services'.[32] In opposition in 1964, Conservative economic policy-makers seemed to do little other than consider the minutiae of tax reform. An expenditure tax was central to these discussions. Thus, in 1965 Iain Macleod, then Shadow Chancellor, argued for 'a switch from direct to indirect taxation to enable us to help the "pacesetters"'.[33] This would be 'so large a revenue raiser that one could take the heat off the income tax'.[34] VAT also appeared a much more 'buoyant' tax than the existing indirect taxes.[35] What was therefore, envisaged was the abolition of selective employment tax (SET) and purchase tax, and their replacement by VAT.[36] This would reverse the current position,

30   Patten interview.

31   Ann Robinson and Cedric Sandford, *Tax policy-making in the United Kingdom: a study of rationality, ideology and politics* (London, 1983), pp. 114–16; J.A. Kay and C.N. Morris, 'Direct and indirect taxes; some effects of the 1979 budget', *Fiscal Studies* 1, 1 (1979), pp. 1–10; A.B. Atkinson, 'On the switch to indirect taxation', *Fiscal Studies* 2, 2 (1981), pp. 1–8.

32   Bow Group, 'The theoretical basis of a tax system', Jun. 1957, the Papers of Lord Jenkin, CAC JENK 4/1/1/2.

33   Macleod note, 'Taxation', 30 Nov. 1965, Oxford, Conservative Party Archive, BOD LCC 1/2/4.

34   Minutes of 8th meeting of Economic Policy Group ('EPG'), 13 Apr. 1967, pp. 3/4, BOD CRD 3/7/6/1.

35   Note on VAT, about 1968, p. 2, BOD CRD 3/7/26/40.

36   Minutes of working conference on VAT, 16 to 18 Jun. 1969, BOD CRD 3/7/26/36.

whereby earning was taxed too much and spending too little, thus 'discouraging effort and initiative'.[37]

Once the Conservatives returned to power in 1970, Anthony Barber (who became Chancellor on Macleod's death in July 1970) emphasised to his officials that the early introduction of VAT was central to the government's objectives.[38] The Heath government's public case for bringing in VAT emphasised its regulatory and efficiency advantages.[39] However, internally the key consideration for Tory ministers was that the introduction of VAT would enable the government to push ahead with reforms to direct taxation.[40] The government duly implemented these proposals, with VAT set at 10 per cent in 1973.

Labour was in government from 1974 to 1979, and reduced the standard VAT rate to 8 per cent, with a higher rate for 'luxury' goods of 25 per cent. In opposition, the Conservatives remained of the view that more emphasis should be placed on indirect taxation.[41] There was some nervousness about the impact of the tax on Conservative voters, and a Task Force was established to review the effect on small businesses.[42] However, the report was positive: VAT was 'a tax better at raising revenue, fairer in its impact on businesses and less onerous on the poor than its predecessors. It is also the preferred tax in Europe.'[43] Towards the end of this period of opposition, there was a strong view in Conservative circles that there should be a 'move to at least a 15 per cent VAT rate'.[44] As Howe, Shadow Chancellor from 1975 to 1979, urged his leader in 1978, 'if the increase is not made on this occasion, it never will be made and we will have lost for good any opportunity of seriously redressing the balance between direct and indirect taxation'.[45]

The Conservative Manifesto in 1979 was bland, saying only that 'we shall ... simplify taxes – like VAT ... We must ... be prepared to switch to some extent from taxes on earnings to taxes on spending. Value Added Tax does not apply, and will not be extended, to necessities like food, fuel, housing and transport.'[46] During the campaign, Labour alleged and the Tories denied that they planned

---

37 Draft EPG final report on taxation, 16 Jan. 1969, BOD CRD 3/7/26/38.

38 Note of meeting between Barber and officials, 26 Jul. 1970, TNA T 171/900, Records of HM Treasury, vol. III A.

39 Robinson and Sandford, *Tax policy-making*, p. 35.

40 E.g. memoranda to Barber by Higgins (Minister of State) 17 Nov. 1970 and Cockfield (economic adviser) 18 Nov. 1970, both at TNA T 328/374.

41 Minutes of meeting on tax strategy, 8 Dec. 1975, CAC THCR 2/6/1/35.

42 Press release, 2 September 1976, BOD CRD 4/4/173. Some small business people thought that 'forcing people to act as unpaid servants of the government' was 'a punishment in perpetuity': letter Gorman to Howe, 23 Sep. 1976, ibid.

43 VAT Task Force report, March 1977, BOD CRD 4/4/151 (it was, however, more onerous on the poor than a progressive income tax).

44 Meeting of Policy Group on Taxation (PGT), 18 May 1977, BOD CRD 4/4/152.

45 Note Howe to Thatcher, 9 Oct. 1978, CAC THCR 1/18/2.

46 Conservative Party, *Conservative general election manifesto*.

to increase massively the rate of VAT.[47] Indeed, Howe went so far as to say that 'we have absolutely no intention of doubling VAT'.[48] This was intended to offer reassurance, in conjunction with the somewhat questionable claim that VAT would not be imposed upon 'necessities' but only upon (by implication) discretionary spending.

Nonetheless, after the Conservative victory in May 1979 the Civil Service understood that VAT was 'the prime runner for raising new revenue', with a possible harmonisation of the rate at 10 per cent or 12.5 per cent.[49] The new government was fiscally cautious, and determined that 'cuts in direct taxation will have to be completely off-set by reductions in public expenditure and increases in indirect tax'.[50] Thatcher pressed for large spending cuts, and expressed herself 'extremely perturbed' by the prospect of a 15 per cent rate.[51] However, Howe explained to her that 'the minimum direct tax package can only be financed with a 15 per cent tax rate'.[52] When they met on 22 May, he argued that this was a unique opportunity to rebalance direct and indirect taxation, whereas Thatcher fretted about the effect on inflation and whether the proposed direct tax cuts were over-ambitious.[53] Howe stuck to his guns. The figures could only work, and the promised income tax cuts be delivered, with a 15 per cent rate. Moreover, the Conservative message about personal choice would be 'easier to get across if the switch to indirect taxation is immediate and ambitious'.[54] At this point, Thatcher gave in.[55] Howe announced the change in his first budget on 12 June 1979, together with substantial cuts in direct taxation.

This process had, therefore, been narrowly confined to Thatcher and Howe, with the latter very much in the driving seat. At least one senior minister lobbied Thatcher against the change, but was ignored: 'there were absolutely no consultations about the shape of the budget'.[56] This fitted into the pattern during the Thatcher period whereby 'big macro-economic decisions were taken by the Chancellor alone or by the Chancellor and the PM'.[57] Moreover, Thatcher herself, whilst rhetorically determined to 'restore incentives by direct

47   David Butler and Dennis Kavanagh, *The British general election of 1979* (London: Macmillan, 1999), pp. 187–8, 297.
48   *The Times*, 30 Apr. 1979, p. 16.
49   Cabinet Secretary's briefing to Thatcher, 4 May 1979, p. 3, TNA PREM 19/29.
50   Lankester memorandum, 8 May 1979, CAC THCR 2/6/2/2.
51   Note of meeting, Thatcher and Treasury ministers/officials, 16 May 1979, CAC THCR 2/6/2/48.
52   Memorandum Howe to Thatcher, 21 May 1979, TNA PREM 19/29.
53   Letter Lankester to Battishill, 22 May 1979, TNA PREM 19/29.
54   Memorandum Howe to Thatcher, 23 May 1979, p. 3, TNA PREM 19/29.
55   Memorandum Howe to Thatcher, 1 Jun. 1979, p. 2, TNA PREM 19/29: 'as we agreed last week, VAT will be increased to a unified rate of 15 per cent'.
56   Jim Prior, *A balance of power* (London, 1986), pp. 119–20.
57   Norman Lamont, *In office* (London, 1999), p. 8.

tax cuts and consequently to tolerate indirect tax increases' was distinctly uneasy about the latter when it came to it.[58]

In a sense this was a shocking policy change. Strictly speaking, 15 per cent was not 'double' the two existing rates of 8 per cent and 15 per cent, but, for the average consumer with little taste for luxury goods it might as well have been. The short-term inflationary effect was sharp: a predicted rise of about 3.5 per cent, with inflation already forecast to reach 13 per cent by the end of 1979.[59] Only Howe was really committed to this change; for example, Douglas Hague, a Conservative economic adviser, had thought as recently as April 1979 that there was a 'consensus that we want to return to a single VAT rate of 10%'.[60] However, in the broader context of Conservative policy as it had evolved since 1964, Howe's position was entirely consistent with the long-standing desire to 'take the heat off the income tax'.

Cutting marginal tax rates

Tory politicians are often nervous about being seen as the party of the wealthy.[61] Of course, few voters are rich. Yet between 1979 and 1988, the Thatcher governments reduced the highest marginal rate of income tax to 60 per cent in 1979, abolished the IIS of 15 per cent in 1984, and then lowered the top rate again, to 40 per cent, in 1988. Altogether the very rich saw their highest marginal rate fall from 98 per cent to 40 per cent in nine years. How and why did the Conservatives do this, and did it represent an abandonment of a pre-existing consensus on progressive taxation?

In 1951 the Conservatives inherited from the Attlee government a tax system with marginal rates as high as 98 per cent. Broadly speaking, the governments of 1951–64 were content to work within this system, which was markedly progressive and redistributive.[62] There were Tory voices raised against this fiscal structure, but they had little effect on policy.[63] However, as already noted, the Party looked at taxation in great detail after 1964. A central theme was a desire to encourage the 'pacemakers' by making the system less progressive. Thus, in 1967 it was thought that it would be possible to achieve a top marginal rate

---

58   Charles Moore, *Margaret Thatcher: the authorized biography*, vol. 1 (London, 2013), pp. 459, 464–6.

59   Memorandum Howe to Thatcher, 23 May 1979, p. 2, TNA PREM 19/29.

60   Memorandum Hague to Howe and Thatcher, 19 Apr. 1979, CAC THCR 2/6/2/79.

61   ORC Reports on Attitudes to Taxation of Jul. 1976 and Feb. 1978, Oxford, BOD CCO 180/9/10/5 and 180/9/10/7. The former report was discussed on 27 Sep. 1976, when it was agreed that 'a perceived Conservative partiality to the rich needs to be countered': the Papers of Lord Howell, CAC HWLL 2/4/1/1.

62   Daunton, *Just taxes*, pp. 229–78.

63   Bow Group, 'The theoretical basis of a tax system', Jun. 1957, CAC JENK 4/1/1/2.

of 70 per cent and abolish the earned/unearned income distinction.[64] By 1970 the income tax package which had evolved was more modest: abolish surtax, increase allowances, and reduce rates. The earned/unearned income differential would remain.[65] In part this was due to fiscal caution: tax reductions had to be balanced elsewhere. Partly, also, the Conservatives wasted a great deal of time investigating, and then abandoning, the idea of a wealth tax.[66] There were a number of problems with this proposal, including the fact that it was 'absolutely moonshine' to imagine the Parliamentary Party accepting it.[67]

The eventually agreed scheme was for a standard rate of 30 per cent, rising in £2,000 increments to produce a top rate of 75 per cent on earned income. Investment income above £5,000 would attract a rate of 90 per cent.[68] However, in order to appreciate what appear at first sight to be very high tax charges on modest earnings, it is important to acknowledge the impact of inflation (see Table 9.3 below). Macleod presented this as 'a complete reconstruction of the whole of the present tax scale ... to make a radical change in the economic climate'.[69] His colleagues were anxious even about the somewhat diluted plan. Keith Joseph worried that this would all benefit the top 1 per cent of earners, which is why 'he had been attracted by an early form of the tax package where the regressive redistribution could be balanced by a wealth tax'.[70] Alec Douglas-Home, a former Prime Minister, thought that very high earners should pay up to 95 per cent, since 'this would mitigate the effects of redistribution, and help with presentation'.[71]

The 1971 budget implemented the agreed tax reform package, including reform and unification of income tax and surtax.[72] Although there was 'an opportunity which may not recur for a generation, to devise a profile of marginal tax rates which is best suited to our economic and social purposes', it was necessary for the highest rate on earned income to be 75 per cent, in order to retain the progressivity of the system and given that a top rate of 90 per cent had been in place for many years.

Nonetheless, when the Conservatives returned to the topic of taxation after 1974, the 1971 reforms represented an important bridgehead. Internally it was believed that Heath's government had 'carried out the most radical programme

---

64   Minutes of 10th meeting of EPG, 11 May 1967, p. 3, BOD CRD 3/7/6/1.
65   'Tax package: the main proposals and our commitments', 29 Jul. 1970, p. 1, BOD CRD 3/7/26/37.
66   Daunton, *Just taxes*, pp. 316–18.
67   Chief Whip, Notes of fourth session of Selsdon Conference, 31 Jan. 1970, p. 4, BOD CRD 3/7/7/7.
68   'Tax package', p. 1.
69   Notes of third session of Selsdon Conference, 31 Jan. 1970, p. 4, BOD CRD 3/7/7/7.
70   Ibid. p. 11, and fourth session, ibid., p. 4.
71   Rough notes of eighth session at p. 15, 1 Feb. 1970, BOD CRD 3/7/7/7.
72   Anthony Barber, *Taking the tide: a memoir* (Norwich, 1996), pp. 103–5.

Table 9.3. Conservative income tax proposals, 1970[1]

Taxable income £ (2018 adjusted)[2]	Rate
0–5,000 (0–76,000)	30%
5,000–7,000 (76,000–106,000)	35%
7,000–9,000 (106,000–137,000)	40%
9,000–11,000 (137,000–167,000)	45%
11,000–13,000 (167,000–198,000)	50%
13,000–15,000 (198,000–228,000)	55%
15,000–17,000 (228,000–258,000)	60%
17,000–19,000 (258,000–289,000)	65%
19,000–21,000 (289,000–319,000)	70%
21000– (319,000–)	75%

Notes
1   Investment income over £5,000 pa (£76,000) was to incur a surcharge of 15 per cent, so that the highest potential charge was 90 per cent
2   Adjusted by reference to http://www.bankofengland.co.uk/education/Pages/resources/inflationtools/calculator/flash/default.aspx.

of tax reform … the country has seen this century'.[73] Those considering policy therefore returned to the business which Barber had left unfinished. The key themes were substantial reductions in the highest rate and the abolition or emasculation of IIS.

So far as rates were concerned, there was widespread agreement that 'the top marginal rates of tax on investment and earned income stand out like a beacon of fiscal absurdity'. The Policy Group on Taxation recommended a top rate of 75 per cent on investment income and 60 per cent on earned income.[74] Ideally, they thought, the top rate should be no more than 50 per cent. After all, 'the harsh reality must be accepted that there is no way of increasing incentives except by making the rich richer relative to the poor'.[75] On these issues, in contrast to VAT, the 1979 manifesto could, therefore, be clear:

> It is especially important to cut the absurdly high marginal rates of tax … the top rate of income tax should be cut to the European average and the higher tax bands widened. To encourage saving we will reduce the burden of the investment income surcharge.

73   Paper 'Taxation', Apr. 1975, BOD CRD 4/4/144.
74   Second Interim Report of PGT, 16 Jun. 1976, CAC THCR 2/6/1/159, par. 8.
75   Progress Report of the PGT, Jun. 1977, CAC CRD 4/4/153.

There had been some discussion of abolishing the IIS. Howe was sympathetic to this idea.[76] The options appeared to be complete abolition or the 'retention of a residual charge as a defence mechanism against a wealth tax'.[77] However, for some Conservatives complete abolition went too far, in conjunction with the proposed sharp reduction of the top rate.[78] There was also general agreement on the need to retain graduated and progressive tax scales, increasing from 30 per cent for income up to £10,000 to 60 per cent above £30,000.[79] Lawson, however, proposed that the system be simplified. There would be two tax bands only: a basic rate of 25 per cent and a higher rate of 40 per cent, once the taxpayer earned seven times the basic tax allowance. This was too heady a mixture for most of Lawson's colleagues, primarily for political rather than economic reasons.[80]

Subject, once more, to the need to win over a wary Prime Minister, the route to the 60 per cent top rate seemed clear following the 1979 election victory. The Civil Service expected that the new government would be 'reducing the top rate to 75 per cent, and revalorizing the bands to April 1973 levels'.[81] Some in the Thatcher entourage advocated a 50 per cent top rate 'while the Opposition remains stunned'.[82] Howe, in keeping with the debates in opposition, argued that a '60% maximum' would 'constitute … an irreducible minimum'.[83] The PM urged caution: it was 'better to concentrate on cutting public expenditure, curbing the rate of inflation and getting the overall balance of the economy right in the first year – with major reductions in income tax being left to the second'.[84] Howe held his nerve and Thatcher yielded, as she had over VAT.[85]

In the 1979 budget, Howe therefore announced the tax rates shown in Table 9.4. Comparison between Tables 9.3 and 9.4 suggests that the difference between the Conservative position in 1970 and 1979 was more apparent than real. Someone with a taxable income of (say) £80,000 in 2018 terms would have been paying a top marginal rate of 35 per cent in 1970 and 50 per cent in 1979. These comparisons can never be entirely accurate, because of the vagaries of inflation, but the broad picture seems clear. It was only the really high earner who was doing much better in 1979. A taxable income over £115,000 (in 2018

76   Undated note by Howe, CAC THCR 2/1/1/31.
77   Meeting of PGT, 15 Jun. 1977, CAC HWLL 2/4/1/1. The Labour government was considering, but did not implement, a wealth tax.
78   Note of meeting, 11 Jun. 1978, the Papers of Sir Adam Ridley, CAC RDLY 2/1/4/1, par. 18.
79   C/Tax 10, 25 May 1978 by Cockfield, the Papers of Peter Cropper, CAC CPPR 1/2/3.
80   Note of 15 May 1978, Lawson to Howe, CAC RDLY 2/1/4/2. Howe was 'sympathetic to this general approach', but cautious on the detail: note of 18 May 1978, ibid.
81   Cabinet Secretary's briefing to Thatcher, 4 May 1979, p. 3, TNA PREM 19/29. It is not clear whether the 75 per cent included the IIS.
82   Note on taxation, probably by Woodrow Wyatt, 8 May 1979, CAC THCR 1/15/3.
83   Memorandum Howe to Thatcher, 21 May 1979, TNA PREM 19/29.
84   Letter Lankester to Battishill, 22 May 1979, TNA PREM 19/29.
85   Memorandum Howe to Thatcher, 23 May 1979, and Memorandum Howe to Thatcher, 1 Jun. 1979, both at TNA PREM 19/29.

Table 9.4. 1979 budget

Income £ (2018)	Rate
0–10,000 (0–50,000)	30%
10,000–12,000 (50,000–60,000)	40%
12,000–15,000 (60,000–75,000)	45%
15,000–20,000 (75,000–99,000)	50%
20,000–25,000 (99,000–124,000)	55%
The remainder (124,000–)	60%

terms) would produce a levy of 55–60 per cent, compared with potential exposure of up to 75 per cent in 1970 on at least part of the income.

Howe did not abolish IIS, but spoke of it with little affection. He raised the threshold to £5,000 (2018: £25,000), noting that 'the justification for retaining the surcharge is itself debatable'.[86] This essentially returned the tax position of investment income to 1973/74, rather than 1970. Whether to retain the surcharge turned out to be the next item on the Conservative agenda, albeit that debate over the 1984 (and 1988) changes was even more perfunctory than in 1979. Lawson, determined to 'be master in his own house' whilst Chancellor, consulted the cabinet hardly at all and Thatcher evasively.[87]

The Conservatives made no mention of abolishing IIS during the 1983 election. In January 1984, Lawson told Thatcher that he 'should like to get rid of' IIS.[88] There was no widespread discussion within government. With little further ado, Lawson took 'a last-minute decision which struck a chord on our own side' to end IIS.[89] He told the Commons:

> The investment income surcharge is an unfair and anomalous tax on savings and on the rewards of successful enterprise. It hits the small businessman who reaches retirement without the cushion of a company pension scheme ... In the vast majority of cases it is a tax on savings made out of hard-earned and fully-taxed income ... I have therefore decided that [IIS] should be abolished.[90]

Differential taxation of investment income had been a feature of the UK tax system since 1907. The principle underlying this distinction was that the

---

86 HC Debs, 12 Jun. 1979, vol. 968, c. 260.
87 Charles Moore, *Margaret Thatcher: the authorized biography*, vol. 2 (London, 2015), pp. 185–7.
88 Lawson memorandum 'Tax reform strategy', 19 Jan. 1984, par. 5, TNA T 530/97.
89 Lawson, *View from No. 11*, p. 350.
90 HC Debs, 13 Mar. 1984, vol. 56, cc. 293–4.

income had not been earned.[91] This principle did not have great appeal to the Conservative Party in the 1970s and 1980s. It was unceremoniously dispatched.

Between 1984 and 1987 the focus of tax policy moved away from the 'pacemakers'. There was much work on the taxation of husband and wife.[92] Some discussion occurred within government on the need to help 'relatively modest salary earners in key management positions'.[93] For the 1987 election, the Conservatives proclaimed that they had 'reduced sharply the absurd top rates of tax inherited from Labour which were causing ... talented people to work abroad'. Their aim was to reduce burden of taxation, and, 'in particular, we will cut income tax still further ... continue ... tax reform'.[94]

As already noted, Lawson used the first budget of the 1987 Parliament to dispense with all income tax rates above 40 per cent, causing delirium among his backbenchers and uproar from his opponents. In preparing this budget, he consulted with the Lord Chancellor on some legal arcana, but otherwise very much drove the process himself. According to Lawson, the budget 'went considerably further than anything Margaret had in mind: her own ambitions were essentially confined to ... reducing the top rate of income tax to 50 per cent'.[95]

What, then, was the effect of these various changes to the highest marginal rates? The most recent figures available (for 2013/14) are that the 98th centile of UK taxpayers had a pre-tax income of £110,000 and the 99th centile were at £159,000.[96] Such taxpayers would have been liable to pay tax at the higher rate of 40 per cent on income between £32,011 and £150,000, and in the latter case at the additional rate of 45 per cent on income over £150,000.[97]

In the period discussed in this chapter, equivalent incomes would have attracted taxation approximately as shown in Table 9.5. This can be only a crude approximation, partly because of the incidence of inflation, but, more importantly, because one cannot know the individual circumstances of each taxpayer. There have also been numerous changes over this period in respect of national insurance, VAT, and other taxes. However, this approximation almost certainly overstates the real change for 98th and 99th centile taxpayers. That is because successive governments over this period restricted or removed numerous reliefs and allowances which were once available and which greatly benefited higher earners. These included relief on pension contributions and mortgage interest, and numerous other means to 'shelter' higher incomes through various

---

91   Daunton, *Just taxes*, p. 23.
92   *The reform of personal taxation*, HMSO, Cmnd 9756, Mar. 1986.
93   Memorandum by Financial Secretary, 17 May 1984, TNA T 530/98.
94   Conservative Party, *Conservative general election manifesto*.
95   Lawson, *View from No. 11*, pp. 821–4.
96   http://www.gov.uk/government/statistics/percentile-points-from-1-to-99-for-total-income
-before-and-after-tax, viewed 29 Nov. 2016.
97   http://www.gov.uk/government/publications/rates-and-allowances-income-tax/income-tax
-rates-and-allowances-current-and-past, viewed 29 Nov. 2016.

Table 9.5. Income tax equivalents (all incomes contemporary)

Tax year	98th centile	Higher rates	99th centile	Higher rates
1973/74	10,000	40%–55%[1]	14,500	40%–65%
1979/80	24,000	40%–55%[2]	35,000	40%–60%
1988/89	46,000	40%[3]	66,000	40%

Notes
1   See Section 66 of Finance Act 1972 for income tax rates and bands for 1973–74.
2   See Table 9.4.
3   Section 24(1) of Finance Act 1988 set the rate for income exceeding £19,300 at 40 per cent.

schemes.[98] A taxpayer with a gross income equivalent to £100,000–£150,000 (in 2018 terms) would, therefore, have been very unlikely to be paying the higher rates which his or her income might, at first sight, be expected to attract.

The most conspicuous beneficiaries of the successive changes have been the very rich, who do not feature in the centile charts at all. Someone with an income of £1 million (2018) would have been liable to pay 75 per cent in 1973/74 and 60 per cent in 1979/80 on large tranches of that income, but after 1988 was obliged to pay no more than 40 per cent. The change was more dramatic still for a person with a large investment income who was no longer subject to the 15 per cent surcharge.

However, whilst Lawson's 1988 tax changes may have reduced his opponents to apoplexy, they were not controversial within the Conservative Party. For Lawson, writing in 1992, the changes were a 'vital part of the … sweeping reform of the supply side of the economy'.[99] Thatcher, a year later, thought them 'a huge boost to incentives, particularly for those talented, internationally mobile people so essential to economic success'.[100] John Major (Chancellor 1989–90 and Prime Minister 1990–97) believed in 1999 that 'the tax changes Nigel introduced [in 1988] were right. They ended the unjustifiably high taxation of income that had hampered investment.'[101] These confident assertions were based on little evidence. There was little data available to show that particular levels of taxation demoralised or drove away the 'pacemakers'.[102]

98   E.g., Lawson, *View from No. 11*, pp. 819–23.
99   Ibid., p. 818.
100   Margaret Thatcher, *The Downing Street years* (London, 1993) p. 674.
101   John Major, *The autobiography* (London, 1999), p. 106.
102   There was little information obtainable on this issue. The IFS did 'lots of work on relationship between incentives and taxation. But that's based on large data sets, you can get from the sources like Family Expenditure Survey … But the number of people in Family Expenditure Survey who paid very high rates of tax is infinitesimal.' Kay Interview.

Conclusions

This chapter has considered three of the central tax changes introduced by the Thatcher governments. Each, one might argue, evidenced the rupture which those governments sought and achieved with the post-war consensus. Rather than the average taxpayer making contributions directly and in proportion to income, the burden was shifted to indirect, essentially flat-rate taxation. Unearned income no longer bore any fiscal stigma. The rich, and especially the very rich, benefited substantially. The Left were very much on the back foot, and had to accommodate themselves to a 'new era'.[103]

However, it is easy but misleading to overstate the extent of this rupture. As we have seen, the Conservatives had been consistently attracted to the introduction and extension of VAT. Nor were they alone in advocating a switch from direct to indirect taxation. In 1975, the Institute for Fiscal Studies had established the Meade Committee. Its very distinguished membership was charged with considering no less than 'the structure and reform of direct taxation'. They recommended a significant switch to expenditure tax.[104] Others took notice of these ideas. The Treasury looked in some detail at the workings of the committee in 1975/76.[105] The Liberals, who had formed a pact with the Labour government in 1977, were pressing for 'a major shift from direct to indirect taxation, on a broad basis'.[106] That government took these ideas on board and by 1977 had 'become publicly committed to correcting the imbalance between direct and indirect taxation'.[107] Arthur Cockfield, the Conservatives' foremost tax expert, thought that Meade had been correct to diagnose the problem – namely that there was 'too much on to income, too little on to expenditure' – but that he had gone too far in proposing 'to shift the balance 100% to expenditure'.[108] Cockfield was, however, encouraged by the positive reception for Meade, which had 'made a <u>massive</u> switch from direct to indirect taxes respectable'.[109]

What the switch from direct to indirect taxation did not do, however, was enable the Conservatives to reduce, or even reshape, the state, which continued to grow in the Thatcher era and beyond. VAT has proved a handy weapon for Tory governments struggling to soften the edges of the poll tax or austerity. The very effectiveness of this tax and its near invisibility have made it a powerful tool for governments that have sought stealthily to increase taxes. As Samuel

103   Richard Whiting, *The Labour Party and taxation: party identity and political purpose in twentieth-century Britain* (Cambridge, 2000), p. 258.
104   *The structure and reform of direct taxation: report of a committee chaired by Professor J.E. Meade* (London, 1978).
105   'Direct tax system: consideration of Meade Committee Report', 1975–76, TNA T 366/4.
106   Memorandum by A. Isaac, 31 Mar. 1977, TNA T 366/532.
107   Note, Donoughue to Prime Minister, 9 Sep. 1977, CAC DNGH 1/1/19.
108   Cockfield, 'The Meade Report', C/Tax 4, 16 Feb. 1978, CAC CPPR 1/2/4.
109   Cockfield Note, C/Tax 3, 12 Feb. 1978, CAC CPPR 1/2/3.

Brittan pointed out in 1975, nineteenth-century liberals were hostile to such imposts since:

> A shift from direct to indirect taxation is a way of concealing from the public the extent to which income is withdrawn from their pay packets and devoted to collective consumption. If I wished to enlarge the share of the state sector I would recommend such a shift.[110]

In relation to reducing the high levels of direct taxation on the rich and those who had large investment incomes, the Conservatives saw themselves completing in the 1980s the work which Barber had commenced in the 1970s. When reviewing policy in opposition, it was thought that 'Britain has created a tax trap for its citizens' out of which the Heath government had started to find an escape route.[111] The Barber reforms were 'needed now as they were then'.[112] Nor was this view wholly confined to the Tories. At its 1977 conference the Confederation of British Industry rejected a resolution from its leadership calling for top rates of 60 per cent on earned income and 75 per cent on investment income, in favour of a single top rate of 50 per cent.[113] In 1979, the Liberals promoted 'Income Tax starting at 20 per cent with a top rate of 50 per cent'.[114] Even within the Labour government, there was concern that high marginal rates discouraged effort, drove talented people abroad, and encouraged tax evasion.

As has been shown, the change between the Barber period and the Thatcher era was less marked than might at first appear. The thinking underlying the Howe and Lawson changes – that incentives and inequality were the wellsprings of economic progress – flowed from mainstream and long-standing Conservative thinking. Most 'salary earners in key management positions' did not see their financial position transformed through these tax changes, even if they were at the 98th or 99th centile in the income distribution. What Lawson had not fully anticipated was the surge in executive pay which would ensue. It is these very highest earners who have gained the most. Thomas Piketty has addressed this issue in proposing an 80 per cent tax on incomes over $0.5 million or $1 million, 'to distribute the fruits of growth more widely while imposing reasonable limits on economically useless (or even harmful) behaviour'.[115]

---

110   Note, 31 Jul. 1975 by Samuel Brittan, 'A comment on chairman's interim report', at BOD CRD 4/4/145, par. 3. Brittan was advising the party's PGT.
111   Note on taxation, about 1975, BOD CRD 4/4/144.
112   Barry Bracewell-Milnes, 'Conservative Party fiscal options', 12 May 1975, BOD CRD 4/4/144.
113   *Britain means business 1977: the full proceedings of the CBI first national conference, Brighton 13–15 November 1977* (London, 1978), pp. 28, 32, 33, 44.
114   *Liberal Party manifesto* (London, 1979).
115   Thomas Piketty, *Capital in the twenty-first century* (London, 2014), p. 513.

10

Britain since the 1970s: a transition to neo-liberalism?

JIM TOMLINSON

At the close of a chapter analysing the policies of the Thatcher government, Martin Daunton remarks that, in relation to public spending levels, 'For all her rhetoric, Mrs Thatcher did not roll back the state.'[1] This statement is an important reminder to us about the need to avoid confusing the rhetoric of politics with the substance of political and policy action. And it is a particularly useful starting point from which to examine the broad claims about the transition in Britain since the 1970s from the predominance of 'Keynesian social democracy' to neo-liberalism.[2] This chapter questions the adequacy of such characterisations, focusing especially on the neo-liberal aim of 'rolling back the state' and changes in public spending.

The first part deals with the issue of 'crisis' and the use of this term to characterise the events of the 1970s. The second analyses ideological and political responses to these events, and what shaped these responses. The third section puts the 1970s into the perspective of subsequent events to see whether indeed what followed this decade shows evidence of a neo-liberal predominance. The final section offers some speculative conclusions.

I

It is uncontentious to see the British economy as 'in crisis' in the 1970s. What matters is the nature of that crisis, given that crises are always constructed;

1   M.J. Daunton, *Just taxes: the politics of taxation in Britain 1914–1979* (Cambridge, 2002), p. 338.
2   R. Skidelsky, ed., *The end of the Keynesian era* (London, 1977); P. Hall, 'The movement from Keynesianism to monetarism: institutional analysis and British economic policy in the 1970s', in S. Steinmo, K. Thelen and F. Longstreth, eds, *Structuring politics* (Cambridge, 1992), pp. 90–113; A. Glyn, *Capitalism unleashed: finance, globalization and welfare* (Oxford, 2006).

accounts of crisis draw on events but require an active process of narration.[3] Section II analyses the way that neo-liberals sought to construct those narratives. This section offers a summary of key economic events around which those narratives were built.

The 1970s did not see a serious crisis of *output*. The recession of 1974/75 was a mild one in comparison with those of the interwar period and the three that have occurred since.[4] Growth of GDP over the decade was little different from preceding or succeeding periods, but with sharp cyclical movements: a period of clearly unsustainable 4.7 per cent annual expansion, followed by a short-lived recession.[5] Of course to contemporaries the recession came as a major shock after twenty-five years of almost uninterrupted expansion. They were also much exercised by the rise in unemployment. By 1971 the figure was clearly heading towards one million, stimulating a policy U-turn, and the recurrence of that figure in 1975 was also a major basis of criticism of the Labour government's policies.[6] Mass unemployment was a particularly sensitive issue in Britain, partly because of the overwhelming proletarianisation of the population, much higher than in other Western European countries, where small farmers and peasants were still significant sectors. This helps to account for the strength of the response to what was, like the fall in output, in long-run perspective a relatively mild change. Unemployment was higher in the recessions of 1920–22, 1929–32, 1979–82, 1990–92 and 2007–10 than under Labour.[7]

There were two key aspects of the economic crisis of the 1970s. First was 'stagflation', the combination of higher unemployment with much higher inflation. In the 'Golden Age' of the 1950s and 1960s inflation averaged about 3 per cent per annum, but after the 1967 devaluation there was a notable upward shift, accelerating again in the boom of the early 1970s, before reaching a peak at 26 per cent in 1975. Second was the growth in the public sector deficit, driven largely by the automatic stabilisers responding to the recession. Again, the contrast with the Golden Age was stark. In those good years there was normally

---

3   C. Hay, 'Chronicles of a death foretold: the Winter of Discontent and the construction of the crisis of British Keynesianism', *Parliamentary Affairs* 63 (2010), pp. 446–70; R. Saunders, 'Crisis? What crisis? Thatcherism and the seventies', in B. Jackson and R. Saunders, eds, *Making Thatcher's Britain* (Cambridge, 2012), pp. 25–42. A broader historical literature emphasises crisis as 'a category within a rhetorical understanding of historical development': J. Shank, 'Crisis: a useful category of post–social scientific historical analysis?', *American Historical Review* 11 (2008), p. 1097.

4   C. Dow, *Major recessions: Britain and the world, 1920–1995* (Oxford, 1998), pp. 14–15.

5   Ibid., pp. 295–9.

6   And famously in 1979 the Conservatives put 'Labour isn't working' as a major slogan at the centre of their election campaign.

7   Post-1971 data are not strictly comparable with those for the interwar period, but peaks of around 17 per cent (1921), 22 per cent (1932), 12 per cent (1984), 11 per cent (1992), and 8 per cent (2010) suggest the relative mildness of the 5 per cent figure in 1975.

a public sector current account surplus, with an overall deficit typically around 2 per cent of GDP, whereas in the 1970s public sector net borrowing peaked at 6.7 per cent (the Public Sector Borrowing Requirement (PSBR), the figure used at the time, peaked at 9.6 per cent). However, the debt/GDP ratio declined in the 1970s, largely as a result of inflation reducing the value of outstanding debt.[8]

Labour came to power in 1974 in the context of the breakdown in industrial relations caused by conflict over the Conservative's incomes policy, part of the post-U-turn policy package. This had led to a miner's strike and the imposition of a three-day working week to reduce electricity consumption. Labour's policy to attempt to resolve the tension between unions and government was the Social Contract, which sought to bargain policies desired by the unions against their acceptance of wage restraint. No formal agreement on such restraint was achieved until union leaders 'stared into the abyss' of accelerating inflation in 1975, when a deal was agreed to limit rises to £6 per week.[9]

Labour's economic inheritance was one of accelerating inflation brought about by the expansionary policies of the Conservative government (reversed only in November 1973), combined with a world commodity price boom and the OPEC (Organization of Petroleum Exporting Countries) oil price rise.[10] Domestically the most important legacies from the previous administration were extraordinarily rapid monetary growth of 20 to 30 per cent per annum, and the pay threshold system. This system guaranteed pay increases to match inflation, and thereby built in a mechanism which made reducing inflation much harder. Critics have seen maintaining the threshold policy as the major error of the new government, but any repudiation would have undermined Labour's key desire to achieve a rapport with the trade unions.[11]

Almost from the beginning of its period of office the Labour government started to shift the focus of its macroeconomic policy from reducing unemployment to combatting inflation. Whilst the fiscal stance was broadly neutral in 1974, by the budget of spring 1975 the Chancellor, Denis Healey, was explicitly rejecting the possibility of an expansionary fiscal policy to combat unemployment:

> I fully understand why I am being urged by so many ... to treat unemployment as the central problem and to stimulate a further growth in home consumption, public or private, so as to start getting the rate of unemployment down as fast as possible. I do not believe it would be wise to follow this advice today

8   C. Allsopp, 'Macroeconomic policy: design and performance', in M. Artis and D. Cobham, eds, *Labour's economic policies 1974–79* (Manchester, 1991), pp. 19–37.

9   P. Ormerod, 'Incomes policy', in Artis and Cobham, *Labour's economic policies*, pp. 56–72.

10   A. Britton, *Macroeconomic policy in Britain 1974–1987* (Cambridge, 1991), pp. 13–17.

11   M. Artis and D. Cobham, 'Summary and appraisal', in their *Labour's economic policies*, pp. 269–70.

... I cannot afford to increase demand further today when 5p in every pound
we spend at home has been provided by our creditors abroad and inflation
is running at its current rate.[12]

Against the background of the growth of public borrowing resulting from the
effects of the automatic stabilisers, Healey cut spending, and, very importantly,
introduced a policy of 'cash limits', which meant departmental budgets were no
longer automatically increased in line with inflation, but were fixed in monetary
terms. This had a big impact on spending, with cuts falling especially heavily
on capital items, especially housebuilding.[13]

By early 1976 the government appeared to have got a grip on the crisis.
The rate of inflation and the PSBR were falling, monetary growth was diminishing, though unemployment was still rising.[14] Despite these improvements
the exchange rate, which had been falling since the pound floated in June 1972,
continued to decline, and did so at an accelerating rate from March 1976. This
acceleration was partly stimulated by a government seeking a further fall to
improve competitiveness, but it quickly got out of control. It was this plunge
which drove the government to seek a loan from the International Monetary
Fund (IMF), and resulted in a long autumn of political dispute over the terms
of the deal to be agreed in return for borrowing from the Fund.[15]

The negotiations with the IMF produced major political traumas in and
brought the Labour party to a crisis point. Yet in terms of the impact on
the trajectory of the economy the loan deal was of limited importance; the
borrowing conditions did not lead to a major reversal of existing policy. As
noted, the stance of policy had been tightening since 1975, with public spending
cuts and the stabilisation of the PSBR. Monetary targeting also predates this
episode.[16] The significance of the loan deal was more than anything to give an
IMF 'seal of approval' to the government.[17]

In the event, public spending fell faster than envisaged, largely as a result of
cash limits. Only half the offered loan was taken up. The deal initiated a notable
rally in the exchange rate, aided by the discovery and exploitation of North
Sea oil. Through 1977 and well into 1978 the evidence suggested an improving
economy, with output expanding, unemployment and inflation falling, and

---

12   House of Commons (*Hansard*), 15 Apr. 1975, col. 282.
13   K. Burk and A. Cairncross, *'Goodbye Great Britain': the 1976 IMF crisis* (New Haven,
1992), pp. 184–8.
14   Ibid., p. 215.
15   Britton, *Macroeconomic policy*, pp. 28–33.
16   S. Ludlam, 'The gnomes of Washington: four myths of the 1976 IMF crisis', *Political Studies*
40 (1992), pp. 713–27; D. Needham, 'Britain's money supply experiment, 1971–73', *English
Historical Review* 130 (2015), pp. 1079–101.
17   Burk and Cairncross, *'Goodbye Great Britain'*, pp. 225–6.

Table 10.1. Major economic indicators, 1974–79

	France	Italy	W. Germany	UK
Output growth (% p.a.)	3.1	2.3	2.7	2.0
Unemployment (%, national definitions)	4.5	6.6	3.6	4.5
Inflation (% GDP deflator)	10.4	16.9	4.3	16.3
Current balance (% GDP)	−0.6	−0.2	1.0	−1.3

Source: Artis and Cobham, Labour's economic policies, p. 267.

the balance of payments deficit declining. Policy helped support this through some fiscal loosening.[18]

But the problem of industrial relations and wage inflation continued. The £6 deal had been followed in 1976 by an agreement to limit increases to 5 per cent, and the following year the figure was 10 per cent. But in 1978 the government sought to reduce inflation further by proposing a 5 per cent ceiling, which was not accepted by the Trades Union Congress (TUC). In practice this ceiling affected only the public sector, where government controlled the budgets. With inflation running at 8–10 per cent, low-paid public sector workers faced a further fall in their real wages, and it was resistance to these cuts which underpinned the 'Winter of Discontent' of 1978/79, and the subsequent Conservative election victory.[19]

To place Britain's economy in context, Table 10.1 sets out British economic performance over the central cycle of the 1970s (the cyclical peak was in November 1973). It suggests a poor performance, but not one entirely out of line with what was happening elsewhere in Western Europe.

II

Up until 1978 the Labour government had some success in overcoming a combination of an appalling economic legacy and external buffeting. But the crisis exposed major problems for the party. It starkly revealed the fragility of the links between the party and the unions, which were crucial to its claim to be the only party that could provide a peaceful resolution of industrial conflict. Some saw this breakdown of relations as fundamentally undermining 'the forward march of labour'.[20] From a different perspective, the key ideologue of British

18 Artis and Cobham, 'Summary and appraisal', pp. 266–77.
19 W. Brown, 'Industrial relations', in Artis and Cobham, *Labour's economic policies*, pp. 213–28.
20 E. Hobsbawm, 'The forward march of labour halted?', *Marxism Today*, Sep. 1978, pp. 279–86.

post-war social democracy, Tony Crosland, argued that 'the party is over', referring explicitly to the impossibility of continuing the expansion of social welfare programmes from the proceeds of economic growth.[21]

In the 1970s this core notion of British social democracy, that a prosperous and expanding industrial economy would provide the resources for a relatively painless expansion of social welfare, came under severe pressure. The profits crisis of 1973–75, to which Labour was forced to respond, gave weight to the argument that without some mechanisms for guaranteeing that prosperity, the dividend of continuous social improvement would have to be curtailed.[22] So in many respects it is right to see the 1970s as the high-water mark for British social democracy, without suggesting that the tradition was entirely exhausted.

Much more important to the immediate fortunes of neo-liberalism was the way the crisis of the 1970s convulsed the Conservative party, and led to the election of Margaret Thatcher as its leader in 1975. The overarching rhetorical strategy that soon emerged under her leadership was twofold. First was an emphasis on the enormous dangers to economic, political, and social stability of inflation.[23] Second was the argument that inflation, alongside Britain's other problems, was not the result of conjunctural circumstances, but was the *culminatory* effect of the whole of the post-war settlement; it was part of the manifestation of British 'decline', which only a radical reversal of policy could effectively address.[24]

The first of these tropes was by no means an opportunistic response to the mid-1970s price explosion. Belief in the destabilising effects of inflation was long-standing amongst supporters of a market economy; such an economy, they thought, could not function if market prices were unstable. This notion was adhered to by neo-liberals, such as Hayek, but was equally associated with Keynes – as Thatcherites pointed out.[25] But the focus on inflation as a dangerous manifestation of underlying ills provided a powerful hook on which to hang criticisms of Labour, which went far beyond the failure to achieve a narrowly defined economic policy objective.

The 'declinist' trope was politically polymorphous. It began on the centre-left as a critique of the Conservative government in the late 1950s and early 1960s,

---

21   K. Jeffreys, *Anthony Crosland* (London, 2000), pp. 179–86.

22   A. Glyn and R. Sutcliffe, *British workers, capitalism and the profits squeeze* (Harmondsworth, 1972).

23   J. Tomlinson, 'Thatcher, monetarism and the politics of inflation', in Jackson and Saunders, *Making Thatcher's Britain*, pp. 62–78; lecture at Preston by Keith Joseph (1974): http://www.margaretthatcher.org/document/1110607.

24   D. Cannadine, 'Apocalypse when? British politicians and British "decline" in the twentieth century', in P. Clarke and C. Trebilcock, eds, *Understanding decline* (Cambridge, 1997), pp. 261–84; E. Green, *Thatcher* (London, 2006), pp. 55–82.

25   F. Hayek, *A tiger by the tail: a 40 years running commentary on Keynesianism* (London, 1972); N. Lawson, Mais lecture 1985, http://www.margaretthatcher.org/document/109504.

linked to the geopolitical uncertainties following the decline of the Empire and before accession to the European Economic Community, and soon spread across the political spectrum; but it was deployed especially by the Right in the 1970s. While not inherently neo-liberal, declinism provided British neo-liberals with an important, because widely resonant, starting point for the critique of the alleged failures of the post-war settlement.[26]

So what more broadly was the relationship between the Conservatives under Thatcher and neo-liberalism? In approaching this issue it is important to stress both the complexity and historical evolution of neo-liberalism. The roots of that ideology lay in three strands of argument: neo-classical economics, Ordo-liberalism, and Austrian Economics, brought together by the belief that the growth of economic planning in the 1930s and 1940s posed a fundamental threat to democracy, and articulated most significantly in the founding of the Mont Pelerin Society in 1947.[27] As Jackson has persuasively argued, the neo-liberalism of the 1930s and 1940s was significantly different to that which dominated in the 1970s and 1980s.[28] Most important in the current context were three characteristics. First, it retained a visceral dislike for trade unions as 'coercive monopolies' whilst its parallel critique of large companies had almost disappeared. This anti-unionism was a long-standing feature of British Conservative politics, but became especially virulent in the 1970s, when trade unions were central villains in the Conservatives 'declinist' account of Britain.[29]

Second, hostility to the welfare state was much more wholehearted in the 1970s and 1980s than previously. In the earlier period neo-liberals were somewhat divided on this issue, but even Hayek, for example, was willing to support a social safety net, while others saw room for much more extensive provision as an important way of sustaining worker support for free markets, and as a quid pro quo for breaking up trade unions.[30] By the 1970s the welfare state was much larger in all Western countries than thirty years earlier. More generally, the state's role in economic and social life had expanded. In response there had emerged a new strand of argument, public choice or 'the economics of politics', which gave a much more thoroughgoing critique of the state and the workings of democracy than had been available in the 1940s, and this strand had been enthusiastically embraced by neo-liberalism.

Thatcherite Conservatives deployed elements of public-choice thinking to contrast political decision-making unfavourably with the workings of the

26   J. Tomlinson, 'The politics of declinism', in L. Black, H. Pemberton and P. Thane, eds, *Reassessing 1970s Britain* (Manchester, 2013), pp. 41–60.

27   D. Plehwe, 'Introduction' to P. Mirowski and D. Plehwe, eds, *The road from Mont Pelerin: the making of the neoliberal thought collective* (Cambridge, MA, 2009), pp. 1–42.

28   B. Jackson, 'At the origins of neo-liberalism: the free economy and the strong state, 1930–1947', *Historical Journal* 53 (2010), pp. 129–51.

29   K. Joseph, *Reversing the trend* (London, 1975).

30   Jackson, 'At the origins'.

market. On the other hand, their conservative politics favoured strong state action in areas such as 'defence' and law and order.[31] As Jackson notes, such a combination was evident in the arguments of the Ordo-liberals in the 1940s, but for them the strong state was not to be used for classic conservative purposes of coercively maintaining social order, but to rigorously sustain a competitive order, including against the machinations of large companies; this was not part of Conservative politics in the 1970s.[32]

The third important shift in neo-liberalism was the rise in prominence of macroeconomics. In the 1930s and 1940s there was a division of opinion amongst neo-liberals on macroeconomic issues, especially on how far they supported Keynesian remedies for unemployment. The attitude was by no means one of wholesale rejection, with even Hayek objecting more on 'technical' grounds than to the spirit of Keynes' proposals.[33] This changed in the late 1960s, especially with the work of Friedman. He advanced claims about the macro-economy that were to be crucial to British politics in the 1970s. First, he argued that, beyond the very short-run, unemployment levels were determined by 'real factors', not by macroeconomic policy, and therefore that, at best, activist fiscal policy was ineffectual. Second, he argued that inflation was 'always and everywhere' a monetary phenomenon, and could only be effectively addressed by control of the money supply.[34]

These arguments became much more potent when inflation rose sharply and as the Conservatives put its reduction at the core of their politics. 'Monetarism' thus became a core feature of 'Thatcherism'. The significance of monetarism did not lie in its specific, instrumental recommendation of controlling the 'money supply' as a way of limiting inflation; instrumentally 'monetarism' in this narrow sense was a resounding failure when applied after 1979, and Friedman strongly rejected the Conservative government's approach to monetary control.[35] But the broader significance of monetarism was as a form of 'statecraft' which enabled Conservatives to detach themselves from negotiating with interest groups, unions, and employers, in pursuit of counter-inflationary goals. It gave them a freedom of manoeuvre which earlier post-war Conservative ideology had lacked.[36]

Monetarism also posed problems for British conservatism. It undermined the long-standing view that one of the problems caused by trade unions was

31   A. Gamble, *The free economy and the strong state* (Basingstoke, 1988).
32   Jackson, 'At the origins', pp. 134, 151.
33   Ibid.
34   M. Friedman, 'The role of monetary policy', *American Economic Review* 58 (1967), pp. 1–17.
35   Friedman, 'Memorandum on monetary policy', Treasury and Civil Service Committee, House of Commons Papers 720 (1980).
36   J. Bulpitt, 'The discipline of the new democracy: Mrs Thatcher's domestic statecraft', *Political Studies* 34 (1989), pp. 19–39.

inflation. In the mid-1970s this analysis was from a Conservative-party view ironic, as the Labour government predicated its policies on the belief that unions *were* key to inflation, and the eventual failure of the Labour government to persuade the unions to agree to lower wage increases was of course the basis of the Winter of Discontent and the triumph of the Conservatives in the following general election.[37] A monetarist analysis of inflation was, however, reconciled with anti-unionism by ascribing to unions both an indirect role in the causing of inflation and responsibility for a whole range of other ills in the declinist framing of Britain's condition.[38]

Clearly neo-liberalism was an important element in Thatcherite conservatism, but the latter was by no means simply derived from the former. It is equally important to note that the growth of neo-liberalism in these years was not a matter of a few senior Conservative politicians being converted by the doctrine and then carrying the ideology into policy on achieving office. This is the narrative suggested by Cockett's pioneering account of the neo-liberal think tanks, especially the IEA, founded in 1957.[39] Undoubtedly the IEA was the key purveyor of neo-liberal ideas in Britain, with close links to the Mont Pelerin Society and publishing a stream of pamphlets that sought to give a layperson's account of neo-liberal thinking on a very wide range of economic and social policy issues. But too much focus on the role of the IEA is misleading in a number of respects.[40] First, while some of the ideas prominent in IEA pamphlets can be seen at work in Thatcherite thinking and eventually policy, others made little headway. Most obviously, a large proportion of the IEA's published output in the 1950s and 1960s was an attack on the post-war welfare state, especially on the 'monopoly' provision of healthcare and public education, with calls for a shift to market-based system such as through the use of vouchers. For reasons returned to in section III below, these proposals made almost no headway. This emphasises the obvious point that while some IEA notions were taken up, others were not, and we need therefore to understand what forces were at work in determining this differential success.

A further problem with the story of a 'heroic' think-tank-based minority slowly permeating sections of the political class with ideas previously deemed wholly marginal is that these ideas found support and influence in a diversity

37   J. Tomlinson, *Managing the economy, managing the people: narratives of economic life in Britain from Beveridge to Brexit* (Oxford, 2017), pp. 187–205.

38   B. Jackson, 'An ideology of class: neo-liberalism and the trade unions, c. 1930–79', in C. Griffiths, J. Nott and W. Whyte, eds, *Classes, cultures and politics: essays for Ross McKibbin* (Oxford, 2011), pp. 263–81; Tomlinson, 'Thatcher, monetarism'.

39   R. Cockett, *Thinking the unthinkable: think-tanks and the economic counter-revolution, 1931–1983* (London, 1994), introduction.

40   Ben Jackson, 'The think-tank archipelago: Thatcherism and neo-liberalism', in Jackson and Saunders, *Making Thatcher's Britain*, pp. 43–61.

of ways beyond shaping the minds of a few Conservative leaders. Ben Jackson and Neil Rollings have shown how the think tanks were closely linked with business, both financially and in personnel.[41]

It is important to emphasise that neo-liberalism was distinct from neo-classical economics, which has always had the potential for diverse interpretations and for underpinning varying political positions.[42] Mirowski has shown how neo-liberalism drew on a *diversity* of economics traditions, embracing not only neo-classicism but also the Austrian School and Ordo-liberalism.[43] None of these latter strands of opinion was strong amongst professional economists in Britain in the 1970s, but one of the successes of the IEA was to mobilise the voice of the minority who did espouse such ideas.[44]

This mobilisation was allied to a major effort to shape media opinion, and a key feature of the 1970s was the key role not of British academic economists, but of economic journalists such as Samuel Brittan, Peter Jay, and David Butt, who drew heavily on American academic economists, including public choice theorists like Buchanan and Tullock.[45] The latter were, arguably, equally important as more mainstream neo-liberal economists, as they gave analytical gravitas to those who distrusted government. These journalists were major conveyors of neo-liberalism to elite thinking generally, but were especially important in the mid-1970s when opinion in financial markets fed directly into the 'credibility' of British fiscal policy, in a context of great leverage for such markets because of the scale of public borrowing in an inflationary environment.[46]

This particular point is well made in Hall's 'institutional analysis', which highlights the conjunctural aspects of the 1970s: growing government borrowing, and hence the heightened significance of 'City opinion', when City opinion was increasingly influenced by neo-liberal financial journalism. Other aspects of Hall's analysis of a 1970s transition from Keynesianism to monetarism are more problematic. He suggests that prior to the 1970s official economic

---

41   Ibid., pp. 46–9; N. Rollings, 'Cracks in the post-war Keynesian settlement? The role of organised business in Britain in the rise of neo-liberalism before Margaret Thatcher', *Twentieth Century British History* 24 (2013), pp. 637–59.

42   See, for example, the very radical use made of notions of 'rent-seeking' in J. Stiglitz, *The price of inequality* (Harmondsworth, 2012).

43   P. Mirowski, 'Postface: defining neoliberalism', in P. Mirowski and Dieter Plehwe, *Road from Mont Pelerin* (Cambridge, MA, 2009), pp. 417–55.

44   Jackson, 'Think-tank archipelago', pp. 50–2; on British economics, see K. Tribe, 'Liberalism and neoliberalism in Britain, 1930–1980', in Mirowski and Plehwe, *Road from Mont Pelerin*, pp. 68–97.

45   D. Lee, ed., *Public choice, past and present: the legacy of James M. Buchanan and Gordon Tullock* (New York, 2013).

46   W. Parsons, *The power of the financial press* (London, 1989); D. Needham, 'Goodbye Great Britain? The press, the Treasury, and the 1976 IMF crisis', in S. Schifferes and R.W. Roberts, eds, *The media and financial crises: historical an comparative perspectives* (London, 2014).

advice was highly concentrated in a Keynesian Treasury, with few other authoritative voices available.[47] However, this draws too sharp a distinction between
theoretical positions and their policy implications. As Bulpitt argued, the key
role of monetarism was to license a withdrawal of the government from direct
bargaining with interest groups, a role which *could* have been played by a
Keynesianism which focused entirely on fiscal and monetary manipulation.[48]
What exposed British-style Keynesianism especially to the neo-liberal critique
was that many of its adherents had gone beyond that macro policy focus to
support incomes and industrial policies: 'Keynesianism plus' policies, which
involved a degree of economic intervention, and state negotiation with interest
groups, which a textbook 'hydraulic Keynesianism' would have avoided.[49]

III

At the level of policy, neo-liberalism achieved some unambiguous victories after
1979. The Thatcher government's desire to 'roll back the state' led to very large-
scale privatisation, selling off publicly owned productive assets in the years after
1983.[50] This was composed both of public corporations and of public housing.

Sales of nationalised industries helped raise revenue and thereby reduce the
PSBR, though revenues amounted to more than 3 per cent of public spending
in only one year, 1988/89.[51] Ideologically important was the attempt to use
these sales to create a 'popular capitalism' by greatly extending personal share
ownership. The initial effects were substantial, with enterprises like British Gas
and British Telecom finding large markets for their shares. By 1997 approximately 22 per cent of the adult population held shares directly, compared
with around 7 per cent in 1979.[52] But the average holding was modest; for
example, British Telecom had 1.4 million shareholders in 2006, but two-thirds
of these held fewer than 800 shares.[53] The aim of a major transformation in
the number of Britons holding substantial equity failed; for the great bulk of

47   Hall, 'From Keynesianism to monetarism'.
48   By 1979 the Treasury was divided in its theoretical allegiances, but the Bank of England
remained strongly Keynesian: its support for Thatcherite policies was based crucially on its desire
to reduce inflation, *not* its support for monetarism: C.A.E. Goodhart, 'The Bank of England view',
in D.J. Needham and A.C. Hotson, eds, *Expansionary fiscal contraction* (Cambridge, 2014), p. 83.
49   For 'Keynesianism plus' see H. Pemberton, *Policy learning and British governance in the
1960s* (Basingstoke, 2004).
50   D. Parker, *The official history of privatization*, vol. 1: *The formative years, 1970–87*
(Abingdon, 2009) and vol. 2: *Popular capitalism, 1987–1997* (Abingdon, 2012).
51   Parker, *Popular capitalism*, p. 505.
52   Ibid., p. 520.
53   Ibid., p. 517.

the population, escaping the 'tyranny of earned income' remained implausible.[54] The trend towards a rising proportion of shares held by institutions, evident since the 1960s, had continued through the period of privatisation; the proportion in the hands of private owners fell from 28 per cent in 1983 to 10 per cent by 2010.[55]

More important, certainly politically, was the sale of public (council) housing at discounts to sitting tenants. Under this policy 1.5 million units were sold, reducing public housing to a largely residual role. This privatisation succeeded by combining three aims in one policy. Housing sales contributed to the reduction in the PSBR, and it gave financial windfalls to purchasers, consolidating electoral support for the Conservatives. Third, it fitted ideologically with notions of extending 'property-owning democracy', an important part of Conservative thinking, especially in regard to housing, since the late nineteenth century and Salisbury's 'villa conservatism'.[56] Sales were concentrated amongst unskilled and semi-skilled workers, whose voting behaviour does seem to have been influenced by the policy.[57]

Up until the 2007 recession, house ownership in Britain was on a rising trend, and was by far the most important form of property ownership. But beyond housing, there has been little spreading of wealth. Overall, wealth inequalities have increased more rapidly in the 'neo-liberal period' than previously.[58]

The most unambiguous success for neo-liberalism was the weakening of trade unions, though this was driven by structural change in the economy as much as by policy. With the successful construction of an anti-union account of the Winter of Discontent, a combination of cumulative legislative restrictions, defeats for key groups of workers (especially the National Union of Mineworkers in 1984/85), and ideological 'de-legitimisation' of union activity saw membership shrink radically.[59]

Also carried through were a wide range of deregulatory measures. The labour market was one area where 'market forces' were given much greater rein, with, for example, the abolition of most Wage Councils which set minimum

54   J. Froud, S. Johal, J. Montgomerie and K. Williams, 'Escaping the tyranny of earned income? The failure of finance as social innovation', New Political Economy 15 (2010), pp. 147–64.
55   Parker, Popular capitalism, p. 520.
56   M.J. Daunton, A property-owning democracy? Housing in Britain (London, 1987). Property-owning democracy is not an inherently Conservative notion: see B. Jackson, 'Property-owning democracy: a short history', in M. O'Neill and T. Williamson, eds, Property-owning democracy: Rawls and beyond (Oxford, 2012), pp. 33–52.
57   D. Butler and D. Kavanagh, The British general election of 1983 (London, 1984).
58   J. Hills, Good times, bad times (Bristol, 2014), pp. 24–8.
59   J. Pencavel, 'The surprising retreat of union Britain', in D. Card, R. Blundell and R. Freeman, eds, Seeking a premier economy: the effects of British economic reforms, 1980–2000 (Chicago, 2004), pp. 181–232.

wages in low-paid sectors.[60] Very important also was the deregulation of the financial system, which underpinned a huge expansion of personal credit in the mid- and late 1980s, supporting the consumption-led recovery from the recession of 1979–81.[61]

Crucial to the advance of neo-liberalism in the 1980s was the repudiation of Keynesian responses to recession. In 1981 the Thatcher government directly contradicted the idea of using fiscal policy to sustain output and employment by introducing a budget aimed at cutting the deficit in the midst of sharply rising unemployment. This decision evoked a major confrontation with a large number of academic economists, but the government stuck to its fiscal constraint.[62] *Politically* this was an important victory for neo-liberalism, even if in overall macro-policy terms the rhetoric of 'the lady's not for turning' was belied by the reduction in interest rates already begun in July 1980.[63]

But from the perspective of more than thirty years later it is evident that this episode did not represent a decisive defeat for 'Keynesianism'. In the recession of the early 1990s the Conservative government under John Major allowed the automatic stabilisers to work, with the effect of a very sharp rise in public borrowing. In the wake of the recession from 2008, British policy went beyond allowing the stabilisers to work, substantially increasing public spending to counteract falling output. Both these later episodes took place when there was no serious inflationary threat, and in that respect the prioritising of low inflation as a policy goal was not compromised. 'Keynesianism without inflation' was politically much less problematic than when it could plausibly be claimed that public borrowing was fuelling a major inflationary surge.[64]

This reordering of priorities between unemployment and inflation has been sustained even as the nostrums of 1970s monetarism about 'controlling the money supply' have been abandoned, with policy based on inflation-targeting by an independent central bank and interest rates as the main instrument of control. The public discussion of economic policy has continued to highlight the importance of employment, whilst the policy framework has subordinated employment goals to the achievement of low inflation.

In the 1950s and 1960s the great bulk of the publications of the IEA were focused on criticising the welfare state; only in the 1970s was there much focus

---

60   This policy was reversed by Labour's national minimum wage in 1998, and the Conservatives changed their line, eventually, in 2014, embracing a 'National Living Wage' to shift some of the burden of wage subsidies back on employers.

61   R. Backhouse, 'The macroeconomics of Margaret Thatcher', *Journal of the History of Economic Thought* 24 (2002), pp. 328–9.

62   P. Booth, *Were 364 economists all wrong?* (London, 2006).

63   D.J. Needham and A.C. Hotson, *Expansionary fiscal contraction: the Thatcher government's 1981 Budget in perspective* (Cambridge, 2014).

64   The inflationary impact of public borrowing is not the only argument deployed against it; also important is the claim that it 'crowds out' the private sector.

on the macro-economy.[65] This critique was coupled to advocacy of radical market reforms, including the breaking up of the National Health Service (NHS), a move to vouchers for schooling, and major restrictions in social security. As envisaged by the IEA, neo-liberal reform of the first two of these, health and school education, has made almost no headway. The NHS continues to be a near 'monopoly provider' and apart from a local experiment or two, vouchers for schools have never been taken up seriously in Britain.[66] The failure of the Thatcher government to pursue the neo-liberal agenda in this regard was noted at the beginning of her period in office, when it was clear that the reasons were electoral. The NHS, in particular, had become sacrosanct.[67]

Since the early 1980s increased expenditure on the NHS has been coupled with various attempts to introduce 'market forces' into the system without threatening the principle of a free service at the point of consumption. In education the trend has also been towards increased expenditure, coupled to progressively removing the role of local government in the running of schools, and with an emphasis on 'competition', but without affecting the principle of free access.[68] Both areas are ones where policy has been shaped by a combination of demography, which has determined levels of demand, and political calculation, where governments have had to recognise the high degree of popular support for free provision.

The pattern in social security has had some parallel with that in health and school education. Expenditure overall has increased, in part because of the demographics of an ageing population driving up spending on pensions. The most striking change in social security since the 1970s has been the rise of a 'new Speenhamland' system of wage subsidies. In the name of improving the incentives to work amongst the unemployed, successive governments have used the tax and benefit system to offset the impact of low wages on household incomes. This began in a small way with family income supplement in 1971, but by 2014 expenditure on tax credits had risen to £27 billion per annum, and £20 billion was spent on housing benefit for those in work.[69] In-work benefits came greatly to exceed payments made to the unemployed, but, in addition, the whole principle of post-war welfare shifted. The classic Beveridge analysis of the sources of poverty suggested the problem fundamentally lay in 'interruption to earnings' (by unemployment, sickness, or old age) along with large numbers of children, the latter to be addressed by 'family allowances' (later

65   Nick Bosanquet, *After the new right* (London, 1983), p. 75.
66   Ibid., pp. 165, 170–1.
67   J. Walsh, 'When do ideas matter? The success and failure of Thatcherite ideas', *Comparative Political Studies* 33 (2000), pp. 500–4.
68   R. Lowe, *The welfare state in Britain since 1945*, 3rd edn (Basingstoke, 2005), pp. 353–64, 415–27; P. Wilding, 'The welfare state and the Conservatives', *Political Studies* 45 (1997), pp. 716–26.
69   Office for Budget Responsibility, *Welfare trends report* (2014), pp. 12, 42, 51.

'child benefit').[70] This analysis always misrepresented the actualities of the labour market, not least in its barely qualified notion of the 'male-breadwinner household'; nevertheless, its fundamental idea that normally paid work would provide a route out of poverty has underpinned thinking across the political spectrum. In contrast 'new Speenhamland' gives a large and expanding role for the state, something difficult to reconcile with notions of a triumphant neo-liberalism.

Employment in Britain has also been shaped by the role of the state in the direct provision of jobs. Most of the 'neo-liberal era' has seen a growth in tax-funded public employment. This growth has been obscured by the problematic way in which public sector employment is defined by the Office for National Statistics, a definition which relies on state *control* of the spending body. More helpful is the definition devised by researchers at the Centre for Research on Socio-Cultural Change (CRESC), in which if more than half of an entity's activities are publicly funded it is deemed a part of the public sector.[71] On this basis they calculate that total state and 'para-state' employment together grew from 5.6 million in 1978 to 8.0 million by 2008, 1.7 million more than the official estimate.[72]

The majority of these jobs have been in education, health, and social care. The expansion can in large part be explained by the high income elasticity of demand for health and education.[73] Fiscal pressures, in combination with market fundamentalist ideology, have meant that this expansion of public sector services has increasingly been done by cheapening labour by contracting-out. So while there have been lots of well-paid and relatively secure public sector jobs, these have been accompanied by burgeoning numbers of low-paid and insecure posts in the para-state sector.

IV

What, overall, can be said about the career of neo-liberalism in Britain since the 1970s?

Since the mid-1970s total public spending in Britain has risen by around 250% in real terms, while as a share of GDP it has fluctuated with the economic

70   A. Cutler, K. Williams and J. Williams, *Keynes, Beveridge and beyond* (London, 1986).

71   J. Buchanan, J. Froud, S. Johal, A. Leaver and K. Williams, 'Undisclosed and unsustainable: problems of the UK National Business Model', CRESC Working Paper Series 75 (Manchester, 2009).

72   J. Froud, S. Johal, J. Law, A. Leaver and K. Williams, 'Rebalancing the economy (or buyer's remorse)', CRESC Working Paper Series 87 (Manchester, 2011), p. 18.

73   W. Baumol, 'Macroeconomics of unbalanced growth: the anatomy of urban crisis', *American Economic Review* 57 (1967), pp. 415–26.

cycle, but with a downward trend from just under 50 per cent in 1975/76 to around 42 per cent in 2016/17. The huge fall in public investment means *current* spending has fallen by perhaps 5 per cent of GDP; but this fall does not reflect cuts in overall social welfare spending. Budgets for health care and education have *risen* as a share of GDP. In social security the aim of squeezing the incomes of the unemployed has been carried through, but overall social security spending has risen in line with GDP.[74] Much of this has come from growing expenditure on pensions, but the most striking change has been the rise in in-work and housing benefits. So overall during the 'neo-liberal era' state spending on welfare has *risen*; we have moved from what David Edgerton called a 'warfare state' in mid-twentieth-century Britain to one which, at least in quantitative terms, more than ever deserves the term 'welfare state'.[75]

Public borrowing, too, has varied with the economic cycle, but at levels significantly *higher* than in the preceding 'Keynesian age'.[76] Of course, much of this has reflected the impact of the automatic stabilisers in a much more unstable macroeconomic environment; but, strikingly, apart from in 1981, these stabilisers have been allowed to operate, or even been reinforced by discretionary fiscal action when recessions have occurred.

As suggested above, the growth of public sector employment, along with the 'new Speenhamland' system, seriously qualifies narratives around 'the triumph of neo-liberalism', which friends and foes alike see as dominating the political economy of Britain since the 1970s. But there is a bigger issue here about neo-liberal notions of the economy. Growing subsidies to employment have gone along with other, very extensive forms of support for the private sector. The basic neo-liberal idea that the private sector is the dynamic part of the economy when untrammelled by government is at odds with the picture of an enormous range of corporate tax breaks and subsidies. Farnsworth shows that while explicit 'industrial subsidies' have tended to decline in significance since the 1980s, tax expenditures remain very substantial, estimated by the Organisation for Economic Co-operation and Development as equivalent to 4.5 per cent of GDP in the UK in 2006. Taken together with *explicit* subsidies, total expenditure on business subsidies by the state exceeds corporate tax payments.[77] As he argues, 'even in the neo-liberal era, businesses have remained heavily dependent on states, and even when some forms of corporate welfare have been phased out, primarily in response to tighter international regulations

---

74   A. Jowett and M. Hardie, 'Longer term trends – public sector finance', Office for National Statistics, Nov. 2014; Office for Budget Responsibility, *Welfare trends*, p. 5.
75   D. Edgerton, *Warfare state: Britain, 1920–1970* (Cambridge, 2006).
76   Public sector net borrowing (unadjusted) peaked in 1993/94 at 7.7 per cent of GDP, compared with 7.0 per cent in 1975/76.
77   K. Farnsworth, *Social welfare versus corporate welfare* (Basingstoke, 2012), pp. 119, 120.

concerning trade-distorting business subsidies, other forms of corporate welfare have taken their place'.[78]

The growth of 'corporate welfare' has gone largely unremarked in the political arena. In this respect, as in others, British policy has *de facto* evolved in a direction difficult to reconcile with the tenets of neo-liberalism. How is this to be explained? One aspect is the distinct politics of neo-liberalism in Britain: its reconciliation with Conservatism. It should be emphasised the degree of contingency in this reconciliation. The early Mont Pelerin and IEA promoters of the doctrine did not see their natural allies as lying in the Conservative party. The IEA, when it set out to permeate its ideas amongst opinion-formers, did not focus on Conservatives, and for a period in the 1950s and 1960s it had close ties with elements of the Liberal party.[79] The close association between neoliberalism and British Conservatives has to be seen as historically contingent; contingent upon ideological shifts and the electoral decline of the Liberals as a political force, coupled with the capture of the leadership of the Conservative party by the Thatcherites, and this in the specific 1970s' environment of high inflation, high public borrowing, and industrial unrest, which gave that leadership the opportunity to take power and pursue (parts of) the neo-liberal agenda.

Hence, neo-liberalism has been *one* underpinning of the New Right in Britain, but that Right's policies have been conditioned not only by other doctrines (such as Burkeian conservatism), but also, and despite Thatcherite disdain for the phrase, a very strong sense of the politically possible in a de-industrialising economy.

78   Ibid., p. 12.
79   P. Sloman, *The Liberal Party and the economy, 1929–1964* (Oxford, 2015), pp. 123–5; B. Jackson, 'Currents of neo-liberalism: British political ideologies and the New Right, c.1955–1979', *English Historical Review* 131 (2016), pp. 823–50.

11

Maplin: the Treasury and London's third airport in the 1970s

DUNCAN NEEDHAM

The chapters in this volume each relate to one of the 'four Martin Dauntons' mentioned in the Introduction. In focusing on an episode of transport history, this chapter goes further back, to Martin's PhD supervisor, Theo Barker. In his appreciation of Barker's career, Martin wrote: 'in Theo's hands history is always human; it is about people making decisions in institutional, economic or political circumstances'.[1] As the debate over Heathrow expansion illustrates, there are few more political decisions than choosing where to locate new airport capacity. The debate was particularly fierce in the 1970s, when the Heath government rejected the findings of the then most expensive public inquiry, the Roskill Commission, and announced that London's third airport would be built on reclaimed land at Maplin Sands in the Thames Estuary. Situated nearly fifty miles from central London, Maplin was the most expensive of the four options shortlisted by Roskill.[2] It was also the least attractive to the airlines. Three years later, with the Maplin Development Corporation having already commenced work on an artificial island, the successor Labour government scrapped the project.[3]

This chapter begins with a brief outline of the post-war debate over the location of London's third airport. It then draws upon Prime Ministerial,

---

1 M.J. Daunton, 'Theo Barker: an appreciation', *Journal of Transport History*, 3rd ser., 19, 2 (1998), p. 99.
2 Roskill estimated that in total Maplin/Foulness would cost £156–197 million more than Cublington (1971 values) largely because of the extra time passengers would spend travelling to the more remote site. In public expenditure terms, the 1971 estimates were similar (£349 million for Foulness versus £373 million for Cublington for a 1980 opening). G.S. Downey, 'Third London airport', 6 Jan. 1971, London, TNA T 319/1239.
3 The 'trial bank' at Maplin Sands is still sometimes visible from Shoeburyness.

Cabinet, and Treasury documents to explain why the Heath government overrode the Roskill Commission to choose Maplin, and why the project was subsequently abandoned. The Treasury was opposed to Maplin from the outset. Nonetheless, the department was criticised for its handling of the venture. In 1974, just before Maplin was written off, former Ministry of Transport economist Christopher Foster argued that Treasury officials had 'failed to perform their function' of scrutinising a major public expenditure project.[4] Former Board of Trade official John Heath further suggested that Maplin was symptomatic of an inability to manage infrastructure projects characterised by 'a long delay between decision and execution, considerable uncertainty, large scale, and government domination'.[5] Did the Treasury fail with Maplin? And what are the lessons for the management of large infra-structure projects today?[6]

The debate over London's third airport

In the immediate post-war years, London was served by seven different airfields: Blackbushe (Hampshire), Bovingdon (Hertfordshire), Croydon, Gatwick, Heathrow, Northolt, and Stansted.[7] A 1953 white paper proposed rationalising the London flying pattern by developing Gatwick as the second major airport to Heathrow.[8] Gatwick was an unexpected choice – the assumption had been that Stansted would house London's second airport. Stansted possessed one of the finest runways in Europe, built by the US Air Force during the Second World War, and had been bought by the Ministry of Civil Aviation in 1949 'with the firm understanding that it would be London's second airport'.[9] Indeed, Gatwick was only chosen over Stansted in 1953 because a period of Cold War intensification meant more military air activity over East Anglia.[10] In 1963 a Whitehall interdepartmental committee confirmed that Stansted remained the

4   C.D. Foster *et al.*, *Lessons of Maplin: is the machinery for governmental decision-making at fault?* (London, 1974), p. 49.
5   Ibid., p. 13.
6   For a recent account of the failure of large-scale British projects, see A.S. King and I.M. Crewe, *The blunders of our governments* (London, 2013).
7   Civilian flights ended at Bovingdon in 1947 and at Northolt in 1954. Croydon ceased passenger flights in 1959, Blackbushe a year later.
8   In 1953 there appeared to be few capacity constraints at Heathrow outside high summer and periods of bad weather. Nonetheless, Stansted would be 'held in reserve' and Blackbushe would be the 'supplementary', Ministry of Civil Aviation, *London's airports*, Cmnd 8902 (London, 1953), pp. 3–4.
9   P. Hall, *Great planning disasters* (London, 1980), p. 17.
10   Ibid.

first choice for when Heathrow and Gatwick reached capacity.[11] As the Minister of Housing and Local Government, Anthony Greenwood, told the House of Commons in 1967:

> at least from 1953 onwards, the assumption was consistently made that Stansted would be the third London airport. That assumption helped to determine the routing of air traffic, including military traffic – hon. Members must remember that there are twice as many military movements as civil movements every day – and also helped to determine the distribution of military airfields and other installations.[12]

Stansted remained the government's first choice until a 1967 white paper recommending its expansion produced a well-organised local protest, threatened a revolt of backbench MPs, and produced an actual rebellion in the Lords.[13] There was also a legal problem. In November 1967 the little-known Council on Tribunals ruled that, since the white paper proposed a new runway alignment, there must also be a new planning inquiry.[14] With Heathrow expected to reach capacity in 1970, and noise levels in parts of West London becoming increasingly intolerable, the President of the Board of Trade, Anthony Crosland, appointed the Roskill Commission in May 1968 'to enquire into the timing of the need for a four-runway airport to cater for the growth of traffic at existing airports servicing the London area, to consider the various alternative sites, and to recommend which site should be selected'.[15]

The Roskill Commission sat from June 1968, issuing summary findings in December 1970 followed by a 276-page report a month later.[16] The Commission's use of the latest techniques in cost–benefit analysis attracted favourable comment. Its choice of Cublington in rural Buckinghamshire did not. An Early Day Motion tabled by a group of MPs opposed to *any* of the three 'inland sites' shortlisted by Roskill attracted 134 Conservative signatures out of a total of 219. As David McKie points out:

11   D. McKie, *A sadly mismanaged affair: a political history of London's third airport* (London, 1973), pp. 73–9.

12   The US Air Force had refurbished the runway in 1956; HC Debs, 29 Jun. 1967, vol. 749, c. 877.

13   In 1967, 258 MPs (including 91 Labour MPs) signed an Early Day Motion condemning the choice of Stansted. For the Lords rebellion, see McKie, *A sadly mismanaged affair*, pp. 132–7. For the local campaign against Stansted, see B. Cashinella and K. Thompson, *Permission to land* (London, 1971).

14   The Council on Tribunals was set up in 1958 to review and report on the constitution and working of public tribunals. Newspaper reports hinted at a deliberate attempt by ministers to forestall Stansted expansion in 1967 by alerting the Council to the different runway alignment to that considered by the 1965–66 local inquiry, McKie, *A sadly mismanaged affair*, p. 140.

15   *Report*, Commission on the Third London Airport (the 'Roskill Commission') (London, 1971).

16   There were a further nine volumes of 'Papers and proceedings'.

There was never any chance when the Roskill Report finally appeared in January 1971 that the recommendation of Cublington would be accepted. Politically it was already stone dead; killed by a combination of mounting public concern about the environment and the existence in the Commons and the Lords of a well-marshalled lobby which would have defeated the Government had it tried to go ahead.[17]

In December 1970 Prime Minister Ted Heath commented that the report 'seems likely to give us a good deal of trouble'.[18] Drawing from his 1940s experience in the Ministry of Civil Aviation, Heath revealed 'I have my own very clear ideas about what will have to be done – and it had best be done quickly', before he conceded 'I will read the report first.'[19] Influenced by the successful campaign against Stansted expansion that had precipitated the Roskill Commission, Heath was 'of the opinion that the pressures on the environment which would be created by a site inland, such as the one at Cublington, would be so outrageous that they must be allowed to outweigh any small financial advantage of a more central site. I therefore favour siting the Airport, if it is necessary, at Foulness.'[20] (During 1972, references to 'Maplin' displaced the less-euphonious 'Foulness'). But Foulness had only made the shortlist at the insistence of one dissenting member of the Roskill Commission, the urban planner Colin Buchanan, who argued that 'it would be nothing less than an environmental disaster if the airport were to be built on any of the inland sites'.[21] It had come thirteenth on the long list, behind Stansted (ninth) whose charms, so evident to successive government ministers, were less apparent to Roskill's technocrats.[22] The airlines would have to be coerced to shift their operations from Heathrow to the Southend peninsula. Maplin might require subsidies simply to break even. And the road and rail links to London would blight a large swathe of South Essex.[23] In its favour were the enthusiastic backing of two private sector consortia (keen to develop a seaport complex to rival Rotterdam's Europoort), support from Essex County Council, and (at that stage) weak local opposition.

---

17   McKie, *A sadly mismanaged affair*, p. 191.
18   E.R.G. Heath, 'The Roskill Report', 24 Dec. 1970, TNA PREM 15/698.
19   'Prime Minister to Robert Armstrong' (telegram), Dec. 1970, TNA PREM 15/698.
20   'E.R.G. Heath to Home Secretary', Dec. 1970, TNA PREM 15/698.
21   Roskill (Note of dissent), p. 159.
22   Hall, *Great planning disasters*, p. 30.
23   Foulness ('place of birds' in Old English) is also the winter abode of much of the world's Brent geese population, with the attendant problem of 'goose ingestion' by aircraft engines.

The Treasury view

While the Roskill Commission was sitting, planning within Whitehall was largely confined to the defence and compensation issues that would be generated by the new airport. The pace quickened with the release of the Commission's preliminary report in December 1970. At Heath's behest, the Ministerial Committee on Regional Policy and the Environment considered the Commission's findings, assisted by a team of officials drawn largely from the Cabinet Office, the Department of Trade and Industry, the Department of the Environment, the Ministry of Defence, and the Treasury. It is from the papers of this team that the 'Treasury view' of Maplin emerges.

While officials had their own opinions on the relative merits of each site and the timing of need, the Treasury as a department was sympathetic to the Roskill conclusion in favour of Cublington. There was also admiration for the sophisticated cost–benefit analysis employed. Nonetheless, officials were aware that despite the economic arguments, the politicians were leaning towards Maplin. The cost–benefit analysis showed that the extra time passengers would spend travelling to and from the Southend peninsula meant Maplin would be viable only with cross-subsidies from the existing South-East airports. While subsidies would reduce the chances of Maplin becoming a 'white elephant', they would do nothing to eliminate the economic disadvantages *vis-à-vis* the other sites shortlisted by Roskill. There would be an opportunity cost to the taxpayer and a misallocation of resources. Treasury Under-Secretary Michael Bridgeman commented: 'to my mind, the case against Foulness is conclusive, and the real debate now ought to be the choice between Cublington and Thurleigh [the third Roskill site in Bedfordshire]'.[24] His colleague Peter Lazarus agreed: 'there is no reasonable doubt about the general conclusions to be derived from the figures which clearly show that Cublington should be the preferred solution'.[25] Indeed, Lazarus was concerned that the Treasury representative on the official committee, Deputy Secretary Raymond Gedling, was taking too soft a line: 'I know that you take the view that Ministers will not in the event be prepared to consider an inland site, but this does not necessarily mean that the Official Committee, which has been charged with looking at the facts, should go out of its way to make it easy for Ministers to reach such a decision.'[26] As Assistant Secretary Gordon Downey pointed out 'from a purely Treasury point of view, I think our list of preferences (in descending order) should be (i) Cublington

24   The fourth Roskill site at Nuthampstead in Essex was quickly ruled out; 'J.M. Bridgeman to Mr Downey', 4 Feb. 1971, TNA T 319/1239.
25   P.E. Lazarus, 'Official team on the third London airport', 4 Feb. 1971, TNA T 319/1239.
26   'P.E. Lazarus to R. Gedling', 2 Mar. 1971, TNA T 319/1241.

(ii) Thurleigh (iii) Foulness (iv) Postpone a decision'.[27] Postponement was the preference of Second Permanent Secretary Sir Samuel Goldman, who wanted to slow down air traffic growth by imposing a tax.[28] This would have the twin benefits of generating a new revenue stream and creating a breathing space for new aircraft technology to develop. This might obviate the need for a new airport altogether.[29]

It all came to naught. On 17 March 1971 the Ministerial Committee on Regional Policy and the Environment agreed with Heath's conclusion in favour of Maplin:

> the recent debates in both Houses of Parliament have shown that we have no chance of obtaining the necessary Parliamentary approval for the building of the [third London airport] if Cublington were chosen as the site, and there is little doubt that opposition on a similar scale would soon build up if we attempted to choose Thurleigh instead.[30]

But Treasury officials had not yet given up. On the eve of the Cabinet discussion, Downey urged the Chancellor, Anthony Barber, to continue pressing the merits of both an inland site and a tax on air travel.[31] Failing that, he was advised to recommend postponing a decision.[32] But with Chief Secretary Maurice Macmillan deciding ahead of the Cabinet discussion that 'the choice of any inland site would be politically impracticable', Treasury officials would have to 'play it long'.[33]

27   G.S. Downey, 'Ministerial committee on regional policy and the environment', 12 Mar. 1971, TNA T 319/1245.

28   Goldman argued that if the rate of motor traffic growth had been slowed down then 'we might have saved enormous sums on capital construction (roads, etc.); saved much spoliation of the environment; and found ourselves with a much less intractable problem than that which confronts us now', S. Goldman, 'Roskill report: third London airport', 21 Dec. 1970, TNA T 319/1238; S. Goldman, 'Ministerial Committee on Regional Policy and the Environment', 12 Mar. 1971, TNA T 319/1245.

29   Cabinet Secretary Sir Burke Trend was sceptical: 'A quite penal rate of tax … would probably have to be imposed before … significant numbers of people could give up their holiday on the Costa Brava and go to Blackpool instead', B.St.J. Trend, 'The third London airport', 24 Mar. 1971, TNA PREM 15/698.

30   'The third London Airport (note by the Secretary of State for the Home Department)', 22 Mar. 1971, TNA CAB 129/156.

31   G.S. Downey, 'Cabinet – third London airport', 24 Mar. 1971, TNA T 319/1242.

32   Officials also raised the spectre of a maladministration finding by the Parliamentary Commissioner against the government if it so obviously overrode the Roskill Commission, 'J.M. Bridgeman to R. Gedling', 2 Mar. 1971, TNA T 319/1241.

33   J.B. Unwin, 'Third London airport', 24 Mar. 1971, TNA T 319/1242.

Playing it long

After the briefest of discussions, the Cabinet concluded in favour of Foulness on 25 March 1971.[34] There were three main issues to resolve before reclamation work could begin: relocation of the army's munitions testing facilities at neighbouring Shoeburyness (and the removal of unexploded ordnance from the runway sites); the precise location of the runways; and the extent of private sector involvement in the project.[35] The army had been testing ordnance at Shoeburyness since the Napoleonic Wars, and was reluctant to leave. After a local planning inquiry ruled out relocation at Pembury on the Pembrokeshire coast in 1971, ministers alighted upon Tain (near Caithness), only for this to be ruled out on political grounds in 1972.[36] Despite trawling through another 85 sites, a replacement for the flat sands of Maplin could not be found, and munitions testing continues there today.

In 1971 the Treasury estimated that each year Maplin was delayed would save at least £22 million in public expenditure.[37] This was increasingly important as it became clear during 1972 that Heath's attempt to grow real GDP by 5 per cent per annum (the 'dash for growth') was overheating the UK economy. Nonetheless, there is little to suggest that Treasury officials conspired to delay Maplin by holding up the relocation of the munitions testing facility. They could rely on the inability of the Ministry of Defence to relocate in the face of local opposition wherever a new site was proposed. But officials were alert to the possibilities for undermining the airport proposal. In early 1973 the Treasury's Margaret Elliot-Binns recommended 'delaying tactics for a few months, while the pressure groups against Maplin do their work, while Ministers find it more and more difficult to find sites for the Shoeburyness facilities and while the pressure on public expenditure tightens'.[38] Assistant Secretary John Slater responded with a minute entitled 'Could we cancel Maplin?', suggesting Treasury officials use the delay to enlist the Chief Secretary's support for 'an immediate reappraisal' of the entire project.[39]

Treasury involvement in selecting the precise location of the runway sites at Maplin was largely confined to costing the options. Officials favoured the

34 Cabinet Office, 'Conclusions of a meeting of the Cabinet held at 10 Downing Street, SW1, on Thursday, 25 March 1971', 26 Mar. 1971, TNA CAB 128/49.
35 There was also the problem of the SS *Richard Montgomery*, wrecked off the Isle of Sheppey in 1944, which contains an estimated 1400 tonnes of high explosive.
36 In November 1972 the Chief Whip Francis Pym noted that 'our political position in Scotland is just as important as the speed of development at Maplin', 'AHW to Mr A.G. Semple', 16 Nov. 1972, TNA PREM 15/1252.
37 J. Bowman, 'The Roskill Commission: economic analysis of the choice of site and timing of need for the third London airport', Apr. 1970, TNA T 319/1238.
38 M.J. Elliot-Binns, 'Maplin', 2 Mar. 1973, TNA T 319/1702.
39 J.F. Slater, 'Could we cancel Maplin?', Mar. 1973, TNA T 319/1702.

cheapest option ('Site A'), the location considered by Roskill, which, being closest to Southend, would mean less-expensive transport links. Site A would also mean less delay, since it was marginally less affected by the army's munitions testing. But precisely because Site A was closer to Southend, ministers rejected it in a favour of a more expensive location, a mile-and-a-half to the north-east. Having bowed to public pressure to select Maplin in the first place, they argued that the cheaper/noisier site would cause further delays by forfeiting the support of the local council.

The third issue to resolve before reclamation work could begin was the extent of private sector involvement. One of Maplin's original boosters was the consulting engineer Bernard Clark. Clark claimed to have been 'mulling over' the idea of a large industrial complex on reclaimed land in the Thames since the 1930s, and had been enthusiastically promoting his plan since the mid-1960s.[40] He had given evidence to the Roskill Commission, where one witness described him as 'a bit of a buffoon' who nonetheless 'always had very good maps'.[41] More plausible was the Thames Estuary Development Company (TEDCO) led by former National Union of Conservative and Unionist Associations chairman Sir John Howard. Howard had appointed to his board representatives both from the Port of London Authority, responsible for developments in the Thames, and Southend Borough Council.[42] TEDCO had also given evidence to the Roskill Commission. The Commission had not been impressed, and the company was forced to withdraw its claim that a combined airport/seaport/industrial complex could be built without any cost to the taxpayer. After contributing the foreshore and seabed in return for an equity stake in the private development company, the taxpayer would bear the full cost should the project fail. The Commission, well aware of Maplin's merits to private sector interests, had 'difficulty in seeing what advantages there are to the taxpayer in such a scheme'.[43] Moreover, given that the state can almost always raise funds more cheaply than the private sector, private sector involvement would likely raise the overall cost.

The Treasury might have been expected to welcome private sector involvement since it would reduce the cost to the public purse. Instead, officials sided with Roskill. Gordon Downey advised that 'the advantages of a Seaport/Airport project claimed by the Thames Estuary Development Co. and others are not such as to justify crediting Foulness with an advantage'.[44] A standalone airport

---

40 Cashinella and Thompson, *Permission to land*, p. 103; Clark's plan was publicised by the *Daily Telegraph* on 21 Jun. 1967.

41 McKie, *A sadly mismanaged affair*, p. 149.

42 TEDCO also included London and Thames Haven Oil Wharves, Rio Tinto, and John Mowlem and Co. A second consortium, Thames Aeroport Group, conducted little detailed planning and appeared to be no more than a pressure group.

43 *Report*, Roskill Commission, p. 126.

44 G.S. Downey, 'Foulness seaport/airport project', 2 Mar. 1971, TNA T 319/1241.

at Maplin held little attraction to the private sector since there would be no profits for years, perhaps decades. The project was of interest only because of the possibility of industrial development and, at the very least, a new seaport. But this would conflict with the government's regional policy, whereby development areas in the outer regions took priority over the South-East. It would also create problems of 'over-crowding' in South Essex. Servicing the airport would require a new town the size of Coventry. Additional industrial development would put further strain on the local economy.

Nonetheless, in keeping with his free market instincts, Heath insisted on giving the private sector every opportunity. He forced Secretary of State John Davies to insert a clause into his April 1971 announcement to 'keep open the option of private capital providing the whole complex'.[45] But after a series of meetings between his junior Minister, Michael Heseltine, and TEDCO, Environment Secretary Peter Walker concluded, as the Roskill Commission and Treasury officials had several months earlier, that 'the TEDCO proposals do not stand up to examination and should be rejected'.[46] Private sector involvement would be limited to representation on the government-sponsored Maplin Development Corporation. However, Heseltine was keen that Maplin should be 'a showpiece of design'.[47] The government should commit itself to 'a prestige project', a phrase almost guaranteed to send a shudder through the Treasury.[48]

A troubled bill

With the Cabinet deciding on the precise runway location and the Maplin Development Corporation taking shape in the summer of 1972, officials could begin drafting the Maplin Development Bill, to be laid before Parliament in the autumn. There was an immediate problem. While the Port of London Authority had the power to build a 'dumping harbour' in the Thames, it could not reclaim land. Nor could the British Airports Authority, which would ultimately own the site. The major reclamation work could not begin until the Maplin Development Corporation had come into legal being, once the Bill had received Royal Assent. But because the development would impact upon specific individuals and groups it was designated a 'hybrid bill'. Private petitions would have to be heard at the committee stage, lengthening the legislative

---

45   P.L. Gregson, 'Third London airport announcement', 22 Apr. 1971, TNA T 319/1244.

46   The TEDCO proposal rested on selling up to 600 acres of reclaimed land per annum. Experience with new towns in the 1960s suggested that 30 acres per annum was more realistic, P.E. Walker, 'Third London airport', 29 Dec. 1971, TNA PREM 15/1251.

47   M.R.D. Heseltine, 'Foulness airport/seaport/industrial complex', Dec. 1971, TNA PREM 15/1251.

48   Ibid.

process.[49] In July 1972 the Government's Parliamentary Agent advised that, to satisfy Parliamentary 'expediency', reclamation work could not start until these petitions had been satisfied.[50] To start work before the committee stage might prejudice the interests of the petitioners, opening up the threat of legal action. But work had to commence in the spring of 1973 if the first runway were to open in 1980 as planned.

The Bill received its first Commons reading on 1 December 1972. The second reading, scheduled for 30 January 1973, was postponed when it emerged at a meeting of the Conservative Aviation Committee that growing backbench opposition might overturn the government's majority. Local opposition was growing as it became clear that the 'world's first environmental airport' would require a large new town and major transport links through an already congested part of Essex.[51] As Shadow Environment spokesman Anthony Crosland pointed out, the road links would mean 'far more homes and families disrupted by bulldozers than Cublington'.[52] MPs from south-east Essex were joined by colleagues who questioned the need for a new airport given that larger, quieter aircraft were already reducing noise pollution around Heathrow.

There was also the recent agreement with the French to dig the Channel Tunnel. Roskill had assumed this would have marginal impact on air traffic. More recent surveys suggested otherwise. Sensing an opportunity, Crosland drafted a 'reasoned amendment' requesting that legislation be postponed until the project had been fully reappraised by the recently formed Civil Aviation Authority (CAA). Having set up the Roskill Commission in 1968, Crosland had subsequently concluded that, while the South-East might need more runways, there was no need for an entirely new airport – and certainly not one in the Thames Estuary:

> the choice of Foulness is totally wrong, on the ground of damage to environment, and particularly the coastline; on the ground of destruction of homes for motorways; on the ground of enormous additional cost; and probably also on the ground of safety ... I prophesy that Foulness, if it is ever built at all, will turn out to be the white elephant of the century, because airlines will not use it.[53]

49 Petitions were received from: Southend Corporation, Rochford Rural District Council, the Royal Yachting Association, the Essex River Authority, Bambergers Ltd (a timber company), and a protest group led by The Defenders of Essex: Department of the Environment, 'Maplin – general review of progress', Mar. 1973, TNA T 319/1702/1.
50 P.E. Walker, 2 Aug. 1972, TNA T 319/1456.
51 The phrase was used by Environment Minister Eldon Griffiths in 1972, HC Debs, 9 Aug. 1972, vol. 842, c. 1747.
52 C.A.R. Crosland, 'The folly of Foulness', *Guardian*, 28 Apr. 1971.
53 HC Debs, 26 Apr. 1971, vol. 816, c. 37.

In the event, Crosland's amendment was defeated, and the Bill passed its second reading on 8 February 1973 with a majority of twenty-three, with five Conservatives voting against the government.[54] Six days later Treasury Under-Secretary Anthony Phelps advised Deputy Secretary Leo Pliatzky that:

> For the moment – just after the successful Second Reading of the Bill – I see no hope of our getting the 1971 decision overturned. But there will be plenty of natural obstacles before the Bill (which is a hybrid one) is passed. If the Bill runs into trouble, or if the public expenditure constraints become much more severe in the next few months, we ought then to see if we can get the whole thing reconsidered before too much money is committed.[55]

Pliatzky replied that the CAA review 'could give grounds for reopening the matter'.[56]

Discussion moved on to whether officials should break cover and enlist ministerial support to undermine Maplin. As John Slater pointed out, 'I do not believe that the Treasury (even if our Ministers were so minded) could "kill" the project without a thorough and very high-level group having firmly recommended in that course.'[57] Either way, it would be better to scrap the project before the contracts for the reclamation work were let. Accordingly, Elliot-Binns advised the new Chief Secretary, Patrick Jenkin, ahead of the Ministerial Committee on the Third London Airport meeting in March 1973, 'to suggest that the timing of the need of the airport should also be examined so as to give an overall assessment of the feasibility, costs and benefits of various opening dates [and] to stress the very large public expenditure implications'.[58] Jenkin agreed that a delay would be 'helpful in the public expenditure context ... popular ... [and] consistent with the latest traffic forecasts', albeit he failed to convince his ministerial colleagues who decided that 'it should remain the Government's intention to achieve the earliest possible opening date'.[59]

The CAA traffic forecast was leaked in April 1973.[60] It came as a surprise to the Prime Minister, who asked 'What is this CAA report I read about which

---

54   The rebels included local MPs, Sir Bernard Braine (Essex South East) and Sir Stephen McFadden (Southend East). *The Times* had earlier estimated that at least 22 Conservatives might rebel, J. Grosser, 'MPs believe Ministers fear defeat on Maplin airport Bill', *The Times*, 29 Jan. 1972.
55   A.J. Phelps, 'Maplin airport', 14 Feb. 1973, TNA T 319/1702/1.
56   Ibid (annotation).
57   J.F. Slater, 'Could we cancel Maplin?', Mar. 1973, TNA T 319/1702.
58   M.J. Elliot-Binns, 'Maplin – general progress', Mar. 1973, TNA T 319/1702/1. Jenkin succeeded as Chief Secretary in January 1973.
59   D.J. Howard, 'Maplin – general review of progress', 26 Mar. 1973, TNA T 319/1702/1; Cabinet Office, 'General review of progress', 27 Mar. 1973, TNA T 319/1702/1.
60   D. Fairhall, 'Secret report could shatter Maplin project', *Guardian*, 21 Apr. 1973.

is to be published shortly and will concern the Maplin project?'[61] The report had been compiled with the involvement of the Department of Trade and Industry (which had always preferred Thurleigh), the British Airports Authority (which owned Stansted), and the British Airways Board (which wanted to stay at Heathrow, but might have been persuaded to shift some operations to Cublington). Heath suspected a plot, especially when told that earlier drafts of the report had been even more hostile to the Maplin project.[62]

The CAA report was critical in turning the tide against Maplin. As Table 11.1 shows, its forecasts of passenger numbers and air transport movements were higher than those used by the Roskill Commission. However, greater 'mixed-mode' runway use, improved air traffic control techniques, and fewer 'general aviation' and 'positioning' flights would mean more efficient use of existing runways.[63] The CAA estimated that the existing South-East runways would be able to handle 502,000 air traffic movements in 1980, well above forecast demand of 488,000.[64] A single runway at Maplin would suffice until at least 1990. But so too would the existing capacity at Stansted and Southend – both of which would have to close to make way for Maplin – and at the underused Luton. The problem was no longer a shortage of runways. It was a shortage of terminal capacity.[65]

On 13 June the government was defeated on a Conservative backbench amendment requiring ministers to 'to delay, vary or desist from construction of an airport on land to be reclaimed as a result of the passage of this Act' should technical developments in aircraft negate the need for additional runway capacity.[66] A week later the Cabinet recognised that 'public opinion was becoming increasingly critical of the Maplin project, partly in terms of the expenditure involved but even more on the grounds that an airport at Maplin was no longer necessary'.[67] The Treasury grasped the opportunity, with Elliot-Binns advising the Chief Secretary that 'we have considerable doubts about

---

61   'E.R.G. Heath to C.W. Roberts', 30 Apr. 1973, TNA PREM 15/1258.
62   Peter Hall refers to a 'London airports lobby', comprising the Department of Trade, the Civil Aviation Authority, the British Airports Authority (and their predecessors), and the airlines that consistently favoured Stansted as the third London airport from around 1950.
63   'Mixed mode' means alternate landings and take-offs on individual runways. 'General aviation' is non-scheduled traffic such as business jets and training flights. Civil Aviation Authority, *Forecasts of air traffic and capacity at airports in the London area* (London, 1973), p. 21.
64   The major change was at Gatwick, where forecast capacity rose from 110,000 air traffic movements in 1980 (Roskill) to 168,000 air traffic movements (CAA). This was primarily because the airlines would rather spread flights more evenly through the day, week, and year than move to Maplin, ibid., p. 10.
65   The introduction of wider-bodied aircraft such as the Boeing 747 also saw the CAA revise the Roskill assumption of terminal passengers per plane in 1980 from 126 to 130.
66   HC Debs, 13 Jun. 1973, vol. 857, cc. 1621–2.
67   Cabinet Office, 'Conclusions of a meeting of the Cabinet held at 10 Downing Street on 21 June 1973', 21 Jun. 1971, TNA CAB 128/52.

Table 11.1. 1980 London airport traffic forecasts and outcome

	Passengers (million)		Air transport movements	
	Demand	Capacity	Demand	Capacity
Roskill Commission (1971)	56.6	61	482,000	478,000
CAA Report (1973)	58	57	488,000	502,000
Maplin Review (1974)	51.2[1]	61[2]	450,000[2]	620,000[2]
Outcome	40		441,173	

Notes

1 'Assessment figure' derived from interpolated range.
2 Estimates for 1990.

Sources: Civil Aviation Authority, *Forecasts of air traffic and capacity at airports in the London area* (London, 1973), pp. 11–13, 23, 26, 35; Civil Aviation Authority, *CAA annual statistics 1980*, pp. 41, 46; Hall, *Great planning disasters*, p. 23; Department of Trade, *Maplin: review of airport project* (London, 1974), pp. 11, 14, 76–7.

whether the project is needed at all'.[68] But while Treasury ministers might have then agreed with their officials, Heath was determined to have his airport in the Thames. He was looking for a relaunch rather than a review.

The government responded to its defeat on the backbench clause by inserting one of its own in the Lords on 20 July. The new clause stated that:

> reclamation cannot be started until the Secretary of State makes a Statutory Instrument subject to annulment; and that the Order should not be made until a report has been laid before Parliament following consultation with at least the Civil Aviation Authority, the British Airports Authority, the National Ports Council, the Port of London Authority and the Maplin Development Authority.[69]

Elliot-Binns commented that this clause would be 'satisfactory from our point of view as it would ensure a thorough review of the project before heavy expenditure was committed', and urged the Chief Secretary to lend it 'strong support'.[70] The soon-to-be-released Maplin consultative documents would reveal the scale of the new town and the transport links (a new six-lane motorway through South Essex) required to service the new airport. The Treasury could use the delay created by consultations required under the new clause to let popular opposition build. Even a basic study could not be completed until June 1974,

68 M.J. Elliot-Binns, 'Maplin airport', 26 Jun. 1973, TNA T 319/1702.
69 M. Hatfield, 'Lords win government concession on Maplin', *The Times*, 20 Jul. 2973.
70 M.J. Elliot-Binns, 'Maplin airport', 26 Jun. 1973, TNA T 319/1702/1.

pushing back the opening of the first runway to at least 1982.[71] If the study covered the possibility of pushing London airport traffic out to the regions, this might delay Maplin by another year. As such, Treasury officials insisted that the report should be 'as searching and fundamental as possible'.[72]

The steamroller grinds to a halt

In October 1973 it was clear that while Maplin might overheat the South Essex economy, Heath's dash-for-growth had already overheated the national economy. GDP grew by 7.4 per cent in 1973, nearly three times Britain's post-war average. In January the LSE economist Alan Walters, who had served on the Roskill Commission, had linked Maplin to rising inflation. Using some heroic assumptions, Walters claimed that, on its own, Maplin would increase inflation by a percentage point.[73] By October inflation was running at 10 per cent, even before the impact of the oil shock that began that month. The Treasury was looking for public expenditure cuts to cool down the economy, and Maplin was an obvious target. When Barber called time on the dash-for-growth with £1.2 billion of spending cuts on 17 December 1973, he did not mention Maplin. But in the Commons debate that followed Conservative MPs appeared to assume that both the airport and the Channel Tunnel would be scrapped.[74]

The oil shock finally brought Maplin to a halt, but not because more expensive jet fuel would reduce passenger numbers. As befitted a scheme that was always more political than economic, it was the politics of the post-oil-shock crisis that stopped Maplin. With the Bill finally receiving Royal Assent on 25 October 1973, Environment Secretary Geoffrey Rippon was keen to let the reclamation contract. But even the most enthusiastic ministers recognised that it would be inappropriate to advertise a £140 million infrastructure contract while the country was enduring another three-day week as the government held out against the miners' claim for a 31 per cent wage rise. On 4 February 1974 the Leader of the House of Commons, Jim Prior, advised, 'we ought to get ourselves out of the wood on these economic and industrial troubles before publishing an advertisement which – even if it appears only in trade and professional journals – is bound to excite political controversy'.[75] Three days later Heath called a General Election on the question of 'Who governs?' He lost.

71   Department of the Environment, 'The Maplin study', Oct. 1973, TNA T 319/2024.
72   M.J. Elliot-Binns, 'Maplin study', 24 Oct. 1973, TNA T 319/2024.
73   A.A. Walters, *The Times*, 1 Feb. 1973.
74   HC Debs, 28 Jan. 1974, vol. 868, c. 112.
75   J.M.L. Prior, 'Maplin advertisement', 4 Feb. 1974, TNA T 319/2024.

Crosland returns to deliver the blow

The prospect of a change of government provided Treasury officials with a further opportunity to undermine Maplin. The Labour Party had come out against the 'Tory prestige project' in its 'Labour 1973' policy document.[76] In their draft briefings for a possible Labour government, officials stressed that:

> the Treasury has all along been sceptical about the need for Maplin and has pressed for the current review to be as searching and fundamental as the timetable allows. There are serious doubts about the economic case for Maplin ... We would not rule out the possibility that it may not be needed at all.[77]

With the new Chancellor, Denis Healey, looking for £1 billion of savings in his first 1974 Budget, the scheme was doomed. Anthony Crosland, now Secretary of State for the Environment, advised Prime Minister Harold Wilson on 18 March that he was halting all further expenditure on Maplin, pending a review.[78] Wilson replied, 'Can we not be more negative more early?'[79] Two days later the Queen's Speech announced that a number of major transport projects were under review. The day after that, Secretary of State for Trade Peter Shore confirmed that Maplin was on the list. A week later Healey confirmed in his Budget speech that there would be no provision for Maplin in 1974/75. On 4 April the consultation documents for the new town and access corridor through South Essex were rescinded.

The Maplin Review was published in July 1974. As Table 11.1 above shows, the forecasts for passenger numbers were below the Roskill estimates. This was partly because of the increased cost of air transport in the wake of the oil shock. But passengers would also be travelling on larger planes. The CAA raised the Roskill estimate of 162 passengers per aircraft to 225. The existing London runways would be able to handle 620,000 movements in 1990, well above forecast demand of 565,000 (including cargo movements).[80] There was no need for Maplin. There wasn't even any need for a second runway at Gatwick. As the CAA had already concluded, the only constraint would be terminal capacity. And it would be much cheaper to build at Heathrow where noise pollution was already falling because of quieter aircraft.[81] In any event, the

---

76   *Labour's programme 1973* (London, 1973).
77   J.M. Bowder, 'Briefing for a new government: the Maplin project', 19 Feb. 1974, TNA T 310/2024.
78   'C.A.R. Crosland to Prime Minister', 18 Mar. 1974, TNA PREM 16/286.
79   'R.T. Armstrong to A.G. Semple', 18 Mar. 1974, TNA PREM 16/286.
80   *Maplin: review of airport project*, 1974, p. 11.
81   A new terminal at Heathrow would cost an estimated £115 million in 1974 versus £400 million for Maplin. The new transport links would take Maplin up to about £1 billion, ibid., p. 42.

existing airports would have to be developed to meet capacity until the day Maplin opened, by then estimated to be 1985. As the review concluded, 'a new airport at Maplin does not obviate the substantial expansion at Heathrow and Gatwick provided for in current development plans'.[82]

Peter Shore formally abandoned Maplin on 18 July. He gave seven reasons:

1. The new, lower forecasts for passenger numbers
2. No new runways would be required at the London area airports until 1990
3. Existing terminal facilities could handle the projected passenger numbers
4. Quieter aircraft would reduce noise around the existing airports
5. Capacity at Heathrow and Gatwick would have to expand regardless of Maplin
6. Developments at existing airports and diversion to regional airports might then cope with further demand
7. The 1974 estimate of Maplin's cost was now £650 million – more than double the next alternative.[83]

The Maplin Development Corporation was wound up in 1976. Despite subsequent attempts by the Greater London Council and others to revive the project, the Planning Inspector at the 1981–83 Stansted Inquiry referred to those still calling for Maplin as 'voices crying in the wilderness'.[84] Nonetheless, the idea of an airport on reclaimed land in the Thames never went away, and several proposals were submitted to Sir Howard Davies' Airport Commission in 2012. None of them made the shortlist, although the Commission did investigate the then Mayor of London Boris Johnson's favoured site at the Isle of Grain, concluding that 'a brand new airport in the Thames Estuary, while appealing in theory, is unfeasibly expensive, highly problematic in environmental terms and would be hugely disruptive for many businesses and communities'.[85]

Conclusions

In his appreciation of his PhD supervisor's career, Martin Daunton recalled how Theo Barker would respond to modish seminar papers on the cultural analysis of semiotics, for instance, with: 'that was all very well, but how much did it cost?'[86] This question has always preoccupied Treasury officials.

---

82   *Maplin review*, p. 55.
83   HC Debs, 18 Jul. 1974, vol. 877, c. 675.
84   Quoted in M. Helsey and F. Codd, 'Aviation: proposals for an airport in the Thames Estuary, 1945–2012', *House of Commons Library* (Jul. 2012).
85   Airports Commission, *Final report* (Jul. 2015), p. 4.
86   Daunton, 'Theo Barker', p. 99.

Christopher Foster and John Heath claimed that the Treasury failed to check public expenditure on Maplin. But how much was actually spent before the project was abandoned in 1974? The 1972 Public Expenditure White Paper included a £1.1 million provision in 1972/73.[87] The 1973 White Paper allocated £6 million in 1973/74, with a further £30.1 million estimated for 1974/75.[88] Healey claimed that scrapping Maplin saved £17 million in 1974/75 so, even allowing for the £1.131 million spent on the Roskill Commission, it appears that, apart from the cost of civil servants' time, total expenditure was less than £25 million. This might seem like good value compared to what would have been spent building a commercially unviable airport. By placing obstacles in the way, and reinforcing the obstacles that others laid, it could be argued that the Treasury helped *save* the taxpayer nearly £1 billion (including the proposed transport links).

What lessons can we draw from Maplin for the handling of infrastructure projects characterised by 'a long delay between decision and execution, considerable uncertainty, large scale, and government domination'? First, governments must listen to their infrastructure stakeholders. None of the major stakeholders wanted an airport at Maplin. Many of them would have stayed at Heathrow, Gatwick, or Luton, doing little to relieve the noise nuisance. Most of them had been planning for a third London airport at Stansted since the early 1950s. The battle over the Competition Commission's 2009 ruling that BAA must sell the airport suggests that, until recently, they still were. The Roskill Commission knew that a new airport could succeed only if it worked commercially as an airport. The Treasury also knew this. The private sector consortia that were interested in Maplin only for its potential as a seaport and industrial complex knew this too. If Maplin had made economic sense, then the airlines would not have baulked at shifting operations from Heathrow and Gatwick. And even if it had worked as an airport, Maplin would have required a major new town and transport infrastructure – unacceptable from a political perspective.

Second, the Treasury can usually play it long. Officials were overruled on the decision to overturn Roskill. They were also overruled on the precise location of the proposed runways. But while Concorde showed that determined ministers can sometimes defy economic gravity long enough to actually give birth to a white elephant, a prolonged subterranean campaign of obstruction can postpone an uneconomic project long enough for its defects to become manifest, until technological advance nullifies the problem, or until a change of government makes the U-turn politically possible. The Treasury used every opportunity to delay Maplin, whether it was the delay presented by the

---

87   There was no separate estimate for 1971/72; 'Public expenditure on third London airport', Nov. 1972, TNA T 319/1702/1.
88   *Public expenditure to 1977–78*, Cmnd 5519 (London, 1973), p. 66; 'Maplin expenditure: 1982 opening date', 7 Sep. 1973, TNA T 319/2024.

relocation of the Shoeburyness munitions testing facility, the need to prove the 'expediency' of the Maplin Development Bill, the promise of a review following the insertion of the 'delay, vary or desist' clause, or the inappropriateness of advertising the reclamation contract during the three-day week. By contributing to delay, the Treasury helped the environmental and economic opponents of Maplin to marshal their arguments and win the debate. The Treasury might not have anticipated the oil shock in late 1973, but one might argue that the project was sufficiently damaged by then such that what followed was a mercy killing.

Third, the solution may well be hiding in plain sight. As the Davies Commission concluded, the best way to relieve congestion at Heathrow is to build a new runway – at Heathrow. Even if Maplin had opened in 1980, an estimated £200 million (in 1974 values) would have been spent at Heathrow and Gatwick to cope with the forecast increase in passengers up to that point. Why invest simply to abandon the results?

Heath's plans for a more dynamic economy, fuelled by public expenditure and lax monetary policy, collapsed during the oil shock, the three-day week, and with electoral defeat in February 1974. Of his grand design for an airport at Maplin:

> Nothing beside remains. Round the decay
> Of that colossal wreck, boundless and bare
> The lone and level sands stretch far away.[89]

---

89   With apologies to Percy Bysshe Shelley.

12

Workfare and the reinvention of the social in America and Britain, c. 1965 to 1985

BERNHARD RIEGER

The Prime Minister saw the Panorama programme last night about 'Workfare' in the US. She was impressed by the way it helped both the unemployed themselves – through the chance it gives them to keep in touch with the world of work, to get out of the house and to do something of value – and the taxpayer, through the work done in return for welfare payments. Many of the unemployed who were interviewed liked it; the cities liked it; the unions often at least did not object and some supported it.

It was in April 1986 – with British unemployment standing at a record 3.3 million – that Margaret Thatcher's evening in front of her Downing Street television set prompted her private Secretary David Norgrove to write a letter recommending workfare to several Whitehall departments. He went on to state that, while 'the adoption of "Workfare" in this country has been studied before ... the arguments for it are very strong'.[1] Clearly Thatcher wished her government to (re)examine an approach to social policy that, in her eyes, promised to address Britain's unemployment problem in a constructive manner.

In the 1980s the notion of workfare began to meander through British social policy discussions. A neologism blending the words 'welfare' and 'work', the term captured a widening desire among policymakers to demand that recipients of social security payments accept employment or risk the withdrawal of benefits. Workfare, in short, required people on welfare to work – or lose financial support. That the British governments of the eighties emerged among the first administrations in Europe to debate workfare seriously as a policy option is hardly a surprise. Since workfare promised to raise the number

---

1   TNA PREM 19/1839, letter, David Norgrove to John Lambert, 8 Apr. 1986. For the figure, see James Denman and Paul McDonald, 'Unemployment statistics from 1881 to the present day', *Labour Market Trends* 104, 1 (Jan. 1996), pp. 1–18.

of Britons in employment, it held out the prospect of reducing the monthly unemployment count that presented a major political embarrassment for the Thatcher government for much of the eighties. Unemployment rose dramatically during the recession in the early part of the decade and remained at high levels until 1986. By promising to integrate welfare recipients into the working population, workfare offered not just an opportunity to reduce unemployment figures; it also appeared to address what many cultural conservatives viewed as a prime cause of a moral crisis that supposedly afflicted post-war Britain. Rather than eradicate materially precarious forms of existence, the expansion of the welfare state, a conventional Conservative critique held, had generated a culture of dependency and dysfunctionality that rendered welfare recipients incapable of leading self-dependent lives.[2] With its emphasis on work, workfare appealed to Conservatives like Margaret Thatcher because it proposed to instil into benefit recipients the skills and values that many on the Right considered prerequisites for national regeneration. In other words, workfare could be viewed as an antidote to the culturally corrosive effects of welfare.

Despite the term's strong appeal among cultural conservatives, the unemployment policies the British government adopted from the mid-eighties did not constitute workfare in a strict sense. When British officials took a closer look, they identified a host of practical and conceptual problems that led them to rule it out. That workfare elicited scepticism in the UK was no accident; implementation problems haunted the concept from its inception. Workfare rose to prominence as part of Nixon's abortive attempt to reform the American welfare system. Indeed, by the mid-eighties, there existed only very few examples of workfare policies, and those that did exist were only rarely considered a success. To understand why workfare retained strong appeal among welfare reformers irrespective of persistent implementation difficulties requires an exploration of the term's surprising origins in United States, as well as its subsequent life in British welfare debates in the eighties. Examining the 'global dynamics of social policies' to which Martin Daunton has recently drawn attention, this story uncovers the limits of international intellectual exchange in the transnational history of welfare reform, and highlights how national contexts shape the reception of political ideas.[3] It also shows how a political recipe that many contemporaries considered flawed could become a

---

2   Raphael Samuel, 'Mrs. Thatcher's return to Victorian values', in T.C. Smout, ed., *Victorian values: a joint symposium of the Royal Society of Edinburgh and the British Academy* (Oxford, 1992), pp. 9–30; Matthew Grimley, 'Thatcherism, morality and religion', in Ben Jackson and Robert Saunders, eds, *Making Thatcher's Britain* (Cambridge, 2012), pp. 78–94; Florence Sutcliffe-Braithwaite, 'Neo-Liberalism and morality in the making of Thatcherite social policy', *Historical Journal* 55 (2012), pp. 497–520.

3   Julia Moses and M.J. Daunton, 'Editorial – border crossings: global dynamics of social policies and problems', *Journal of Global History* 9 (2014), pp. 177–88. Social policy is also a prominent theme in M.J. Daunton, *Progress and poverty: an economic and social history of*

shorthand among social scientists and the wider public for a wide range of policies that, in the words of Jamie Peck, comprise 'welfare-to-work programs and ... work-oriented welfare regimes'.[4] As such, the term 'workfare' points towards the manifold initiatives in social policy through which governments in affluent societies have sought to recast the rights and responsibilities of their citizens in recent decades, an ongoing process that sociologist Stephan Lessenich has considered a comprehensive 're-invention of the social'.[5] Workfare highlights a broader political trend since the seventies to link social rights to stringent conditions and reflects a growing expectation that individuals requiring material support assume responsibility for their lives. Although at first sight resembling Victorian efforts to control the poor by linking 'relief' to a work requirement in the workhouse, these recent initiatives differ from this historical antecedent in two important respects: they have aimed – firstly – to reduce significantly more generous benefits deriving from firm legal entitlements by – secondly – mobilising the state bureaucracy that had greatly expanded to administer a far more comprehensive welfare regime after 1945.

Workfare in the US

The term 'workfare' first appeared in American media in reports about Charles Evers' campaign to be elected to the House of Representatives in the spring of 1968. Although Evers did not win the third district of Mississippi, his candidacy attracted national attention. A seasoned activist and organiser for the National Association for the Advancement of Colored People (NAACP), he was the first African American to contest this district. It had been held until recently by segregationist John Bell Williams, who had just gained the governorship of Mississippi. By mobilising 75,000 black voters in a white electoral stronghold, Evers openly challenged Mississippi's racial order. Evers, whose guards exchanged gunfire when his house was attacked by whites during the election campaign, was well aware of the risks he was taking. After all, he was the brother of Medgar Evers, whom white supremacists had murdered for his voter registration drives in Mississippi in 1963. As reporters followed Charles Evers, they were not only impressed by his accounts of boycott activities and his successful business ventures (including the Medgar Evers Shopping Center in Jackson); they also noted his unorthodox approach to welfare. 'One of Evers' programs is what he calls workfare.' Evers, a writer for *Harper's* explained,

Britain, 1700–1850 (Oxford, 1995) and M.J. Daunton, *Wealth and welfare: an economic and social history of Britain, 1851–1951* (Oxford, 2007).

4   Jamie Peck, *Workfare states* (New York, 2009), p. 10.

5   Stephan Lessenich, *Die Neuerfindung des Sozialen: Der Sozialstaat im flexiblen Kapitalismus* (Bielefeld, 2013), pp. 73–128.

had coined the term to convey his conviction 'that everybody ought to work for what he gets'. This did not mean that Evers wanted to abolish welfare programmes altogether. Rather, their reach needed to be reduced. According to Evers, welfare 'ought to exist only for those can't work or for whom no jobs can be made available'. Evers' definition of who was capable of working was clearly very wide. The correspondent for *Harper's* noted that Evers asked a 'one-legged Negro' if 'he would be willing to work, handicapped though he is, if he had a job he could handle'. After the man replied 'perhaps reluctantly' that he would accept a job, 'Evers replie[d] quietly, "Then we're going to get work for you."'[6]

While Evers never outlined a comprehensive concept for a workfare programme, the idea of linking welfare and work took up wider contemporary concerns. The Civil Rights Movement is best known for its struggle to advance political citizenship rights, but its leaders insisted that removing the obstacles barring most African Americans from access to the labour market presented an equally important aim. Indeed, Civil Rights campaigners noted with apprehension that the gaps between the median incomes as well as employment rates of whites and blacks widened significantly between the mid-fifties and the mid-sixties. In 1962 Whitney Young of the National Urban League feared that African Americans might 'end up with a "mouthful of rights and an empty stomach"' unless legislation addressed the causes of socio-economic hardship. It was thus no coincidence that the famous 1963 March on Washington, which culminated in Martin Luther King's 'I have a dream' speech, demanded 'Jobs and Freedom'. By promising to 'get work' for fellow African Americans, Evers placed himself squarely in the Civil Rights Movement's quest for jobs.[7]

Although Evers identified a lack of employment as a part of racism's legacy, his solution diverged from the proposals aired by the majority of black activists. While most Civil Rights supporters considered Federal social policy programmes the most promising tool for combatting the effects of racism on the labour market, Evers emphasised the importance of private enterprise. His campaign against discrimination, he told a journalist, included the equality of rights to pursue commercial ventures: 'If whites can have businesses, blacks can have them,' he stated. Beyond generating personal wealth, stimulating business activity could ease racial tension by raising a community's prosperity level. Money, he declared, 'can change a racist place into a non-racist one', but, first and foremost, building black businesses advanced racial emancipation and liberation. After he had opened the Medgar Evers Shopping Center, he

---

6   Robert Canzoneri, 'Charles Evers: Mississippi's representative man?', *Harper's Magazine*, Jul. 1968, pp. 67–74. Another report on Evers can be found in *Christian Science Monitor*, 26 Feb. 1968, p. 1.
7   On the Civil Rights Movement and social inequality, see Thomas C. Holt, *Children of fire: a history of African Americans* (New York, 2010), pp. 331–8.

recalled, 'the black shoppers came by the dozens to buy their groceries, and the whites ... were so angry they could have died'.[8] Charles Evers, for one, considered himself an entrepreneur, whose father – a lumber contractor – had instilled a staunch work ethic into his offspring: 'He never gave us anything,' Evers remembered. 'I always worked for everything.'[9] Placing himself in the American tradition of the 'self-made' man, Evers praised regular employment as the foundation for the conduct of individual life.[10] It was thus only consistent for him to promote 'workfare' schemes that, in contrast to most proposals of Civil Rights advocates, stressed the individual duty to work rather than an obligation on the government's part to offer material help in combating poverty.

Evers fervently supported the Democrats throughout the sixties for their commitment to racial equality, but his pro-business outlook as well as his emphasis on work and self-dependence established contact points with a resurgent Conservative movement in the US that contributed to Richard Nixon's election to the Presidency in 1969. Nixon's success resulted not only from concern about the radical student movement and the emergence of black power and violent social unrest including urban rebellions by racial minorities. It also marked widespread opposition to the expansion of Federal social security spending that culminated in Lyndon B. Johnson's 'war on poverty'. Dating back to the New Deal in the thirties, the core welfare programmes were the Food Stamp scheme providing the neediest with basic staples, and Aid to Families with Dependent Children (AFDC). Initially conceived in 1935 as a measure to assist a small number of non-working poor white widows with children, after the Second World War AFDC primarily supported divorced, deserted, or never married mothers and their offspring. Between 1960 and 1969 claimant figures rose from 3 million to 6.1 million. In part this increase occurred because AFDC became accessible to African American women and men, not least due to pressure from the Civil Rights movement and the Democrat Federal governments headed by Kennedy and Johnson.[11]

Irrespective of the circumstance that both men and women could draw on AFDC in the sixties, a growing chorus of politicians, social scientists, and commentators focused on the circumstance that the programme provided support for unmarried, non-white mothers in economically deprived inner cities, some of which, including Watts, Harlem, Detroit, and Newark, became sites of rebellion. AFDC, a prominent line of reasoning maintained, undermined

8   Charles Evers with Grace Halsell, *Evers* (New York, 1971), pp. 4, 154.
9   Canzoneri, 'Charles Evers', p. 71.
10 On this tradition, see Jeffrey Louis Decker, *Made in America: self-styled success from Horatio Alger to Oprah Winfrey* (Minneapolis, 1997).
11 Premilla Nadasen, Jennifer Mittelstadt, and Marisa Chappell, *Welfare in the United States: a history with documents* (New York, 2009), pp. 24, 42. See also Elizabeth Hinton, *From the War on Poverty to the War on Crime: the making of mass incarceration in America* (Cambridge, MA, 2016), pp. 27–62.

family values by allowing single mothers access to welfare payments. Welfare, an influential report on 'The Negro Family' by Lyndon Johnson's advisor Patrick Moynihan argued in 1965, unwittingly fuelled an expansion of single-parent households, and thereby perpetuated a 'culture of poverty' among African Americans who according to Moynihan had no chance of escaping from a self-perpetuating 'tangle of pathology'.[12] Conservatives dismissed the possibility that a high proportion of single-motherhood among African Americans may have been the result – rather than the cause – of poverty. They argued forcefully that welfare did not eradicate destitution, but undermined family values and the work ethic among America's urban poor. In other words, social security payments were held to fuel a corrosive moral crisis, and unmarried African American women with children were cast as its most notable manifestation.

In August 1969 Richard Nixon launched a plan to tackle what he called a pervasive 'social crisis' through a comprehensive reform of the 'bureaucratic monstrosity' that welfare had allegedly become. Drawing on Moynihan's advice, he used a televised state-of-the-union address to propose replacing AFDC with a federally funded system of 'family assistance' that would guarantee every poor American a minimum income. Nixon's plan was highly ambitious because it aimed to extend welfare payments far beyond the ranks of the jobless without means. As the president explained, the 'benefits [of the new system] would go to the working poor, as well as the non-working; to families with dependent children headed by a father, as well as to those headed by a mother'. Given its wider range, the plan was, by Nixon's own admission, 'expensive', but it promised to deal with what he considered one of the cultural roots of contemporary poverty. In sharp contrast to current welfare arrangements which, according to Nixon, created 'an incentive for desertion' because fathers had to leave their offspring 'to make [them] eligible for welfare', his proposal strengthened the family because it expressly permitted male heads of households to claim benefits. Nixon's welfare reform thus amounted to a classically conservative move that strove to resolve a social problem by promoting highly conventional family values.

At the same time, Nixon assured his backers that his initiative would not result in an expanded army of passive welfare recipients because it included 'a work requirement and a work incentive'. To begin with, Nixon's proposal stipulated that welfare recipients who took a low-paying job would be allowed to retain 50 per cent of their gross earnings up to a certain threshold, while they currently only retained a third of their incomes derived from paid employment. The plan also promoted work by offering higher benefit payments to those who accepted low-income jobs. Nixon professed optimism about the efficacy of his scheme to render low-paying jobs attractive through welfare support.

---

12   D.P. Moynihan, *The Negro Family: the case for national action* (the 'Moynihan Report') (Washington D.C., 1965).

'With such incentives,' he surmised, 'most recipients who can work will want to work.' And those who could not be induced to take up jobs through incentives would face the threat of having their welfare payments withdrawn. As long as 'suitable jobs' were available, Nixon demanded, 'everyone who accepts benefits must also accept work ... The only exceptions would be those unable to work, and mothers of pre-school children.' The president was convinced that his approach to welfare offered a solution to poverty-related social issues by strengthening individual initiative. 'We cannot talk our way out of poverty; we cannot legislate our way out of poverty; but this nation can work its way out of poverty. What America needs now is not more welfare but more "workfare",' he said to summarise his proposal, before restating its central motif: 'Poverty must be defeated without sacrificing the will to work.'[13] Nixon thus replicated Evers' idea to link welfare payments to a willingness to accept paid employment, so as to strengthen a sense of self-dependence.

It is unclear how the word 'workfare' entered into the vocabulary of the Nixon administration. Nixon's speechwriter William Safire claimed to have been unaware of Evers' formulation as he introduced the term into the administration's welfare plans.[14] What, however, is clear is that from the summer of 1969 'workfare' became a highly divisive part of American political language – irrespective of Nixon's failure to push most of his welfare reforms through. Fellow Conservatives baulked at the proposal when they realised that it would double the number of benefit recipients to about 20 million. Rather than slim down the welfare bureaucracy, Nixon was set to bloat it even further, commentators on the Right feared.[15] While Conservatives worried that Nixon was about to add to an overbearing federal state, white Southern Democrats undermined the bill in the Senate because it required state legislatures to implement measures broadening welfare provisions for African Americans. They regarded Nixon's initiative as yet another Federal interference with states' rights in the South that was bound to fan a conflict that had repeatedly poisoned relations between state and federal governments ever since Brown vs. Board of Education in 1954.[16] Civil Rights activists meanwhile attacked the president for creating the false impression that his initiative would push substantial numbers of welfare recipients into employment. Since, as they pointed out, 'suitable jobs' were scarce commodities in areas with a high proportion of people on welfare, forcing benefit recipients to accept workfare was beside the point. After all, an absence of employment opportunities, 'discrimination and low pay

---

13   The full text of the speech is in *Boston Globe*, 9 Aug. 1969, p. 5.
14   *New York Times*, 17 Jul. 1988, p. A8.
15   For a comment along these lines by renowned Conservative James J. Kilpatrick, see *New York Times*, 15 Jan. 1970, p. C7.
16   See the reports on Senate debates in *New York Times*, 28 Apr. 1972, p. 24; ibid., 29 Apr. 1972, p. 1.

[were] the real causes' of poverty, a comment in the *Chicago Defender* stressed. Nixon's initiative struck the pressure group National Urban League as 'punitive, censorious, moralistic', regarding 'people in economic need' as 'lazy, shiftless and unwilling to contribute to their own support'. Although Nixon's address had studiously avoided the topic of black women on welfare rolls, activists were enraged because the bill insinuated that black women were unwilling to work when millions of them already held down low-wage jobs to make ends meet.[17]

Since Nixon's welfare bill managed to alienate a remarkable number of political groupings, most of its suggestions ended up on the legislative dust heap – with one significant exception. At the end of December 1971, the president could sign into law a stipulation that allowed Federal states to implement workfare regulations as part of their welfare regimes.[18] An early experimental implementation in the state of New York revealed the practical challenges of conducting workfare programmes. A report from 1973 pointed out that only 8 per cent of the state's 1 million welfare recipients had found work through workfare, citing a lack of jobs as well as 'a lack of skills' as the main factors that prevented wider success.[19] Such obstacles, however, did not lead backers, who could count Ronald Reagan among their staunchest supporters, to turn against workfare. As governor of California, he championed a workfare programme entitled 'Community Work Experience' between 1971 and 1975 that required welfare recipients to accept 'public jobs' such as 'swimming pool attendants, road clean-up crew members, geriatric aide, watchman and various clerical positions'. Hailed by Reagan as 'one of the most innovative and far-reaching elements of our welfare reform programs' for 'reintroduc[ing] the work ethic into our way of life', it managed to place a mere 9,600 Californian welfare recipients in public employment. The programme's relative lack of achievement derived not only from a limited number of public positions that were available; it was also materially unattractive to people on welfare because the scheme failed to offer payments in addition to benefits if candidates accepted a job. The material incentive that had been a hallmark of Nixon's workfare plan was thus absent from Reagan's version. Instead his variant of workfare strongly relied on punitive aspects, especially by threatening to withdraw public payments.[20]

Workfare's limited impact in California did not stop Reagan from promoting it in his domestic policy agenda as president. Indeed, among those encouraging Reagan to implement workfare schemes was none other than Charles Evers, who had switched his political allegiance to the Republicans after Reagan had

17 *Chicago Defender*, 19 May 1971, p. 17; 23 May 1970, p. 32.
18 *New York Times*, 29 Dec. 1971, p. A1.
19 *New York Times*, 20 Apr. 1973, p. A34.
20 *New York Times*, 18 Mar. 1981, p. A22; *Washington Post*, 30 Mar. 1981, p. A4. Reagan's successor discontinued the programme.

announced his candidacy.[21] In 1981 Reagan called on Congress to release funds that would allow state governments to create 800,000 public jobs for welfare recipients. The 1981 Omnibus Budget Reconciliation Act opened the door to federally funded workfare programmes with firm employment requirements. Reagan's drive for workfare culminated in the 1988 Family Support Act, which made such programmes mandatory for Federal states accepting Federal funding for welfare. By the late eighties, the only welfare recipients excluded from workfare measures were the disabled and mothers with children below the age of three.[22]

American notions of 'workfare' thus possessed several important characteristics. The concept emerged from highly charged debates about gender, race, and poverty, casting black unmarried mothers as the embodiment of a moral crisis supposedly affecting American cities in the sixties. Rather than associate the causes of deprivation with structural socio-economic factors and racial prejudice, Conservatives attributed destitution to a self-perpetuating culture of poverty. Crucially, the welfare system did not solve America's poverty problem but, according to this line of reasoning, deepened it by weakening family ties and undermining the work ethic. The solution, then, involved reforming welfare regulations to strengthen the family, encourage self-dependence and promote a willingness to work among the poor. By creating an obligation to perform work in return for public material support, workfare recalibrated the relationship between the individual and the state to address what Conservatives viewed as a moral problem. The concept proved a profoundly controversial approach not only because it ascribed to the poor a considerable share of responsibility for their predicament; it also initially elicited scepticism among American Conservatives because it expanded the political reach of the state. The Right, however, soon embraced workfare because it imposed compulsory work on those at the bottom of society, thereby promoting a morality of self-dependence that Conservatives expected to strengthen public order. By the late eighties, workfare had become deeply entrenched in American politics.

Workfare in the UK

While workfare had been discussed in the US since the late sixties, it took until the early 1980s for British political circles to take note. Unlike their American counterparts, British politicians did not begin to discuss workfare in the context of debates about poverty. Instead the term entered into British political discourse at a time when spiralling unemployment presented a major national concern.

21   Charles Evers and Andrew Szanton, *Have no fear: the Charles Evers story* (New York, 1997), pp. 291–2.
22   Richard K. Caputo, *U.S. social policy reform: policy transitions from 1981 to the present* (New York, 2011), pp. 29–43, esp. pp. 37–8.

Between Thatcher's first election victory in May 1979 and January 1982, official unemployment rose from 1.3 million to over 3 million. In the summer of 1986 the count still hovered around 3.3 million – and Thatcher's critics held the government directly responsible for this development.[23] Responding to the recession at the beginning of the eighties with tax increases and interest-rate hikes to combat inflation, opponents argued, had raised the value of the pound, triggered business collapses, and deepened the downturn. Labour MP Jack Ashley was only one of many who accused the government of considering 'unemployment as the necessary price to be paid for reducing inflation' in 1981.[24]

The surge in unemployment triggered a sustained search for policies to combat this trend. Although the Conservatives internally acknowledged that high-interest policies had amplified the recession of the early eighties, they saw unemployment as part and parcel of Britain's wider economic problems that, according to Thatcherites, reflected excessive state intervention in business, disruptive trade unions, an expanding welfare regime, and burdensome taxation. In its analysis of Britain's economic ills, the government regarded unemployment as an indicator of inflated labour costs. Embracing a supply-and-demand model, Thatcher's administration understood unemployment as an oversupply of labour, for which demand was insufficient because the price of work, i.e. the level of wages, was too high. Reducing unemployment, this analysis implied, required lower wages.[25] In Conservative eyes the fact that a large part of the unemployed consisted of low-skilled men added to the challenge. Due to their lack of qualifications these men could only hope to find badly paid work. For many of them it was more lucrative, the government found, to rely on benefits than accept low-skilled work. By establishing a minimum income threshold, the social security system, government officials argued, suppressed the laws of supply and demand in the labour market, thereby directly fuelling unemployment. Only once the welfare system no longer shielded low-skilled men from badly paid work would demand for workers increase among employers, and only then would unemployment fall. An internal memorandum by Alan Walters, Margaret Thatcher's influential economic advisor, put this line of reasoning as a rhetorical question: 'Does not everyone believe that were real wages in Britain to fall 10 or 15 per cent, there would be a most dramatic reduction in unemployment?'[26]

---

23   For the figures, see Denman and MacDonald, 'Unemployment statistics from 1881', pp. 5–18.
24   *Hansard*, HC Debs, 6th series, vol. 7, cc. 272–3. On the impulses behind Thatcher's anti-inflationary policies, see Jim Tomlinson, 'Thatcher, monetarism and the politics of inflation', in Jackson and Saunders, eds, *Making Thatcher's Britain*, pp. 62–77.
25   For more detail on the internal debates, see Bernhard Rieger, 'Making Britain work again: unemployment and the remaking of British social policy in the eighties', *English Historical Review* 133, 562 (2018), pp. 634–66.
26   TNA PREM 19/525, Alan Walters, 'Unemployment measures proposed in E(81)74', note, n.d., par. 4.

Beyond distorting market mechanisms the welfare system also fuelled what many Conservatives considered a moral problem. By protecting the unemployed from absolute poverty, the benefit system, numerous followers of Margaret Thatcher were convinced, suppressed an appreciation of hard work, thrift, and self-dependence – all values that formed the epicentre of the Prime Minister's moral universe. Thatcher for one viewed herself as engaged in a quest for not just economic but also moral regeneration. In 1982 she emphasised this point in a private conversation with Ferdinand Mount, who was about to take up his post as her chief policy advisor: 'We really have to address … the values of society. This is my real task, to restore standards of conduct and responsibility … Personal responsibility is the key.'[27] Mount fully agreed. A memo reviewing unemployment, which he had co-authored with Alan Walters, lamented a widespread 'why-work-syndrome' among benefit recipients as a prime cause for high levels of joblessness.[28] Put differently, the welfare system eroded the work ethic of the poor.

It was in the context of attempts to lower unemployment that workfare ideas caught the attention of the British government. Within the administration, Alan Walters, who probably heard of workfare while at Johns Hopkins University in the second half of the seventies, emerged as an early cheerleader. When a Conservative policy group explored recipes against unemployment reported in preparation for the election campaign in 1983, he and Mount wrote to Thatcher the previous autumn that 'we all agree that some kind of Workfare scheme would be desirable to bring hope and purpose to the long-term unemployed'.[29] Despite this warm welcome, considerable insecurity and ignorance surrounded workfare in Britain. For instance, no one in the administration addressed the fact that the concept owed its origins to American attempts to break up a supposed 'culture of poverty' among African American women. The problem that concerned Whitehall differed fundamentally: rather than deprivation among non-white women, it was unemployment among working-class men that British politicians regarded as their central concern. Ethnic minorities were over-represented among those out of work, but government discussion about unemployment paid them little attention.[30] In terms of gender, race, and social issue, British and American workfare schemes were trained at rather dissimilar targets.

That the government did not dwell on these fundamental points reflects a remarkable lack of knowledge about workfare in Whitehall. Only two days

27   Ferdinand Mount, *Cold cream: my early life and other mistakes* (London, 2009), pp. 288–9.
28   TNA PREM 19/1157, Alan Walters and Ferdinand Mount, 'Unemployment: the next steps', note, 27 Sep. 1982, p. 1.
29   TNA PREM 19/1157, Walters and Mount, 'Unemployment', p. 4.
30   Yaojun Li and Anthony Heath, 'Minority ethnic men in the British labour market (1972–2005)', *International Journal of Sociology and Social Policy* 28, 5/6 (2008), pp. 231–44.

after Walters had recommended workfare in principle did the British embassy in Washington send a two-and-a-half page outline of existing American schemes, which subsequently provided the foundation for government discussions.[31] That the administration had to turn to the diplomatic service for basic information on a new social policy instrument highlights the national focus of Thatcher's government as well as the limits of transatlantic intellectual exchange between Conservatives at the time. Although Thatcherites and Reaganites shared a general political horizon, there were clearly large areas of American policy debate about which the British side possessed hardly any knowledge.[32]

If, as the government argued, unemployment resulted from inflated wages levels as well as an emasculated work ethic among those without a job, workfare appeared to offer a tool to change both. The threat of withdrawing welfare payments could be used to push people into employment and initiate a cultural change among those on welfare, parts of the government hoped. Implementing workfare policies would, a note to the Prime Minister explained, tackle 'a something for nothing mentality' because people on 'welfare benefits would no longer regard ... [them] as a free good'. As such, workfare was suited to counter a 'debilitating dependence on welfare'. While no panacea, 'it could be of such transforming nature ... that it may change significantly the whole ethos and approach to work and a whole way of life generally'. Workfare schemes thus promised to counteract a wider cultural malaise that, in Conservative readings of recent British history, exacerbated the nation's social problems. At the same time, the policy promised to 'bring down unemployment ... [by] creating new jobs'. Since most of the jobs for workfare participants would be part of the low-wage sector, workfare would 'reduc[e] wage levels' in the economy in general, thereby stimulating hiring among employers.[33] Workfare, it appeared to some in Whitehall, offered a political tool to address both dimensions leading Conservatives held responsible for mass unemployment: it could impose conservative values including the need for hard work and self-dependence on broad sections of the British population, as well as lower unemployment by stimulating the demand for labour in the wider economy.

Despite this positive assessment, the government decided against implementing workfare schemes in the early eighties. Much of the policy debate unfolded in the autumn of 1982 when the Conservatives began to prepare for the general election campaign of 1983. In this situation the government shied away from a policy that was bound to generate conflict. Supporters warned the

---

31   TNA PREM 19/1157, 'US Welfare Programmes, telegramme number 3189', 29 Sep. 1982. Much of the information reappeared verbatim in TNA PREM 19/1157, Adrian Smith, 'Workfare', note, n.d.

32   For an emphasis on transatlantic co-operation, see James E. Cronin, *Global rules: America, Britain and a disordered world* (New Haven, 2014), pp. 92–120.

33   TNA PREM 19/1157, Smith, 'Workfare', par. 2.

Prime Minister against the controversial nature of workfare. Alan Walters drew Thatcher's attention to the 'political difficulty' of 'secur[ing] the support for a scheme which includes the denial of benefit to non-participants'.[34] Workfare's punitive dimension, Conservatives were aware, risked inflaming social tensions at a time of economic hardship because large sections of the population, as an internal report complained, held 'that there is an absolute right (at worst) to maintain living standards'.[35] With a general election on the horizon these warnings were enough to shelve workfare schemes.

Although the British economy registered substantial growth in the mid-eighties, the unemployment count remained stubbornly above the 3-million mark. It is thus no surprise that Margaret Thatcher revisited workfare as a potential solution at the time. There was agreement in government circles that joblessness required a new approach, but officials again cautioned against workfare. This time they focused on the role of publicly funded, large-scale job creation. If the government wished to initiate a cultural shift towards self-dependence and a more robust work ethic by forcing the unemployed into jobs, it had to make a sufficient number of positions available in the first place. As Alan Walters and Ferdinand Mount had already pointed out in 1982, the government would have to display a strong 'administrative will to set up [a Job] Pool'.[36]

This task was fraught with difficulties. Whitehall officials lacked confidence that charity organisations and local councils, which would have to implement the programme, would support a mandatory employment scheme. According to the Department of Employment, the charitable sector worried that a workfare programme would not furnish it with 'reliable and cooperative' workers. Due to the compulsory nature of the scheme, many candidates for employment, charities predicted, would be unwilling and unmotivated employees.[37] From this perspective, workfare amounted to a risky gamble that put the national government at the mercy of charities and local agencies. If these bodies refused to co-operate, Downing Street would ultimately be held accountable. Beyond raising organisational problems, workfare also required substantial public spending that expanded the national government's economic role significantly. As an advisor warned in 1986, 'the state is taking on the responsibility of employer of last resort for welfare claimants'.[38] This circumstance was bound to provoke resistance among a group of politicians who regarded state

34 Walters and Mount, 'Unemployment', p. 4.
35 TNA PREM 19/525, CPRS, 'Unemployment: issues for discussion and decision', note, Sep. 1982, p. 4.
36 Walters and Mount, 'Unemployment', p. 4.
37 TNA PREM 19/1161, Department of Employment, 'Employment measures', note, n.d., p. 3. Walters and Mount had raised the same point in 1982. See Walters and Mount, 'Unemployment', p. 4.
38 TNA PREM 19/1839, David Willetts to Margaret Thatcher, note, 9 May 1986, p. 1.

interventionism as one of the causes of Britain's economic problems. In light of substantial pragmatic and ideological doubts, the Conservative government refrained from implementing workfare plans – much to Margaret Thatcher's regret.

Nonetheless, it would be wrong to dismiss the government's internal workfare debates of the eighties as inconsequential. In September 1985 Thatcher entrusted erstwhile property entrepreneur Lord David Young with the task of lowering unemployment by appointing him as Employment Secretary. Plans he presented in November focused on reducing the number of the long-term unemployed, an overwhelmingly male group that added over 1 million to the total. Young suggested that every benefit recipient who had been out of work for over a year should be called for an interview at a Jobcentre to assess their situation. At the end of the conversation, the unemployed would be presented with four options. They could sign up for training, select a position in the government's long-running job-creation scheme entitled 'Community Programme', accept a subsidised low-wage job, or sign up for a 'Jobclub', which would offer support in a targeted search for work. Crucially, candidates refusing all four options risked the suspension of their welfare benefits because, Young emphasised, they could be considered as not 'available for work', which provided the legal requirement for out-of-work welfare payments. Rather than only inform the long-term unemployed of opportunities, the interview process also introduced a significant disciplinary dimension because it was suited to identifying welfare recipients who were unwilling to work.[39]

Thatcher was initially hesitant to embrace Young's proposals because, with the exception of 'Jobclubs', they relied mostly on existing initiatives such as the 'Community Programme' and training courses to combat unemployment. That she had hoped for something more innovative is evident in her continuing propagation of workfare while Young's plan was discussed.[40] Young disagreed with the Prime Minister, explaining that his proposals were new because, in contrast to current arrangements, they contained rewarding *and* punitive elements: 'we will be working with a combination of carrots and sticks,' he stated. The disciplining components of his programme would not receive extended public coverage, he continued, for tactical reasons. To prevent public resistance, 'we must exercise great care that the sticks are never seen'. He insisted that his plans were suited to address the supposed culture of welfare-dependency that so greatly concerned the Prime Minister. 'We must tackle the will to work.'[41] It

39   TNA PREM 19/1839, David Young, 'A strategy for enterprise and employment', note, 1 Nov. 1985, p. 4.
40   TNA PREM 19/1839, letter, Norgrove to Lambert, 8 Apr. 1986; PREM 19/1569, minute, Andrew Turnbull to D. Norrington, 20 May 1985.
41   Young, 'A strategy for enterprise and employment', note, 1 Nov. 1985, p. 4.

took Young until May 1986 to draw the Prime Minister onto his side, when he assured her that workfare 'had an inherent appeal' because it 'expose[d] those who are not genuinely unemployed' and gave 'unemployed people a chance to keep alive their working habits and skills'. At the same time, he emphasised that his current proposals pursued exactly these goals – albeit without the associated political risks of launching workfare in a strict sense. In addition to reminding the Prime Minister of workfare's financial costs and administrative complexities, he feared that 'the Opposition and the trade union movement ... [would] misrepresent ... Workfare as "slave labour" or a return to the workhouse'. By generating public outrage, he predicted, Thatcher's opponents would derail the government's agenda.[42] In other words, the Secretary for Employment took credit for a plan that minimised resistance and sidestepped financial risks, yet pursued the same moral aims as workfare plans that prompted welfare recipients to accept low-paid work to promote a culture of self-dependence. This line of reasoning eventually convinced Margaret Thatcher, and she went along with the solution Young had designed.

Conclusions

American workfare concepts thus acted as an important stimulus in the reframing of British unemployment policies in the 1980s. That the concept had taken shape in debates about poverty among African Americans that construed black single mothers as a social problem group did not diminish its appeal in the eyes of British Conservatives. British politicians wrestled primarily with long-term unemployment among men, but they were interested in workfare because it promised to reverse what Conservatives on both sides of Atlantic considered a pernicious cultural result of existing welfare arrangements. By offering material protection against poverty and the loss of employment, the social security system had allegedly yielded deleterious moral effects by undermining an individual work ethic and a desire for self-dependence among benefit recipients. American and British Conservatives were drawn to workfare because it threatened those unwilling to accept jobs as a precondition for welfare support with the withdrawal of payments. Workfare shifted the core function of welfare from material protection against social risk towards the imposition of conservative values in pursuit of moral regeneration. Moreover, some Tories also hoped that by directing people out of work towards low-wage labour with the help of workfare, the measure would contribute to an erosion of wage levels that many Conservatives considered a prerequisite for a fall of unemployment figures.

42   TNA PREM 19/1839, David Young, 'Workfare', note, 2 May 1986, pp. 1, 3–4.

British Conservatives had more than one reason for not implementing workfare schemes in the eighties. Beyond raising the prospect of practical and administrative difficulties, workfare demanded major public expenditure, and thus stood in tension with a reduction of the state's economic weight, an aim the Tories regarded as central to their economic reforms. While compatible with a quest for moral regeneration, workfare clashed with Conservative economic policies for Britain's economic revival. Similar tensions did not afflict early workfare debates in the US due to an absence of a widespread sense of economic malaise in the late sixties. Furthermore, the circumstance that British unemployment policies targeted (white) working-class men predisposed the Conservative administration against implementing workfare schemes. Lord Young cautioned against workfare because he feared that its implementation would generate vocal resistance among the Labour Party and trade unions – both institutions that considered white working-class men as their prime constituency. Conservatives in the US did not have to apprehend similarly well-organised opposition because American workfare proposals targeted black women, who strongly relied on the Civil Rights movement for advocacy. With the splintering of African American activism in the late sixties, black organisers lost much of their political ability to mass mobilise against Conservative plans for welfare reform in the US.[43] Workfare plans thus faced less organisational and ideological resistance in the US than in Britain.

Nonetheless, workfare ideas prompted British Conservatives to develop unemployment policies that addressed the moral malaise that supposedly underpinned the nation's high levels of joblessness while sidestepping the pitfalls associated with the American concept. When the Tories unveiled new proposals in 1985, they steered clear of further job creation, but introduced regulations allowing the withdrawal of welfare payments. Only those who conformed to a conservative moral agenda by demonstrating a strong desire to work were now deemed worthy of material support. British Conservatives thus began to recast the relationship between the unemployed and the state by linking benefit payments to conditions. By giving to the state stronger regulatory powers to impose behavioural norms that would render the unemployed more self-dependent, British politics recalibrated the relationship between individual social rights and duties. To be sure, welfare regulations routinely embraced the assumption that citizens had a duty to work. The debates and reforms of the eighties made this point with renewed force by simultaneously reforming and mobilising the welfare agencies that had expanded so significantly after the Second World War. This incipient re-invention of the social hinged on a transformation of the rights and responsibilities that link state and society. Rights came to be far more contingent upon the fulfilment of certain responsibilities.

43   Daniel T. Rodgers, *Age of fracture* (Cambridge, MA, 2011), pp. 111–43.

Workfare was important in this process not only because it set the United States on a path of welfare reform that culminated in the abolition of AFDC under Bill Clinton in 1996;[44] it also sharpened the search for social policies in Britain that would weaken the protective function of the welfare system and emphasise the need to accept work as a precondition for benefits, thereby prefiguring a wider policy shift that has by now become a feature of welfare in virtually all affluent societies.

44   R. Kent Weaver, *Ending welfare as we know it* (Washington, 2000).

13

Charity and international humanitarianism in post-war Britain

MATTHEW HILTON

In *Charity, self-interest and welfare in the English past*, Martin Daunton assembled a collection of authors committed to demonstrating the ever-changing nature of welfare provision over the centuries.[1] Martin clearly set out the differing forms of welfare provision – commercial, public, charitable, and household – with the balance between the four never being fixed. Indeed, in Jo Innes' contribution, the precise nature of the mix between these different forms of welfare was never a source of agreement.[2] While commentators might concur that all four served a purpose, the respective weight given to each one has always been in contention. In this chapter I focus on the relative weight given to charitable relief, and probe the nature of the mixed economy of welfare when that model of relief was taken abroad – by British charities, voluntary associations, and non-governmental organisations focused on humanitarian relief and long-term aid and development. In the latter half of the twentieth century they maintained a strong presence in the former territories of the British empire, though tragedy respects no borders, and organisations such as Oxfam, Christian Aid, and Save the Children came to operate in virtually every country the world over.

In Martin's introduction, he was keen to move away from older debates about charity and philanthropy that focused on their roles as agents of social control. Instead, the volume recognised the positive role charity could play in, for instance, the formation of new middle-class identities and in the opportunities

---

1   M.J. Daunton, 'Introduction', in M.J. Daunton, ed., *Charity, self-interest and welfare in the English past* (London, 1996), pp. 1–22.
2   Joanna Innes, 'The "mixed economy of welfare" in early modern England: assessment of the options from Hale to Malthus (c. 1683–1803)', in ibid., pp. 139–80.

afforded to women in the public sphere otherwise denied to them.[3] In writing of the late nineteenth century Martin observed that, like today, charity constituted an incredibly diverse sector. It was, however, also the 'golden age' of philanthropy, as Frank Prochaska has argued. Prochaska has estimated that the middle classes spent a larger amount of their income on charity than on any item in their budget except food.[4] Donations did not just come from the affluent. New research is showing the extent to which the British public as a whole responded to poverty and suffering at home and abroad.[5] But precisely because charity was just one pillar of the mixed economy of welfare, the history of charity is intricately bound up with the history of capitalism, a point Martin has returned to in his other works on the history of political economy.[6] Here we need to remind ourselves that whatever the virtues or effects of the charitable impulse in the late nineteenth century, it flourished at a time of some of the most extreme inequalities in the distribution of wealth.

In the early twenty-first century global wealth inequalities are of a scale comparable to those experienced at the national level in the late nineteenth. We are also witnessing some quite spectacular instances of giving around the world, not only originating from the West. There is a literature on both of these subjects, yet the two are rarely brought together. Led very much by Thomas Piketty's intervention on the history of capital is a profusion of books and articles on inequality across the humanities and social sciences.[7] Likewise there have been an increasing number of works focusing on 'giving well', 'effective altruism', and 'strategic giving'.[8] Yet there are few studies which continue to

3   Brian Harrison, 'Philanthropy and the Victorians', *Victorian Studies* 9, 4 (1966), pp. 353–74; R.J. Morris, 'Voluntary societies and British urban elites, 1780–1850: an analysis', *Historical Journal* 26 (1983), pp. 95–118; plus his *Class, sect and party: the making of the British middle class, Leeds 1820–50* (Manchester, 1990); Martha Vicinus, *Independent women: work and community for single women, 1850–1920* (London, 1985); A. Summers, 'A home from home: women's philanthropic work in the nineteenth century', in S. Burman, ed., *Fit work for women* (London, 1979), pp. 33–63; S. Koven, 'Borderlands: women, voluntary action and child welfare in Britain, 1840 to 1914', in S. Koven and S. Michel, eds, *Mothers in a new world: maternalist politics and the origins of welfare states* (London, 1993), pp. 94–135.
4   Frank Prochaska, *Christianity and social service in modern Britain: the disinherited spirit* (Oxford, 2006); Frank Prochaska, *The voluntary impulse: philanthropy in modern Britain* (London, 1988).
5   Sarah Roddy, Julie-Marie Strange, and Bertrand Taithe, 'The charity-mongers of modern Babylon: bureaucracy, scandal, and the transformation of the philanthropic marketplace, c.1870–1912', *Journal of British Studies* 54 (Jan. 2015), pp. 118–37; Rebecca Gill, *Calculating compassion: humanity and relief in war, Britain 1870–1914* (Manchester, 2013).
6   M.J. Daunton, 'The future direction of British history: thinking about economic cultures', *History Workshop Journal* 72, 1 (2011), pp. 222–39.
7   Thomas Piketty, *Capital in the twenty-first century* (Cambridge, MA, 2014).
8   Peter Frumkin, *Strategic giving: the art and science of philanthropy* (Chicago, 2006); Patricia Illingworth, Thomas Pogge, and Leif Wenar, eds, *Giving well: the ethics of philanthropy* (Oxford, 2011).

bring charity and capitalism together. For the late twentieth and early twenty-first centuries there is an absence of studies of the 'mixed economy' of welfare like those on the late nineteenth century found in Martin's collection and many other works. In this chapter I take my cue from much of this more well-established literature, and also Thomas Haskell's influential essays on the history of capitalism and humanitarianism. Over thirty years ago he argued that the particular forms which humanitarianism has taken were as much the product of underlying, changing material circumstances as they were a reaction to a particular disaster or timeless impulse of compassion. New techniques became available which were able to 'change the conventional limits' within which people felt 'responsible enough to act'.[9]

I will outline some of the history of charitable humanitarianism since the 1960s, and the role of British agencies within this. I particularly will explore what the British public was doing when it gave aid to the relief of suffering abroad, both in the short and the longer terms. I will ask what purpose charity served for those who gave either their time or their money, and what it meant for the wider public. Of course this is only one small entry point into a broader debate about the role of charity within capitalist societies, but by examining the affective economies of charitable giving it is possible to explore the effects of humanitarian sensibilities too. As will be seen, the British public has undoubtedly been a nation of givers, private voluntary donations enabling the rise to prominence of some really quite massive modern NGOs, as well as pressuring the government to act on overseas aid, even amidst periods of austerity. But public attitudes to suffering abroad, admittedly extraordinarily difficult to pin down, have remained only skin deep. Increasingly affluent British citizens have certainly given, and given much. But they have done do so in ways which arguably do not disturb the bases upon which their own comfort rests. Charitable agencies working at blurred boundaries between humanitarianism and development have always presented themselves as a means to an end, either through the stimulus they would provide to state intervention or through the self-help schemes they hoped would ultimately become self-sustaining. But charity has proved to be the end as well as the means. The one clear consequence of the rise of humanitarian philanthropy has been the political, cultural, social and economic legitimacy conferred upon it. Charities have done much to expose the inequities of global wealth, but it seems the only persistent outcome of the public's charity has been its unreflective maintenance in the mixed economy of global welfare.

9   Thomas L. Haskell, 'Capitalism and the origins of humanitarian sensibility', 2 parts, *American Historical Review* 90, 2 and 3 (1985), pp. 339–61; 547–66.

Rise of charities and NGOs in the aid business

Any overview of charitable humanitarianism cannot but conclude that Britain has been, and continues to be, a nation of givers. There has been a long tradition of supporting philanthropic humanitarians in their overseas adventures. Rooted in mission stretching back to the eighteenth century, humanitarianism was transformed in the nineteenth with the foundation of the International Committee of the Red Cross in 1863 and its British wing in 1870, as well as the Quakers' Friends War Victims Relief Committee (1870) and the Salvation Army (1864). After the First World War, the Save the Children Fund (1919) became the first of what many would later recognise as the modern NGO. It was joined in 1942, during the Second World War, by the Quaker-inspired Oxford Committee for Famine Relief (Oxfam). Christian Aid was created in 1945 as Christian Reconstruction in Europe, and, amidst a wider spirit of post-war internationalism, Victor Gollancz established the Association for World Peace in 1951 to campaign for peace and development; it became War on Want in 1952.

The growth of these organisations since the Second World War has been spectacular. By 1970 the leading seven aid and development charities (Oxfam, the Red Cross, Save the Children, War on Want, Christian Aid, Tearfund, and CAFOD – the Catholic Agency for Overseas Development) had a combined income of over £100 million (at 2009 prices). Thereafter, with the increasing proportion of official aid being directed through the charities, that growth was even more impressive. These seven charities alone had a combined income approaching £1 billion at the beginning of the twenty-first century.[10]

Yet much of the growth relied on large injections of cash from the donating public. Oxfam alone was raising around £100 million a year from the public by the early 1980s. It was an early adopter of aggressive fundraising techniques, ploughing monies raised into ever more prominent publicity campaigns. As early as 1949 it appointed a full-time professional advertiser, Harold Sumption. His reports and those of his successors were analysed in depth in numerous Oxfam committees, as strategies for communicating with the variously identified publics were planned and executed in great detail. It also knew how to attract the maximum amount of publicity, and has constantly relied on celebrity endorsements to endear it, especially to the young. When it launched its twenty-first anniversary 'Hunger £million' campaign in 1963, for instance, its key staff were accompanied by the Beatles and a then-youthful Oxford student, Jeffrey Archer.[11]

Undoubtedly, faith has been a key motivator behind humanitarian and

---

10   Matthew Hilton, Nicholas Crowson, Jean-François Mouhot, and James McKay, *A historical guide to NGOs in Britain: charities, civil society and the voluntary sector since 1945* (Basingstoke, 2012), p. 49.
11   Maggie Black, *A cause for our times: Oxfam, the first fifty years* (Oxford, 1992).

development aid donations. Christian Aid was joined by CAFOD in 1962 and by Tearfund in 1968, which emerged out of the Evangelical Alliance. A strong Quaker presence at the foundation of Oxfam persisted within the organisation for many years, and even the ostensibly secular War on Want drew on the resources of faith groups to sustain its network of local organisations. The Quakers were particularly influential in the Bradford and Sheffield chapters, while the Iona Community was a major backer of the Scottish Committee based in Glasgow.[12]

Such considerations ought not to detract from the more routine, everyday, and semi-conscious acts of giving that have also characterised charitable humanitarianism. Long before the non-cancellation of direct debit arrangements became a reliable source of steady funding, Save the Children was reaching out to millions of ordinary working-class donors. By the 1960s the organisation was being run with an impressive administrative efficiency that enabled it to sustain a network of around 600 local branches. Most significantly, it had agreed a deal with the Trades Union Congress to allow union members to volunteer a small portion of their pay packets on a regular basis. The Penny-a-Week scheme might not have done much to instil a deep internationalist mindset among the hundreds of thousands of working men and women who signed up to it, but it ensured that Save the Children's finances became extremely robust. In the mid-1950s, 40 per cent of all the charity's cash donations were coming straight from the factory floor.[13]

The examples of routine, everyday forms of giving across all sections of the population are countless, but there has been a persistent direction of this altruism to the humanitarian sector. Indeed, the cumulative totals of all this giving have continued to be impressive. By the end of the twentieth century, the charitable humanitarian sector as a whole in Britain (or at least those aid and development charities listed in the top 500 charities) was raising £1 billion annually from the public.

This growth in the sector has not come as an alternative to official forms of assistance. Charity and government have complemented one another in the mixed economy of welfare. At the height of empire charities embarked on poverty reduction in hand with the state. Echoing many of the dilemmas over state–NGO relations today, Fischer-Tiné argues that the Salvation Army became inseparable from the state at the turn of the twentieth century, especially as it engaged in increasing amounts of sub-contracting work such as running prisons in Canada and re-educating former convicts in various imperial territories.[14]

---

12 Matthew Hilton, James McKay, Nicholas Crowson, and Jean-François Mouhot, *The politics of expertise: how NGOs shaped modern Britain* (Oxford, 2013), p. 221.

13 Save the Children Fund, *Annual report, 1954–1955* (London, 1955), p. 5.

14 Harald Fischer-Tiné, 'Global civil society and the forces of empire: the Salvation Army, British imperialism, and the "prehistory" of NGOs (ca. 1880–1920)', in Sebastian Conrad and

Disasters and other emergencies have required close co-operation. During the Second World War the voluntary agencies collaborated through the Council of British Societies for Relief Abroad (COBSRA), which liaised closely with the British government. It went on to play a prominent role in ensuring that the United Nations Relief and Rehabilitation Administration (UNRRA) would make good use of the services of the voluntary societies.[15]

At the end of empire charities were brought in to assist with the processes of decolonisation. As the late imperial state retreated from its social, economic, and welfare commitments, charities that had formerly focused on emergency relief were invited in to run hospitals and mother and infant clinics, and to provide relief from suffering and instigate micro-level schemes to alleviate poverty. In extreme cases charities risked being closely associated with activities that were used to condemn colonial violence. As the British authorities in Kenya failed to deal with the chaos of their brutal suppression of Mau Mau, agencies such as Save the Children and the Red Cross were invited in to run rehabilitation camps, particularly for innocent children caught up in the mass arrests.[16]

Charity was also imagined as a handmaiden to new forms of international government. In the 1960s, the United Nations first Development Decade acted as a spur to the growth of British humanitarian charities. Dr Binay Ranjan Sen, Director General of the Food and Agriculture Organization of the United Nations (FAO), initiated the Freedom from Hunger Campaign in 1960 to draw the world's attention to global poverty. While it was essentially an educational campaign, it also sought to enrol citizens into the fight against poverty. National Freedom from Hunger Campaigns (FFHCs) were launched around the world, with many more local committees. In Britain alone 1,000 committees were established.[17]

The FFHC acted as a catalyst for NGOs to shift the focus of their work from relief to development. The campaign 'sought a worldwide partnership among like-minded groups, not for emergency relief or handouts but for

Dominic Sachsenmaier, eds, *Competing visions of world order: global moments and movements, 1880s–1930s* (London, 2007), pp. 29–67, p. 53.

15   Matthew Frank, 'Working for the Germans: British voluntary societies and the German refugee crisis, 1945–50', *Historical Research* 82, 215 (2009), pp. 157–75; Johannes-Dieter Steinert, 'British humanitarian assistance: wartime planning and postwar realities', *Journal of Contemporary History* 43, 3 (2008), pp. 421–35.

16   SCFA A147: T.W. Boyce, 'Report on proposals from the Government of Kenya for the re-establishment of SCF aid', 16 Aug. 1960; CAA CA/A/4/3: Christian Council of Kenya, Annual Report, 1955–56; Janet Lacey, Report on visit to Kenya in January 1955 at the request of Dr R.C. Mackie to discuss the possibility of Inter-Church Aid participation in rehabilitation schemes planned by the Christian Council of Kenya', 14 Mar. 1955.

17   Anna Bocking-Welch, 'Imperial legacies and internationalist discourses: British involvement in the United Nations Freedom from Hunger Campaign, 1960–70', *Journal of Imperial and Commonwealth History* 40, 5 (2012), pp. 879–96.

self-generated agricultural development'.[18] The local FFHC committees raised money for specific projects. War on Want, Christian Aid, and Oxfam were the three voluntary agencies most closely connected with the British Freedom from Hunger Campaign. According to Maggie Black, FFHC helped NGOs 'recast their own role to confront the challenge of world poverty, and to join in the development crusade as partners of the big brothers in the UN system'.[19]

At the very ends of empire then, the mixed economy of imperial relief was being both reimagined and reinforced. FFHC consolidated the legitimacy of the charitable presence in social welfare programmes of newly independent states, backed by the authority of the new institutions of global development associated with the UN. But this legitimacy was conferred also by the British state. Certainly, British charities occasionally fell foul of the Charity Commissioners. Oxfam and Christian Aid were investigated a number of times for seemingly overstepping their charitable remit by engaging in activities others argued were too political in controversial arenas such as South Africa and Palestine. But the overall trend was one of an official embrace of the voluntary sector. The FFHC set precedents for state–voluntary sector partnerships, which would expand enormously from the 1970s, especially when the Joint Funding Scheme (JFS) was launched by the Labour government in 1975. Its guidelines were developed in consultation with the leading NGOs. The scheme consisted of the co-funding (usually 50 per cent) of new projects submitted by British charities 'aimed at the long-term improvement of conditions of the poorest groups of people in developing countries, and not just for welfare or relief'.[20] In 1977 guaranteed block grants were also introduced to the larger NGOs, beginning with Oxfam and Christian Aid that year, and extended to CAFOD in 1979 and Save the Children Fund in 1985. The importance of the JFS, and the block grant within it, steadily increased. By the end of the 1980s the block grant was responsible for over 70 per cent of all JFS Funds, and in 1989 'the JFS translated into support for more than 900 projects in over fifty countries, and included fifty projects specifically concerned with women'.[21] Around 100 charities were eligible to submit for co-funding.

This was but part of a larger international shift to private–public alliances. By 1980 public grants from OECD governments to voluntary organisations had reached $1.5 billion.[22] Moreover, charities were increasingly being praised for their work by the official agencies. In 1974, the UN Development Programme embraced NGOs as 'a "partner" in the field level effort', and the World Food Programme began to expand massively the number of its NGO partnerships

18   Black, *Cause for our times*, p. 70.
19   Ibid.
20   Peter Burnell, *Charity, politics and the third world* (London, 1991), p. 208.
21   Ibid., p. 209.
22   Brian Smith, *More than altruism: the politics of private foreign aid* (Princeton, 1990), p. 4.

(by 2003 it was working with 2,000 NGOs).[23] The Development Assistance Committee of the OECD estimated that at the start of the 1980s virtually every member country had created a system for channelling official funding through NGOs, and it further sought out ways for 'strengthening partner institutions'.[24] The 1980 Brandt Commission championed the opportunities of partnership.[25] In 1987 the Brundtland Commission called for the greater use of NGOs' specialist knowledge and skills.[26] Bertrand Schneider even went so far as to tell the Club of Rome that NGOs' grassroots initiatives were the means by which the 'barefoot revolution' would be brought about.[27]

This mixed economy of welfare bolstered public donations. Indeed the quarter century after 1980 has been regarded as something of a golden age for international humanitarian charities, in a manner not dissimilar to the statements made about British philanthropy in the late nineteenth century. Various studies have traced the level of charitable giving over the period.[28] One estimates that over the 26-year period from 1978 to 2004, contributions to development charities increased sevenfold in real terms.[29] By the end of this period the top 200 fundraising charities that focused on overseas development and emergency relief received nearly £1 billion in donations and bequests, which was equal to approximately a quarter of the figure for the UK government's Official Development Assistance (ODA) at that time.[30] This growth in support has clearly been the consequence of heightened awareness of events around the world, brought to the attention of the public through highly professionalised media campaigns.[31]

23   BOD (OXFAM) PRG.2.2.1: United Nations Development Programme, 'Field level relations: general summary of consultations with Europe-based organizations', 1 Jul. 1974; D. John Shaw, *The world's largest humanitarian agency: the transformation of the UN World Food Programme and of food aid* (Basingstoke, 2011), p. 203.
24   Rutherford M. Poats, *Twenty-five years of development co-operation: a review of the efforts and policies of the members of the Development Assistance Committee* (Paris, 1985), p. 151; OECD, *Voluntary aid for development: the role of non-governmental organisations* (Paris, 1988), p. 11.
25   Independent Commission on Development Issues, *North-south: a programme for survival* (London, 1980), p. 65.
26   World Commission on Environment and Development, *Our common future* (Oxford, 1987), pp. 326-39.
27   Bertrand Schneider, *The barefoot revolution: a report to the Club of Rome* (London, 1988).
28   W. Arulampalam *et al.*, *Donations for overseas development – evidence from a panel of UK charities*, University of Southampton Working Paper, 2009; Anthony B. Atkinson *et al.*, *Charitable giving for overseas development UK trends over a quarter century*, Institute for the Study of Labor Discussion Paper, 2008; Richard Atkinson and Amy Eastwood, *Public attitudes to overseas giving: does government make a difference?*, Southampton Statistical Sciences Research Institute Applications & Policy Working Paper, 2007.
29   Arulampalam *et al.*, *Donations for overseas development*, p. 2.
30   Ibid.
31   Atkinson and Eastwood, *Public attitudes*, p. 1.

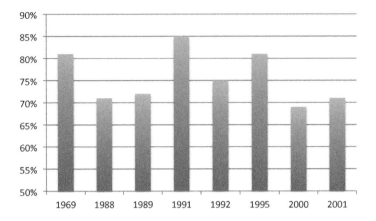

Figure 13.1. Public support in the UK for helping developing countries.

Source: Ida McDonell, 'United Kingdom', *Development Centre Studies public opinion and the fight against poverty*, North-South Centre of the Council of Europe, OECD, 2003, p. 219.

Public attitudes to giving

What the public thinks about charities, international aid, and the mixed economy of welfare is much more difficult to ascertain. Certainly the public has given, but what has this support meant in terms of wider understandings of the inequalities of wealth around the world? It is difficult to know what lies behind donations. Opinion polling data are notoriously unreliable sources. Questions are inconsistent, respondents are unwilling to state that they are actively against the relief of poverty, and support and recognition of an organisation does not necessarily amount to a full understanding of precisely what a charity does, particularly in regard to lobbying and advocacy.

That said, the data that are available – and which are far more complete for the decades since the early 1980s than before – suggest that attitudes to aid and development have been remarkably consistent. As a basic measure, surveys conducted since the late 1960s have generally found high levels of public support for helping developing countries (see Figure 13.1). Irene Rauta's study for the Office of Population Censuses and Surveys, conducted in 1969, found that four-fifths of the population were in favour of the idea that the richer countries of the world should help the poor.[32] Yet Rauta concluded that actual awareness of developing country problems was 'superficial' and 'rudimentary'. She found that many people assumed aid to be mainly about dealing with

32   I. Rauta, *Aid and overseas development* (London, 1971), p. 7.

disasters, and that aid was essentially a form of 'hand out'. That is, aid as charity (and which could also come second to charity that begins at home) could be 'turned off and on' rather than be a fixed commitment arising out of a sense of being 'all part of one world community'. Her conclusions have been broadly replicated ever since. Moreover, while surveys have found persistently high support for the idea that the rich should help the poor, when that question has been focused on the British government support has been much less. Just a few years later, T.S. Bowles found similar high levels of support for aid in principle, but just 46 per cent of the public were in favour of official UK government aid.[33] Connected to this was a mistaken sense of the importance of charity, with the public believing that the main NGOs played a much greater role in development assistance than was actually the case. Bowles further noted that people were particularly attracted to Oxfam because of its reputation for efficiency, and to Save the Children because of its stated focus on the relatively less controversial area of childhood suffering.

While actual understanding of developing world issues has remained high among committed supporters, surveys have found repeatedly both a lack of general awareness of the causes of poverty and a relatively simplistic belief in the role played by charities: alleviating suffering rather than contributing to long-term development. This is why when support for government aid has fluctuated and declined, most recently as a consequence of the financial recession, support for private charities has conversely increased. When charities expanded enormously from the 1980s, boosted by government grants and then by a surge in public donations following Live Aid and other such mass appeals, it did not follow that public understanding deepened. Indeed, one VSO report of 2001 on the 'Live Aid legacy' even found the reverse to be true. It concluded that 80 per cent of the public associated the developing world with famine and disaster, consisting, in short, of 'starving children with flies around their eyes'. Furthermore, the nature of charitable appeals had encouraged a view of victims of famine as being 'less human' while a 'false sense of superiority' had increased among the public based on a notion of a 'powerful giver and grateful receiver'.[34]

To be sure, there are many gradations within this notion of a homogenous public. Various studies have found that Conservative Party supporters and the over fifty-fives are much less likely to support government aid than the young. Women are more likely to support aid, both public and private. People from families with traditions of giving to charities are also much more likely to continue doing so. But for all groups the importance of the media, of public appeals, the mobilisation of celebrities, and the human interest story in the press have proven key ways of encouraging people to give more, whatever their existing level of support.

33 T.S. Bowles, *Survey of attitudes towards overseas development* (London, 1978), p. 13.
34 VSO, *The Live Aid legacy: the developing world through British eyes* (London, 2001), p. 3.

But while it is easy to dismiss public support for charities as superficial, the nature of that support is complicated. What is clear is that the public has deliberately chosen to support these charities over others. On an individual level, people have been very engaged with overseas charities, particularly in terms of charity membership and giving. In a study conducted by Johanna Lindstom and Spencer Henson in March 2011, a panel was asked about the level and nature of their engagement with charities in the UK during the previous twelve months. The results show that charities working on overseas aid and disaster relief were very much supported by the public, being the most popular cause for regular donations. In addition, a high number of people were members of these charities (second only to animal welfare charities).[35] The annual UK Giving Survey, conducted by the Charities Aid Foundation and the National Council for Voluntary Organisations, has consistently found that overseas development has been one of the three most popular causes.

However superficial their understanding of the underlying issues of aid and development might be, people have nevertheless made deliberate choices to support humanitarianism over other good causes. The active nature of these choices cannot be overlooked or simply dismissed. In the work I conducted with colleagues at the University of Birmingham we showed how the myriad contributions to NGOs and charities – however small – collectively constituted a form of political engagement that was significant. Central to this was a reconceptualisation of trust. That is, we took an approach that, unlike for theorists of social capital, trust does not have to be seen as the consequence of membership; it might just as easily be the cause of membership. People have made deliberate decisions to trust certain types of organisation over others. Arguably this is what the public has decided to do in recent decades, and it explains why trust in charities when dealing with overseas aid has come to be so much higher than that in government. It also explains the differences within the public, and the acts of discrimination that take place when it comes to trusting. Younger people, women more than men, those who are educated, well-travelled, live in cities, and have been brought up by parents with similar attitudes to aid are all more likely to give and to support the wider charitable objectives. Given these consistencies of finding across polling data, it is easy to conclude that attitudes to aid are rather engrained, and explain why phenomena such as 'aid fatigue' rarely manifest themselves.

While it can be argued that the public has chosen to trust charities, what it has chosen to trust them to do is another matter. Surveys that have reported on high levels of trust in humanitarian charities have also found that most people think charities are engaged in relatively innocuous caring roles that we associate with

---

35   Johanna Lindstom and Spencer Henson, *What does the public think, know and do about aid and development? Results and analysis from the UK Public Opinion Monitor* (Institute of Development Studies, Oct. 2011), p. 9.

traditional forms of philanthropy. The reading we can take from such evidence, as the British voluntary sector has itself worried, is that trust is maintained in charities precisely because they are not seen as political actors in any traditional sense. And this explains too the discrepancies in knowledge about the various aspects of development work. The most recent polls reveal high levels of public concern about single issues such as debt, fair trade, landmines, and child labour – awareness that is closely linked to civil society advocacy in the United Kingdom. They indicate little or contradictory awareness of issues of economic interdependence, the multidimensional nature of development, and the decline in global ODA levels. There is consistency in opinion about the level of government commitment to poverty reduction in developing countries, where 43 per cent of the respondents said UK spending was about right, and 30 per cent found it too low. Poverty eradication in developing countries was for 68 per cent a moral issue, conceived as a personal one best expressed through a limited view of what constitutes charitable endeavour.[36]

As so many have concluded for particular moments in time, we can only similarly conclude for the period as a whole. Public attitudes have persistently been 'two dimensional', as Glenner et al. put it: the public's views 'are often underpinned by stereotypical attitudes towards poverty, or particular countries, and a strong moral sense that at times appears close to superiority and contrasts between "us" and "them", which can work to undermine a sense of shared empathy'.[37] It is why, in the years after the financial crisis, support for government assistance began to be seriously called into question, while support for charities remained consistently high. It also helps to explain why the valorisation of charity as a solution for the problems of global poverty has continued to increase.

The critique of charity

One way of explaining this two-dimensional aspect of support for charity is to locate it within a more general public debate about the proper role of charity. Certainly this was the case in the nineteenth century, if not in subsequent decades too. Yet the post-war history of charitable social welfare in Africa and other parts of the world has made no clear articulation as to the proper role and extent of charity. There have been no latter-day equivalents of the public poor law and private Charity Organisation Society. There has been no articulation of the 'new philanthropy', no third volume on voluntarism to accompany a

---

36   Ida McDonnell, Henri-Bernard Solignac Lecomte, and Liam Wegimont, *Public opinion and the fight against poverty* (Development Centre Studies, OECD, 2003), p. 218.
37   Glenner et al., *Understanding public attitudes to aid and development* (IPPR & ODI, 2012), p. 2.

modern-day Beveridge's plans for the welfare state. There has been no attempt to demarcate the blurred lines between the public and the voluntary sector in a mixed economy of welfare.[38] So while the existence of a global mixed economy mirrored that of the domestic one in the previous century, the difference is that, in the late twentieth and early twenty-first, there were far fewer attempts to delineate with any precision the nature of this mix.

Moreover, in the scholarship of modern-day philanthropy there has been little critique of charity. Those who have studied nineteenth-century philanthropy have been as much concerned about understanding the theoretical role and effects of charity as the contemporaries they study. Gareth Stedman Jones, for instance, wrote of the 'deformation of the gift' relationship in his *Outcast London* as alms-givers worried about the 'demoralisation' of the poor through a profusion of uncoordinated relief.[39] But notwithstanding Slavoj Zizek's ironic condemnation of charity as the perverted logic of 'liberal communism', it seems the long tradition of attacking charity's 'multitude of sins', in Oscar Wilde's phrase, has long since been eclipsed by the inexorable rise of the charitable humanitarians.[40]

It has not always been the case, particularly in regard to development debates more generally. The left has charged that aid has been used to promote capitalism and maintain the economic balance of power in the West. Ultimately aid is held to promote neo-colonialism or, as Kwame Nkrumah put it, 'the last stage of imperialism'.[41] And from the right, critics of aid have argued it to be an inappropriate and damaging government intervention in the market which, left alone, would eventually bring economic prosperity to all.[42] In earlier decades even ministers for Overseas Development waded into debates about the fundamental purpose and effects of aid. But it is a long time since accusations of charity as being a mere 'sticking plaster' over deeper structural issues

---

38 Geoffrey Finlayson, 'A moving frontier: voluntarism and the state in British social welfare', *Twentieth-Century British History* 1 (1990), pp. 183–206; Bernard Harris, *The origins of the British welfare state: society, state and social welfare in England and Wales, 1800–1945* (Basingstoke, 2004); Pat Thane, *The foundations of the welfare state*, 2nd edn (London, 1996); Geoffrey Finlayson, *Citizen, state and social welfare in Britain, 1830–1990* (Oxford, 1994); Jane Lewis, *The voluntary sector, the state and social work in Britain: the Charity Organisation Society/Family Welfare Association since 1869* (Aldershot, 1995); Susan Pedersen, 'Gender, welfare, and citizenship in Britain during the Great War', *American Historical Review* 95, 4 (1990), pp. 983–1006.

39 G. Stedman Jones, *Outcast London: a study in the relationship between classes in Victorian society* (Oxford, 1986), p. 252.

40 Slavoj Zizek, 'The liberal communists of Porto Davis', *In These Times*, 11 Apr. 2006; Oscar Wilde, 'The soul of man under socialism', 1891.

41 Kwame Nkrumah, *Neo-colonialism: the last stage of imperialism* (London, 1965); C.R. Hensman, *Rich against poor: the reality of aid* (London, 1971); Teresa Hayter, *Aid as imperialism* (Harmondsworth, 1971).

42 Peter T. Bauer, *Dissent on development: studies and debates in development economics* (London, 1971); Peter T. Bauer, *Equality, the third world and economic delusion* (London, 1981).

were a common expression.[43] When Save the Children commissioned social-realist filmmaker Ken Loach to produce a fiftieth anniversary film in 1969, they were askance when he studied their work in Africa and accused them of crudely and inappropriately imposing western values on the recipients of their aid. The charity banned the film for over forty years, and instead sought the assistance of their patron, Princess Anne, and the children's TV show *Blue Peter* to commission another film that they felt better reflected the benefits to the poor of their philanthropic initiatives.[44]

Charities themselves have been more willing to discuss the problematic nature of the gift relationship, particularly when mediated through images of suffering. The sector has long been concerned with the images it has peddled to sell poverty alleviation. As Francis Khoo, the Secretary General of War on Want in the 1990s, put it, 'I baulk at the poverty of images in our images of poverty.'[45] The rhetorical tropes associated with mission and earlier waves of humanitarianism have persisted, especially through the visual imagery NGOs have continued to publish. Before and after pictures continued, for instance, even though they could homogenise suffering, render the recipient passive, and legitimate the heroic intervention of the aid worker. In a moment of candid self-referentiality, one Oxfam field officer described the starving people of Congo in 1966 as 'looking like advertisements for Oxfam'.[46] This problem has not gone away. The sector has been very aware of its problematic, homogenising images and has done much to try and counteract them. Guidelines on advertising and imagery have regularly been published to suggest a more complex interaction between North and South, and to show to the public that the alleviation of poverty involves far more than the heroic acts of donation and assistance. Yet charities also know what sells. The machinery of aid mobilises particularly at times of disaster, and images that depoliticise suffering are precisely the ones that raise the most cash. Charities constantly find themselves in a bind – eager to raise cash so that they can assist and protect, but doing so in ways that do not raise a broader awareness of the underlying issues in the political economy of global inequality.

These issues have only been exacerbated with the further massive injections of cash into the sector from the public since the Live Aid phenomenon of the 1980s. Critiques now directed at the sector are less about the fundamental logics of charitable assistance and the unequal nature of the gift relationship than they are about specific aspects of NGO activity that can be called into question. The rise of celebrity humanitarianism, for instance, has provoked particular ire. It

43 Judith Hart, *Aid and liberation: a socialist study of aid politics* (London, 1973).
44 Matthew Hilton, 'Ken Loach and the Save the Children film: humanitarianism, imperialism and the changing role of charity in postwar Britain', *Journal of Modern History* 87, 2 (2015), pp. 357–94.
45 Cited in Burnell, *Charity, politics and the third world*, p. 18.
46 BOD (OXFAM) PRG/1/3/1: T.G. Brierly, 'Kikwit, Kwilu: report', 20 Jul. 1966.

has been alleged that while Hollywood endorsement might raise funds, it does nothing to improve actual engagement with development issues and perhaps, even worse, reduces it to a level of superficiality alike to just shopping.[47]

Instead, charity has found new champions. Even while official forms of aid become less popular, the moral legitimacy of the philanthropist appears as secure as the political legitimacy of the neoliberal world order of which he or she increasingly seems a part. Billionaires set up foundations in their own name while former presidents tell us how giving can change the world. Such is the moral and political value attributed to charity as a corollary of the free market that some have claimed for 'philanthrocapitalism' the same utopian goals formerly attributed to the ideological movements of the previous century.[48] But philosophers are encouraging us all to behave like billionaires, channelling funding according to our own individual preferences. 'Effective altruism' helps us to make more informed choices and to direct our funding to those NGOs we identify for ourselves as the most efficient, helping to rein in those charities that newspapers such as the *Daily Mail* and *Daily Express* have long accused of wasting our donations on salaries and bureaucracy.[49] The trust that has been placed in charities to 'do good' on our collective behalf is being replaced with individual scepticism. But this is a scepticism aimed at single charities rather than charity as a whole. We can keep on giving, but with our own individual preferences – and prejudices – directing and switching our decisions as rapidly as an investor might speculate on the stock exchange.

Conclusion

Catherine Hall, in *Civilising subjects*, brilliantly delineates the attitudes to racial difference in the mid-nineteenth century. The monolithic image of the suffering slave that raised so much humanitarian compassion had to be rethought once he and she were made free. The reality of equality was dealt with differently than the theory. A new vocabulary of racial difference and hierarchy was articulated, often by those former anti-slavery activists, in order to restore a social order to be based on social and physical difference rather than physical oppression.[50]

---

47 Ilan Kapoor, *Celebrity humanitarianism: the ideology of global charity* (London, 2013).
48 Bill Clinton, *Giving: how each of us can change the world* (London, 2008); Robert H. Bremner, *Giving: charity and philanthropy in history* (New Brunswick, NJ, 1996).
49 Peter Singer, *The life you can save: how to play your part in ending world poverty* (London, 2009); Peter Singer, *The most good you can do: how effective altruism is changing ideas about living ethically* (New Haven, 2015); William MacAskill, *Doing good better: effective altruism and a radical way to make a difference* (London, 2016).
50 Catherine Hall, *Civilising subjects: metropole and colony in the English imagination 1830–1867* (Oxford, 2002).

One might expect a similar re-articulation of racial differences in the transition from empire to independence. Arguably the 'afterlives of empire' have done that as race continues to be a battleground over meaning and difference.[51] But in one particular area we can observe a different trajectory to that which Hall identified. The languages of racial differencing have instead been homogenised in the post-colonial world. Whereas the image of the starving African child exemplifies this homogenisation of suffering, it arguably represents a more troubling one-size-fits-all approach to development that has been a persistent critique within and beyond the aid industry.

Charity has a role in the imagination of suffering and the alleviation of poverty. For all that sector leaders have lobbied, campaigned, and sought to persuade the public and politicians of the underlying and deeper issues associated with poverty, they have relied on a donating public that has offered them much support, albeit in a highly circumscribed manner. Moreover, that sector has been actively encouraged by governments keen to partner with it, although here too there has been an attempt to constrain the role of charity, be it through funding restrictions or persistent policing of an organisation's proper charitable remit through the interventions of the Charity Commissioners.

Charity has assumed a role in the mixed economy of welfare, though it is one that has been reined in both by the donating public and by its partners in the alleviation of suffering. The sort of charity practised in international development has always presented itself as a means to an end, either through the stimulus it would provide to state intervention, or through the self-help schemes it has hoped will ultimately become self-sustaining. But charity has proved to be the end as well as the means, and the one clear consequence of the rise of humanitarian philanthropy has been the political, cultural, social, and economic legitimacy conferred upon it. Thus the donating public has arguably supported a system of global poverty reduction that seeks to complement rather than contradict the systems of power within the global market. Charities have done much to expose the inequities of global wealth, but it seems the public have turned to their wallets and purses in ways in which the only persistent outcome of their emotional and political reactions is the maintenance of charity itself in the mixed economy of global welfare.

51 Jordanna Bailkin, *The afterlife of empire* (Berkeley, 2012); Bill Schwarz, *Memories of empire*, vol. 1: *The white man's world* (Oxford, 2011).

14

Discounting time

MARTIN CHICK

I first heard of Martin Daunton in 1983 during a postgraduate research seminar chaired by Theo Barker at the LSE. Discussion turned to the Post Office, and someone mentioned that Martin was writing its history. Even then the mention of Martin's name carried a quiet authority with it, with no one in the room doubting that what Martin wrote would be of the highest quality. Yet, because I was not the most outgoing of creatures, I was not to meet Martin until 2006. Sitting in a hostel in Dali, China in January 2006 and, as one does, checking through my university email, I noticed an invitation from Martin to give a paper to the modern economic and social history seminar at Cambridge. I accepted the invitation, and so began the first of several happy visits to stay with Martin and Claire at Trinity Hall. Later that same year, Martin and I both gave papers to a UK–Russian seminar on state and industry relations at the International Economic History Congress in Helsinki. In 2009 I began work on the final volume of the *Oxford economic and social history of Britain*, to which Martin had already contributed two volumes, as well as being the general editor of the series. Throughout the long process of writing my volume, Martin endured sporadic bursts of email from me on topics ranging from John Hicks and what became the IS/LM model, to the likely rates of return on the technology shares gathered together in the Scottish Mortgage investment trust. Throughout, Martin has remained good humoured, well-informed and highly perceptive, qualities which abound in his writing.

This chapter examines one of the main concerns of the fifth volume of the *Oxford economic and social history of Britain*, which I am currently finishing. Its concern is with time, and in particular with the increasing use of 'discounting' over time by post-World War II UK governments in their approach to the management of public expenditure. While other approaches to the accommodation of the future, such as insurance, take precautions to mitigate the risk and magnitude of contingent future events, the practice of discounting differs in valuing not the risk and its cost, but instead the income and the returns from the future in terms of the present. Formally, discounting is the valuation of the future income and costs expressed in their current or present value. In valuing the future in terms of the present, given certainty, the interest rate will be used. Given the presence of uncertainty a discount rate is chosen which for most projects is likely to be higher than the rate of interest. The tendency is to presume that the needs of today have a greater value than those of the future. This approach is underpinned by impatience, an assumption of economic growth, rising per capita income such that the marginal utility of income falls, faith in technological progress, and a mixture of risk and uncertainty. In western Europe, the industrial application of discounting was begun in the 1950s in companies like Courtaulds, Esso, and Rio Tinto Zinc, as well as in nationalised industries such as Electricité de France.

The particular purpose of this study of the government's use of discounting is to provide one means of analysing the longer-term change across UK post-World War II history in the nature and scope of what the UK state did. For much of the post-war period, as Martin Daunton has noted for 1979–96, for all of the political noise, the share of GDP accounted for by public expenditure remained broadly unchanged.[1] However, within that total the nature of the expenditure changed considerably. Almost from the start of the post-World War II period, as the economist Dennis Robertson noted, the Attlee government assumed a significantly greater influence over the allocation of resources across time. Addressing the Liverpool Statistical Society on 11 January 1952, Robertson observed:

> It seems to me that the most significant economic difference between the England of 1950 and the England of 1910 in which I began to study economics does not lie in the vast extension of social services, nor in the fact that certain branches of industrial activity have been nationalised, nor even in the greater preoccupation with high employment as the supreme objective of policy, though it is not unconnected with any of these things. It lies rather in the fact that the State has claimed the right and assumed the duty of making and implementing on behalf of the community one of the most fundamental of economic choices, namely the distribution of productive resources between present and future uses. In other words it has taken upon itself the responsibility for determining the rate of growth of the community's real capital.[2]

This issue of how resources were distributed across time concerned economists like Hayek, Keynes, and Ramsey in the interwar period. Frank Ramsey's 1928 paper entitled 'A mathematical theory of saving' was considered by Keynes to be 'one of the most remarkable contributions to mathematical economics ever

---

1   M.J. Daunton, *Just taxes: the politics of taxation in Britain* (Cambridge, 2009), p. 338. Jim Tomlinson, *Managing the economy, managing the people* (Oxford, 2017), p. 76.
2   D.H. Robertson, 'British national investment policy', in D.H. Robertson, ed., *Utility and all that* (London, 1952), pp. 116–31, p. 116.

made'.[3] In it, Ramsey considered the temporal issue of what proportion of its income a society should save for the purposes of investment. This formed an important contribution to discussions of how the present should value the future in terms of the present. One question which immediately arose was whether benefits in the future should be regarded as having the same value as those in the present. In short, should one 'discount' the future? One argument for doing so was that as a function of economic growth, a future society would be richer than the present one.

Keynes also emphasised this idea in a paper, 'Economic possibilities for our grandchildren', which was written in 1928 and read to a student society at Ramsey's old school of Winchester College.[4] In the paper Keynes underlined the importance of compound growth. In a sense, discounting looks from the future back to the present, whereas compound growth gains power as it moves from the present to the future. For both Keynes and Ramsey, the object of striking the right balance between consumption in the future and investment for the future was to attain a position of Bliss. Philosophically Ramsey was reluctant to 'discount later enjoyments in comparison with earlier ones, a practice which is ethically indefensible and arises merely from the weakness of the imagination'. However, Ramsey did accept that since trade-offs between present and future would be made, then discounting would occur.

In the immediate post-World War II period, there was little use of such discounting practices within government. Public housing was built and financed with loans from the Public Works Loan Board, and the rents charged reflected pooled average costs. Nationalised industries were simply required to cover their costs, taking one year with another, which again encouraged the use of average cost pricing with little pressure for any real return to be earned on assets. Schools, hospitals, universities, and roads were funded from the public purse and, aside from the entry fee of road vehicle duty, use of the investment and service was not paid for at the point of consumption. There was a sense in which the state performed a collectivist, provisionist function financed by general taxation.

Over time, that was to change. Provision diminished as the state sold public housing and encouraged those seeking housing to do so in the private rented sector, armed if need be with housing benefit. Nationalised industries were required from 1961 to earn a return on their existing assets, and from 1967 to apply test discount rates to proposed projects. From the 1980s, nationalised industries were also privatised. In health, rates of return on operations and treatments formed the basis of the quality-adjusted life year (QALY) approach to resource allocation. In higher education, students began to pay tuition fees.

---

3   F.P. Ramsey, 'A mathematical theory of saving', *Economic Journal* 38, 152 (1928), pp. 543–59. D.H. Mellor, ed., *F.P. Ramsey* (Cambridge, 1990), pp. xi, xv.
4   J.M. Keynes, 'Economic possibilities for our grandchildren', in J.M. Keynes, *Essays in persuasion* (London, 2010), pp. 321–2.

Why did such changes occur? In part because as expenditure on social security and the National Health Service grew as a proportion of public expenditure, especially from the 1970s, so a corresponding pressure fell on the remaining components of public expenditure. As shares of GDP, public expenditure on social security rose from 6.5 per cent in 1969–70 to 11.8 per cent by 2014–15, while health absorbed 3.5 per cent in 1969–70 and 7.4 per cent in 2014–15. In responding to such pressure from health and social security expenditure, an increasing use was made of discounting, both in appraising proposed fixed capital investment projects and also in evaluating the size and appropriation of benefits from expenditure in health and education.

Part of the state's response to the changing and increasing pressures on public expenditure was not simply to apply discounted approaches to proposed investment, but also to scale back its entire public fixed capital investment activity. In the early post-war period, public net investment rose steadily from 2 per cent of GDP in 1949–50 to a peak of 7.6 per cent of GDP in 1967–68. However, thereafter it fell, and public net investment virtually ground to a halt in 1999–2000. While it did pick up proportionately in the middle of the first decade of the twenty-first century, the high percentage share in 2009–10 reflected the slump in GDP. This fall in investment was complemented by a shift in the ratio of current to investment spending from 10:1 in 1958–59 to 118:1 in 1988–89, before it fell back to 70:1 in 2000–01 and 19:1 in 2007–08.[5] In part the withdrawal of the state from investment was physically visible in the privatisation of housing and, to a lesser extent, nationalised industries. Between 1950 and 1991 there was a switch-round in the source of investment in housing. Whereas in 1950 investment in private dwellings accounted for 3.4 per cent of total fixed capital investment in housing and public investment accounted for 16.3 per cent, by 1994 these contributions had been reversed, with 18.2 per cent private and 2.7 per cent public.

As direct investment activity by the state fell, so too did its interest in encouraging substitute private fixed capital investment grow. This required a shift from providing public funding up front, to instead offering private investors streams of income as a rate of return in the future. Perhaps the best known instance of this approach was the Private Finance Initiative (PFI). Announced by Chancellor Norman Lamont in his Autumn Statement of 1992, this enabled a stream of services to be purchased from a provider, rather than through up-front public financing. Politics apart, one argument made was that construction and other risks were being transferred to private industry, although it came at a price. It was not clear why construction risks could not be guarded against in contracts with contractors or why concern at the risks of raising money should be particularly problematic. By taking a stream of services from PFI providers, a

---

5 Rowena Crawford, Carl Emmerson, and Gemma Tetlow, *A survey of public spending*, IFS Briefing Note, BN 43, p. 16.

risk premium had to be built into the price reflecting the risk that future governments might not honour or want the contracts and their services. The political hue of governments could change, and governments in western Europe had walked away from nuclear power. Such risks and the difficulties of specifying service requirements made these incomplete contracts of higher risk than the risks arising from construction or finance, but this higher risk was bundled up in the total risk pricing assessment for the whole project.[6]

If finding new 'off the books' means of financing 'public' investment was one response to public finance constraints, another was subjecting all proposed fixed capital investment and expenditure to discounted appraisal. In the UK this discounted approach had been developed in the nationalised electricity industry, notably during the 1960s, both to provide the Treasury with influence over technological choices (thermal vs. hydro) and partly to compensate for difficulties in pricing electricity at long-run marginal cost. The approach that was developed in the 1960s in the nationalised industries began to be applied beyond these industries in the 1970s. One area targeted by the Treasury was the NHS. While the dominant cost of a hospital was that of labour, as a lumpy, fixed investment, hospitals increasingly had Treasury investment appraisal techniques applied to them. In the language which the Treasury increasingly visited on the Department of Health and Social Security (DHSS), the decision to build (close) a hospital represented a marginal addition to (subtraction from) an entire existing system whose social discounted costs and benefits required appraisal. This approach came as something of a shock to the DHSS in the 1970s, which had never previously attempted any such systematic cost–benefit analysis of the social rate of return on large-scale capital projects.[7]

As the Treasury fought its case with the DHSS, the usual arguments about the type and level of discount rate to be used ensued. However, here was a pragmatic recognition that while the intricacies of test discount rates, social time preference rates, and other conceptual approaches to expressing the future in terms of the present might not always be followed closely by politicians and administrators, nonetheless the use of a discount-rate approach seeped through into their decision-making via a process of political osmosis. The chosen test discount rate (TDR) affected the numbers which were fed to senior officials and ministers over a period of months and sometimes years leading up to a decision, and 'these numbers do affect the climate of opinion and hence the preferences of the decisions makers, even though these preferences are perceived as essentially "political" or "'gut feelings'".[8]

6   Peter Jackson, 'The private finance initiative', The David Hume Institute, Occasional paper no. 64, Feb. 2004, pp. 16–17.
7   'Investment appraisal techniques for the Health Capital Programme', par. 14, TNA T 379/74.
8   Ibid.

Discounting was not simply applied to fixed capital investment projects, but also to the size and allocation of the benefits of any expenditure. Increasing attention was paid to the balance between the public cost of expenditure and the public–private split of any benefits. In health and education, this coincided with the Treasury view that not only were there diminishing returns to additional expenditure, but that many of the gains of this additional expenditure went to private individuals rather than to any wider public good. Treasury scepticism of the marginal benefits of education was of long standing. Over time it did accept that there was an association between economic growth and expenditure on education, but in the shorter term Treasury officials were very sceptical of any such causal effect.[9] Even if a direction of causation did exist, it might run from economic growth to educational expenditure: that as economies grew richer, so more was spent on education as a form of consumption. Prior to World War II, this view of educational expenditure as in part a form of consumption was common, and it lingered on within the Treasury after the war. While politicians pushed for the raising of the school-leaving age, Treasury economists questioned the marginal benefits. The school-leaving age was raised from fourteen to fifteen in 1947, and not further to sixteen until 1973. That twenty-six years intervened between raising the school-leaving age from fifteen to sixteen in part reflected such concerns. In 1963 the economist Maurice Peston captured some of these (welfare) economic concerns in a paper written for HM Treasury's Committee on the Economics of Education.[10] Quite what the marginal benefits were of additional expenditure on education, and to whom they went, suffused the Treasury economist Ralph Turvey's lengthy review in 1964 for the Treasury of Gary Becker's book *Human capital*, which was published that year. If anything, Turvey thought that the social rate of return was probably understated, as Becker tended to capture only the direct returns, all effects on the output of other people being excluded – Einstein's gifts to the world for example.[11] While an association could be observed between the average cost of education and average earnings at various ages for groups with eight, nine, ten etc. years of education, it was much more difficult to get from this to estimates of the marginal social rate of return, not least because of a need to correct for ability, the non-educational portion of income, and allowance for the fact that the marginal return was below the average return.[12]

This same concern with the public–private division of benefits also came

9 'Education and economic growth', note, Peter Vinter, Sep. 1961, TNA T 298/277.
10 M.H. Peston, 'The school leaving age', HM Treasury Committee on the Economics of Education, 4 Oct. 1963, pars 2 and 3, TNA T 227/1348, C.E.E. (63)6.
11 R. Turvey, 'Returns to investment in education', 1964, TNA T 298/277.
12 'Washington Conference: economic growth and investment in education', comments by R. Turvey to Mr. Hopkin, par. 6, TNA T 230/536.

increasingly to suffuse discussion of further investment in higher education. Responding to the 1963 expansionary Report of the Committee on Higher Education chaired by Lionel Robbins of the LSE, the Treasury sought justification for this additional claim on resources which it regarded as 'really very large indeed'.[13] If they were implemented, the Treasury feared that the Robbins Report's proposals would increase spending on higher education from 0.8 per cent of GNP in 1965 to 1.6 per cent in 1980, on an assumption of 4 per cent annual growth in GNP. The Treasury questioned whether, if the future benefits of higher education went mainly as private benefits to individual graduates, those graduates should not in turn contribute to the cost of their higher education. Ultimately the Robbins Committee remained neutral on such matters, although Lionel Robbins himself favoured a student loan scheme and higher fees. While his eponymous report 'recommended that the level of fees should be raised so that in future they covered at least 20 per cent of current institutional expenditure', Robbins admitted that 'Some of us would prefer to see the proportion greater. I do not think I shall be guilty of gross impropriety if I reveal that I was one of the "some". I should like to see the proportion much higher.'[14]

Some in the Treasury thought higher fees plus loans to be superior to the simple substitution of loans for grants, or to a graduate tax, the aim being to restrict the public subsidy to the 'social' element in higher education costs. At the end of 1971 there was discussion of introducing a graduate tax, although there was concern that government did not have sufficiently reliable information about the lifetime earnings of graduates so as to be able accurately to forecast the yield of such a tax; on these grounds it was considered inferior to a loan scheme.[15] Throughout the 1980s and 1990s evidence of a lifetime earnings premium accompanied by a growing view that most of the gains went to private individuals continued to encourage talk of student loans and fees. The 1997 Dearing Report emphasised the extent to which the gains made from higher education went to the private individual, although in fact there were little high-quality empirical data which allowed the social and private benefits of higher education to be separated out and weighted.[16]

As the future benefits of expenditure were discounted back to the present on a marginal basis, so too did they encourage these discounted returns to be expressed, where possible, on a disaggregated and potentially individual

13 'Robbins Report', note by R.W.B. Clarke, 13 Sep. 1963, par. 10i, TNA T 227/1618.

14 Lionel Robbins, 'Recent discussion of the problems of higher education in Great Britain', in Lionel Robbins, *The university in the modern world* (London, 1966), pp. 17–39, pp. 31–2.

15 'PAR: Higher education', Note, M.S. Levitt to Miss Forsyth, 13 Dec. 1971, par. 2, TNA T 227/3658.

16 N. Barr and I. Crawford, 'The Dearing Report and the government's response: a critique', *Political Quarterly* 69, 1 (1998), pp. 72–84. Stephen Machin and Anna Vignoles, *What's the good of education? The economics of education in the UK* (Princeton, 2005), p. 91.

basis. In health, not only was there the same impetus as in higher education to distinguish between the public and private benefits of treating patients, but there was also in the development of a QALY approach to allocating health resources between patients, a logical tendency to identify the private benefits enjoyed by individual patients.[17] QALYs combined an assessment of the cost of an operation or procedure, with an assessment of the ability of an individual to benefit, with the duration of this weighted benefit being expressed in terms of added life years.[18] Added life years reflected both life-expectancy and a quality adjustment (as weights indicating the healthiness of the expected life years). In theory QALYs enabled inter-technology comparisons to be made, the theory being that setting the marginal cost per QALY as near as possible to equality across all technologies was an important step towards maximising health gains. Thus technologies with a 'low' marginal cost per QALY were to be preferred to those with a 'high' marginal cost per QALY.[19]

While the QALY approach focused on the monetised private benefits of treating one person rather than another, those benefits necessarily lay in a future from which they were discounted backwards. In thinking of how to prevent individuals being killed on the roads, there was a shift in the temporal perspective from which the loss of life was considered. At around the same time as nationalised industries were required to move from an *ex post* required rate of return on existing assets to the application of an *ex ante* TDR to proposed new investment, so too was there a shift between an *ex post* and an *ex ante* valuation of life occurring in the government's Road Research Laboratories. From the interwar period until the 1960s an *ex post* approach had been used to calculate the monetary cost to society of an 'average' accident.[20] In thinking *ex post* about someone's death, the calculation made concerned the future loss of output and income minus the consumption which no longer occurred. In shifting to an *ex ante* approach, the concern was not with the death, but rather with its prevention. This value of prevented fatality (VPF) approach, which measured the benefit of keeping an individual alive who, but for the introduction of some safety measure, would have been dead, used a gross measure of output rather than netting out consumption. Since the individual was alive

---

17   Some of the origins of such an approach can be found in Kenneth Arrow's 1963 *American Economic Review* article on 'Uncertainty and the welfare economics of medical care' and in Martin Feldstein's 1966 book of his doctoral dissertation, M.S. Feldstein, *Economic analysis for health service efficiency* (Amsterdam, 1966).

18   A.J. Culyer, 'The normative economics of health care finance and provision', *Oxford Review of Economic Policy* 5, 1 (1989), pp. 34–58.

19   Richard Cookson and Karl Claxton, eds, *The humble economist: Tony Culyer on health, health care and social decision making* (York, 2012), pp. 108–9, 122.

20   D.J. Reynolds, 'The cost of road accidents', *Journal of the Royal Statistical Society*, series A, 119, 4 (1956), pp. 393–408.

and able to enjoy his/her consumption, this consumption was a benefit to him/her and, since he/she was a member of society, a benefit to society.[21]

The *ex ante* valuation of the VPF substantially raised the value of life used in appraising the benefits of road improvements.[22] In 1970 the valuation of a life saved was almost doubled, with the valuations in 1970 prices being £17,000 for a fatality, £900 for a serious injury, and £30 for a slight injury.[23] Expressed in 2004 prices, the VPF of a road fatality rose from £37,500 in 1952 to £1,384,500 in 2004, a 37-fold increase. As an *ex ante* approach to preventing fatalities was adopted, so it became tempting to distinguish between the economic value of the individual lives which were being saved. This value arose from their annual output and the number of expected future years of work. It became possible to differentiate the VPF by age, income, and gender. So, for example, motorcyclists tended to be young men whereas pedestrian casualties were weighted towards old people and children. In economic terms, the young and employed were worth more than the old and retired; the individual motorcyclist or car occupant was worth more than the individual pedestrian.[24]

As the economic value of workers increased, so too did the value of their time. Such concerns affected decisions on investment in transport, and raised new issues concerning the measurement of the rate of return on capital. In as much as net transport investment enabled travel times to be reduced, it represented an uncommon instance of a rising marginal efficiency of investment.[25] The time-saving aspect of putative transport projects, both for users of new transport links and for users of existing capacity from which demand had shifted, made proposed projects very suitable for cost–benefit analysis (CBA), as too did the social costs and benefits of transport. There had been notable exercises in the application of CBA, such as to the proposed construction of the Victoria underground line in London.[26]

The factoring-in of the value of time and of time savings became of increasing importance in transport infrastructure projects, although it was vulnerable to entering a vicious logical spiral. As productivity growth raised the value of time, so more time-saving transport investment might be justified. Such investment by the current generation also benefited future, wealthier generations whose productivity and value of time would consequently increase. In turn, they should invest in more time saving. As the government economist

21 'The prediction and evaluation of road accidents', paper by R.H. Bird, 16 Aug. 1965, par. 11, TNA MT 120/186; 'Accident cost valuation', no date or signed author, pars 9, 12, TNA MT 92/481.

22 'Accident costs', J. Jukes, 19 Aug. 1970, par. 10, TNA MT 92/404.

23 'Differentiation of road casualty costs', paper by L.E. Dale, 3 Dec. 1970, TNA MT 120/186.

24 'Differentiation of road casualty costs', memo, L.E. Dale, 30 Dec. 1970, pars 4, 6 TNA MT 92/404.

25 'The value of time through time', paper, J.L. Carr, 12 Jan. 1970, par. 1, TNA T 316/85.

26 C.D. Foster and M.E. Beesley, 'Estimating the social benefit of constructing an underground railway in London', *Journal of the Royal Statistical Society* 126 (1963), pp. 46–58.

J.L. Carr commented in 1970, it 'seems superficially nonsensical to argue that, the richer we expect our children to be, the more we should deprive ourselves (and the children) of present benefits in order to build more roads so that they can drive everywhere faster in the 1980s than in the 70s, and so on ad infinitum'.[27] One route from the vicious towards a more virtuous circle involved the recognition that as productivity, per capita income, and the value of time rose in the future, then so too would the value set on scarce assets, notably good property in desirable locations and, arguably, amenity (unspoilt countryside). Such developments would increase the opportunity–cost value of new roads and externalities.

Assumptions about continuing economic growth underpinned approaches to discounting. In the absence of growth, or even negative growth, the assumptions and the discounting would change. Many such arguments emerged in the heated exchanges on the economic response to global warming. In the UK in July 2005 the UK government appointed a team led by the economist Nicholas Stern to examine the economics of climate change. In the absence of any action, the Stern Report estimated the overall costs and risks of climate change as equivalent to losing 5 per cent of global GDP each year 'now and forever'. If the range of risks and impacts was widened, then the potential estimated damage could rise to 20 per cent of GDP or more. In contrast Stern estimated that the cost of taking action to reduce greenhouse gas emissions and avoiding the worst impact of climate change could be limited to 1 per cent of global GDP each year.[28] Central to the estimation of both the loss of income likely to be caused by climate change and to the cost and timing of action to reduce greenhouse gas emissions was the social discount rate used in the Stern Report. At 1.4 per cent this social discount rate was controversially very low, and given that it reflected only the possibility of extinction (being hit by an asteroid or whatever), then effectively the report's social discount rate could be regarded as being zero. Many critics of Stern who favoured a 'ramped' approach to the problem of climate change assumed that economic growth would continue, and that income would be higher in the future.[29]

One aspect of the use of social discount rates in environmental policy is a little curious. It concerns nuclear waste. If a nuclear waste dump was to leak in 100 years' time at a cost of £1,000 million at a discount rate of 8 per cent the present value of the damage caused by the leaked material 100 years from now would be £450,000. Or as Parfit characterises the effect of discounting the future:

27   'Value of time in transport investment appraisals', note, J.L. Carr, 5 Jan. 1970, TNA T 316/85.
28   Nicholas Stern, *The economics of climate change: the Stern Report* (London, 2006), pp. ix, xv.
29   William Nordhaus, 'The Stern Review on the economics of climate change', paper, 17 Nov. 2006, p. 3.

We shall not be troubled by the fact that some nuclear waste will be radio-active for thousands of years. At a discount rate of five per cent, one death next year counts for more than a billion deaths in 500 years. On this view, catastrophes in the further future can now be regarded as morally trivial.[30]

This raises serious doubts as to the ethical validity of using discounting in this manner. While the discounting of benefits may be a valid activity for the present generation, it essentially reflects a choice made as to when benefits (and how many) are received and what the present generation is prepared to forego in consumption in the interim. It is less clear that the cost of a nuclear waste dump leaking in the future is equivalent to that cost/benefit trade-off grounded in consumption. While it is valid to discount the financial cost of constructing a nuclear power station against the discounted benefits in terms of the value of future electricity output, it is not at all clear why one should discount the damage of a nuclear waste leak. One is a financial cost, the other is a risk, and a risk probably based on an assumption of finding a technological solution to the nuclear waste problem. It is also a cost relating to loss of life and danger to health. If it is expressed in terms of human life, then certainly if productivity has increased over the intervening years, it is more likely that each lost life has an economic value higher than the value of life today.

In its adoption of the theory of discounting, government pragmatically emphasised the opportunity costs of different fixed capital investment projects, within a political context of public finance constraints. Discounting provided a rationale and means for reining in public expenditure, working most effectively on its capital investment projects. In weighting the present value of the future benefits of investment in human capital, a tempting dichotomy was drawn between its private and public benefits. Certainly, if higher education was to be expanded, then unless there were equivalent benefits to economic growth, it was likely that arguments for the private financing of private benefits would be advanced. That this argument was born of pragmatism suggested that theoretically the question of who financed higher education was largely a matter of political choice.

In the use of QALYs the choice was economic and also ethical. The future benefits were related to the economic value of the individual, as were altered temporal approaches to evaluating and discounting the benefits of road improvements designed in part to save lives. In similar vein time savings arising from road improvements or construction also rested on a discounted valuation of the benefits accruing for particular groups of individuals. Economic growth which raised the economic value of humans in the future sat uneasily with some of the rationale for the use of discounting in the present. If humans were of greater value in the future, then it was less obvious why a discount rate would be used

30   Derek Parfit, *Reasons and persons* (Oxford, 1984), p. 357.

which left a degraded environmental legacy to them. It was not simply an issue of how future negative growth would affect current discounting, but also that in terms of the natural capital stock that is the environment, it was unclear why a discount rate which postponed projects designed to mitigate the effects of climate change and thereby caused a deterioration in that natural environmental stock would be chosen. The application of an opportunity–cost approach to choosing discount rates in the present emphasised the comparative flows of income in the future. The pragmatic adoption of discounted approaches to comparing alternative uses of resources in the present, especially in the context of public finance constraints, was apparent. Arguably where an approach to comparing the flow of income from capital projects and expenditure became ambivalent was in its approaches to evaluating the value of current flows of activity on the quality of a future stock.

15

The material politics of energy disruption: managing shortages amidst rising expectations, Britain 1930s–60s

HIROKI SHIN AND FRANK TRENTMANN

On 25 December 1962, thousands of people, from Lancaster to mid-Wales, celebrated Christmas by candlelight. The electricity supply had collapsed. In the St Margaret's Road area of Prestwich, the power went out at lunchtime and was reinstated only at 4:30 a.m. Elsewhere the power outages ranged from three to 23 hours.[1] In the early 1960s, Christmas Day often saw a great surge in demand for electricity. Even though industrial use was less, residential demand for cooking Christmas dinner and heating put tremendous pressure on the National Grid. A major cause of supply failure, according to Philip Chantler, under-secretary of the Electricity Division of the Ministry of Power at the time, was the steady increase in the number of appliances in households, which was pushing up electricity demand by around 10 per cent annually.[2] For most of the year, appliances were rarely switched on simultaneously. It was this diversity of use, Chantler noted, that enabled the grid to supply all customers. Once a cold spell coincided with a national holiday, however, a 'collapse of diversity' followed, inevitably leading to a disruption of supply.

As Martin Daunton has shown for the gas industry in Victorian Britain, public utilities operated within material politics that involved the state, business, and consumers.[3] Energy disruptions provide an interesting extension of this work because they make visible the core values and interests under-pinning the material politics of a particular era that are often hidden or taken

---

1   'Thousands celebrated by candlelight', *Guardian*, 27 Dec. 1962.
2   P. Chantler, 'Interruptions in electricity supplies, Christmas, 1961', 1 Jan. 1962, TNA POWE 14/374; 'Heavy electric power demand', *Financial Times*, 28 Dec. 1961.
3   M.J. Daunton, 'The material politics of natural monopoly: gas in Victorian Britain', in M.J. Daunton, *State and market in Victorian Britain: war, welfare and capitalism* (Woodbridge, 2008), pp. 111–27.

for granted. If there is not enough energy to satisfy everyone, who should be supplied first and whose needs should be curtailed? What are the basic needs to be protected, and which can be sacrificed? In short, disruptions illuminate the very fabric of 'normality'.[4] Energy disruptions are politically and morally charged moments during which different groups of users mobilise a language of equity, fairness, and justice. This chapter follows disruptions and the career of this moral language from the interwar years through the Second World War and into the 'affluent' 1960s.

The development of the modern energy system in industrialised nations is often described as a constant expansion of supply with a corresponding growth in demand. With regard to residential energy in particular, the spectacular rise of electricity consumption over the last century is largely attributed to the success of utility providers and appliance manufacturers in cultivating demand. 'The turbines were, in effect, supply in search of demand,' as Thomas Hughes famously put it in his history of networks of power.[5] In reality, modern energy systems rarely developed the way supply engineers had imagined. Especially from the mid-twentieth century, demand started to catch up with and sometimes even surpass supply. The early vision of the development of power networks was based on the idea that the main demand would come from industry and be merely supplemented by off-peak demand from households. Yet electrification and the rise of domestic demand, especially since the Second World War, created the risk of Chantler's collapse of diversity, not only on national holidays, but on regular working days, too.

The coordination of supply and demand has been a crucial issue in modern energy systems, applying equally to coal, gas, and electricity. Failure of coordination leads to energy disruption. It would be wrong to think of disruption in terms of total stoppage or disintegration. Rather, disruptive events often lead to 'punctuated cooperation' in society, in the words of the sociologist Hendrik Vollmer, triggering mechanisms that restore order.[6] In this chapter, we expand on this insight to consider the political mechanisms and repair work that operate during energy disruptions. Between the technical cause of a supply failure and society's response lies the world of politics, which mediates how a disruption is diagnosed and tackled. The politics of disruption works both

4   See Frank Trentmann, 'Disruption is normal', in Elizabeth Shove, Frank Trentmann and Richard Wilk, eds, *Time, consumption, and everyday life* (Oxford, 2009), pp. 67–84; Heather Chappells and Frank Trentmann, 'Disruption in and across time', in Elizabeth Shove and Frank Trentmann, eds, *Infrastructures in practice* (London, 2018).

5   Thomas Hughes, *Networks of power: electrification in western society, 1880–1930* (Baltimore, 1983), p. 364. See also Astrik Kander, 'Energy transitions in the twentieth century', in Astrid Kander, Paolo Malanima and Paul Warde, eds, *Power to the people: energy in Europe over the last five centuries* (Princeton and Oxford, 2013), pp. 249–86.

6   Hendrik Vollmer, *The sociology of disruption, disaster and social change: punctuated cooperation* (Cambridge, 2013). See also Chappells and Trentmann, 'Disruption'.

in the short term (in response to an immediate emergency) and in the longer term (initiating plans and policies to anticipate or prevent future disruptions). It leaves its mark on business decisions, consumer expectations, and networks and supply. Energy disruption, we argue, should therefore be understood not as an aberration from the norm but as an element that has helped shape what we think of as a 'normal' energy system.

Emergency planning in interwar Britain

Britain's policy for responding to energy disruption was established on the basis of the Emergency Powers Act of 1920. Although the act was created in response to coal shortages during the First World War, its main remit concerned civil emergencies and strikes in key industries. During the 1926 general strike a limited effort was made to conserve fuel by an official order restricting the industrial and domestic consumption of coal and other fuels. A Central Coal Emergency Committee and the Mines Department of the Board of Trade were given power to control fuel resources, and house coal delivery was limited to 1cwt per week.[7]

The impact on British households of the general strike and the miners' strike of the same year was limited, since they took place outside the peak winter demand for house coal.[8] Several electricity power stations, however, did join the general strike. London's electricity workers were particularly militant, especially in Labour-controlled areas such as Battersea and Bermondsey.[9] More than 1,000 naval sailors, petty officers, and civil volunteers were sent to thirty-three London power stations to maintain operations.[10] The situation of provincial power stations is less clear, although there were some contemporary reports of electricity power cuts.[11] The fisheries and the ship-building industry in Scotland were hit by lack of electricity and steel plates.[12] Generally speaking, however, the official restriction of electricity consumption – which prohibited the use of electricity 'beyond the minimum reasonably requisite' – was primarily an effort to save coal. The public did not feel any urgency to save electricity, and the official restriction order was frequently ignored. In

---

7   'Mines department coal emergency organisation prepared in 1930', TNA POWE 26/209; 'Mines department emergency organisation', 2 Sep. 1935, TNA POWE 26/307; *Board of Trade Journal*, 3 Jun. 1926, pp. 593–4.

8   *Western Daily Press*, 4 Jun. 1926.

9   *Electrical Times*, 3 Jun. 1926, p. 649.

10   Frank Ledger and Howard Sallis, *Crisis management in the power industry: an inside story* (London, 1995), p. 17.

11   Ibid., p. 17.

12   *Aberdeen Journal*, 16 Jun. 1926.

Westminster, most shops were lit by electric lamps at night. Not surprisingly, the electricity industry was opposed to strict restrictions. The *Electrical Times* argued that, while more visible, electric lighting consumed less coal than gas cookers.[13]

When renewed concern arose about strike action in 1931, during the world depression, the official emergency organisation was overhauled. In its review of the 1926 arrangements, the Mines Department concluded that 'it was not a success'.[14] The department wanted to have greater control over the distribution of coal during an emergency. Regional coal distribution was to be supervised by divisional fuel emergency officers, appointed by local authorities. The lesson from the 1926 general strike was clear: if a similar coal stoppage were to take place in winter, it would have a devastating impact on national life. The stock of house coal would last for three weeks only.[15]

In the middle of the state's rethink, the household energy situation itself was slowly changing. By 1937 there were 11 million gas and 9 million electricity consumers, but their diffusion remained highly uneven. In that year a market survey by the British Gas and Coke Company found that more than 90 per cent of working-class homes in London were heated by coal grates. Only one in six working-class households had a gas fire installed, and only one in twenty-eight had an electric fire. And for those with gas and electricity, the use remained limited. Gas was primarily used for cooking. 60 per cent of the surveyed households with electricity used it almost exclusively for lighting and barely at all for heating (3.5 per cent), cooking (4.3 per cent), and hot water (2.4 per cent).[16]

In 1926 the Electricity Supply Act laid the foundation for the National Grid, which started operation in 1933 through a series of connected regional grids. Still, Britain's electricity supply system remained volatile, with frequent accidents and technical failures. A fire at the generating and distributing station at Kingston-on-Thames on 14 December 1938, for example, caused a blackout within a seven- to eight-mile radius. Hundreds of electrified homes were unable to cook. Some schools were closed due to the lack of heating, and theatres and cinemas shut their doors.[17] Most electricity supply failures were localised, but the network was also vulnerable at the national scale. While the progress of electrification improved the load factor (the average load divided by the peak load) – it rose from 28 per cent in 1922 to 35.5 per cent in 1938 – it also saw

---

13   *Electrical Times*, 23 Sep. 1926.
14   'Mines department emergency organisation', 2 Sep. 1935, TNA POWE 26/307.
15   'Minutes of Heating and Ventilation Group', 6 Mar. 1942, TNA DSIR 4/295; Department of Scientific and Industrial Research, 'Pre-war trends in domestic fuel usage', 30 Mar. 1942, TNA DSIR 4/1926; Neil Buxton, *The economic development of the British coal industry: from industrial revolution to the present day* (London, 1978), p. 174.
16   London Press Exchange Limited, 'Social and fuel survey in working class families', 1937, TNA POWE 28/43, pp. 27, 34, 44.
17   *The Times*, 15 and 16 Dec. 1938.

increased demand at peak hours. In December 1938, the National Grid narrowly escaped collapse when a sharp cold snap in late December drove electricity demand close to maximum generating capacity. The crisis was avoided, but only just, by transferring power from the north to the central and southern parts of the country.[18]

Wartime debates on fuel control

With the outbreak of the Second World War, the threat of energy disruption became constant. During the war coal output declined from 235 million tons in 1939 to 186 million tons in 1945, chiefly because of the loss of manpower in the coal industry. Available coal was diverted to the armed forces and munitions factories, leaving less fuel for industry and households. Shortages were particularly severe in the latter stages of the war, and pushed the government to look at rationing of household fuel. This galvanised a public debate about the moral economy of coal and its 'fair' use in the home, as well as about the proper relationship between households, energy users, and the state.

The wartime administration of fuel was initially based on plans drawn up by the Mines Department in the early 1930s. A household fuel rationing scheme was introduced on 7 September 1939, followed by petroleum rationing two weeks later.[19] Under the Fuel and Lighting Order, an allowance for house coal was set, starting at two tons per year for a single household. The same order stipulated that electricity and gas users should not consume more than 75 per cent of what they had used the previous year.[20] The restriction turned out to be short-lived, however. The electricity and gas industries claimed that they had already suffered significant losses through the evacuation of their customers and cutbacks in street lighting. To recover, they would have to raise the unit price of gas and electricity, which would cripple war-related production.[21] By November 1939 the restrictions on residential electricity and gas were lifted.

In 1941 the coal situation started to deteriorate. Coal output dropped by 18 million tons.[22] In June 1941 Alfred Hurst, the Secretary for Mines, suggested that the Mines Department consider rationing domestic fuel, including coal, electricity, gas, and other fuels.[23] He proposed a coupon or points rationing

---

18   Leslie Hannah, *Electricity before nationalisation* (London, 1979), p. 141.
19   Electricity Commissioners, *War period report of the Electricity Commissioners* (London, 1946), p. 55.
20   'Rationing of fuel', *The Times*, 21 Sep. 1939.
21   'Report by the Joint Gas and Electricity Committee', Jan. 1940, TNA POWE 14/19.
22   Buxton, *Economic development*, p. 174; B.R. Mitchell, *British historical statistics* (Cambridge, 1988), p. 249.
23   'Rationing', 12 Jun. 1941, TNA POWE 16/103.

system, such as had already been introduced for some foods and clothing.[24] This scheme applied rationing to a group of interchangeable commodities, allowing consumers to obtain articles according to their needs and preferences.[25] It was believed to be fair because it prevented wealthy consumers from increasing their total consumption by purchasing a greater quantity of uncontrolled items.[26]

The decision about household fuel rationing in early 1942 landed with the newly appointed president of the Board of Trade, Hugh Dalton. He expected a deficit of at least 3.2 million tons of coal, the equivalent of 1.5 per cent of total annual demand.[27] Although Dalton was convinced that a saving of 8 million tons could be achieved with the help of a comprehensive rationing scheme, he was also conscious that rationing would be politically sensitive. Dalton decided to seek the assistance of William Beveridge. In his plan for comprehensive household fuel rationing, Beveridge broadly followed the earlier sketch drawn up by the Mines Department. He based the 'need' of families on the size of their premises, and the number of rooms and residents.[28] For example, a family of five living in a house with five rooms would receive 57cwt equivalent of coal plus a personal ration of 7.5cwt per year per head.[29] This amounted to about 1.8cwt per week, which was considerably less than the 2.35cwt per week the average working-class family consumed at the time.[30]

The initial public response to domestic fuel rationing was encouraging. A Mass Observation survey conducted in late March 1942 found 70 per cent of respondents to be in favour of fuel rationing and only 10 per cent against it.[31] The situation quickly changed when Dalton prematurely commented on the rationing scheme in parliament without waiting for the submission of Beveridge's report. His remarks created the impression that fuel rationing would be harsher than expected. Through a leak from Wade Hayes of Edmundsons, a large electrical manufacturer, the British public learned that the supply industries were opposed to the scheme. A joint committee from the gas and electricity industries condemned plans to ration fuel according to the number of rooms as inequitable and impracticable.[32] It ignored the size of the family,

24   'War emergency measures: domestic rationing schemes for fuel, lighting and power', 27 Jul. 1941, TNA POWE 16/103.
25   Stephen Broadberry and Peter Howlett, 'Lessons learned? British mobilisation for the two world wars', Draft paper for conference to Honour Mark Harrison, 2014, p. 25.
26   'War emergency measures', 27 Jul. 1941, TNA POWE 16/103.
27   William Hancock and Margaret Gowing, *The British war economy* (London, 1949), p. 471.
28   'Rationing', 12 Jun. 1941, TNA POWE 16/103.
29   *White paper on coal* (London, 1942), Cmd 6364, pp. 10–11.
30   Wartime social survey, 'Heating of dwellings inquiry', Mar. 1942, TNA POWE 17/34.
31   Mass Observation, 'Report on fuel rationing', 6 May 1942, p. 1. *The Mass Observation Online*, File 1243.
32   Hannah, *Electricity before nationalisation*, p. 303; Keith Clements, ed., *The moot papers: faith, freedom and society* (London, 2010), pp. 554–5.

and different individual needs and patterns of consumption.[33] Public support quickly evaporated. In a second Mass Observation survey in late April, 68 per cent now disapproved of the rationing scheme as unnecessary and impractical.[34] The publication of the fuel rationing report helped to alleviate public fears, but only up to a point. In early May the support for the scheme stood at 25 per cent, but 48 per cent were still opposed, and the remaining 27 per cent had no opinion or were 'doubtful'.[35]

Mass Observation found that better-off respondents in particular tended to be critical of fuel rationing.[36] However, another survey, this one conducted by the government itself, pointed to more general public opposition to state intervention. More than a quarter of those opposing the scheme felt that fuel matters should be 'left to one's own judgement'.[37] The *News Chronicle* warned that the scheme would be run by 'Little Hitlers'.[38] There was a pronounced gender divide. While 44 per cent of male respondents disapproved of the scheme, only 28.5 per cent of female respondents did so, an interesting gap since women's opposition to austerity measures after the war has been credited with the shift from Labour to Conservative politics.[39] By early May 1942 the issue had become highly politicised. In parliament, Conservative MPs mounted an assault on the Beveridge scheme, which they claimed was a socialist subterfuge to nationalise the coalmines and to put the entire fuel distribution under state control.[40]

According to the historian and Conservative politician Philip Goodhart, the government's main concern was that the scheme might undermine its parliamentary support.[41] However, the debate over fuel rationing reached well beyond party politics. Opposition from the 1922 Committee, a group of Conservative backbenchers, was another part of the supply industry's sustained battle against government intervention. The political debate was also driven by concerns over equity. Beveridge himself raised the issue of the inequitable nature of fuel rationing.[42] He later likened the proposal to 'an attempt to ration

33 'Why the scheme is inequitable', 9 Sep. 1941, TNA POWE 33/1324.
34 Mass Observation, 'Report on fuel rationing', p. 2.
35 Ibid., p. 3.
36 Ibid., p. 5.
37 Wartime social survey, 'Fuel rationing', May 1942, TNA POWE 17/34, p. 3.
38 *News Chronicle*, 11 Oct. 1939.
39 Wartime social survey, 'Fuel rationing', p. 3. For the post-war years, see Ina Zweiniger-Bargielowska, *Austerity in Britain: rationing, controls, and consumption, 1939–1955* (Oxford, 2000).
40 Angus Calder, *The people's war: Britain 1939–1945* (London, 1969), p. 284.
41 Philip Goodhart, *The 1922: the story of the Conservative backbenchers' parliamentary committee* (London, 1973), pp. 114–19.
42 William Beveridge, *Fuel rationing* (London, 1942), Cmd. 6352; William Beveridge, *The pillars of security and other war-time essays and addresses* (London, 1945), p. 195.

the whole of the food (including bread) of a people whose individuals vary in height from 1 foot to 20 feet'.[43]

In the light of these difficulties, Dalton was forced to retreat. By the end of 1942 the government's strategy in the 'battle for fuel' had shifted to moral suasion, with official campaigns urging people to reduce their fuel consumption to meet 'fuel targets'.[44] Such appeals had limited success. Instead of reducing their overall consumption, many people simply switched from controlled house coal to uncontrolled fuel, especially electricity. Increased electricity consumption, in turn, strained the supply situation further. Between 1939 and 1945 domestic electricity consumption grew by a stunning 48 per cent, in spite of a wartime ban on electricity suppliers signing up new customers. On 11 January 1944 national supply failed to meet demand for the first time since the establishment of the National Grid.[45] A year later, the Ministry of Fuel and Power and its regional controllers were forced to issue a warning that without reductions in consumption, it might not be possible to meet demand.[46] The warning went unheeded, and on three days in late January 1945 southern England experienced supply cuts that lasted for up to two hours each. The public rejection of comprehensive fuel rationing effectively amounted to an acceptance of interruptions in electricity supply. As a Sussex housewife wrote to *The Times*: 'no coal or coke, and consequently no fires or hot water. It is then that one has recourse to the electric immerser and electric fire.'[47]

Fuel shortage and continuing austerity in post-WWII Britain

The implicit choice of one form of disruption over another had unintended consequences, as did the wartime shift from one fuel to another. The increased demand for electricity made disruptions a constant headache in the immediate post-war years, just as domestic consumers were becoming increasingly locked in to the grid. At the same time, disgruntled consumers were also becoming more vocal. Once peace returned, Britons expected their quality of life to improve. Instead, the late 1940s were marked by continued austerity, shortages, and black outs.

The Second World War set the course for Britain's domestic energy consumption in peacetime. Restrictions on the sale of house coal continued. The consumption of house coal fell from 44 million tons in 1941 to 31 million tons in 1946. At the same time, the coal consumed in the process of generating

43   'Memorandum on fuel restrictions', n.d., TNA POWE 17/58.
44   Wartime social survey, 'The battle for fuel', 1943, TNA POWE 17/34.
45   *Electrical Times*, 14 Nov. 1946, p. 653.
46   *Hull Daily Mail*, 25 Jan. 1945.
47   *The Times*, 29 Jan. 1945.

domestic gas and electricity increased by 4.5 million tons. The total primary energy consumption of coal, therefore, fell by only 8.5 million tons during the course of the war.[48] Coal output recovered slowly from the wartime loss of manpower and low productivity. In 1946, it stood at 190.1 million tons, 34.2 million tons below the figure in 1940.[49] In October 1946, the government began to appeal to industrial consumers to economise their use of coal. In addition, the government's coal distribution plan tried to distribute coal to users according to their importance for the national economy.[50] While demand for coal from the iron and steel industries, coke ovens, railways, and collieries was to be fully met, supply to other industries was cut by between 5 per cent and 12.5 per cent. By February 1946, the situation had turned into a crisis. On top of coal restrictions, electricity consumption was now restricted as well. The new cut applied to all consumers, including domestic ones.[51] Only 'essential industries' were exempted. Industrial output fell by about 25 per cent for lack for coal and electricity.[52]

For the government, cutting domestic electricity posed the greatest challenge. The wartime experience of the abortive rationing scheme had taught ministers and civil servants to be cautious about tampering with domestic fuel. As house coal consumption had already been reduced to a 'bare minimum', in the words of G.L. Watkinson, deputy-secretary at the Ministry of Fuel and Power, the government was reluctant to make further cuts.[53] In fact, households received more coal in February 1947 than in the previous year; in London, deliveries were up by 12 per cent.[54] Any saving in household consumption therefore had to come from electricity and gas. As Watkinson noted, consumers were 'rush[ing] to install electrical gadgets' to circumvent the restrictions on house coal.[55] In mid-February, the Cabinet Fuel Committee considered rationing as a way to reduce non-industrial consumption, but the wartime political muddle over the Beveridge plan had unnerved the government.[56] Other options, such as a raising prices or a fuel tax, were dismissed as affecting low-income families disproportionately.

---

48   G.L. Watkinson, 'Domestic fuel rationing draft proposals', 13 Feb. 1947, TNA T 273/305.

49   Mitchell, British historical statistics, p. 250.

50   For Britain's broad resource allocation policy, see Martin Chick, Industrial policy in Britain, 1945–1951: economic planning, nationalisation and the Labour governments (Cambridge, 1998), pp. 41–7.

51   Alec Cairncross, Years of recovery: British economic policy 1945–51 (Michigan, 1985), p. 368.

52   Ibid., p. 374.

53   Watkinson, 'Domestic fuel rationing draft proposals'; Labour Party, Fuel crisis: the facts (London, 1947), p. 7.

54   'Fuel crisis: stocks rise but weather worsens', TNA POWE 10/426.

55   Watkinson, 'Domestic fuel rationing draft proposals'; Labour Party, Fuel crisis, p. 8.

56   Cabinet Fuel Committee, 'Plans for avoiding a fuel crisis in the winter of 1947–1948: memorandum by the Prime Minister', TNA PREM 8/443.

Instead, the government decided to restrict electricity consumption during designated hours. From 10 February 1947, the use of electricity in domestic and commercial premises was prohibited between 9 a.m. and 12 noon and between 2 p.m. and 4 p.m., with statutory sanctions for offenders.[57] Enforcing these restrictions, however, was easier said than done. As electricity cuts had to be operated by supply mains units, households that happened to be on the same supply mains as a hospital or other 'essential' industries could not be cut off. Respect for the restrictions was patchy. A Mass Observation investigator noted how a medical student in South London virtuously studied for her final exam in a 'dim room' even though her electricity supply was not cut because of proximity to a children's hospital. At the same time, a nearby neighbour 'kept her refrigerator on all the time'.[58]

Attacks were immediate, and expressed through a language of equity and justice. One Labour MP, Mrs Middleton (Plymouth, Sutton), argued that prohibiting the use of electricity during particular hours ignored the real-life needs of working housewives like herself. After leaving the House of Commons, she was obliged to stay up 'until one o'clock, two o'clock or even three o'clock in the morning, in order to do the cooking, ironing and other things which needed to be done'.[59] The restriction order, she said, was designed to turn 'housewives of this country into a class of law breakers and law evaders'. Male workers, in turn, resisted government efforts to move one third of industrial electricity demand outside regular working hours through the introduction of night shifts.[60] They were particularly averse to 'fluctuating meal arrangements', the chief inspector of factories noted.[61] In factories where hours were staggered, managers tended to limit the number of workers on night shifts.[62]

The coal situation began to improve at the end of March, not because the British public had made any significant fuel savings, but because coal output was rising.[63] Indeed, officials reported that the 'novelty' of restriction was wearing off and a growing number of domestic consumers were ignoring them altogether.[64]

These months in early 1947 witnessed the first national-scale energy

---

57 'Restrictions on the use of electricity, gas and central heating', Feb. 1947, TNA POWE 14/488.
58 'Fuel situation 1947, panel responses', N1020, Mass Observation archive (University of Sussex), SxMOA 1/2/8/5/C.
59 *Hansard*, vol. 436, 1 May 1947, cols 2202–3.
60 *Hull Daily Mail*, 26 Feb. 1947. See also Ministry of Labour, *Report of the Electricity Sub-Committee of the Joint Consultative Committee 1947* (London, 1947), esp. p. 6.
61 *Annual report of the chief inspector of factories for the year 1947* (London, 1949), Cmd. 7621, p. 101.
62 *Annual report of the chief inspector of factories for the year 1948* (London, 1949), Cmd. 7839, p. 123.
63 Cairncross, *Years of recovery*, p. 373.
64 'Meeting of Inter-Departmental Policy Committee', 21 Feb. 1947, TNA POWE 10/246; Cabinet Fuel Committee, 'Economies in domestic consumption of gas and electricity: memorandum by the Minister of Fuel and Power', 15 Jul. 1947, TNA PREM 8/443.

disruption in peacetime. It forced the government and supply industry to face up to what turned out to be the persistent problem of peak load, created by the shift in domestic consumption from coal to electricity. On 30 January 1947, the demand on the National Grid reached 10,920 MW, a 20 per cent rise above the previous year's high.[65] The capacity available, however, was a mere 9,092 MW. The highest peak usually occurred in the morning between 8 a.m. and 10 a.m. A smaller hike happened in the evening, around 6 p.m. The principal reason for the narrowing of the supply margin was the wartime backlog in the construction of new generating plants. This left only one remedy: load shedding. The load could be 'shed' either by reducing the system's voltage or by shutting down supply in some areas. And load shedding had to be conducted before demand reached maximum supply capacity, otherwise the generators broke down. In 1946, forty-six such controlled disruptions occurred in England and Wales.

It is striking that, despite some discussion in Cabinet, official policy shied away from interfering with domestic consumption. A partial exception was the government's attempt to reduce peak-time domestic consumption by raising purchase tax. Originally introduced in 1940 to divert resources to the war effort, purchase tax was reduced in October 1945 as part of a wider post-war relaxation of controls. As a result, the production of electric irons, electric fires, electric kettles, and vacuum cleaners saw a significant boost in 1946.[66] In his budget speech on 15 April 1947, Dalton reintroduced a purchase tax of 66⅔ per cent on a wide range of appliances; only lighting appliances, wireless sets, and electric clocks were exempted. The decision caused an outcry from Conservative and Labour MPs. Labour's Barbara Castle (Blackburn) urged the government to reconsider the imposition of a tax on 'such an essential household commodity as the electric iron'.[67] Other MPs pointed out that the purchase tax on cookers and heaters pushed up rents and the cost of new homes. But these attacks were able to change Dalton's mind only so much. He withdrew the purchase tax on some appliances such as kettles, irons, wash boilers, and refrigerators, but retained the 66⅔ per cent purchase tax on immersion heaters, storage water heaters, and space heaters, alongside a 33⅓ per cent tax on washing machines, lighting fittings, and vacuum cleaners.[68]

By now, domestic electricity had become the subject of popular politics. Electric appliances promised to save time and energy for 'the harassed housewife today'.[69] On 6 June 1947, 3,000 angry housewives from the British Housewives' League met at the Royal Albert Hall to denounce Emmanuel Shinwell as the minister of 'no power' and John Strachey as the minister of

65 *Electrical Times*, 13 Feb. 1947, pp. 194–5.
66 'Consumers' supplies and purchase tax', *The Economist*, 6 Jul. 1946.
67 *Hansard*, vol. 438 (1947), col. 1844.
68 *The Economist*, 21 Jun. 1947.
69 *Hansard*, vol. 438 (1947), col. 1852.

'no food'.[70] Frustration was spreading. The electricity restrictions interfered with theatres, cinemas, and some sporting events; exceptionally, cricket matches continued as normal. Television and radio broadcasts were curtailed, and the publication of periodicals was suspended altogether for a few weeks in spring 1947. Conservative politicians accused the Labour government of treating the consumer as of no importance.[71] The Prime Minister, Clement Attlee, was forced to announce that his government had no intention of imposing compulsory cuts on domestic electricity and gas.[72]

For all their complaints, though, domestic consumers were hardly innocent victims of austerity. Their growing use of electricity at home was partly responsible for the peak problem. That electricity consumption continued to increase after 1947, when coal production improved, suggests that people chose electricity not because house coal was scarce, but increasingly for its convenience.[73] Even though the fuel crisis of 1946/47 did not recur, electricity supply remained precarious the following year. In the East and West Ridings, industrial consumers complained that they bore the brunt of the peak reduction while domestic and commercial consumers were off the hook.[74] In response, the government mounted a 'fuel target' campaign, and raised the purchase tax on refrigerators and vacuum cleaners from 33⅓ per cent to 50 per cent, and that for space and water heaters from 66⅔ per cent to 75 per cent.

In July 1948 the Clow Committee, appointed by the government to study the electricity peak, reviewed the options for controlling domestic electricity demand through technical instruments and changes to the tariff structure.[75] For example, it recommended 'ripple control', which allowed grid controllers to switch off individual consumers' supply mains remotely.[76] Another proposal was to use differential pricing according to the season and time of day.[77] Neither of these recommendations elicited support from utilities or their customers. Not only did the winter tariff trial scheme infuriate unwitting consumers who were taken by surprise on receiving a substantial bill, but the experiment barely managed to reduce peak consumption.[78]

---

70 *The Times*, 7 Jun. 1947; *LIFE*, 23 Jun. 1947, p. 35.
71 For example, *Hansard*, vol. 426 (1946), col. 133. See also Zweiniger-Bargielowska, *Austerity in Britain*, p. 207.
72 'The winter coal budget', 30 Sep. 1947, TNA PREM 8/443.
73 Buxton, *Economic development*, p. 233.
74 TNA T 229/48.
75 Ministry of Fuel and Power, *Report of the committee to study the electricity peak load problem in relation to non-industrial consumers* (London, 1948), Cmd 7464 (Clow Report).
76 Clow Report, p. 10.
77 Ibid., pp. 17–18.
78 Leslie Hannah, *Engineers, managers and politicians: the first fifteen years of nationalised electricity supply in Britain* (London, 1982), pp. 36–7; Martin Chick, *Electricity and energy policy in Britain, France and the United States since 1945* (Cheltenham, 2007), p. 74.

In the late 1940s and early 1950s, shortages were mainly a problem of the peak load. There were 62 occasions of load shedding in 1947, 88 in 1948, 77 in 1949, and 204 in 1950. Energy officials were concerned that their fuel policy was being eroded by industry's resentment of having to carry a disproportionately heavy burden. In the world of politics, however, proposals for a new committee that would be responsible for commercial and domestic as well as industrial electricity went nowhere.[79]

The situation was exacerbated by the fast-changing pattern of energy use in households during these years. Coal remained the principal household fuel, but was now increasingly supplemented by electric heating. A survey of heating practices in 1948–49 found that, even though living rooms were still predominately heated by coal, electric heating was now commonly used in bedrooms. Electric fires were also used for short periods to top up the heat of the coal fire.[80] Between 1945 and 1949, the proportion of households spending more than £15 per annum on electricity doubled.[81]

Domestic consumers started to be openly criticised, especially by industry. The purchase tax for space and water heaters was raised to 100 per cent in April 1948. In November 1950, the Minister of Fuel and Power, Philip Noel-Baker, acknowledged that the electric fire was 'the most serious contributor to the winter load problem'.[82] By this time, over 15 million electric fires were in use. The electricity utility's publicity organisation, the Electrical Development Association (EDA), tried to appease the growing number of critics through a campaign asking people to switch off their electric fires during peak hours and promoting night-storage heaters.[83]

The coal situation in 1950 was nearly as bad as in 1946, and the expectation of a cold winter led many to predict a severe fuel crisis. In order to build up sufficient coal stock for winter, the government drastically curtailed coal exports as early as August 1950.[84] Load spreading arrangements, including rota schemes for industrial users, were put in place across the country, but failed to prevent a large number of load shedding incidents. In November 1950 the Midland Regional Board for Industry reported that there was 'a widespread loss of confidence by industry in the ability of the Electricity Authorities to settle their problems'.[85] The Northern Regional Board received numerous complaints

79 Robens to Noel-Baker, 8 Jun. 1951, TNA POWE 14/361.
80 Leslie Wilkins, *Domestic utilization of heating appliances and expenditures on fuels 1948/49* (London, 1951), p. 2.
81 Ibid., p. 2.
82 'Memorandum of interview', 30 Nov. 1950, TNA POWE 14/355.
83 Anna Carlsson-Hyslop, 'Past Management of energy demand: promotion and adoption of electric heating in Britain 1945–1964', *Environment and History* 22 (2016), pp. 75–102.
84 Cairncross, *Years of recovery*, p. 368.
85 Midland Regional Board for Industry, 'Electricity load shedding', 2 Nov. 1950, TNA BT 171/220.

from firms and other bodies about 'excessive' load shedding.[86] In January 1951, firms were asked to reduce 20–25 per cent of their peak electricity consumption, but load shedding persisted.[87] M.P. Murray of the Ministry of Fuel and Power warned of 'signs of revolt' from industrial and commercial users.[88] In May the National Union of Manufacturers threatened legal action against the supply authority, following a report from the union's Nottingham representative that small textile and engineering firms were suffering from constant power cuts and were falling behind on overseas orders.[89]

In 1951 the official policy of electricity restrictions lay in ruins. Industrialists blamed the supply authority for failing to build sufficient generation capacity and criticised the government for its lenient treatment of domestic consumers. The Southern Regional Board attacked the Electricity Board for encouraging the public to purchase immersion heaters and electric fires.[90] The United Nations' *Economic survey of Europe in 1951* was scathing about Britain's uncoordinated policy. The report stressed that it resulted in inequity between households using solid fuel (which was still controlled) and those with increased electricity consumption (which was uncontrolled).[91] But at a time when Labour was struggling to hold on to power, raising the electricity tariff would have been suicidal.[92] The root of the problem, then, was a clash between the imperatives of fuel policy and electoral politics. Voters were, after all, domestic consumers, but their rising demand for electricity exacerbated the peak problem, and caused disruption for industries and export earnings at a time of a dollar shortage. This in turn meant fewer resources for upgrading the energy infrastructure, which meant more volatility and load shedding. It was a vicious circle, and the Labour government lacked a strategy for breaking out of it.

Energy disruption in the affluent society

On 22 June 1951, Caroline Haslett, the president of the Electrical Association for Women (EAW), gave a speech at the British Electrical Power Convention in Brighton. Haslett lauded electricity as a driving force for social progress, offering both 'economic and social advantages in saving man-hours and woman-hours in factory and home'. A housewife in an electrified home, she said, was able

---

86 'Minutes of the Northern Regional Board', 25 Jun. 1951, TNA BT 171/220.
87 *Electrical Times*, 4 January 1951, p. 30.
88 Murray to Carpenter, 11 Jan. 1950, TNA POWE 14/366.
89 *Electrical Times*, 24 May 1951.
90 Southern Regional Board for Industry to J. Macdonald, 3 Nov. 1950, TNA BT 171/220.
91 United Nations Department of Economic Affairs, *Economic survey of Europe in 1951* (Geneva, 1952), p. 170.
92 Turnbull to Plowden, 1 Jun. 1950, TNA T 229/225.

to save about twenty-four working hours a week.[93] Her speech came at a time when Britain was still reeling from electricity shortages earlier in the year. It expressed the growing animosity toward continuing austerity amidst the rising consumer expectations that were to characterise the 1950s.

The Conservatives' victory in the October 1951 general election reflected public discontent with austerity.[94] The new government was soon faced with another difficult winter, with 236 occasions of load shedding – only marginally fewer than the year before.[95] Once the worst of the winter crisis had subsided, there was a strong backlash against electricity restrictions. The Ridley Committee on National Fuel Policy, which had been appointed under the Labour government in July 1951 but reported in September 1952, signalled the near-end of post-war austerity.[96] The report not only recommended capacity-building, but concluded that 'the aim of all production is to provide what people want'.[97] The authorities should not interfere with freedom of choice, regardless of the cost of fuel: 'any attempt to determine ... the pattern of the consumers' fuel use would meet formidable problems of enforcement, both because of administrative difficulties and on grounds of equity.'[98] The committee's conclusion was in line with the position taken by consumer bodies like the EAW, which argued that the freedom of the housewife to choose methods and appliances should not be restricted by a national fuel policy.[99]

The Ridley Committee's advocacy of freedom of choice encouraged the EDA and the British Electrical and Allied Manufacturers' Association (BEAMA) to intensify their campaigns against the purchase tax.[100] Three decades earlier, in the 1920s, freedom of choice had emerged as a principle championed both by the electricity and the gas industries to secure a level playing field for fuel provision in council housing.[101] By the 1950s, the electricity industry used it to regain the ground lost during the period when electricity was restricted. Broader policy concerns, however, militated against a simple abolition of purchase tax. The Ministry of Fuel and Power warned that if the winter peak problem recurred, the government would be criticised for having been overhasty.[102] More

---

93 'Electricity – a factor in social progress', *Electrical Age*, Oct. 1951, p. 533.

94 See Zweiniger-Bargielowska, *Austerity in Britain*, pp. 227–34.

95 British Electrical Authority, *Annual report* (1952), p. 37.

96 Chick, *Electricity and energy policy*, p. 10.

97 *Report of the committee on national policy for the use of fuel and power resources* (Ridley Report) (London, 1952), Cmd. 8647, p. 13.

98 Ibid., p. 53.

99 'Consumers' choice', *Electrical Age*, Oct. 1952, p. 721.

100 See the Ministry of Fuel and Power's correspondence with the EDA and BEAMA in TNA POWE 14/380.

101 Frank Trentmann and Anna Carlsson-Hyslop, 'The evolution of energy demand: politics, daily life and public housing, Britain 1920s–70s', *Historical Journal* 61, 3 (Sep. 2018), pp. 807–39.

102 L.G. Vedy to H. Cox, 21 Jul. 1953, TNA POWE 14/380.

significantly, the purchase tax was an important anti-inflationary measure for the Treasury.[103] In addition, it also improved Britain's precarious balance of payments situation by diverting steel and non-ferrous materials such as copper and zinc away from domestic appliance manufacturing to exports that earned precious foreign currency.[104]

More generally, policy and politics started to move away from electricity demand control. There was a gradual improvement in load management. Above all, a more liberal attitude towards electric heaters was gaining ground. Expert opinion about the effect of electric heating on the peak problem mellowed. In 1953, Murray echoed the increasingly influential view that the contribution of electric fires to the peak problem had been exaggerated.[105] Electric appliances even came to be seen as 'a coal saver'.[106] BEAMA stressed that most consumers used electric heaters for only 150 to 200 hours per year.[107] The already high number of appliances owned also meant that most new purchases were replacements that did not worsen the peak load problem. And electricity was clean, a not insignificant factor at a time when the campaign for smoke abatement was making headway. The Beaver Committee on air pollution recommended electricity use instead of dirty solid fuel, adding further weight to the case against the purchase tax.[108]

In the late 1950s electricity supply became more stable, but shortages would return with a vengeance in the early 1960s, when the peak problem was exacerbated by industrial action and extreme weather. Christmas 1961 was marked by widespread supply failure.[109] Another Christmas blackout followed in December 1962, when the grid system in the Greater Manchester area was overwhelmed by peak demand – the blackout which opened this chapter. A month later, in January 1963, the Electrical Trades Union adopted 'work to rule', prompting more serious power cuts such as a widespread load shedding on 13 January, which affected London, the Home Counties, Bristol, South Wales, and East Anglia. The Central Electricity Generating Board appealed to housewives to postpone their Monday washing, or at least to put off ironing until later in the week.[110] But the worst was yet to come. During the week following 20 January, the 'big freeze' iced up insulators in switching stations and on overhead lines,

103   Memorandum by E. Sharp, 30 Dec. 1952, TNA POWE 14/380.
104   T.B.A. Corley, *Domestic electrical appliances* (London, 1966), p. 46; 'Hire purchase restrictions', Jan. 1952, TNA T 229/735.
105   'Purchase tax', 15 Dec. 1953, TNA POWE 14/380; M.P. Murray, 'Purchase tax on fuel appliances', 24 Jul. 1953, TNA POWE 14/380.
106   A.G.F. Farquhar, 'Reduction of purchase tax on electric fires', 11 Jan. 1954.
107   'The cooking and heating loads of an integrated electricity supply system', *BEAMA Journal*, Aug. 1952, p. 236.
108   Committee on Air Pollution, *Report* (London, 1954), Cmd. 9322, p. 22.
109   Chantler, 'Interruptions in electricity supplies, Christmas, 1961'.
110   'Washday appeal to housewives', *Guardian*, 14 Jan. 1963.

causing the most serious dislocation yet on the National Grid: one-fifth of customers were disconnected.[111]

The electricity crisis in 1963 was short, and did not lead to a major revision of policy. While the 1963 Select Committee on Nationalised Industries recognised the need for limiting peak demand, it tasked the electricity utilities with developing loads 'to improve the overall economy of the industry'.[112] Within the newly named Ministry of Power (created in 1957), the earlier debate about distributive justice had given way to a calculation of cost and benefits, and a belief in the efficient working of the market. Philip Chantler of the ministry argued that if the country's electricity supply was to be equipped with the capacity to withstand 'the rare spells of extremely cold weather in our normally temperate climate, the cost would be enormous, and might not be justifiable in a booming economy, persistently short of capital resources'.[113]

Conclusion

Energy disruption was hardly a problem confined to Britain. In the 1960s electricity peak load became a high-profile issue internationally. In 1963 the Economic Commission for Europe published *The covering of peak loads in electricity supply networks*, a report that showed how the growth in demand and subsequent narrowing of supply margins during peak periods posed problems for countries across Europe. Britain's winter peak was, however, particularly pronounced. The country's maximum winter load in 1958–59 was 21,600 MW, almost double the corresponding figure for West Germany (12,800 MW) and three times that of Italy (7,000 MW).[114] In May 1965 a symposium was held in Istanbul to consider how to meet 'rapidly-growing requirements for electric power'.[115] The meeting was attended by 215 delegates from twenty-one capitalist and socialist countries and various international bodies. Delegates discussed the prevalence of the peak load problem in different political regimes, and their different responses. In the USSR, for example, a central committee allocated power to different classes of consumer during shortages. In France, by contrast,

---

111 'The battle of the "big freeze"', *Central Electricity Generating Board Newsletter*, No. 27 (Mar. 1963).
112 *First special report from the Select Committee on Nationalised Industries: the electricity supply industry* (London, 1964), p. 3.
113 Chantler, 'Interruptions in electricity supplies, Christmas 1961'.
114 Economic Commission for Europe, *The covering of peak loads in electricity supply networks* (New York, 1963), Annex II.
115 'Economic Commission for Europe, Committee on Electric Power, *Symposium on special problems in meeting rapidly-growing requirements for electric power*, 2 vols (1965).

only heavy industrial consumers, such as the electro-metallurgical and chemical industries, were subject to supply reduction in 1963.[116]

Since then the risk of grave power disruption has been increased by what the sociologist Charles Perrow has described as a 'normal accident'.[117] Modern society's dependence on highly complex networked systems has made inter-locked critical infrastructures vulnerable to knock-on effects that spread across the entire system. The American Northeast blackout in November 1965 showed the powerful impact of a normal accident on a society dependent on electricity.[118] However, as this chapter has illustrated, energy disruption extends well beyond a story of technological failure. It was not always the case that people had no choice but to wait quietly for their supply system to be fixed and for the lights to go back on. Energy disruption has social aspects as well. They involve the contestation over who should have energy and whose demand for power should be curtailed. Allocating scarce energy to one group of consumers inevitably creates shortages for others. Moral concerns about fair shares and just distribution were a critical feature in the British debate during the Second World War, and defeated attempts to introduce fuel rationing. In the post-war years, this moral debate extended to a conflict between industrial and private consumers, with the former accusing the latter of not doing their part. It was only during the mid and late 1950s that this moral discourse of fairness gave way to an economic argument that made growth the litmus test of policy. The distribution of resources and burdens when the lights went out, moreover, helped shape what we think of as 'normal' when the lights are on. Disruption was part of the 'normal' process that policymakers and supply authorities used to plan for future interruptions to supply. Consumers were by no means absent from the discussion. The changing patterns of energy consumption shaped the way disruptions occurred. With their growing reliance on electrical heaters and rising expectations of thermal comfort, domestic consumers aggravated the peak problem after the Second World War.

Today, economic and technical discussions continue to dominate the political and public debate about energy problems. Moral discussion of equity and justice, such as energy justice for vulnerable households, is sidelined. This chapter reminds us that there is nothing inevitable about this. Just as decarboni-sation and decentralisation are calling into question the future of modern infra-structures, so shortages and disruptions might prompt a return to questions of distributional justice.

---

116   Ibid., vol. 1, p. 22.
117   Charles Perrow, *Normal accidents: living with high-risk technologies* (updated edn, Princeton, 1984).
118   David Nye, *When the lights went out: a history of blackouts in America* (Cambridge, MA, 2010).

The published writings of Martin J. Daunton

Books

Coal metropolis: Cardiff, 1870–1914
Leicester: Leicester University Press, 1977, 260 pp

House and home in the Victorian city: working-class housing in English cities, 1850–1914
London: Edward Arnold, 1983, 320 pp

Royal Mail: the Post Office since 1840
London: Athlone Press, 1985, 388 pp

A property-owning democracy? Housing in Britain
London: Faber and Faber, 1987, 148 pp

Progress and poverty: an economic and social history of Britain, 1700–1850
Oxford: Oxford University Press, 1995, 620 pp

Trusting Leviathan: the politics of taxation in Britain, 1799–1914
Cambridge: Cambridge University Press, 2001, 438 pp

Just taxes: the politics of taxation in Britain, 1914–1979
Cambridge: Cambridge University Press, 2002, 406 pp

Wealth and welfare: an economic and social history of Britain, 1851–1951
Oxford University Press, 2007, 656 pp

State and market in Victorian Britain: war, welfare and capitalism
The Boydell Press, Woodbridge, 2008, 341 pp

Edited (with introductions)

Councillors and Tenants: local authority housing in English cities, 1919–1939
Leicester: Leicester University Press, 1984, 223 pp

Housing the workers, 1850–1914: a comparative perspective
Leicester: Leicester University Press, 1990, 297 pp

Charity, self-interest and welfare in the English past
London: UCL Press, 1996, 262 pp

with Rick Halpern:
Empire and others: British encounters with indigenous peoples, 1600–1850
London: UCL Press and University of Pennsylvania Press, 1999, 400 pp

with Bernhard Rieger:
The meanings of modernity
Oxford and New York: Berg, 2000, 250 pp

Cambridge urban history of Britain, volume III, 1840–1950
Cambridge: Cambridge University Press, 2000, 1026 pp

with Matthew Hilton:
The politics of consumption: material culture and citizenship in Europe and America
Oxford and New York: Berg, 2001, 320 pp

with Frank Trentmann:
Worlds of political economy: knowledge and power in the nineteenth and twentieth centuries
Basingstoke: Palgrave Macmillan, 2004, 275 pp

The organisation of knowledge in Victorian Britain
Oxford: Oxford University Press for the British Academy, 2005, 434 pp

with Amrita Narlikar and Robert M. Stern:
Oxford handbook on the World Trade Organization
Oxford: Oxford University Press, 2012, 880 pp

with Marc Buggeln and Alexander Nützenadel:
The political economy of public finance: taxation, state spending and debt since the 1970s
Cambridge: Cambridge University Press, 2017, 328 pp

Articles

'The Dowlais Iron Company in the iron industry, 1800–1850'
Welsh History Review 6, 1 (1972), pp. 16–48

'Suburban development in Cardiff: Grangetown and the Windsor Estate, 1857–75'
Morgannwg 16 (1972), pp. 53–66

'Aristocrat and traders: the Bute Docks, 1839–1914'
Journal of Transport History, new ser., 3 (1975), pp. 65–85

'House ownership from rate books'
Urban History Yearbook (1976), pp. 21–7

'Inter-union relations on the waterfront: Cardiff, 1888–1914'
International Review of Social History 22,3 (1977), pp. 350–78

'The Cardiff Coal Trimmers Union, 1888–1914'
Llafur 2, 3 (1978), pp. 10–23

'Jack Ashore: seamen in Cardiff before 1914'
Welsh History Review 9 (1978), pp. 176–203

'The building cycle and the urban fringe in Victorian cities: a comment'
Journal of Historical Geography 4 (1978), pp. 175–81

'Miners' houses: South Wales and the Great Northern coalfield, 1880–1914'
International Review of Social History 25, 2 (1980), pp. 143–75

'Down the pit: work in the Great Northern and South Wales coalfields, 1870–1914'
Economic History Review, 2nd ser., 34,4 (1981), pp. 578–97

'Experts and the environment: approaches to planning history'
Journal of Urban History 9 (1983), pp. 233–50

with N.J. Morgan:
'Landlords in Glasgow: a study of 1900'
Business History 25 (1983), pp. 264–86

'Toil and technology in Britain and America'
History Today (April 1983), pp. 24–9

'Rowland Hill and the Penny Post'
History Today (August 1985), pp. 31–7

'Australian merchants in the City of London, 1840–90'
The City and Empire, II, Collected Seminar Papers No. 36, Institute of Commonwealth Studies, 1987, pp. 134–42

'Cities of homes and cities of tenements: British and American comparisons, 1870–1914'
Journal of Urban History XIV (1988), pp. 283–319

'Home loans versus council houses: the formation of American and British housing policy, 1900–20'
Housing Studies 3 (1988), pp. 232–46

'Inheritance and succession in the City of London in the nineteenth century'
Business History XXX (1988), pp. 269–86

'A lakásviszonyok Nagy- Britanniában B, 1850–1939'
Történelmi Szemle 3 (1987–88), pp. 351–65

'Gentlemanly capitalism and British industry, 1820–1914'
Past & Present 122 (1989), pp. 119–58

'Firm and family in the City of London in the nineteenth century: the case of F.G. Dalgety'
Historical Research 62 (1989), pp. 154–77

'Health and housing in Victorian London'
in W.F. Bynum and R. Porter, eds, *Living and dying in London,* supplement 11 of *Medical History* (1991), pp. 126–44

'Debate: gentlemanly capitalism and British industry'
Past & Present 132 (1991), pp. 170–87

'Inside the Bank of England'
Twentieth-Century British History 6 (1995), pp. 344–58

'How to pay for the war: state, society and taxation in Britain, 1917–24'
English Historical Review 111 (1996), pp. 882–919

'Industry in London: revisions and reflections'
London Journal 21 (1996), pp. 1–8
[guest editor of special issue on *Industry in London, 1750–1945*]

'London, state power and economic change, 1680–1900'
Ninoshi Kenkyu 404 (1996), pp. 3–31 [in Japanese]

'Middle-class voluntarism and the city in Britain and America'
Journal of Urban History 22 (1996), pp. 253–63

'Payment and participation: welfare and state-formation in Britain, 1900–51'
Past & Present 150 (1996), pp. 169–216

'Churchill at the Treasury: remaking Conservative fiscal policy, 1924–29'
Revue Belge de Philologie et d'Histoire 75 (1997), pp. 1063–83

'Virtual representation: the History of Parliament on CD-rom'
Past & Present, 167 (May 2000), pp. 238–61

'Michael Young and meritocracy'
Contemporary British History 19 (2005), pp. 285–91

'Britain and globalization since 1850: I, Creating a global order, 1850–1914'
Transactions of the Royal Historical Society, 6th ser., 16 (2006), pp. 1–38

'Britain and globalization since 1850: II, The rise of insular capitalism, 1914–1939'
Transactions of the Royal Historical Society, 6th ser., 17 (2007), pp. 1–33

'Britain and globalization since 1850: III, Creating the world of Bretton Woods, 1939–1958'
Transactions of the Royal Historical Society, 6th ser., 18 (2008), pp. 1–42

'Britain and globalization since 1850: IV, The creation of the Washington consensus'
Transactions of the Royal Historical Society, 6th ser., 19 (2009), pp. 1–35

with J. Dutta and T. Aidt:
'The retrenchment hypothesis and the extension of the franchise in England and Wales'
Economic Journal 120 (2010), pp. 990–1020

'The future direction of British history: thinking about economic cultures'
History Workshop Journal 72 (2011), pp. 222–39

With Julia Moses:
'Editorial — border crossings: global dynamics of social policies and problems'
Journal of Global History 9 (2014), pp. 177–88

'Questioning Leviathan: restructuring the state in Britain since 1970'
East Asian Journal of British History 5 (2016), pp. 29–50

Chapters in books

'Towns and economic growth in eighteenth-century England'
in P. Abrams and E.A. Wrigley, eds, *Towns in societies*
Cambridge: Cambridge University Press, 1978, pp. 245–77

'Public place and the private space: the Victorian city and the working-class household'
in D. Fraser and A. Sutcliffe, eds, *The pursuit of urban history*
London: Edward Arnold, 1983, pp. 212–33

with M. Wagner:
'Jedermanns Geldschäfte prompt, sicher und billig zu besorgen: Die Bestimmungsgrößen unterschieldlicher Rentabilitat öffentlicher Unternehmungen am Beispiel der britischen und österreichischen Postsparkasse, 1885–1914'
in R. Tilly, ed., *Beiträge zur quantitaven vergleichenden Unternehmensgeschichte*
Göttingen: Klett-Cotta, 1985, pp. 131–45

entries on D.A. Thomas and Evelyn Murray
in D.J. Jeremy, *Dictionary of business biography: a biographical dictionary of business leaders active in Britain in the period 1860–1980*
London: Butterworths, 1984–86

'Labour and technology in South Wales, 1870–1914'
in C. Baber and L.J. Williams, eds, *Modern South Wales: essays in economic and social history*
Cardiff: University of Wales Press, 1986, pp. 140–52

'Coal to capital: Cardiff since 1839'
in P. Morgan, ed., *Glamorgan county history, volume VI: Glamorgan society, 1780–1980*
Glamorgan History Trust, 1988, pp. 203–24

'Urban Britain'
in T. Gourvish and A. O'Day, eds, *Later Victorian Britain*
Basingstoke: Macmillan, 1988, pp. 37–67

'Income flows, the family economy, and survival strategies'
in P. Scholliers, ed., *Real wages in nineteenth and twentieth century Europe: historical and comparative perspectives*
Oxford: Berg, 1989, pp. 143–8

'Housing, 1750–1950'
in F.M.L. Thompson, ed., *Cambridge social history of Britain, II: People and their environment*
Cambridge: Cambridge University Press, 1990, pp. 195–250

'Rows and tenements: American cities, 1880–1914'
in M. Daunton, ed., *Housing the workers, 1850–1914: a comparative perspective*
Leicester: Leicester University Press, 1990, pp. 249–86

'Comment'
M.A. Crew and P.R. Kleindorfer, *Rowland Hill's contribution as an economist*
in Crew and Kleindorfer, eds, *Competition and innovation in postal services*,
Dordrecht: Kluwer, 1991, pp. 13–15

'Financial elites and British society, 1880–1960'
in Y. Cassis, ed., *Finance and financiers in European history, 1880–1960*
Cambridge: Cambridge University Press, 1992, pp. 121–46

'Finance and politics: comments'
in Y. Cassis, ed., *Finance and financiers in European history, 1880–1960*
Cambridge: Cambridge University Press, 1992, pp. 283–90

'London und die Welt'
in Kulturstiftung Ruhr Essen, *Metropole London: Macht und Glanz einer Weltstadt, 1800–1840*
Recklinghausen: Verlag Aurel Bongers, 1992, pp. 21–38,
and
'London and the world'
in C. Fox, ed., *London: world city, 1800–1840*
London: Yale University Press, 1992, pp. 21–38

'The City and industry: the nature of British capitalism, 1750–1914'
G. Alderman and C. Holmes, eds, *Outsiders and outcasts*
London: Duckworth, 1993, pp. 185–206

'Vorstadt, Gesellschaft und der Staat: London in den zwanziger Jahren'
in P. Alter, ed., *Im Banne der Metropolen*
Göttingen: Vandenhoeck und Rupert, 1993, pp. 87–110

'"A kind of tax prison": rethinking Conservative taxation policy, 1960–70'
in M. Francis and I. Zweiniger-Bargielowska, eds, *The Conservatives and British society, 1880–1990*
Cardiff: University of Wales Press, 1996, pp. 289–315

'Theo Barker: an appreciation'
Journal of Transport History, 3rd ser., 19, 2 (1998), p. 99

'Trusting Leviathan: British fiscal administration since 1842'
in V. Braithwaite and M. Levi, eds, *Trust and governance*
New York: Russell Sage Books, 1999, pp. 102–34

'Society and economic life'
in Colin Matthew, ed., *Short Oxford history of the British Isles: the nineteenth century*
Oxford University Press, 2000, pp. 41–82

'The wealth of the nation'
in Paul Langford, ed., *Short Oxford history of the British Isles: the eighteenth century*
Oxford University Press, 2001, pp. 141–180

'The material politics of natural monopoly: consuming gas in Victorian Britain'
in M. Daunton and M. Hilton, eds, *The politics of consumption: material culture and citizenship in Europe and America*
Oxford and New York: Berg, 2001, pp. 69–88

'Taxation and representation in the Victorian city'
in R. Colls and R. Rodger, eds, *Cities of ideas: civil society and urban governance in Britain*, 1800–2000
Aldershot: Ashgate, 2004, pp. 21–45

'What is income?'
in J. Tiley, ed., *Studies in the history of tax law*
Oxford and Portland: Hart Publishing, 2004, pp. 3–14

'The fiscal-military state and the Napoleonic wars: Britain and France compared'
in D. Cannadine, ed., *Trafalgar in history: a battle and its afterlife*
London: Palgrave, 2006, pp. 18–43

'Tax transfer: Britain and its empire, 1848–1914'
in H. Nehring and F. Schui, eds, *Global debates about taxation*
London: Palgrave, 2007, pp. 137–57

'Taxation, state and society in comparative perspective, 1750–1950'
in A. Nützenadel and C. Strupp, eds, *Taxation, state and civil society in Germany and the United States from the eighteenth to the twentieth century*
Baden Baden: Nomos, 2007, pp. 205–27

'Land taxation, economy and society in Britain and its colonies'
in J. Avery Jones, P. Harris and D. Oliver, eds, *Comparative perspectives on revenue law: essays in honour of John Tiley*
Cambridge: Cambridge University Press, 2008, pp. 197–218

'A tale of two conferences: the International Trade Organization, GATT and world trade'
in F. Trentmann, ed., *Is free trade fair trade: new perspectives on the world trading system*
London: Smith Institute, 2009, pp. 34–46

'From Bretton Woods to Havana: multilateral deadlocks in historical perspective'
in A. Narlikar, ed., *Deadlocks in multilateral negotiations: causes and solutions*
Cambridge: Cambridge University Press, 2010, pp. 47–78

'Welfare, taxation and social justice: reflections on Cambridge economists from Marshall to Keynes'
in R. Backhouse and T. Nishizawa, eds, *No wealth but life: welfare economics and the Welfare State in Britain, 1880–1945*
New York: Cambridge University Press, 2010, pp. 62–88

'The inconsistent quartet: free trade versus competing goals'
in A. Narlikar, M. Daunton, and R. Stern, eds, *The Oxford handbook on the World Trade Organization*
Oxford: Oxford University Press, 2012, pp. 40–63

'The Shoup mission: the context of post-World War II debates over international economic policy'
in W. Elliot Brownlees, Eisaku Ide, and Yasunori Fukagai, eds, *The political economy of transnational tax reform: the Shoup mission to Japan in historical perspective*
New York: Cambridge University Press, 2013, pp. 402–25

'Afterword: mercantilism and the Caribbean Atlantic world economy'
in A.B. Leonard and D. Pretel, eds, *The Caribbean and the Atlantic world economy: circuits of trade, money and knowledge, 1650–1914*
Basingstoke: Palgrave Macmillan, 2015, pp. 290–304

'Cambridge and economic history' and 'John Harold Clapham (1873–1946)'
in Robert A. Cord, ed., *The Palgrave companion to Cambridge economics, vol. I*
London: Palgrave Macmillan, 2017, pp. 157–86; 423–54

'Creating a dynamic society: the tax reforms of the Thatcher government'
in M. Buggeln, M. Daunton and A. Nützenadel, eds, *The political economy of public finance*
Cambridge: Cambridge University Press, 2017, 328 pp. 32–56

'Mismanaged chimneys: nuisances in Victorian Britain'
in Chris Wrigley, ed., *The Industrial Revolution and industrialisation revisited: Cromford, the Derwent Valley and beyond*
Cromford: Arkwright Society, 2017, pp. 29–42

'Time and history'
in *Balzan Papers* 1
Florence: Olschki, 2018, pp. 259–80

'Thomas Gibson Bowles v Bank of England (1913): A modern John Hampden?'
in John Snape and Dominic de Cogan, eds, *Landmark cases in revenue law*
Oxford: Hart Publishing, 2019, pp. 99–118

'Nutrition, food, agriculture and the world economy'
in Naomi Lamoureaux, ed., *The Bretton Woods Agreement: together with scholarly commentaries and essential historical documents*
New Haven: Yale University Press, forthcoming 2019, pp. 145–72

entries on Walter Boyd, Sir John Clapham, Sir Mark Collet, Sir Daniel Cooper, Frederick Dalgety, Henry Gibbs (first Baron Aldenham), Alexander Henderson (first Baron Faringdon), John Hubbard (first Baron Addington), Ephraim Lipson, William Manning, Sir Leo Chiozza Money, Sir Evelyn Murray, Sir Charles Sikes and William Thompson
in *Oxford dictionary of national biography*
Oxford: Oxford University Press (online edn)

Index

PEOPLE, MARKETS, GOODS:
ECONOMIES AND SOCIETIES IN HISTORY

ISSN: 2051-7467

PREVIOUS TITLES

1. *Landlords and Tenants in Britain, 1440–1660:*
Tawney's Agrarian Problem Revisited
edited by Jane Whittle, 2013

2. *Child Workers and Industrial Health in Britain, 1780–1850*
Peter Kirby, 2013

3. *Publishing Business in Eighteenth-Century England*
James Raven, 2014

4. *The First Century of Welfare:*
Poverty and Poor Relief in Lancashire, 1620–1730
Jonathan Healey, 2014

5. *Population, Welfare and Economic Change in Britain 1290–1834*
edited by Chris Briggs, P. M. Kitson and S. J. Thompson, 2014

6. *Crises in Economic and Social History: A Comparative Perspective*
edited by A. T. Brown, Andy Burn and Rob Doherty, 2015

7. *Slavery Hinterland: Transatlantic Slavery and*
Continental Europe, 1680–1850
edited by Felix Brahm and Eve Rosenhaft, 2016

8. *Almshouses in Early Modern England:*
Charitable Housing in the Mixed Economy of Welfare, 1550–1725
Angela Nicholls, 2017

9. *People, Places and Business Cultures:*
Essays in Honour of Francesca Carnevali
edited by Paolo Di Martino, Andrew Popp and Peter Scott, 2017

10. *Cameralism in Practice: State Administration*
and Economy in Early Modern Europe
edited by Marten Seppel and Keith Tribe, 2017